D1703642

LOUIS VUITTON
ARCHITECTURE
AND INTERIORS

ARCHITECTURE AND INTERIORS 2

LOUIS VUITTON ARCHITECTURE AND INTERIORS

FRÉDÉRIC EDELMANN, IAN LUNA, RAFAEL MAGROU
AND MOHSEN MOSTAFAVI

Rizzoli
NEW YORK

New York · Paris · London · Milan

First published in the United States of America
by Rizzoli International Publications, Inc.
300 Park Avenue South, New York, NY 10010
www.rizzoliusa.com

All rights reserved. No part of this
publication may be reproduced, stored
in a retrieval system, or transmitted in
any form or by any means, electronic,
mechanical, photocopying, recording,
or otherwise, without prior consent of
the publishers.

Louis Vuitton: Architecture & Interiors
Texts by Frédéric Edelmann, Rafael Magrou,
& Mohsen Mostafavi, Copyright © 2011,
Louis Vuitton Malletier; other text
Copyright © 2011, Ian Luna.

Printed in Hong Kong SAR

2011 2012 2013 2014 2015 / 10 9 8 7 6 5 4 3 2 1
Library of Congress Control Number:
2011926895
ISBN: 978-0-8478-3652-9

Editors: Ian Luna & Lauren A. Gould
Managing Editor: Ellen Nidy
Editorial Assistants: Mandy DeLucia,
Kayleigh Jankowski
Production: Kaija Markoe, Eugene Lee
Translation Services: Molly Stevens,
Rebecca Cavanaugh, Andrea Torres
Perdigón & Nicolás Alvarado
Editorial Coordinator for French Edition:
Catherine Bonifassi

For Louis Vuitton
Director of the Heritage Department:
Antoine Jarrier
Head of Publications: Julien Guerrier
Editor: Valérie Viscardi
Picture Library Manager: Marie-Laure Fourt,
assisted by Amandine Jochem and
Camille Nicolas

Louis Vuitton would like to extend its appreciation to the following individuals, and particularly to Serge Alfandary, Marie Barace, Pietro Beccari, Caroline Bellemare, Lionel Berruyer, Cédric Bouron, Élise Bracq, Isabella Capece-Galeota, Yves Carcelle, May Chen, Eléonore de Boysson, Cécile Durieux, Georgina Edminston, Isabelle Franchet, Séverine Fritsch-Fontanges, Jun Fujiwara, Kaori Fuse, Tara Hannert, Ben Huang, Stanley Hunter, Édith Jarboua, Mayumi Khoda, Stéphane Leveaux, Victoria Ling, Maud Lomnitz, Jean-Marc Mansvelt, Emmanuel Mathieu, Lucy Myners, Roberta Polato-Rossi, Solène Reymond, Marie Saito, Élodie Spitz, Johnny Tan, Kaori Umezawa, Joanne Yau, Rhoda Wong, & Marie Wurry

Special thanks to the Louis Vuitton Architecture and Real Estate Departments for their active contribution:
David McNulty, Christian Reyne and Aurore Baulier, Marine Billet, Loïc Bouchard, François-Régis Colombani, Dak Coutts, Elise Delestre, Maria Elena Fanna, Abir Fawaz, Nathalie Fremon, Walter Giulio, Kar-Hwa Ho, Thierry Lemoine, Valérie Merceron, Alain Michaux, John Mulliken, Salamata N'Diaye, Rudi Novello, Zeynep Ozandag, Nicolas Paschal, Patrick Pimont, Laetitia Perrin, James Poon, Stéphanie Rainaut, Odile Rignault, Magali Rougier, Boris Schebesch, Céline Sidibe, Samuel Singer, Kazuhiro Takamiya, & Stuart Young

The editors would like to extend their gratitude to the following individuals:
Patrick Li, Daniel Wagner, Seth Zucker, Bettina Sorg, Meriem Soliman, Christina Yang, Toshiko Mori, Catherine Bonifassi, Molly Stevens, Rebecca Cavanaugh, Andrea Torres Perdigón, Nicolás Alvarado, Susan Chua, Lester Koh, Jane Acheson, Suneeta Gill, Edith Taichman, Bryan Dorsey, Roger Howie, Maria Wilthew, Uli Wagner, Craig Greenberg, Gay Gassman, Stephane Muratet, Pierre Brullé, Jimmy Cohrssen, Marie Iida, Yuko Machida Nathalie Tollu, & Marianne Lass

Design: Li, Inc., New York

AUTHOR AND ARCHITECTS' BIOGRAPHIES 6

FOREWORD
BY MOHSEN MOSTAFAVI 8

PROJECTS 9

JAPAN 10

A CONVERSATION WITH
JUN AOKI AND MOHSEN MOSTAFAVI 70

ASIA-PACIFIC 72

A CONVERSATION WITH
PETER MARINO AND MOHSEN MOSTAFAVI 118

UNITED STATES 120

A CONVERSATION WITH
DAVID MCNULTY AND MOHSEN MOSTAFAVI 140

EUROPE 142

A CONVERSATION WITH
CHRISTIAN DE PORTZAMPARC AND FRÉDÉRIC EDELMANN 190

HEADQUARTERS BUILDINGS 192

A CONVERSATION WITH
CHRISTIAN REYNE AND RAFAEL MAGROU 212

INDUSTRIAL BUILDINGS 214

CODES: SKINS, FAÇADES AND SIGNAGE 240

LOUIS VUITTON—ARCHITECTURE,
FASHION, AND FABRICATION
ESSAY BY MOHSEN MOSTAFAVI 242

SKINS 246

FAÇADES 248

SIGNAGE 264

PROJECT CREDITS 268

ILLUSTRATION CREDITS 271

AUTHORS

Frédéric Edelmann was born in 1951. Edelmann is a journalist and has been a critic at *Le Monde* since 1977. He curated the exhibition *Chicago Architecture (1833–1983)* as well as the exhibitions *Dans la ville Chinois, Regards sur les mutations d'un empire* and *Portrait d'une nouvelle génération d'architectes chinois* (Cité de l'Architecture, Paris, Barcelona & Valencia, 2008). He is the co-founder of the organizations AIDES (in 1984), ARCAT-SIDA (1987), and was co-founder with François Bloch-Lainé, then president (1994-1997) of the organization Patrimoine sans Frontières (PSF). Named Chevalier of the National Order of the Legion of Honor, he was awarded the Prix National for architectural criticism (1990), and is an associate member of the Académie d'Architecture.

Ian Luna is a writer and critic based in New York and is the author of several books on architecture, design and fashion. Most recently, he was the general editor and a contributing author to *Louis Vuitton: Art, Fashion and Architecture* (2009) for Rizzoli. His previous books include *A Bathing Ape* (2008) with Nigo; *Tokyolife: Art and Design* (2008), with Toshiko Mori; *On the Edge: Ten Architects from China* (2007) with Yung Ho Chang; *Retail: Architecture and Shopping* (2005); *Imagining Ground Zero: The Official and Unofficial Proposals for the World Trade Center Site* (2004), with Suzanne Stephens; and *New New York: Architecture of a City* (2003). He has lectured on urbanism and architectural history at the MIT School of Architecture and Planning and the Yale School of Architecture, and is an occasional critic and correspondent for a number of publications in Japan and China, including the print and digital editions of *Studio Voice, High Fashion* and Japan *Tokion*.

Rafael Magrou was born in 1971. An architect-observer, Magrou is a critic of change in the contemporary world. He practices as a specialized journalist, curator and teacher in architecture schools (ENSA Paris-Malaquais, and Columbia University). He writes for different publications including *L'Architecture d'Aujourd'hui, AMC, MARK* and *EXÉ*.

In 2007, he was the curator of *Scènes d'architectures*, the French pavilion at the 7th São Paulo International Architecture Biennial; in 2008, for the *Nouveaux Albums des jeunes architectes et paysagistes*, and in 2009, co-curator for *Habiter écologique* at the Cité de l'Architecture et du Patrimoine, Paris. He is preparing an exhibition-installation in Nantes on the theme of Sport to open in summer 2012.

As a writer, he has contributed to the following anthologies: *Les Arpenteurs de l'Europe* (Actes Sud), *Nouvelles formes d'habitat en Europe* (Arc En Rève/Birkhauser); and edited the monograph on the choreographer Frédéric Flamand (Actes Sud). His most recent publication is *Habiter un container* (Edilarge/France Ouest, 2011).

Mohsen Mostafavi is an architect and educator, and is currently the Dean of the Harvard Graduate School of Design and the Alexander and Victoria Wiley Professor of Design. He was formerly the Gale and Ira Drukier Dean of the College of Architecture, Art and Planning at Cornell University where he was also the Arthur L. and Isabel B. Wiesenberger Professor in Architecture. Previously, he was the Chairman of the Architectural Association School of Architecture in London. Mostafavi is a member of the trustees of the Van Alen Institute, and serves on the steering committee of the Aga Khan Award for Architecture. At Harvard, he co-chairs the Common Spaces Committee, is a member of the University's Committee on the Arts and the Standing Committee on Middle Eastern Studies. He chairs the North American jury of the Holcim Foundation Awards for Sustainable Construction. Previously he served on the design committee of the London Development Agency (LDA), the jury for the RIBA Gold Medal, and the advisory committee on campus planning of the Asian University for Women. His research and design projects have been published in many journals, including *The Architectural Review, AAFiles, Arquitectura, Bauwelt, Casabella, Centre, Daidalos*, and *El Croquis*. He is co-author of *Delayed Space* (with Homa Farjadi, Princeton Architectural Press, 1994); and *On Weathering: The Life of Buildings in Time* (with David Leatherbarrow, MIT, 1993) which received the American Institute of Architects prize for writing on architectural theory. Mostafavi's recent publications include: *Ecological Urbanism* (Lars Müller Publishers, 2010); and *Implicate and Explicate: Aga Khan Award for Architecture* (Lars Müller Publishers, 2011).

ARCHITECTS

Jun Aoki is an architect and principal at Jun Aoki & Associates. Having graduated from Tokyo University in 1982, Jun Aoki worked at Arata Isozaki & Associates before establishing his own Tokyo-based practice in 1991. With a mandate to do "anything that seemed interesting," Aoki emerged as one of the critical figures in Japanese architecture in the mid-1990s, and his works include a series of houses, public architecture, and commercial buildings, as well as a number of award-winning commissions from Louis Vuitton. Major works include the Mamihara Bridge in Kumamoto (1995), the Fukushima Lagoon Museum in Niigata (1997, which won him one of his first Architectural Institute of Japan Annual Awards), the Aomori Museum of Art (2006) and the SIA Aoyama Tower in Tokyo (2008). His first monograph *Jun Aoki Complete Works 1* was published in October 2004, simultaneously with another book *Harappa to Yuuenchi* (Vacant Lot and Amusement Ground), a collection of his writing. The second monograph, *Jun Aoki complete Works 2*: was published in 2006. He was recently awarded the Japanese Minister of Education's Art Encouragement Prize and was the recipient of The Good Design Award for the SIA Tower.

Shigeru Ban was born in Tokyo, and in 1971 received his architectural degrees from the Southern California Institute of Architecture and the Cooper Union School of Architecture in New York before joining Arata Isozaki's firm in 1982. Ban established his own practice in Tokyo in 1985.

Shigeru Ban's innovative use of paper as a principal structural element in architecture forever transformed international building codes. His studio was an early, practical advocate for using renewable resources. With a portfolio spanning three decades, Ban demonstrated that cardboard tubes could transcend their workaday use as molds for concrete columns, to form the interior and exterior cladding of a building, or even constitute a building's entire frame. This experience contributed to some of his most iconic architecture, from the Paper House (1995), to the Centre Georges Pompidou-Metz (2009), the temporary Papillon Pavilion for Louis Vuitton's Paris flagship (2006) and provisional housing for earthquake survivors in Haiti and Northeastern Japan (2010-2011)

Ban has taught at Tama Art University, Columbia University, Keio University, Amherst College, Harvard University Graduate School of Design and is presently a visiting professor at Cornell University. Ban was the recipient of the Thomas Jefferson Medal in Architecture in 2005 and was inducted in 2010 into the French Order of Arts and Letters.

Grégoire Gilliot was born in 1971 and is a graduate of the École d'Architecture de Paris Belleville (UP8). After several years of practice in different agencies (Igloo, Pascal Sirvin, WB Architecture) and on different types of projects (hotel accommodation, housing, sports facilities, school buildings and universities), he joined the firm of Gilles Carnoy in 2005. This collaboration allowed him to discover the business side of real estate and more specifically the construction of industrial sites dedicated to logistics and the manufacture of luxury leather goods.

He collaborated on the development and construction of the Cergy Eole Site, an environmentally friendly storage facility for Louis Vuitton in the town of Cergy Saint Christophe, which was certified HEQ, and has also delivered a pristine production workshop in Marsaz.

Zaha Hadid is the Founding Director of her London-based firm, Zaha Hadid Architects. She consistently pushes the boundaries of architecture and urban design, and her work experiments with new spatial concepts, intensifying existing urban landscapes in the pursuit of a visionary aesthetic that encompasses all fields of design, ranging from urban scale through to products, interiors and furniture. Best known for her seminal built works (Vitra Fire Station, Rosenthal Centre for Contemporary Art, BMW Central Building, Phaeno Science Center, and MAXXI: Italian National Museum of XXI Arts, and most recently, the Guandong Opera House in 2011), her central concerns involve a simultaneous engagement in practice, teaching and research. Hadid has held the Kenzo Tange Chair at the Graduate School of

Design, Harvard University; the Sullivan Chair at the University of Illinois, School of Architecture, Chicago; guest professorships at the Hochschule für Bildende Künste in Hamburg; the Knolton School of Architecture, Ohio and the Masters Studio at Columbia University, New York. In addition, she was made Honorary Member of the American Academy of Arts and Letters, Fellow of the American Institute of Architecture and Commander of the British Empire, 2002. She is currently Professor at the University of Applied Arts in Vienna, Austria and was the Eero Saarinen Visiting Professor of Architectural Design at Yale University.

Kumiko Inui graduated from the Architecture and Planning course of Tokyo National University of Fine Arts and Music in 1992, and from Yale Graduate School of Architecture in 1996. She worked at Jun Aoki & Associates from 1996 to 2000, when she set up her own architectural practice, Office of Kumiko Inui. She gained recognition for her first independent work, the renovation of Kataokadai Nursery (2001), and followed it up with a series of acclaimed residential and commercial projects. Among these are a number of retail commissions that have since become iconic structures in their contexts, including the exterior of Christian Dior Ginza boutique (2004) as well as the Louis Vuitton stores in Kochi, in Shikoku (2003), Taipei, Taiwan (2004), and on Canton Road, in Hong Kong (2008). Her most recent publication, *Episodes* was published by INAX in 2008. As an educator, she has taught at Tokyo University, Showa Women's University in Tokyo, and is currently a visiting professor at the Oslo School of Architecture.

Kengo Kuma completed his master's degree in Architecture at Tokyo University in 1979, and was a visiting scholar at Columbia University from 1985 to 1986. He established Kengo Kuma & Associates in 1990, and as an educator, has been a professor at the Faculty of Science and Technology, Keio University, since 2001. A key figure in contemporary Japanese design, his major built works include the Kirosan Observatory (1995), Water/Glass (1995, AIA Benedictus Award), the Stage in Forest, and Toyoma Centre for Performing Arts (1997, Architectural Institute of Japan Annual Award 1997), Stone Museum (2000, International Stone Architecture Award 2001), Museum of Hiroshige Ando (2000, Togo Murano Prize). He received the 2002 International Spirit of Nature Wood Architecture Award from Finland for his contribution to timber architecture.

Peter Marino is the principal of Peter Marino Architect, PLLC, an internationally acclaimed architecture, planning and design firm founded in 1978 and based in New York City. Marino holds an architecture degree from Cornell University and began his career at Skidmore Owings & Merrill, George Nelson and I.M. Pei/Cossutta & Ponte.

Peter Marino's design contributions in the areas of commercial, cultural, residential and retail architecture emphasize materiality, texture, scale, light and the constant dialogue between interior and exterior. He is widely known for his residential and retail designs for the most iconic names in the fashion and art worlds. In 2010, Marino received the American Institute of Architects New York Chapter Interiors Honor Award for Chanel Robertson Boulevard in Los Angeles, and in 2008, received the American Institute of Architects (AIA) Awards of Merit for Ermenegildo Zegna New York and Louis Vuitton Hong Kong in addition to a Citation for Design for Fendi Beverly Hills. In 2007, Mr. Marino received an AIA National Honor Award for Louis Vuitton, Hong Kong and an AIA Design Award for Fendi, Rome. Marino sits on the boards of the New York Foundation for Architecture, the Venetian Heritage Foundation and the International Committee of the L'Union Centrale des Arts Décoratifs, and was recently appointed to the U.S. General Services Administration's National Register of Peer Professionals as part of its Design Excellence Program.

David McNulty graduated from University College of Dublin School of Architecture in 1985, then moved to Paris where he worked for Marcel Breuer Architects, Christian de Portzamparc and Chaix & Morel before joining Louis Vuitton to establish the Architecture Department in 1998. He contributed to the Adolf Loos exhibition in Dublin in 1985 and to the Figurative Architecture exhibition in Paris in 1987.

Christian de Portzamparc was born in Casablanca in 1944, and is an architect and urbanist. In 1994, de Portzamparc was the first French architect to receive the highest honor in architecture, the Pritzker Prize. He is a Commander of the Order of Arts and Letters, an Officer of the Order of Merit, and a Chevalier of the National Order of the Legion of Honor. His awards include Grand Prix d'Architecture de la Ville de Paris (1990), the Grand Prix National d'Architecture (1998) the Grand Prix de l'Urbanisme (2004) and he is an honorary member of the American Institute of Architects. From single buildings to neighborhoods, the city is a founding subject of his work, which he develops around three major and recurring themes. The first of these are *Symbol buildings*, which bring together, attract, and cohere the great urban landscape, especially large public works like the headquarters of the Conseil Régional Rhône-Alpes in Lyon (2006-2011) and cultural projects like the Cité de la Musique, Parc de la Villette, in Paris (1984–1995). The second theme is represented by *Sculptural Towers*. Since the Marne-la-Vallée water tower in 1971, Christian de Portzamparc has pursued his sculptural investigations based on the theme of verticality, as seen in The LVMH tower in New York (1995-1999). The third theme, *Small Neighborhoods and City Parts*, investigates theoretical and practical research on methods that bring the city into being, which de Portzamparc has called the "open block." These explorations informed the transformation of urban parameters in Paris, in the Masséna Seine neighborhood on the left bank (1995-2010), and in Brussels, on the Rue de la Loi. In Montpellier, de Portzamparc designed the ground plan for Les Jardins de la Lironde and is one of twenty architects involved in a major urban scheme in Manhattan, masterplanning a four-block project called Riverside City Center.

Christian Reyne studied architecture in Nanterre (UP2) from 1983 to 1987, working during this period with the architecture firm LPA in Paris. Spending three years from 1988 as a building supervisor, in 1991 he joined GV, the marketing arm of LVMH in order to develop the company's building department. It was at this time that he first collaborated on Louis Vuitton industrial projects before permanently joining the company in 1995 as Director of Real Estate. Since then, Christian Reyne has headed numerous projects, notably the renovation of the Louis Vuitton headquarters in Paris, of the Champs Élysées building, as well as twelve leather goods, shoe workshops and logistic centers in France and abroad.

Named Associate Director at the Louis Vuitton Foundation for Creation by Bernard Arnault in 2007, he currently heads the construction project conceived by Frank Gehry in the Bois de Boulogne in Paris.

Jean-Marc Sandrolini was born in Algiers, and founded his firm in 1980. A graduate of the École Nationale des Beaux-Arts in Paris in 1976, he had a private practice in Paris between 1978 and 2002, which transitioned into a limited liability architecture firm later that year. An architectural advisor at the Conseil d'Architecture, d'Urbanisme et d'Environnement de l'Indre between 1981 and 1985, he is Vice President and Secretary General of the Association Architecture et Maîtres d'Ouvrage.

FOREWORD
MOHSEN MOSTAFAVI

Fashion and architecture have had an increasingly closer liaison recently. But the current fascination of the one for the other—architecture as the prop for the display of fashion, and fashion as the prerequisite for all that is architectural—has only helped to mask the longevity of their association. If popularity and newness are considered as the main characteristics of fashion, then it is undeniable that architecture has for a long time been pursuing similar aspirations. At least, this is one way to consider the crisis of architectural styles in Europe during the nineteenth century, when the authority of the classical tradition was largely supplanted by the search for new styles. The result was a proliferation of popular stylistic revivals, each of which could in some ways be seen as part of a specific trend, or a form of fashion.

At the same time, the notion of architecture as the setting for the selling of goods has an equally long history. One such connection between architecture and retail is linked with the evolution of the department store. The mass production of all manner of goods made it necessary for department stores to construct special and often exotic displays that created an aura of uniqueness around the objects for the consumer.

In the more recent past, it is the architecture of minimalism that has provided the most explicit and significant contribution to the reciprocal relationship between fashion and architecture. In many ways the abstraction and literal emptiness of minimalism has been an ideal setting for the valorization of fashion—a technique not dissimilar in its impact to the exotic settings of nineteenth-century department stores, both ultimately leading to the construction of desire.

If minimalism focused on the solitude of reification, Louis Vuitton's strategy has been to create desire on a scale approaching a new mass hysteria. At least this seems to be the case in Japan. Before the opening of the new Louis Vuitton store in Omotesando in 2002, in the heart of Tokyo, thousands of people waited patiently to gain entry into this Aladdin's cave. Many slept on the pavement outside the store for two nights or more in anticipation of acquiring their favorite limited edition items.

In contrast to the recent emphasis on interior spaces for the display of fashion, the architectural explorations of Louis Vuitton documented in this volume primarily concern the outside of buildings, their appearance—with a few notable exceptions. Louis Vuitton has so far had a policy of fitting their stores across the world with similar interiors that provide a consistent image of understated luxury. It is against the stability of these repeatable interiors that the company has been developing its explorations with the external skin over the last decade.

These developments, however, must be seen as part of a longer and more systematic architectural project. Because of the nature of the work—fashion—it is inevitable that this project will always be in transition. Nevertheless, the architectural achievements of the last few years have revealed a number of additional topics that will need to be addressed over time. The connections between the inside and outside of the buildings, the size and scale of their operations, the flexibility and temporality of their interiors: these are examples of the types of questions that will in part draw their responses from the dynamics of circumstance, including those of the marketplace of architecture.

The organizational structure for handling architectural projects at Louis Vuitton is different from most other brands. The main difference is the presence of an in-house Architecture Department that acts as architect and/or client, depending on the project. In reality, even when the Architecture Department commissions outside designers its involvement is directly architectural, interventionist yet supportive. This unusual condition is allied with the fact that the company has, at least up to now, only worked with architects who have been willing to fully participate in an ongoing collaborative project. In marked contrast to those companies that have used "signature" architects, the architectural projects of Louis Vuitton can be seen to be based on an evolutionary co-development of the LV brand and its own distinct architectural identity.

We are now at a period when the luxury retail store has become a crucial forum for architecture. A previously off-limits relationship has now found mutually beneficial common ground. Through the realization of numerous projects, the Architecture Department at Louis Vuitton has been involved in establishing this new territory, and continues to pursue the exploration of architecture in a continually changing present.

Japan, Tokyo Omotesando, Jun Aoki & Associates, 2002

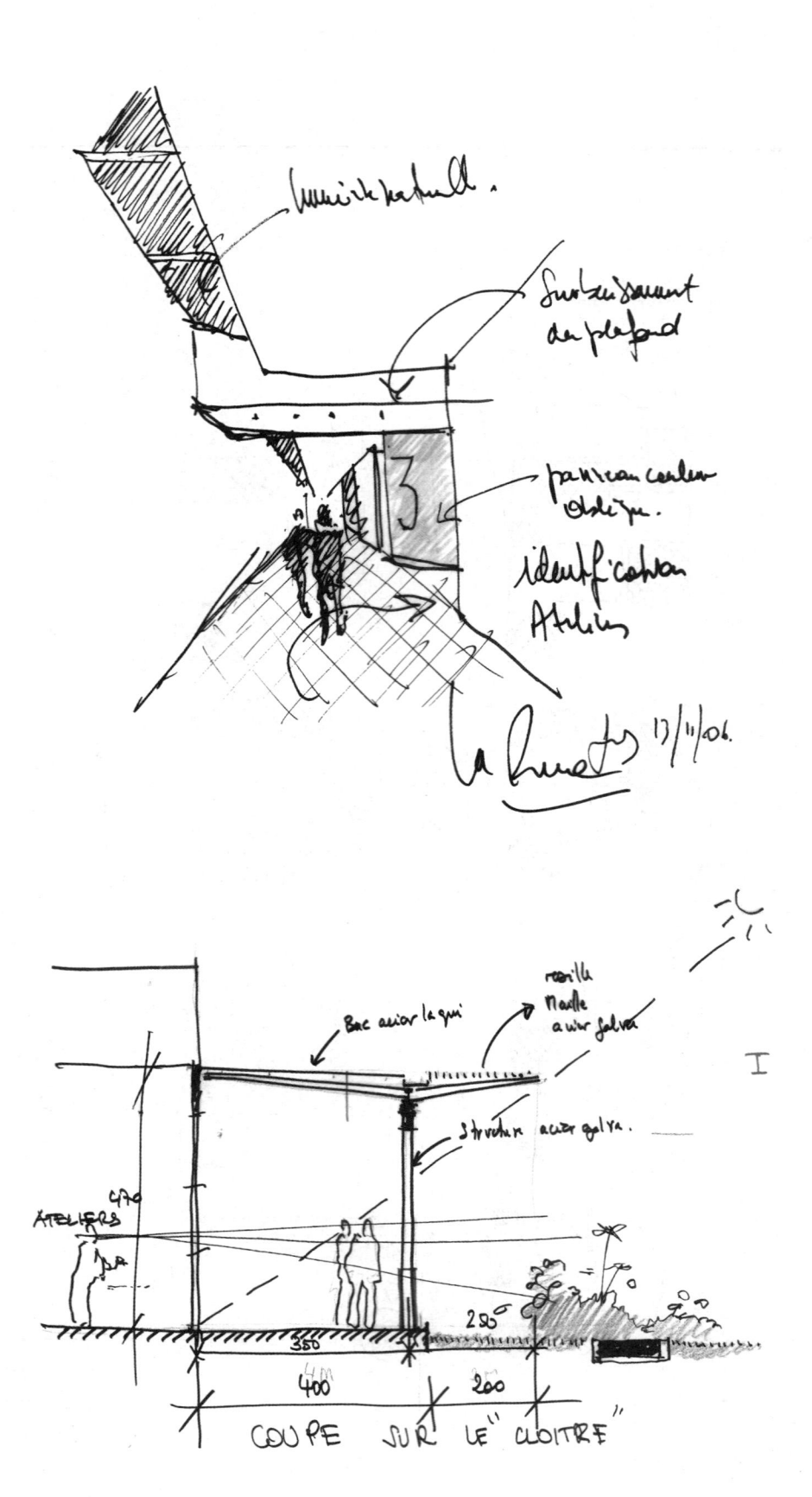

Italy, Fiesso d'Artico Shoe Manufacturing Facility, Jean-Marc Sandrolini, 2009

Japan, Tokyo Omotesando, Jun Aoki & Associates, 2002

No.

Date

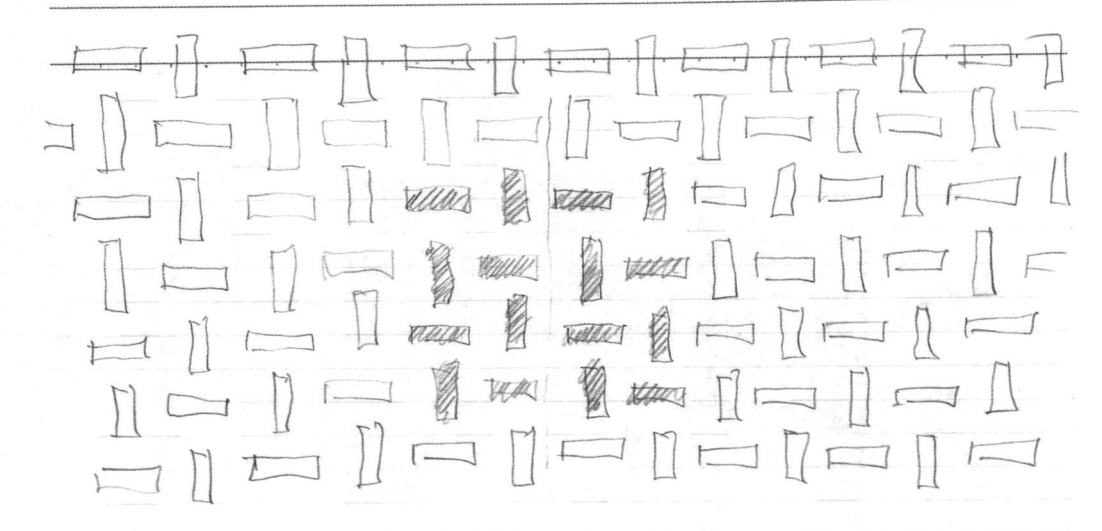

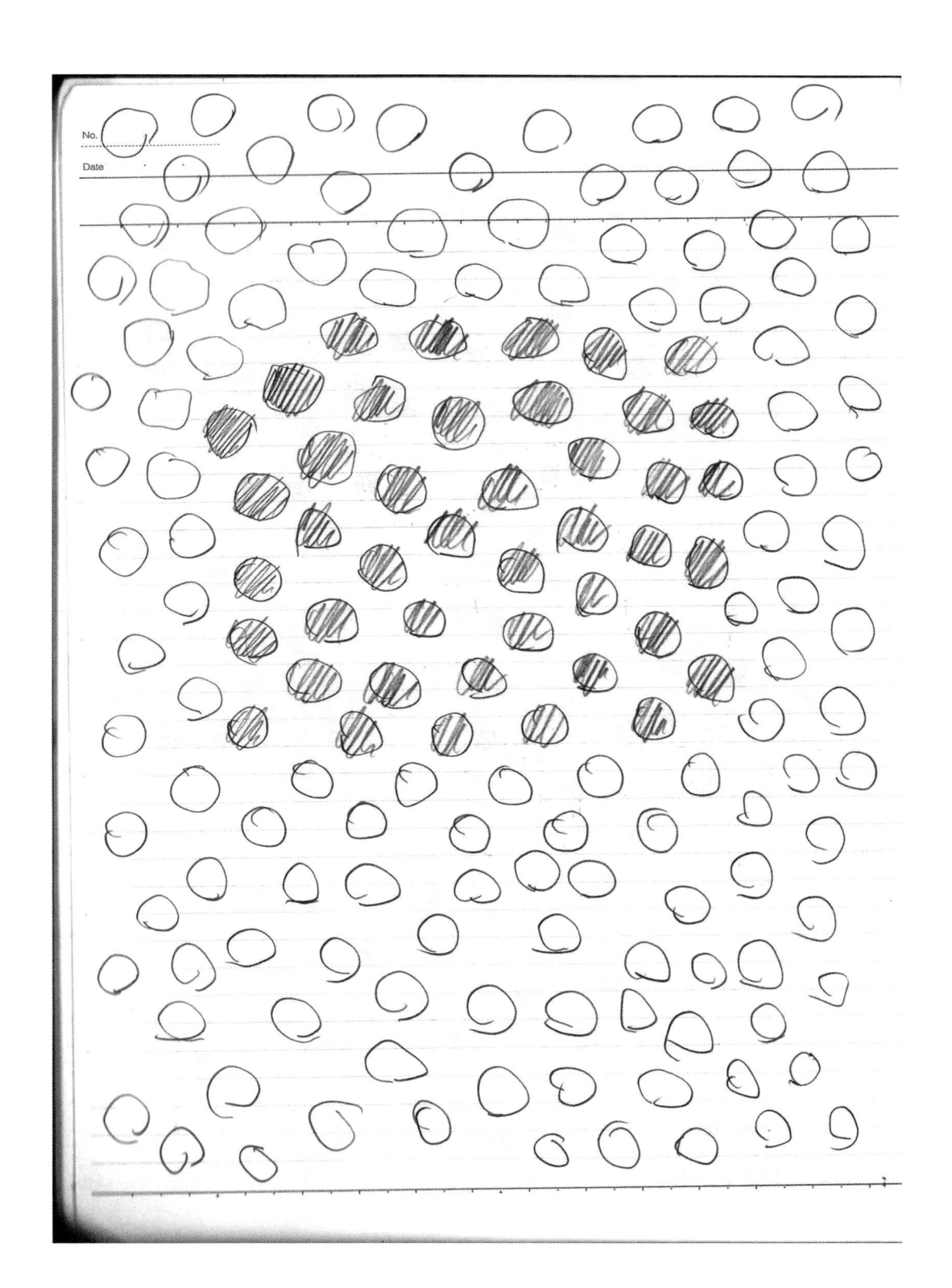

Japan, Tokyo Namiki Dori, Jun Aoki & Associates, 2004

No.
Date

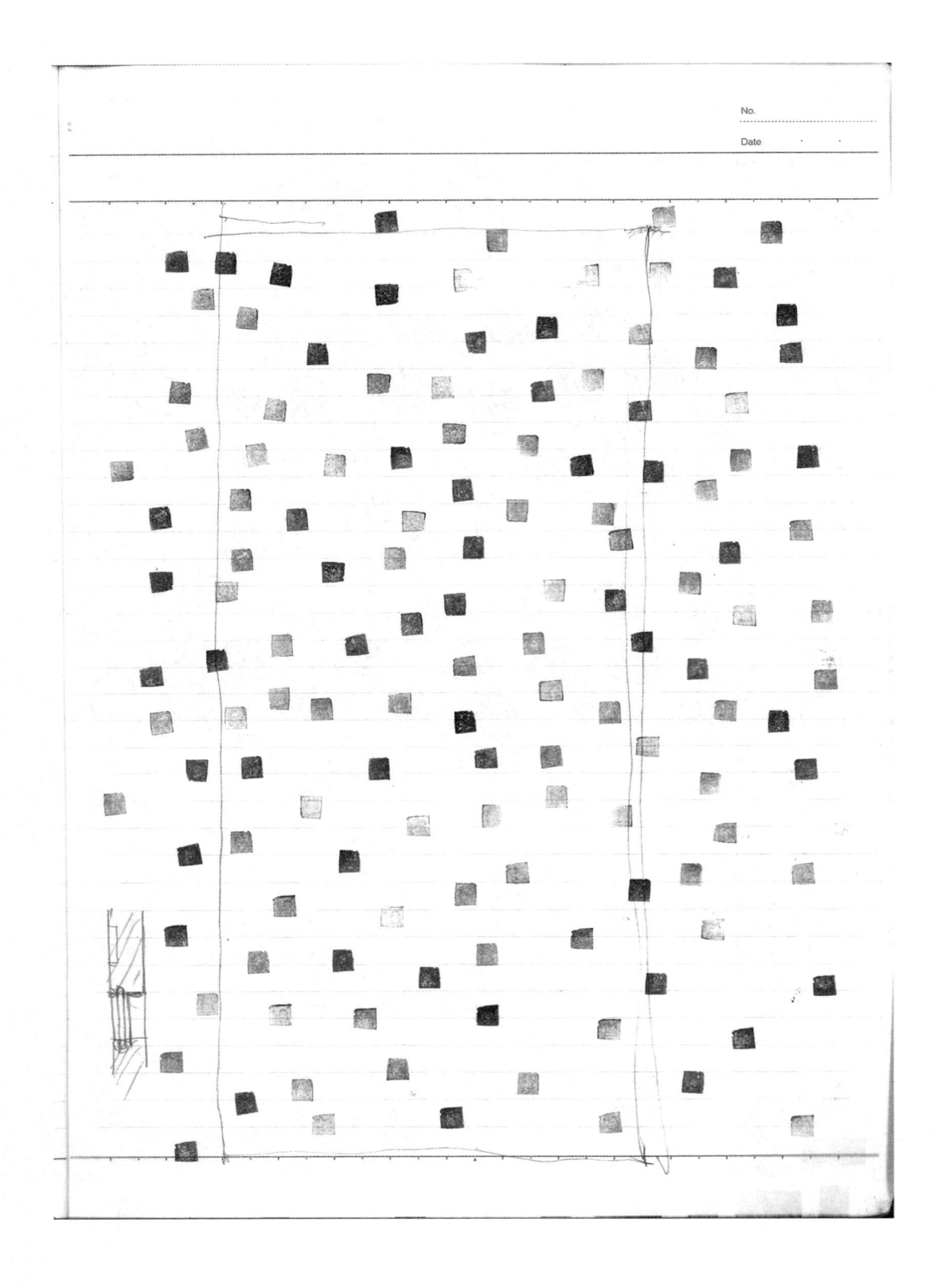

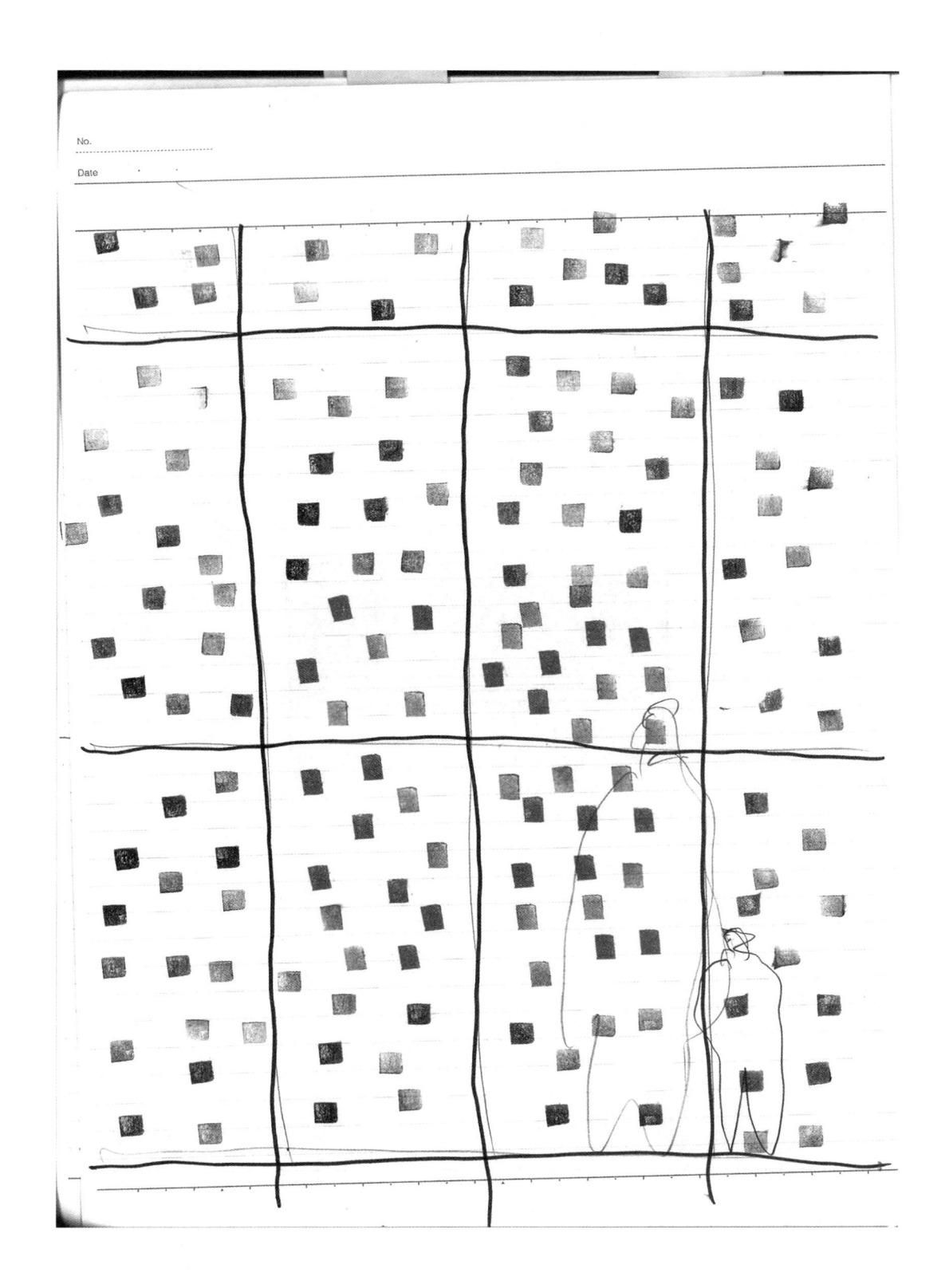

Japan, Tokyo Namiki Dori, Jun Aoki & Associates, 2004

No.
Date

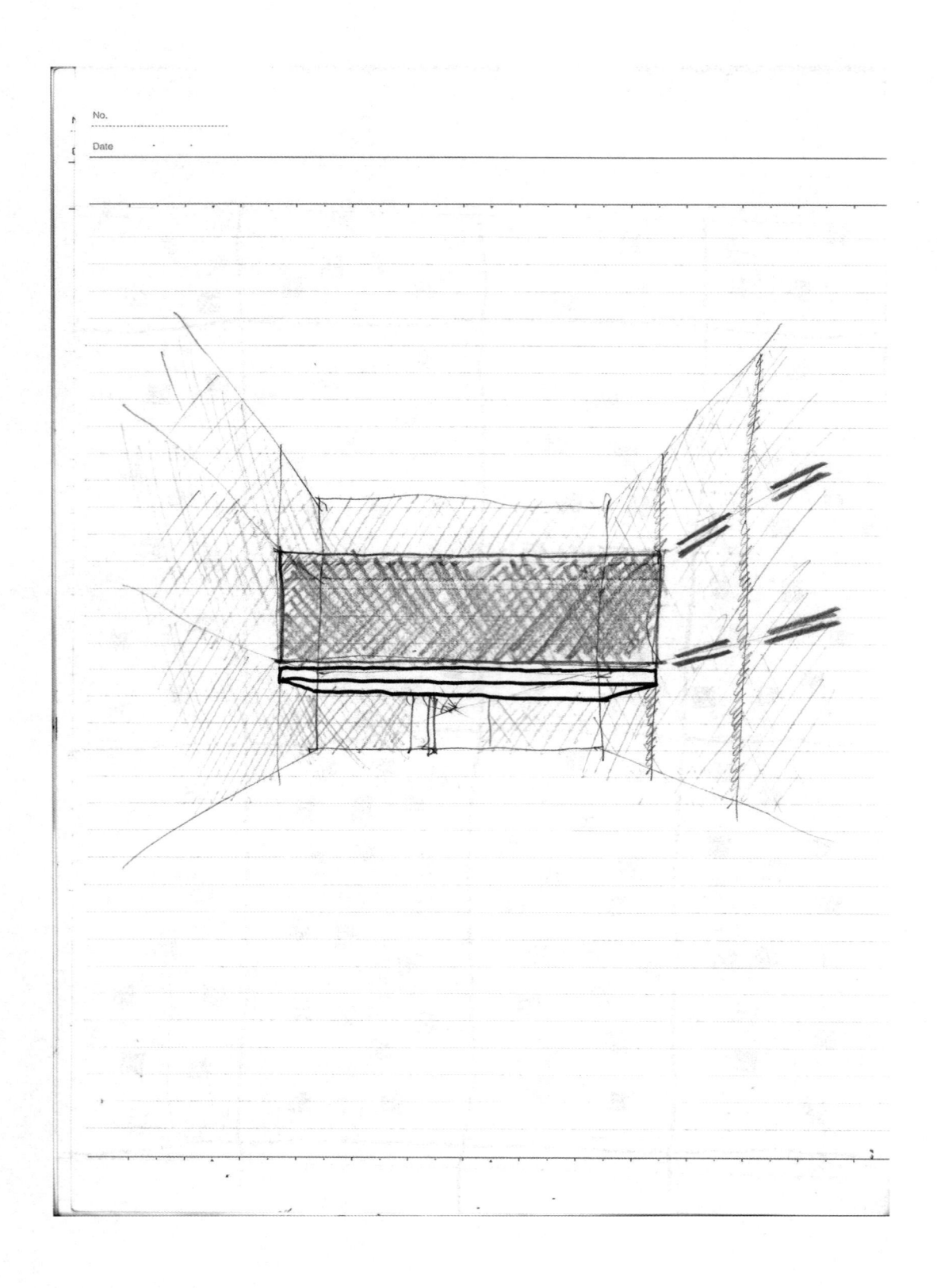

No.

Date

Japan, Tokyo Omotesando, Jun Aoki & Associates, 2002

26/APR/2002
No 1

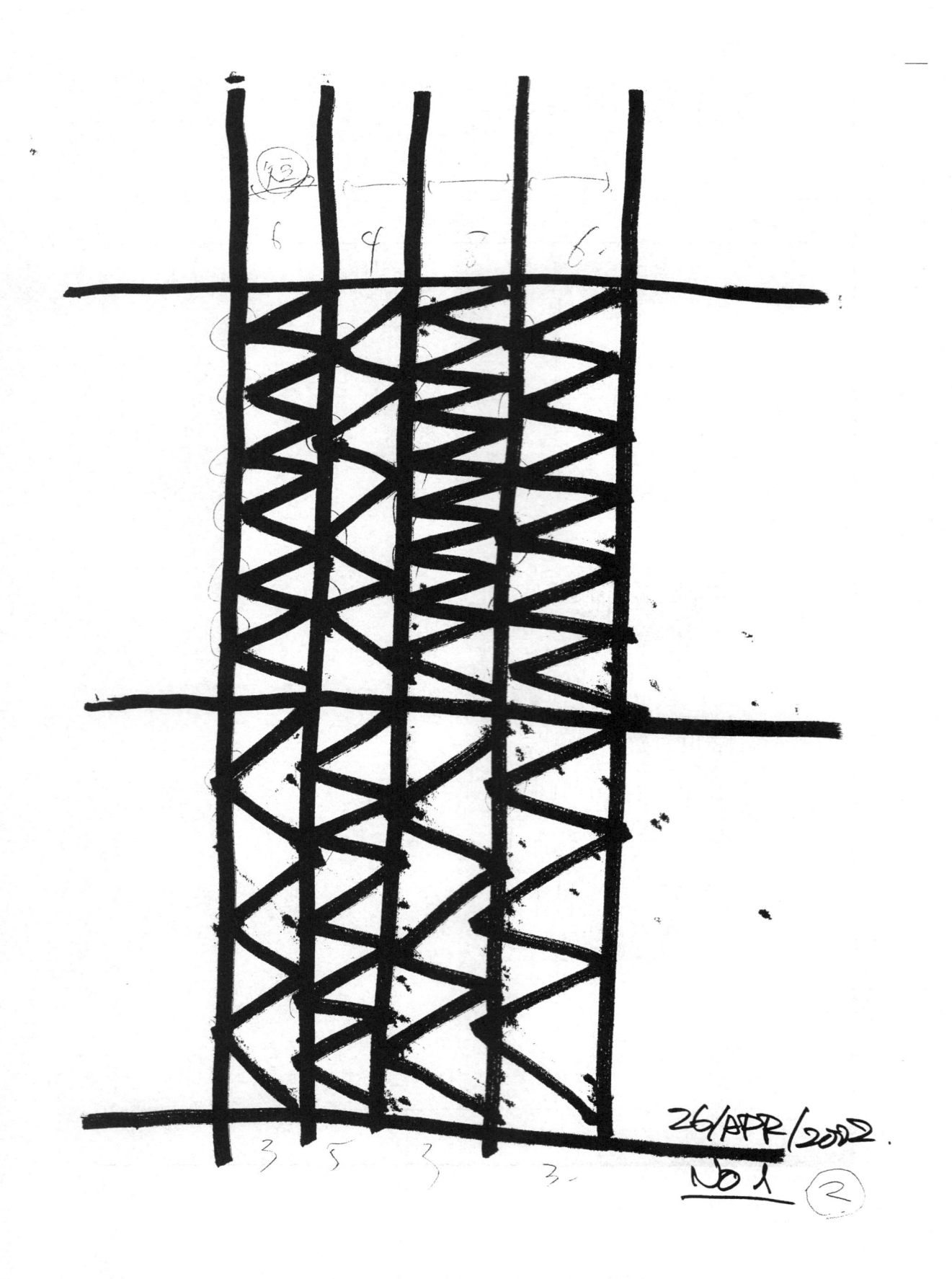

Japan, Tokyo Omotesando, Jun Aoki & Associates, 2002

No.
Date

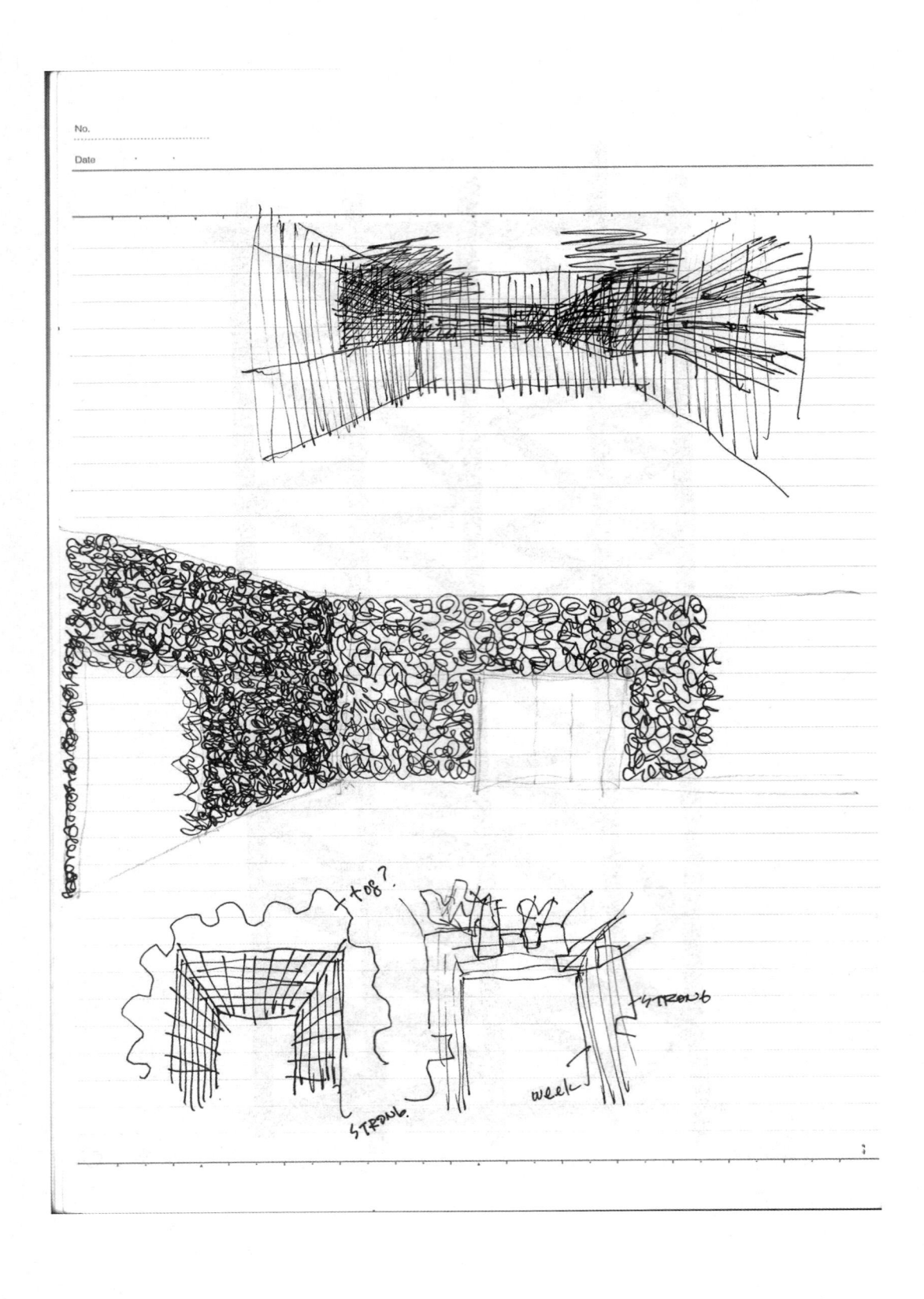

strong. weak STRONG

Japan, Tokyo Roppongi, Jun Aoki & Associates, 2003

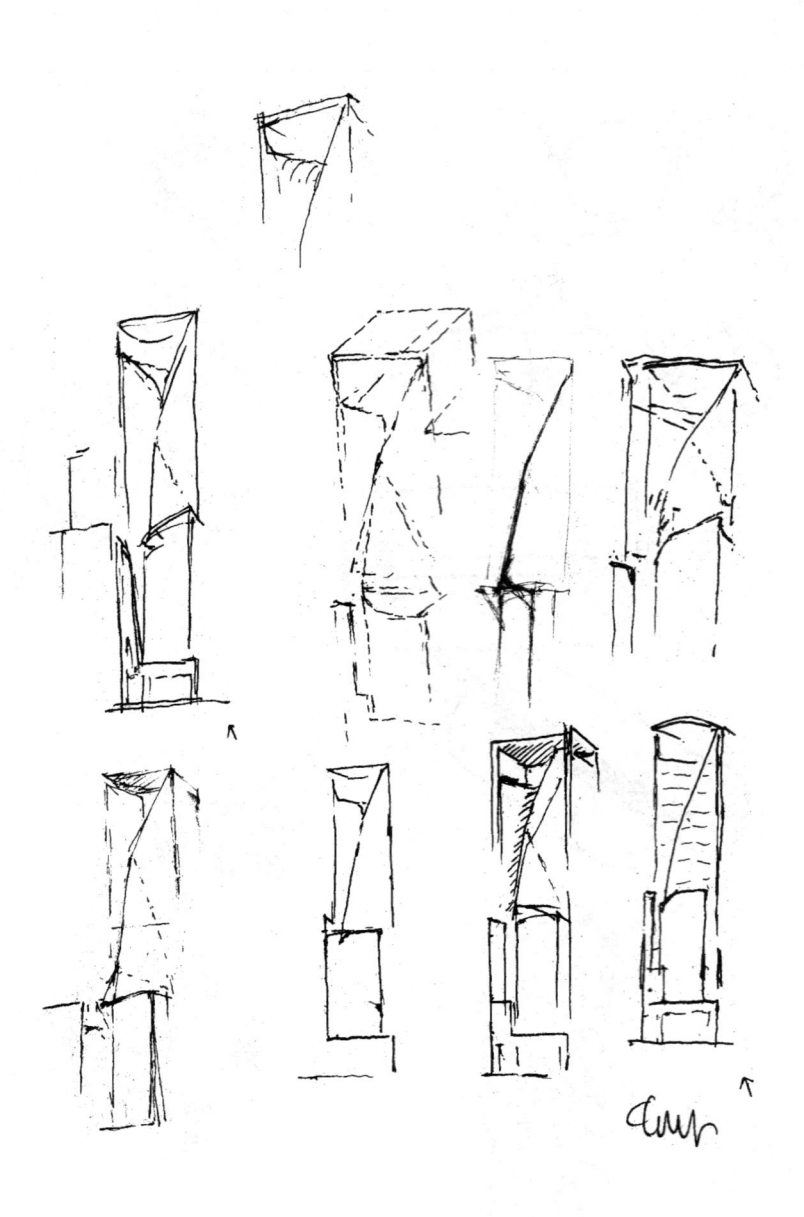

New York LVMH Tower, Atelier Christian de Portzamparc, 1999

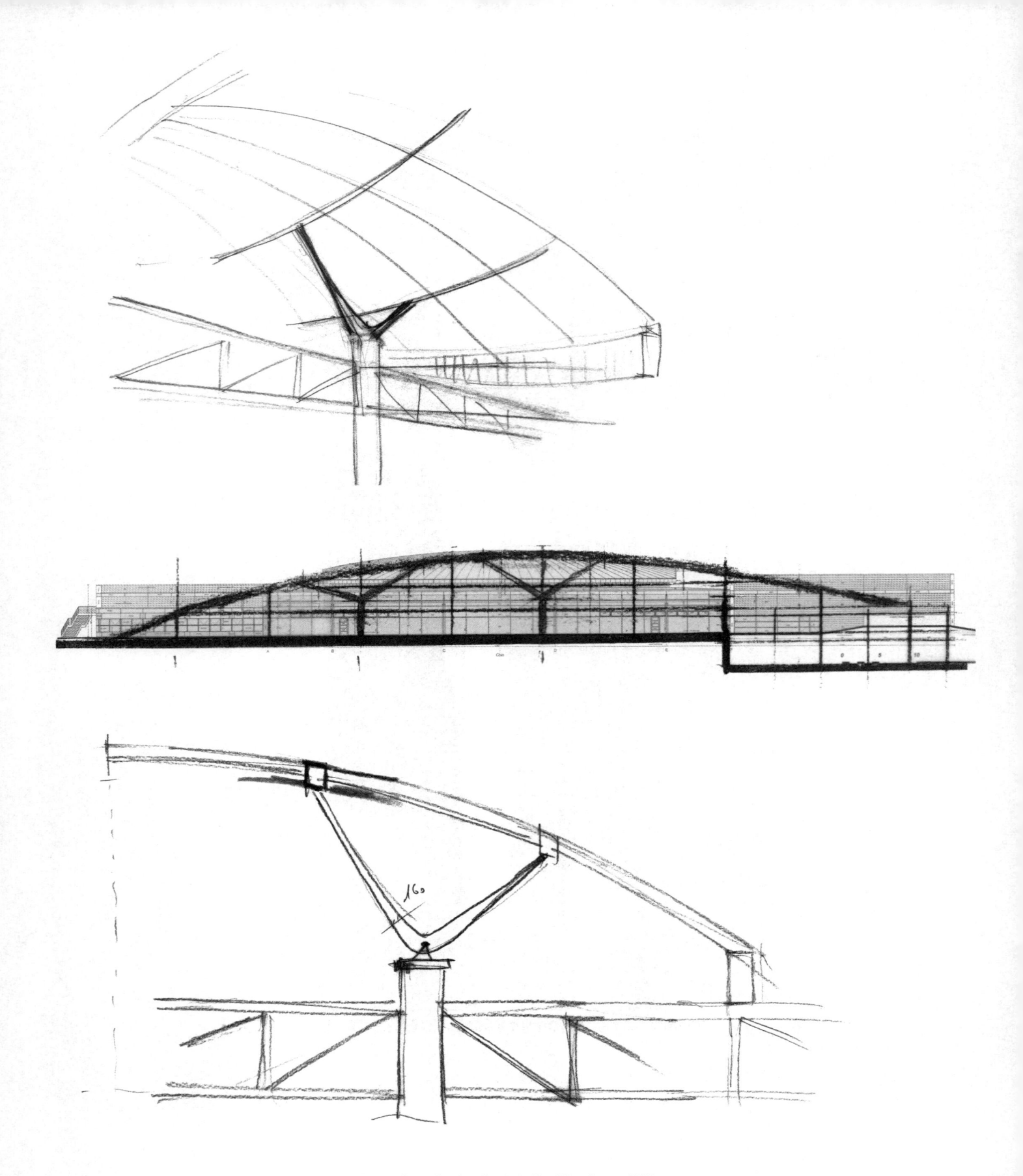

France, Ducey Leather Goods Atelier, Gilles Carnoy, 2002

PROJECTS
JAPAN
ASIA PACIFIC
UNITED STATES
EUROPE
HEADQUARTERS
INDUSTRIAL

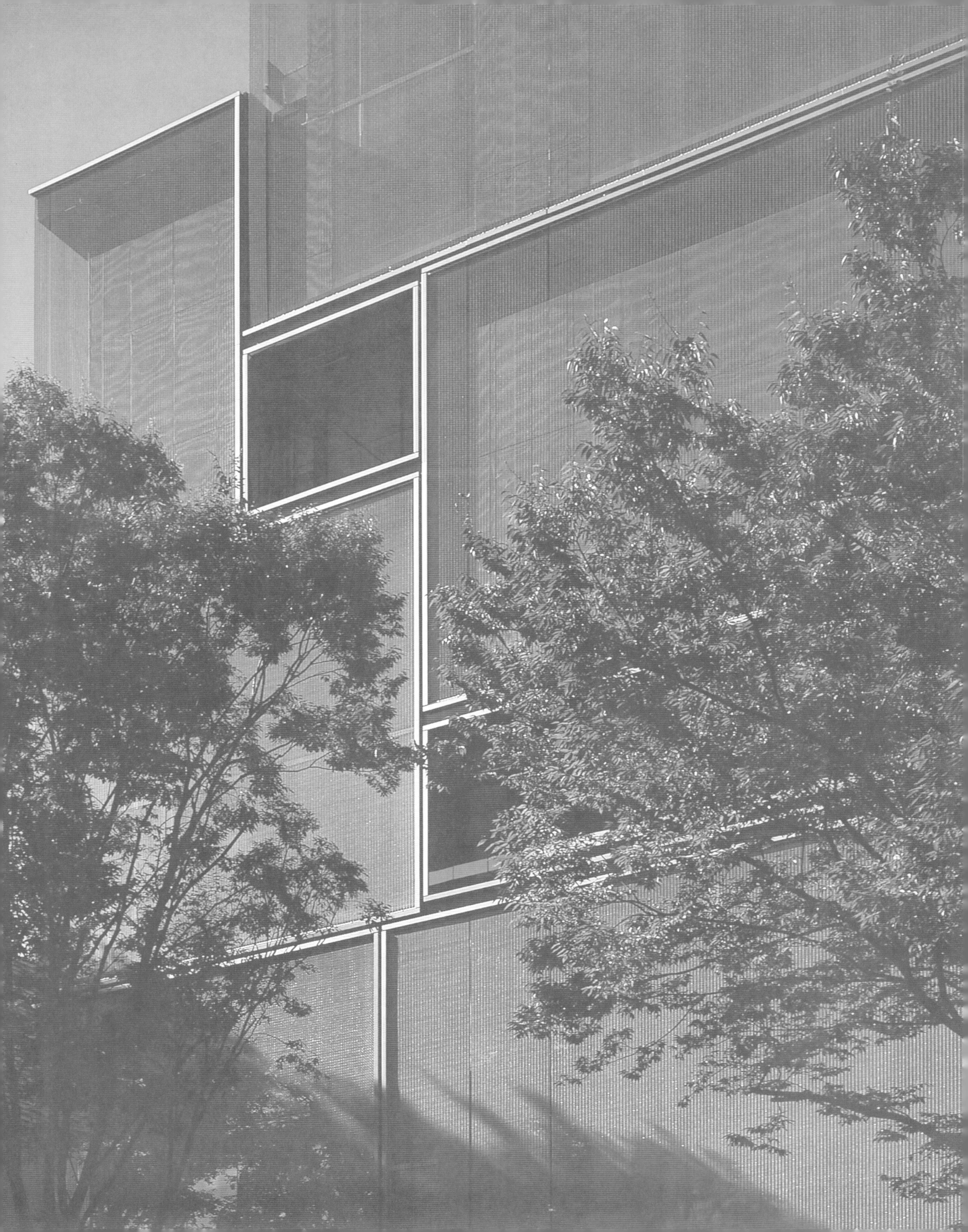

JAPAN
KOBE *KYORYUCHI*
NAGOYA *SAKAE*
TOKYO *OMOTESANDO*
TOKYO *ROPPONGI*
TOKYO *NAMIKI DORI*
OSAKA *MIDOSUJI*

KOBE KYORYUCHI

architects
THE LOUIS VUITTON
ARCHITECTURE DEPARTMENT
2010

text by
FRÉDÉRIC EDELMANN

The inhabitants of Tokyo rarely head southwest of Honshu to the Kansai region, the site of many great battles and the birthplace of imperial capitals, Nara (*Heijo-kyo*) and Kyoto (*Heian-kyo*). If they catch the Shinkansen on the Tokaido line, it's for business, and never, or seldom, to take in a cultural heritage largely spared by the war—and the focus of tourism in the Land of the Rising Sun. Are Osaka and Kobe more familiar to them? Like Tokyo and Yokohama, the two cities also form a sizable conurbation, a landscape of ports, warehouses, factories, a wealth of blue-gray tones, and a disorderly order from which there emerges from time to time an architectural surprise that's difficult to classify. In which category does the new Louis Vuitton store fall? In a category of moderation distinguished by gray marks of restraint. This controlled form is interrupted only by a few openings through which Louis Vuitton's codes can be immediately seen and understood; ever evolving, they are a constant in most stores.

Here, as on the other side of the world, architecture is not understood as an autonomous object, even if everything is precisely designed and premeditated, like a church façade; one has to come close and truly feel it, like the inside of a chest that inevitably opens little by little. At night, the lantern effect obtained by the internal illumination of the monograms on the façade stands out amidst the austerity of the city's chic neighborhood, a prefecture with a population of 1.5 million, or nearly 3 million if one includes the outskirts. These are the potential customers.

Every major city in Japan is equipped with its own sounds and even its own stores, and here, as elsewhere, the Louis Vuitton store was conceived of in response to the specificity of the city. This is a city influenced by a Western presence, where fashion has always been a serious passion, marked by somber colors such as navy blue, black, white and gray, while at the same time Osaka, a city known for its performers, evolved into exuberance and color. The Kobe Collection—fashion week in Kobe—has become very popular, causing a flood of trade to Shanghai and Southeast Asia. In such a context, it wasn't very hard for Louis Vuitton to find its place.

The city is sandwiched between the sea and mountains, traversed by railways and highways; the inhabitants, anchored in a provincial but prestigious past, have grown accustomed to this landscape regulated by the economy. During the day, except on weekends, activity on the streets seems to ebb, and it's hard to recognize central areas other than train stations or large hubs, whether spontaneous or artificial. There are centers though, and not insignificant ones; take, for example, the one that formed at the heart of a large neighborhood on the artificial island of Rokko, an eclectic mix of large hotels, hospitals, a university, and a fashion museum that was installed to add a touch of cultural life. Whether they're adventurous in spirit or know the aging institutions of Rokko Island out of habit, taxi drivers, happily in their seventies, might forget what they're doing and take you to the fashion museum… even though you asked to be taken to the Louis Vuitton store. The local television stations might have also confused them.

The real Louis Vuitton is located more to the North, in what is still known as Kobe's ancient central ward (*Chuo-ku*), even if after the devastation of World War II and the 1995 earthquake, the concept of old might seem a bit displaced. Everything is new and clean in this neighborhood, which has attracted every major international fashion brand. It's the Kobe equivalent to the Champs-Élysées or, to Tokyo's Ginza, Roppongi and Omotesando. But the words *Kyu Kyoryuchi* (former foreign settlement) and *Kyomachi*, the name taken for the new store, do not resonate in a neutral way. Around Louis Vuitton, the district extends from east to west along Nakamachi Street and from north to south along Naniwa Avenue, the former name of Osaka when—during the 7th and 8th centuries—Kobe, its twin sister, served as a capital for the first rulers of a Japan that was still fragmented. Through its toponomy, the neighborhood evokes the past and the sea; *Naniwa* is also the name of the first battleship to join the ranks of the Imperial Navy in 1883, whose imperial status required a distinct design and whose military function meant that it was one of the most fearsome ships of the time. As in Osaka, this is the crossroads of various worlds that came from the sea: battleships, pirates, yachts, and luxury cruises. In each case, copper had to be polished and the decks carefully washed.

Was all this behind Louis Vuitton's approach to Kyomachi? The first store was developed in 2003 on the same side of Nakamachi street, but on the other side of Naniwa. Skillfully designed by the architects Barthélémy & Griño, you couldn't even see the four-level parking garage above, a common trait of other buildings in the neighborhood since the earthquake. Here, the lot was hidden by large bands of simple colors, arranged in a square, and at random. At the corner where the avenue and street met, there was an excavated cube, a kind of gully protecting passersby and clients who were invited to enter the 800 square-meters of the store. Six years later, Louis Vuitton crossed the street to occupy a portion of the space left vacant by the collapse of the Oriental Building and its hotel in 1995.

Among the Louis Vuitton stores in Japan, the new Kobe store, opened on March 3, 2010, has become a point of reference. It's the first in Japan to have reached the enviable status of "Maison"—the ninth such location in the world—with a surface area of 1200 square meters. The Louis Vuitton Maison, that singular sound, refers to the distinctiveness of the first store in Paris and the chic elegance that its tightly maintained name has never ceased to evoke.

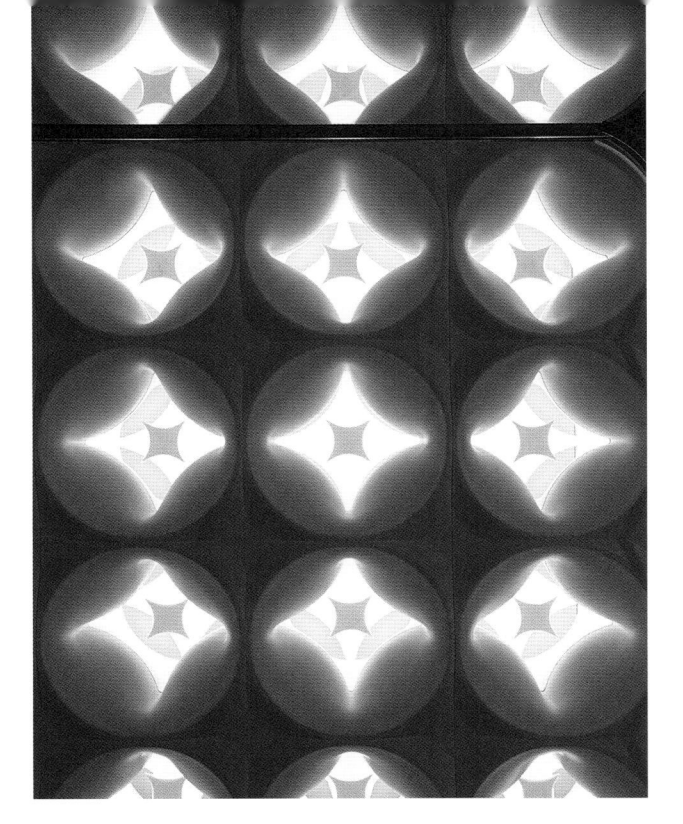

The same avenue, a street crossed; a funny crossover. This was not the company's first undertaking of this kind; at Vuitton, the lifespan of a store and its interior design is never more than six years: materials get used and eyes become weary, both for clients and the sales teams attending to them. This is the price (costly but indispensable) of the vigilance necessary to not let the dust settle—neither physically nor morally—in the fickle world of luxury and fashion. Just as with every move or new establishment, the Louis Vuitton adventure in Kobe has its own specificities. The neighborhood itself, its toponymy retaining the scent of the sea, plays its part. The theme of maritime travel in the store comes as no surprise.

Other factors were also in play. First, the flow of people and cars on the street surged alongside the first store, adhering to the one-way direction of Nakamachi street. The new building goes against the current. Its entrance, also excavated and symmetrical with the first one—which has become virtual—greets clients head on. In addition, the sales area increased in size by approximately 200 square meters. As a result, the "net" is wider and better placed. In six years, the range that Louis Vuitton has to offer has also increased substantially. More clothes (Vuitton Ready to Wear was born in 1998), accessories and bags to present has multiplied and increased the challenges of merchandising.

On the avenue, the building has a more solid, more structured appearance. Even though it has neighbors, the store imparts an urban autonomy, enhanced at night by the intensity of light emanating from it. Crowning the building is an architectural ornament, the design of which is borrowed from the International Style, meaning that it's smooth and straight like a ruler. The façade, as is company norm, plays off of the famous monogram, its multiple flowers creating a rhythmic design that can be identified from afar, as the principle is so frequent and recognizable. It is built on the principle of symmetry—in fact a false symmetry—between the avenue and the street. On one side, a window obscures any view of the inside. On the other, a side entrance—proportional to the window—permits direct access to a world of travel and the sea.

However, it's at the corner where everything happens. The codified universe of the brand draws on the classic principle of the rounded staircase (here a spiral), monumental and unavoidable. Both an element of décor and a sign, it is doubled in effect by a succession of platforms, which rise more slowly and are less spectacular, allowing one to discover, like different autonomous worlds, the Louis Vuitton universe. Tables, displays, and the Bag Bar act as shelves where every object informs you of their rarity and delicate balance.

In theory, there are only two floors. The succession of mezzanines, the way they open (or don't) towards one another, the way they sometimes observe each other—a cream-white universe for women, a warm wood universe for men—are there to pique and accompany your curiosity, fueled by the fact that the principal areas of the store are immediately perceptible as soon as you walk through the entrance. The upper part of the stairwell, conceived of as a treasure chest, adopts a stylistic "vocabulary" that in fact escapes all technical vocabulary. Between the aeronautic dressing room, the cage for exotic birds, the merry-go-round, and the jewelry box, the area plays well with transparency.

Curves call for curves. The transition from the orthogonal spaces could only be accomplished through a light and very noticeable element: a long, ribbon-sculpture by the American artist Alyson Shotz. Its title, borrowed from Einstein, is *A Curve in Space and Time*. The piece solves the equation. At more than 20 meters long, composed of countless translucent and mirrored fragments, the sculpture—sensual and cold, changing with time and light—sets the tone in this Kobe symphony.

p. 10 Maison Louis Vuitton Tokyo Omotesando, façade detail
p. 13 curtain wall detail
p. 14 exterior views of west façade
p. 15–19 interior views of Bag Bar, stair and main retail areas. Installed along the stair is Alyson Shotz's *A Curve in Space and Time* (2010)

KOBE KYORYUCHI

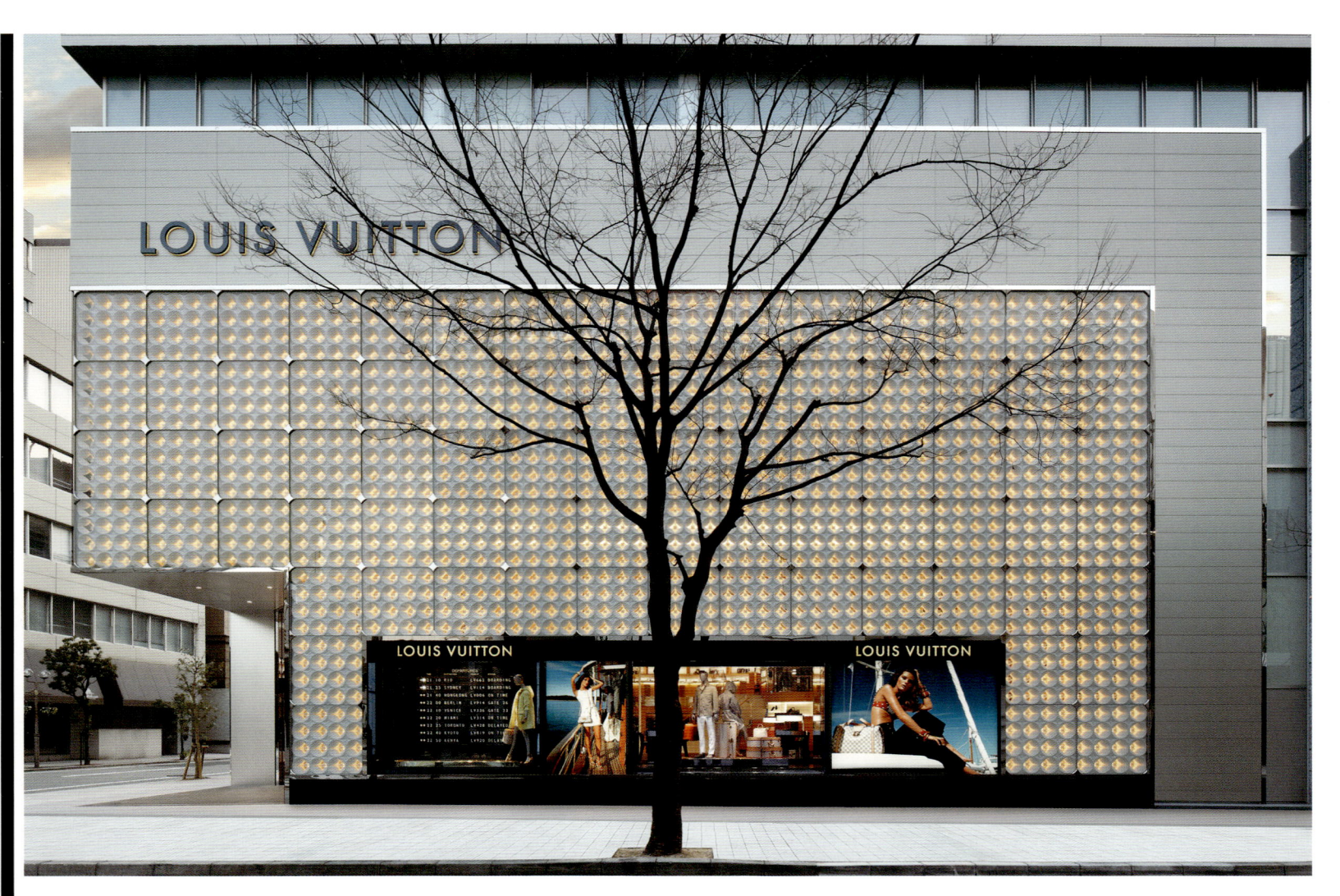

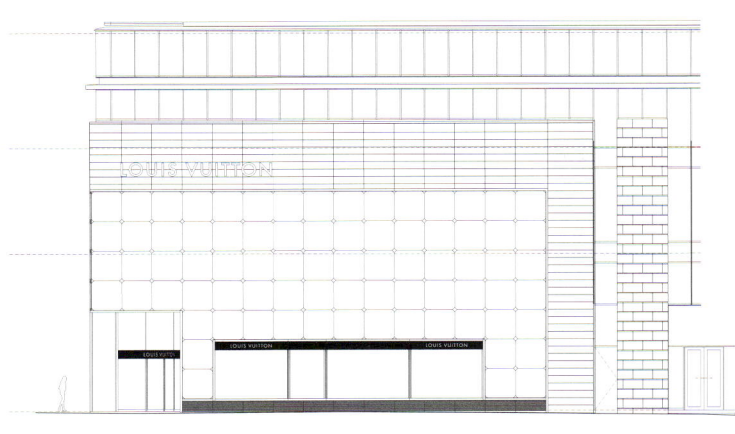

WEST FACADE ELEVATION

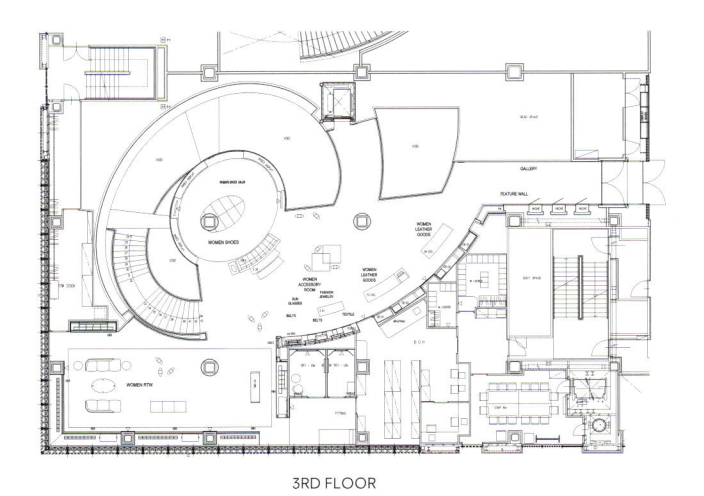

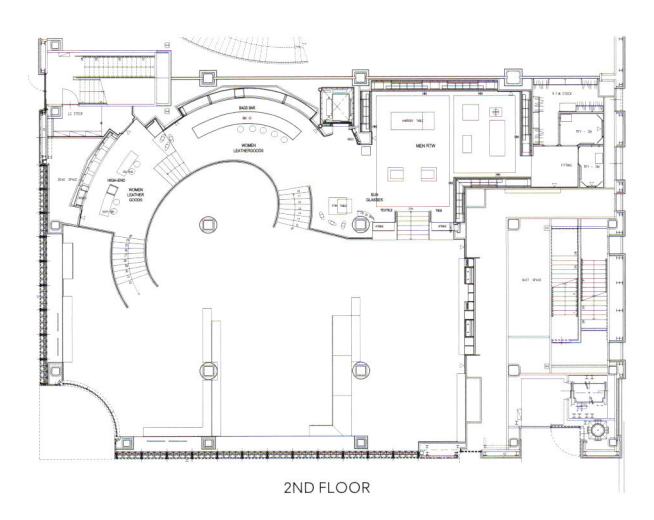

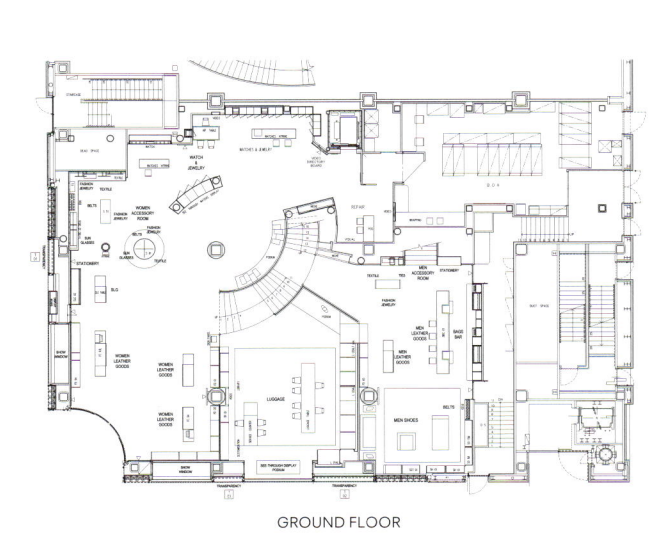

3RD FLOOR

2ND FLOOR

GROUND FLOOR

ARCHITECTURE AND INTERIORS 15

KOBE KYORYUCHI

JAPAN

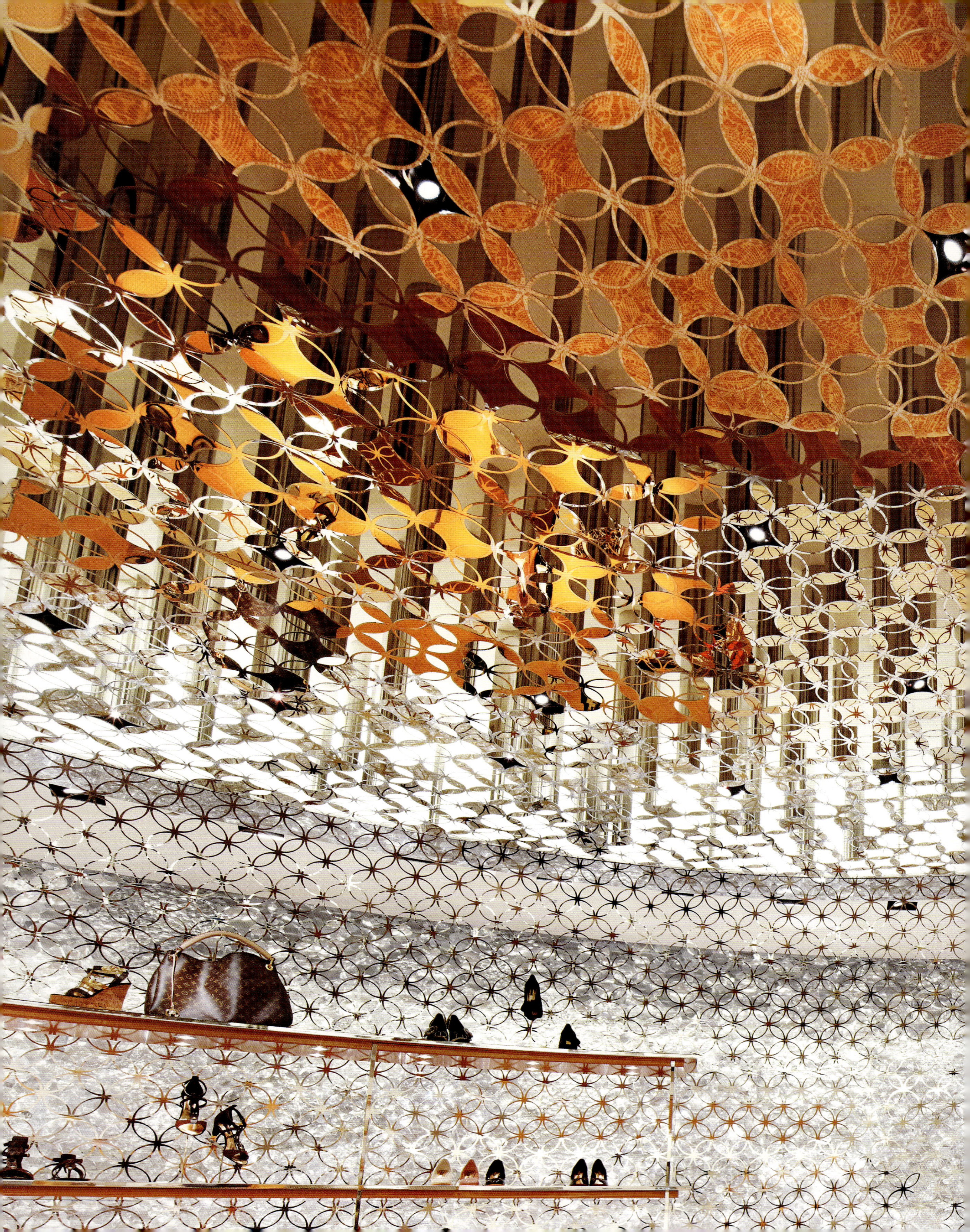

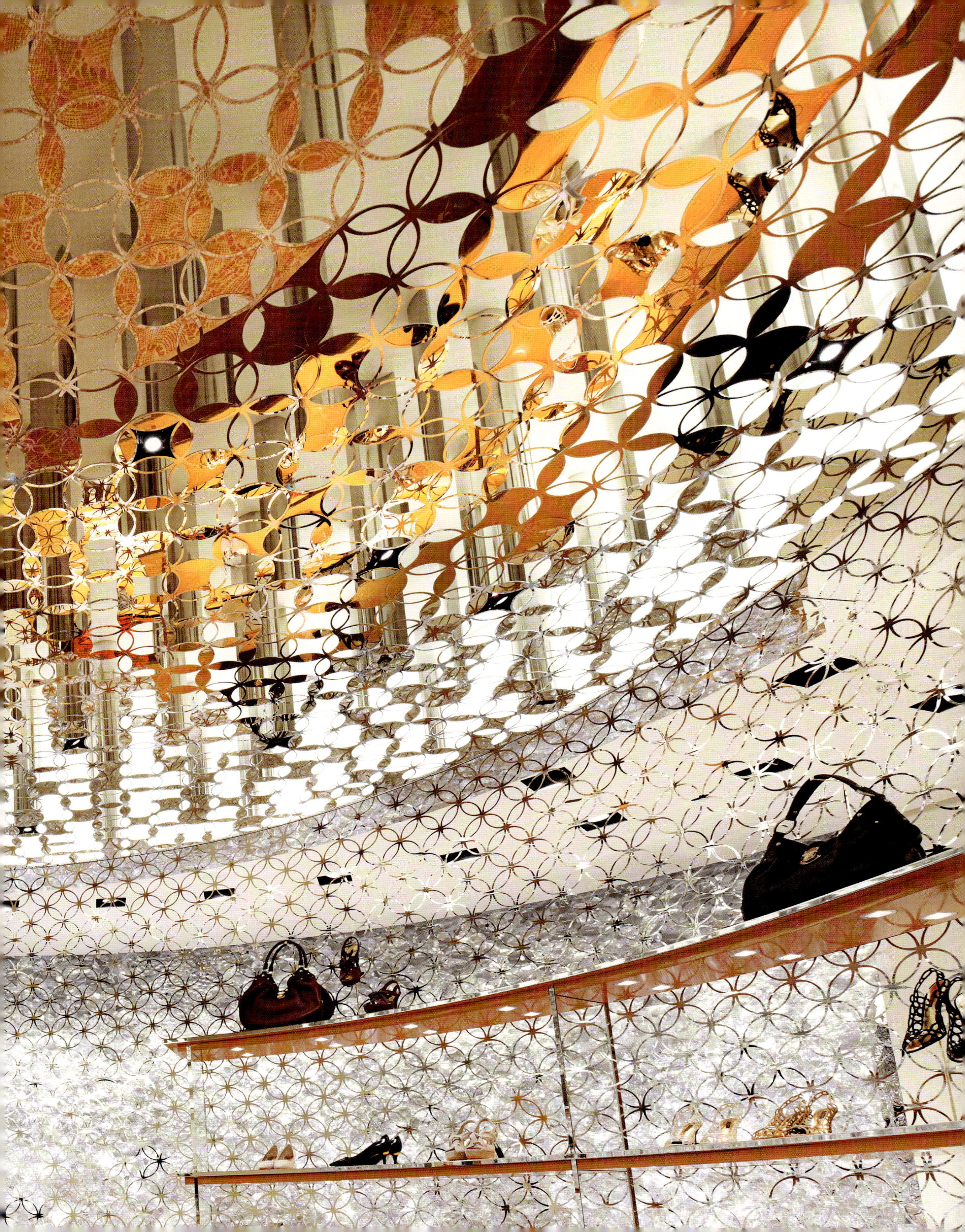

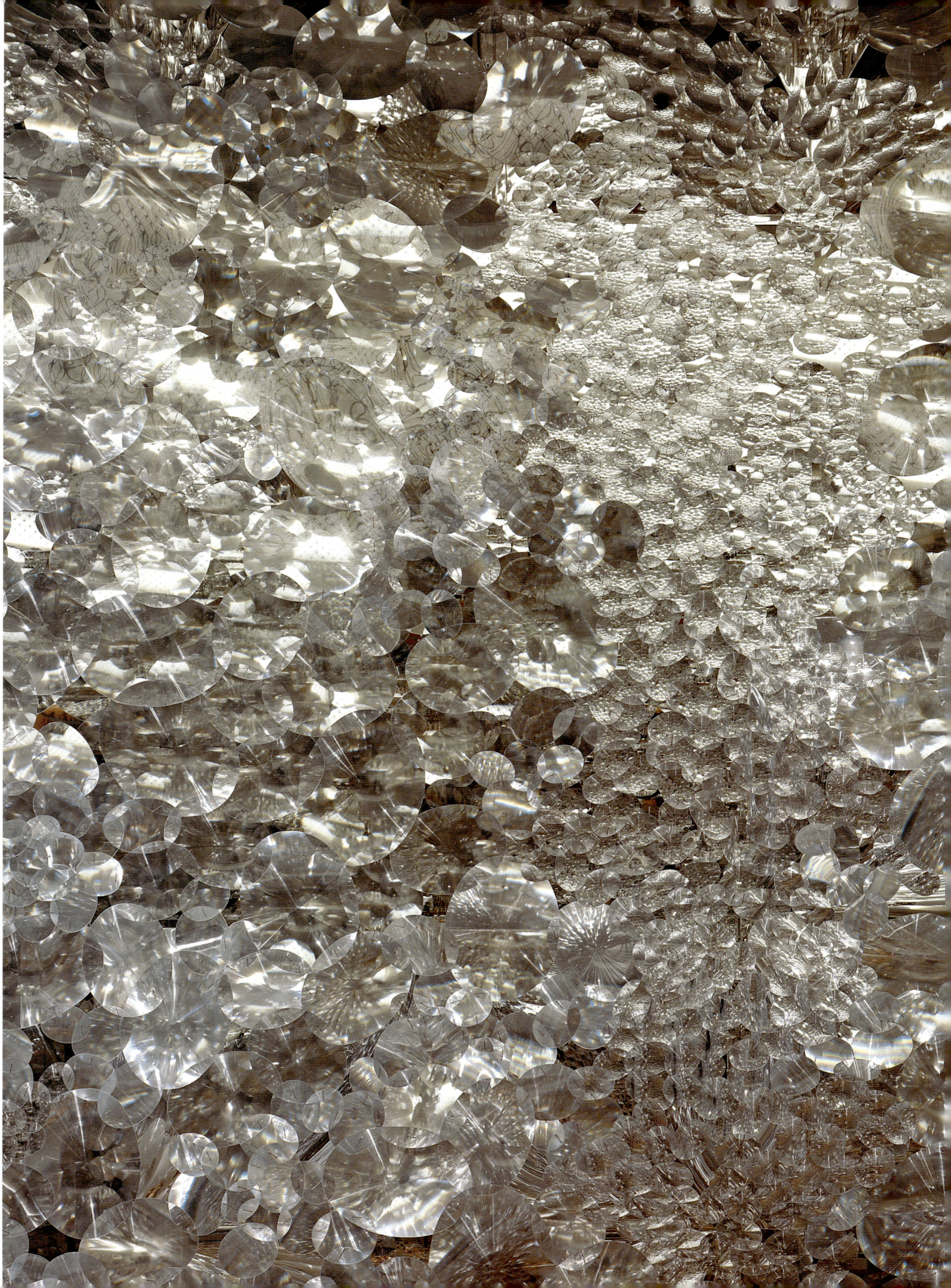

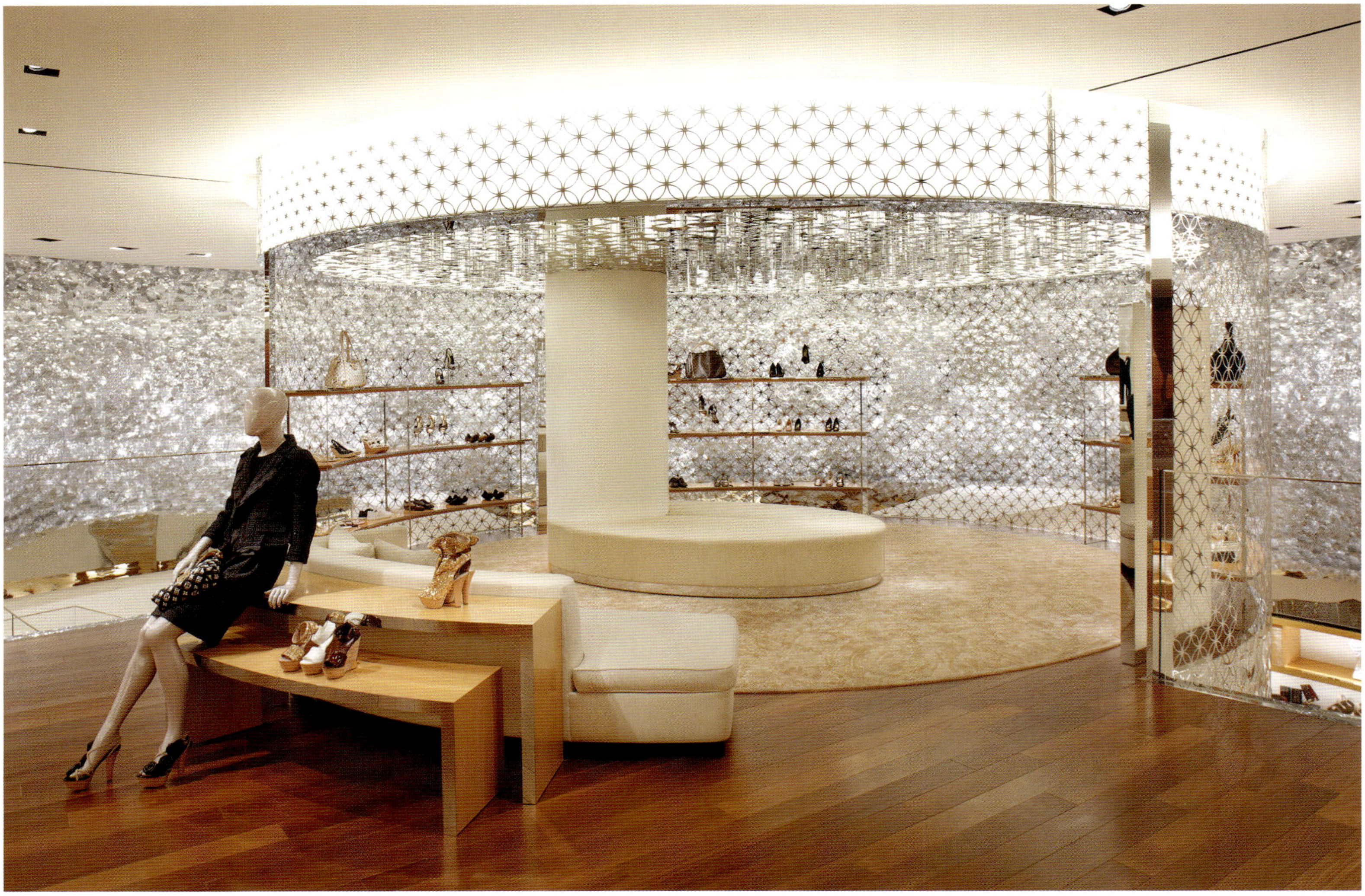

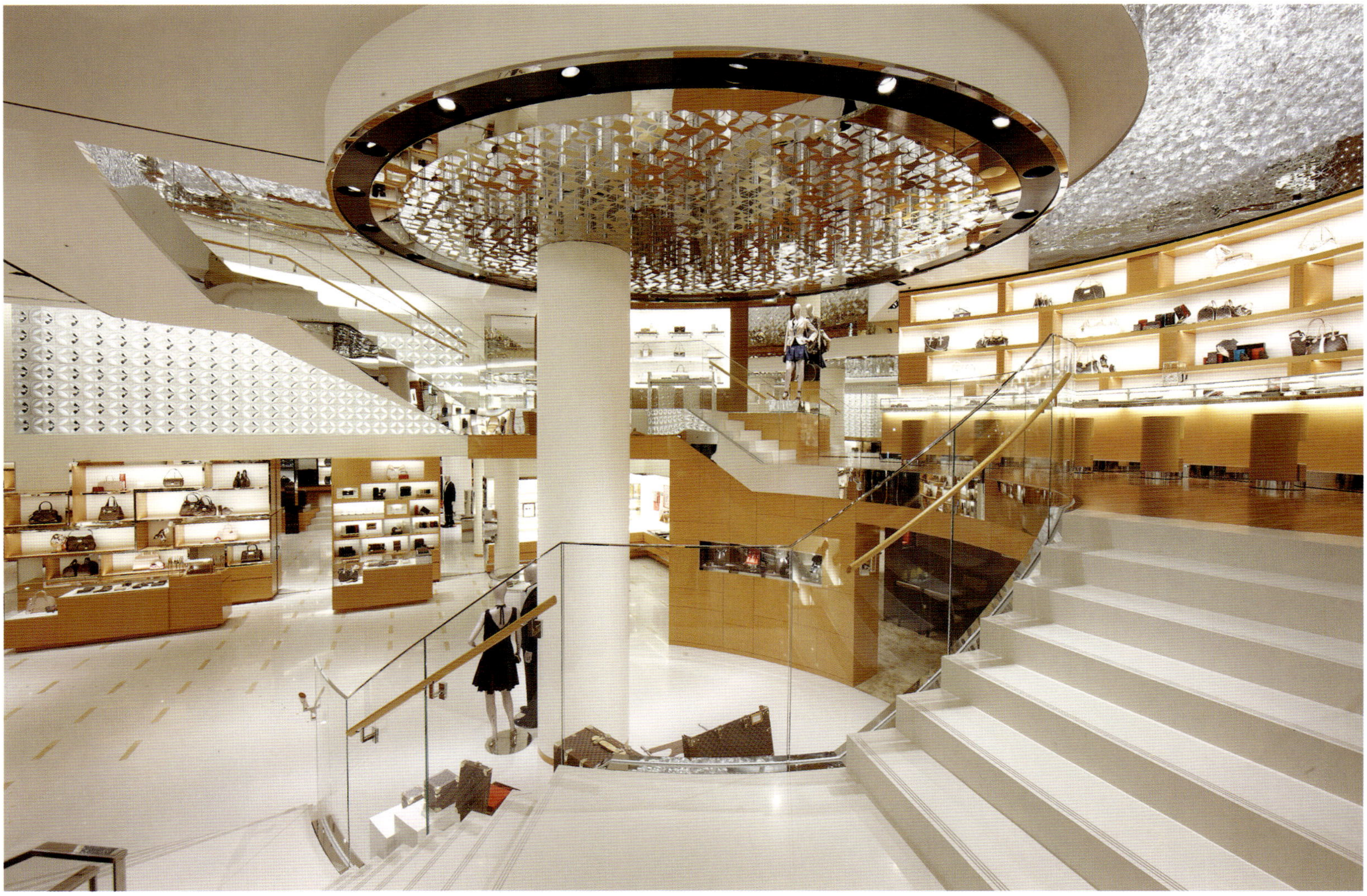

KOBE KYORYUCHI

JAPAN

NAGOYA SAKAE

architects
JUN AOKI & ASSOCIATES;
THE LOUIS VUITTON
ARCHITECTURE DEPARTMENT
1999

text by
RAFAEL MAGROU

In Nagoya, situated an hour and a half outside of Tokyo via the Shinkansen bullet train, there's an address that every taxi driver knows: from the station, ask for Louis Vuitton Sakae and you'll be sure to arrive at your destination. This is surprising, since this boutique isn't part of a department store—as is usually the case in Japan. Having become iconic since its construction in 1999, this architectural object is extraordinary because of its isolated, if not insular, position. Located in the heart of downtown Nagoya, it has become a point of reference not because of its dimensions, but because of the singularity of its materiality. Or, to be more precise, of its immateriality.

Within the diverse fabric of Japan's second largest city, the capital of the Aichi Prefecture and the town that gave us *pachinko* —that form of pinball gambling that the Japanese so love—the Louis Vuitton Sakae store stands apart from the bustling Otsu-dori, an area that attracts a clientele that's eclectic, but frenetic when it comes to shopping. Although one can find the monogrammed brand in the Mitsukoshi and Matzuzakaya department stores—the Japanese equivalents of Paris's Galeries Lafayettes—Sakae keeps away from the hubbub and offers a moment of rest to more discreet clients. The store can therefore maintain a level of service that regulars and newcomers, often demanding about hospitality, have come to expect.

At the corner of Hisaya-dori and Nishiki-dori, this lone *ex nihilo* building is Louis Vuitton's first freestanding building in Japan. At the same time, it inaugurated the start of a long-term collaboration between Louis Vuitton and the architect Jun Aoki, who has since designed landmarks in Hong Kong, on Omotesando & Namiki-dori in Tokyo, and on Fifth Avenue in New York, which rest among the brand's strongest symbols, and are also presented here in this book. Relatively unknown at the time, Jun Aoki was retained during a competition launched by Louis Vuitton for the Nagoya site. For this project, the architect received little help from the heterogeneous context where he was to incorporate this new building; bordered by an open-air parking lot, there were no elements offering tangible support of what was to become the new emblem of the fashion house.

Starting from the checkerboard (Louis Vuitton's leather motif designed in 1888), Jun Aoki imagined a magic box, with a moiré surface that would attract attention without disturbing it. Nagoya Sakae could be described as an autonomous monolith, the skin of which is composed of overlapping checkered patterns. But, that would reduce the design to its most primitive level. In fact, the double façade is the result of a subtlety and precision that is both graphic and dimensional. The first, outer layer presents a skin of floating glass, a single panel without horizontal joints, enhanced by one-inch squared tiles that alternate between transparency and translucency; the second layer, which is opaque, reveals a checkered pattern of equal dimensions that remains slightly different due to its printed, black and white surface. Keeping a distance of precisely one meter between the two layers, the architect achieved a subtle kinetic effect, in which there alternates interplays of transparency, reflection and translucency. The structure and its support beams disappear, giving way to the city's different overlapping layers which appear like a living tattoo on the boutique façade: in one spot, there is a telecommunications tower resembling the Eiffel Tower, in another, a large Ferris wheel belonging to a megastore off in the distance. What's more, the incorporation of display windows doesn't disturb the dynamic thanks to their mirrored sides and unadorned panes that rest on the outer wall. Without the use of image technology —in 1998, neither LED nor large-scale plasma screens were available—this optical casing combines the static and the dynamic, procuring a true visual *satori*. Even the surrounding keyaki elm leaves are taken aback by their own beauty and movement in this moiré mirror, seemingly astonished by the longevity of the "leather flowers" imprinted on the windows. One must note that this was the first time that the brand concept was applied to an entire building, in which the façade became the entire showcase, literally speaking.

Furthermore, the scale of the building participates in it own way: Jun Aoki wanted a building that remained within human range. Although he clearly reduced the shelving and thereby, in a certain manner, selected the clientele, the decision was made not to build upward. Balance was found by digging down into the earth in order to retain proportions suitable to the "house." This stance also upholds the logic of offering the best service to visitors, following the philosophy of *wabi sabi*—a principle derived from Zen Buddhist concepts that espouse peaceful simplicity as a means of positively influencing existence. Synonymous with sophistication, an extreme quality of order emanates from the building. This was enhanced by the renovation of the interior, unveiled in September 2010, which was reorganized to promote the values of reception and perception to their highest possible levels.

Immediately upon entering, the ground floor is devoted to leather goods of varying scales and nuances, discernable by their colors and textures. Three chandeliers in Murano glass, the first of which was made at the GUM department store in Moscow, provide a sought-after evanescence. Framed within a line of dark wood, they create an enduring association with craftsmanship and the custom-made. Semi-circular counters are arranged into various display units, while the Bag Bar establishes a central, autonomous structure that gives off a public air in the front, and a more private ambience towards the rear. On one side, the continuous stone of the floor alternates with inserts of darker strips, a common characteristic of many Louis Vuitton stores, although the London store on New Bond Street rests as the most handsome example of this effect. On the other side, a teak parquet floor in a large chevron design lends a unique vibration to the space. The stucco surface of the walls, delicately scuffed, envelop a wooden composition dominated by African Walnut, and connected to a textile tapestry bearing a diamond pattern—an homage to the fleeces that adorned ancient trunks. Each material, each detail, is recorded in a "bible," whose contents are particularly rich for Japanese buildings, and which constitutes an encyclopedic collection of architectural elements kept secret by the department of Architecture at Louis Vuitton.

The furniture, inspired by the work of designer Paul Dupré-Lafon (1900-1971), creates a bridge between Art Deco and the Modern Movement and emits sophistication—using accents of palm wood, lacquer plaques and horn. It offers a luxurious presentation for the latest in women's footwear. The relief is accentuated by lines of bamboo that underline the display cases, making you believe that each piece is destined to be yours. Mirrors inevitably take the stage in the jewelry space—a lounge in which a bouquet of flowers, ephemeral jewels, is enthroned.

Since the store's opening, the clientele has so evolved that the glass monolith stamped with checkered motifs has been enriched by a more distinctive masculine personality. Created in the midst of the store's interior renovations, the lower level was imbued with a "jazz spirit." Nevertheless, it perfectly suits the usual treatment of basement spaces, which are often associated with those smoky clubs that thrive on a particular sound "born in Japan" by Japanese jazzmen, who used to wear black glasses and even went as far as to paint their faces black, and broke away from their American idols to compose innovative and avant-garde music. Through a separate entrance, distinguished by a hall connecting to the main building, a shimmering stairway invites visitors into a cavernous universe, immersed between walls that are seemingly soaked in cigarettes and bear metallic strips of a decidedly masculine air. The passageway is highlighted by the name of the brand in slender, backlit letters—calligraphy that announces the excellence of this distinguished club. A piano surrounded by urban photographs of Paris and New York couch the notoriety of the premises. The Bag Bar, exclusively dedicated to men, is a three-dimensional checkerboard sculpted in space, with Corian cubes carved to accentuate the relief effect. Wooden patterns present products against a sandstone background, the layers and undulations of which evoke inspiring landscapes. In the back, camouflaged behind a showcase displaying the latest designs directly from the shoe factory at Fiesso d'Artico, there is a VIP salon with unexpectedly plush textile rugs. In this exclusively male universe, where wood predominates, lighting is key to the structure of the space—whether it's incorporated into the furniture or disseminated by Art Deco table lamps whose traits alternate between a decidedly underground atmosphere and one straight out of *Bird*, the biopic on Charlie Parker directed under the experienced eye of Clint Eastwood. What emanates is a melody that is very *East End Blues*.

p. 21 façade detail showing the optical effects created by the damier patterns fritted on the exterior double-glass wall
p. 22 top to bottom: exterior view and façade detail,
p. 23 façade details
p. 24–25 exterior view at dusk
p. 26–27 interior views of stair, Bag Bar and Women's Universe

NAGOYA SAKAE

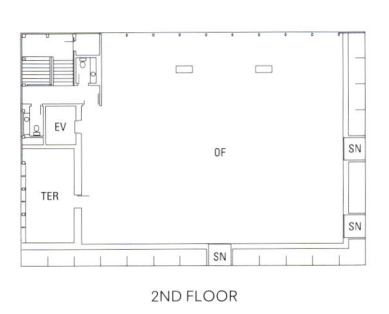

2ND FLOOR

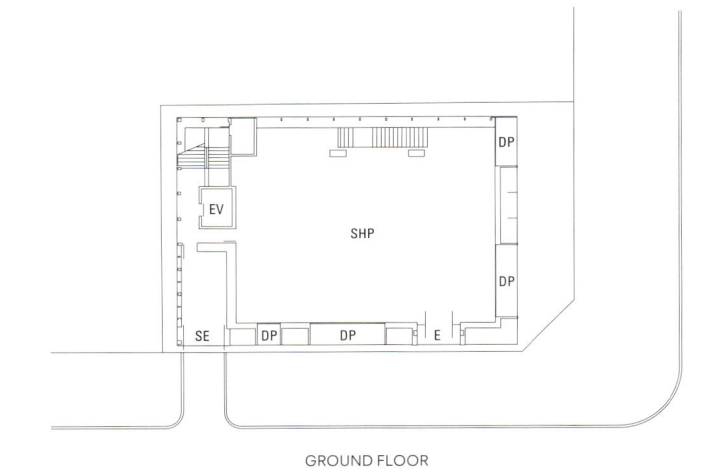

GROUND FLOOR

ARCHITECTURE AND INTERIORS 23

NAGOYA SAKAE

JAPAN

JCB
JCB CARDS
an
アルバイト発見マガジン[アン]
LOUIS VUITTON
LOUIS VUITTON

NAGOYA SAKAE

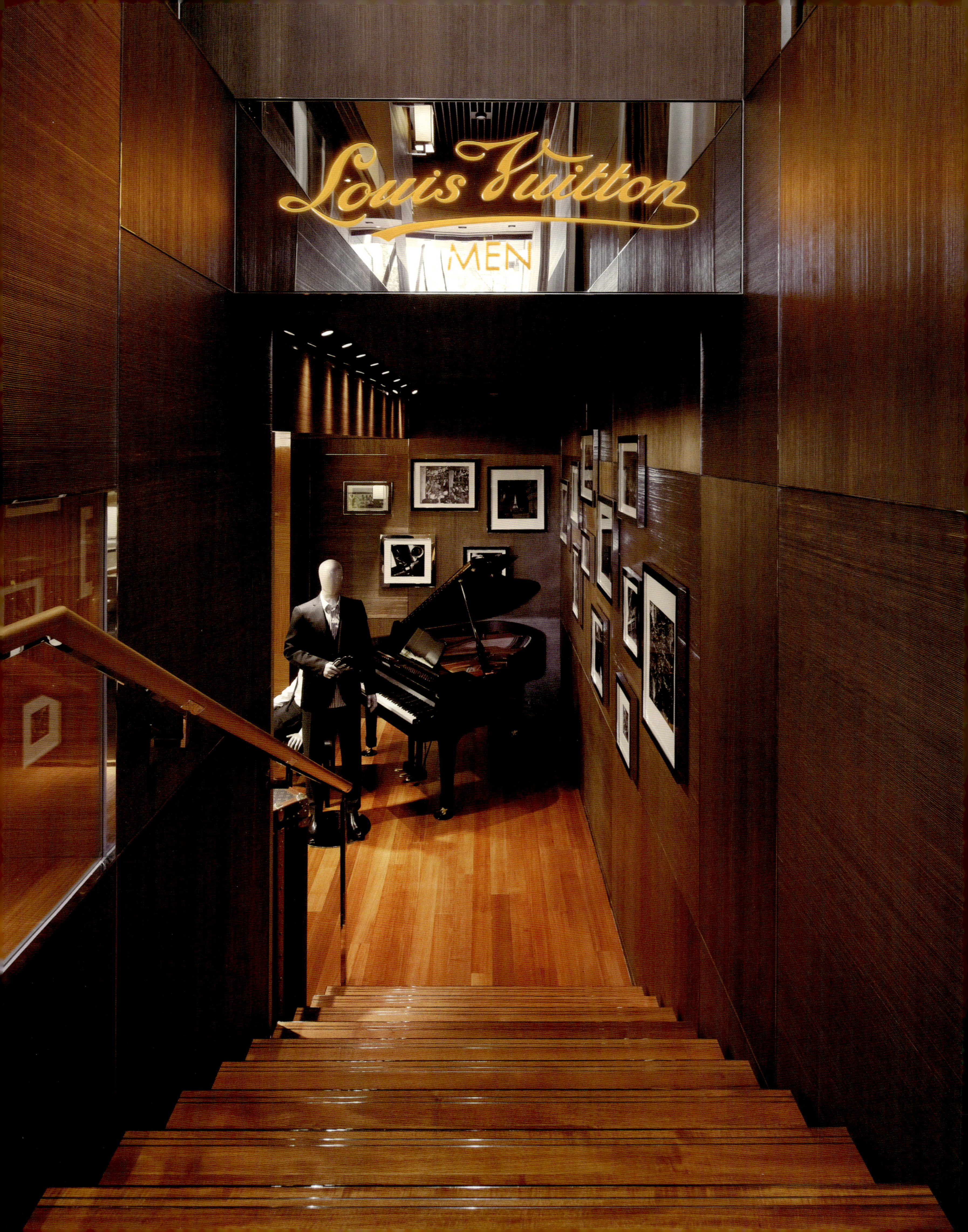
Louis Vuitton
MEN

NAGOYA SAKAE

TOKYO OMOTESANDO

architects
JUN AOKI & ASSOCIATES;
THE LOUIS VUITTON
ARCHITECTURE DEPARTMENT
2002

text by
FRÉDÉRIC EDELMANN

Jun Aoki's relationship with Louis Vuitton began with the Nagoya store, which opened in 1999. The architect had already developed the building envelope, a kind of façade that doesn't reveal its materiality to the eye. In this regard, the project for the Louis Vuitton store in Omotesando, inaugurated on August 21, 2002, certainly attained an unrivaled perfection, and it hasn't aged a bit since. Despite the arrival in 2003 of the Prada store, a structure built by the Swiss duo Herzog & de Meuron that drew all the attention of critics—and Toyo Ito's Tod's not long after that—Jun Aoki's building has quietly made its mark on Omotesando, and indeed, has become an architectural reference point for all of Tokyo. The store designed for Dior by SANAA, the firm of Kazuyo Sejima and Ryue Nishizawa, recipients of the Pritzker Prize in 2010—conveys a message of similar sophistication, however contradictory, as its interior bears almost no relationship to the architecture. Across from the Louis Vuitton store, on the other side of the avenue, Tadao Ando, another Pritzker Prize winner, designed a shopping center for developer Minoru Mori called Omotesando Hills. Horizontal in format, it is so at odds with the neighborhood's typology, that it seems more or less not a part of it.

When it opened, Louis Vuitton Omotesando was the brand's seventh "global store" in Japan, and its forty-fourth store altogether, but was billed as the largest one in the world, offering 900 square-meters of retail space, and 340 square-meters of exhibition space and VIP areas. Day and night, the building—located between a lofty church and an ordinary building covered in white tile, but without common ownership to meet earthquake regulations—asserts a presence that is at once strong and reassuring, mysterious and customary, even if only because of the name Louis Vuitton, which is supremely famous in Japan.

What's the recipe here? Aoki has in fact combined two devices that are almost contradictory. The façade is designed as a stack of trunks of various sizes, waiting on a dock to be loaded onto a boat. The narrative reference to Vuitton's celebrated trunks is absolutely explicit on this level. The initial model is eloquent in this respect: bags in various colors ranging from beige to dark brown, marked with monograms and flowers. Their number is somewhat difficult to establish (seven, eight?) because between two trunks there remains a seemingly empty space that, once the project was finished, would have become a terrace, or an entrance. One must add to this figure the trunks that are hinted at by the sides of the building, which are approached in the same fashion. The model is reminiscent of the temporary hoarding installed on the Champs-Élysées Maison while the new Paris store was under renovation: a façade that also consisted of huge, imitation trunks.

Springing from this rather playful but steady heap, Aoki designed a façade measuring 32 meters high by 25 meters wide; in other words, following the template of buildings in this district of Tokyo—something that would be contradicted very quickly by Omotesando Hills. The architect then transformed the trunks into rectangles made abstract through the use of metal and glass. Not just any metal, this is the taut steel mesh on conveyor belts, the kind normally used in a variety of industrial situations. Aoki already explored the idea in Seoul, which can also be found in many buildings designed by the French architect Dominique Perrault. The weave of the mesh varies depending on the spaces it hides and is reflected in large windows that are each treated in their own way: clear, frosted, copper-colored. At night, these semi-transparent, moiré surfaces—depending on the interior lighting—resemble different types of Japanese lanterns. To speak of the true elegance of the building, we are led to forget any of this typology, and driven instead into the abstract universe of Mondrian and of the De Stijl movement. The considerable amount of work rendered on the façade, which clearly evokes luxury but without falling into the trap of glitzy excess, is echoed by the organization of the building's interior architecture. Aoki very rightly speaks of spaces, even boxes, rather than floors, for inside you'll find a series of volumes of irregular sizes and forms within its 21-meter depth. All the more so, these spaces don't necessarily correspond to the divisions suggested on the façade.

Ten levels, two of which are below ground, flow into each other, sharing the functions of the store. From the basement to the highest floor accessible to them, clients travel through spaces of varying heights, the equivalent of one to three stories, connected by flights of stairs that are alternately central and lateral. Whatever the volume, each space is ample and rigorously geometric, with an accent on horizontal features that are sometimes reinforced by double rows of shelving. Areas for shoes, men's bags and purses, watches, jewelry and ready to wear are arranged to convey a feeling of tranquility and respite. As a counterpoint to twenty-five masterpieces from the Louis Vuitton collections—old or recent trunk models and exceptional luggage imbued with the spirit of travel—the furniture punctuates the space, convincing the public that a good traveler is also someone who knows how to stop, looking in the distance, through the surrounding windows.

The light-colored tones of the universe created for women are interrupted on the fifth floor by the warmer, woody tints of the men's space, presented here in the same way as in all Louis Vuitton stores. It is a space where sport, the sedentary form of travel, becomes an element of surprise and curiosity; a table-soccer game revamped in leather, a punching ball also in leather, a stationary bike carefully covered by Vuitton's saddle-makers (gently) shake up the atmosphere.

Access to the VIP lounges, hidden at the end of a winding route, is carefully isolated, as are support services—stock room, workshops, parking. They can hardly be spotted because their doors and designs practically disappear. In the world conceived by Vuitton's in-house architectural department, which is relatively spare in comparison to Peter Marino's work, every client is the master of his space, or at least of the space that they can perceive.

At the fifth level, however, one is far from being at the end of the journey. If, until now, there's been an obvious link between each floor or landing, here the world of Louis Vuitton becomes more limited; other keys are required. The store's lounge combines the best of Japanese architecture with the efficiency of Louis Vuitton's architects. The design is impeccable, the geometry perfect, and the details and materials are of a rare quality. In one corner stands the trunk of Pierre Savorgnan de Brazza, discoverer of the Congo and humanistic explorer, who is still waiting for his museum to open in Brazzaville. In the lofty space of the room, the furniture refers to a less adventurous luxury, carrying the names of prestigious artists like Mies van der Rohe. A large terrace opens out onto a view of this Tokyo neighborhood. To the left are the colorful youth at Harajuku, the amusing models of artist Takashi Murakami—one of the company's favorite artists, whose work filled the Omotesando store in 2009. To the right, One Omotesando, the Japanese headquarters of Louis Vuitton, built by Kengo Kuma. And beyond Minami-Aoyama the extension of the avenue, at the end of which is Kuma's renovation Nezu Museum, completed in 2009 in one of the rare, once private, parks of Tokyo.

One accesses the Espace Culturel via a dynamic, inlaid corridor—an assemblage of *trompe l'oeil* cubes straight out of the Italian Renaissance. This optical effect is, to say the least, disconcerting; almost as much as the large hall that crowns the Omotesando store: a parallelpiped measuring nearly nine meters high, fifteen meters long, and ten meters wide. This space is dedicated to temporary exhibitions of contemporary art. Here there's another view of the neighborhood's urban sprawl: a priceless collection of architecture, with its minor and major masterpieces, its jokes, its surprises and its perpetual movement of destruction and reconstruction.

p. 28 interior view of Louis Vuitton hall on the 7th floor, clad in the woven fabric screen designed by Yoko Ando in 2002
p. 30 top to bottom: locator plan; scale model describing the massing strategy of stacked trunks; concept rendering
p. 31 entrance view
p. 32 exterior view at night

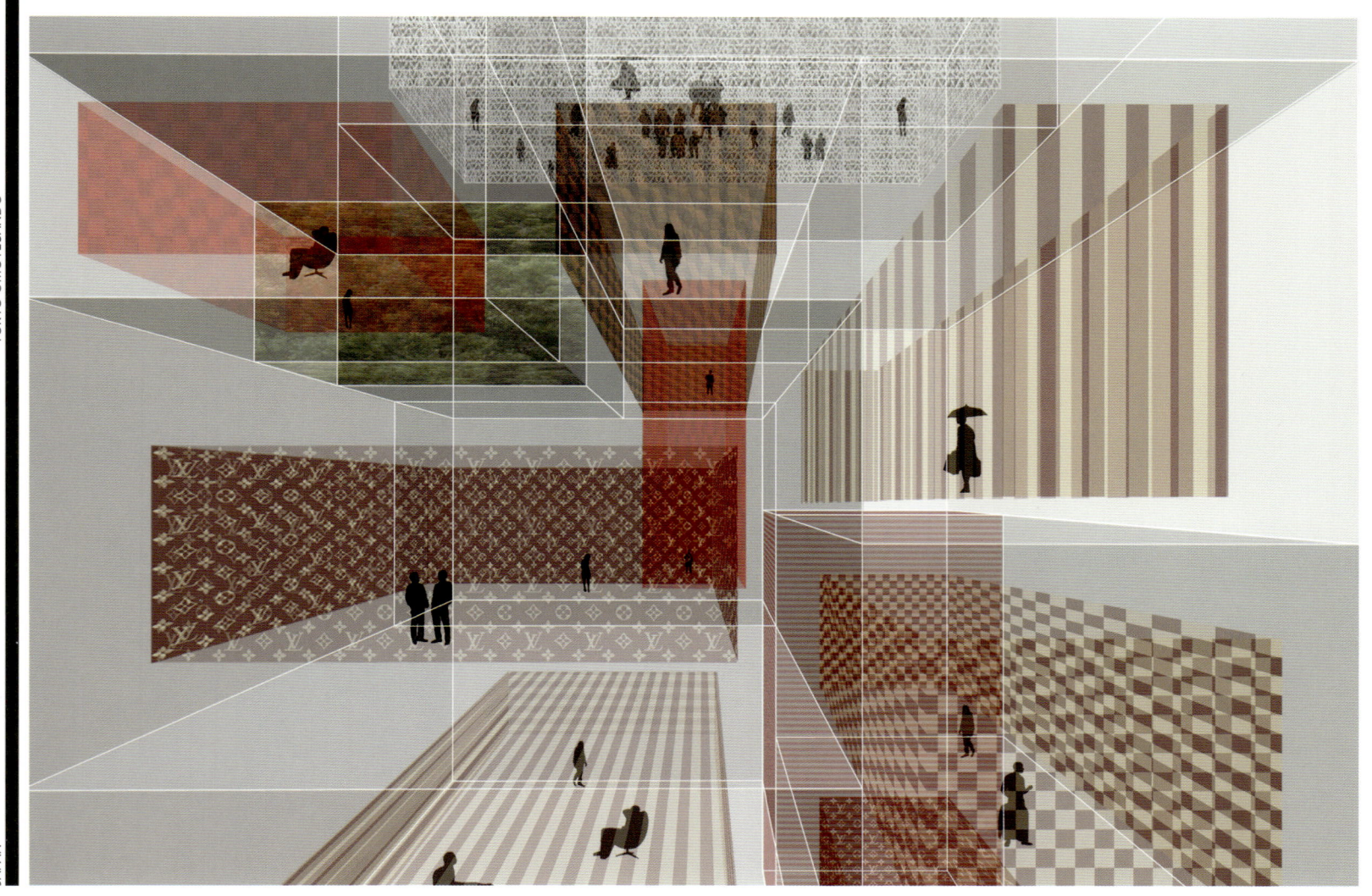

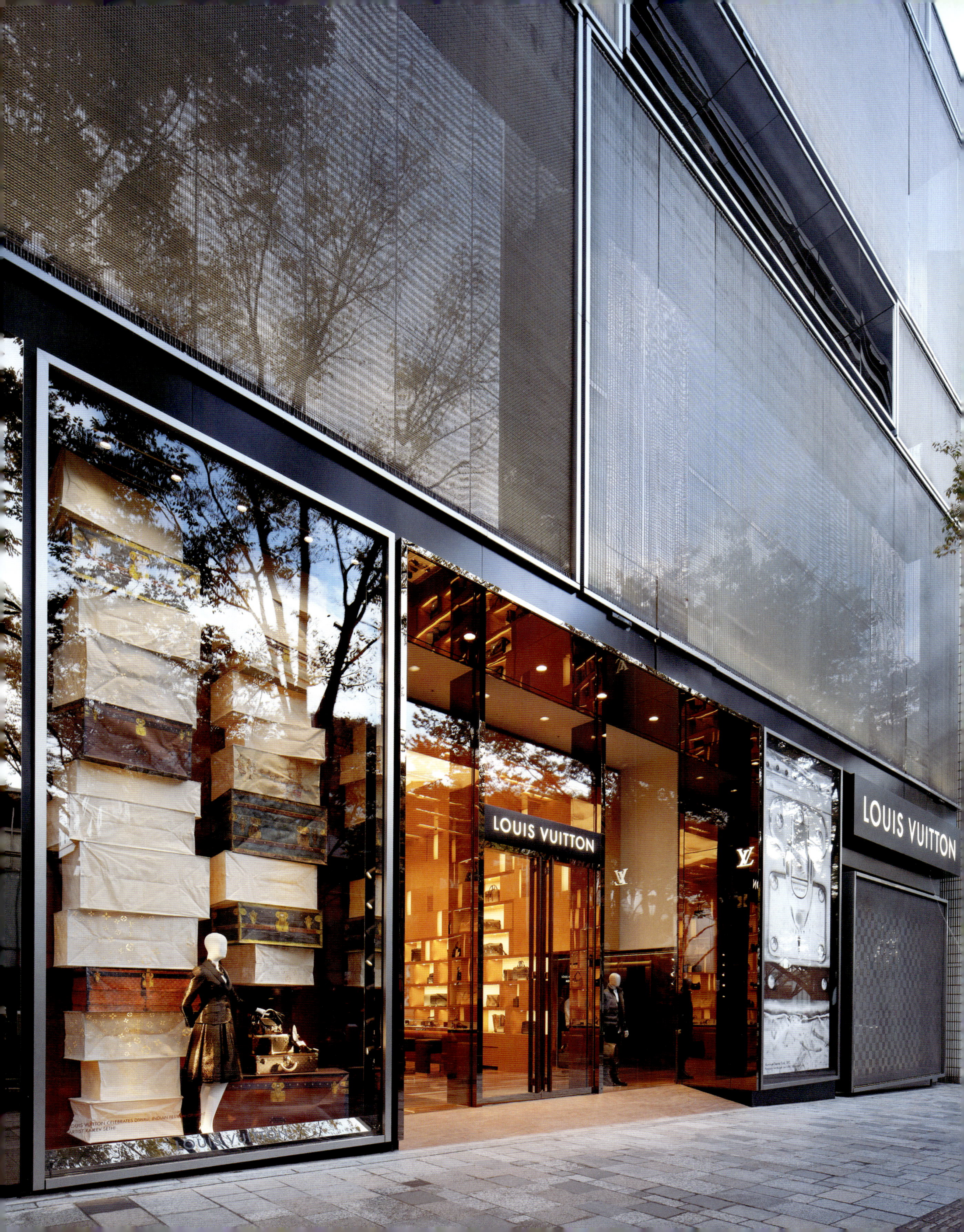
LOUIS VUITTON
LOUIS VUITTON

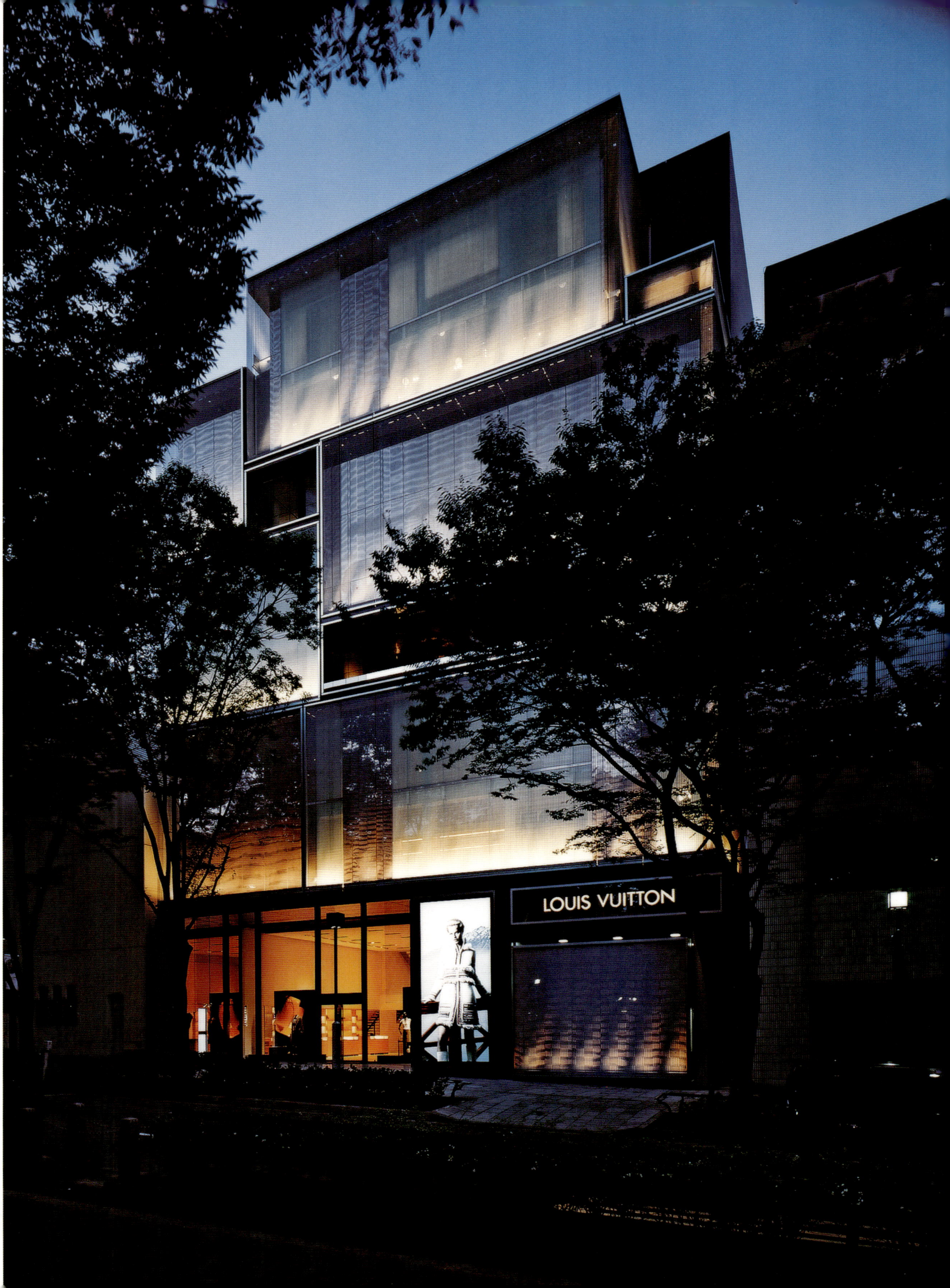
LOUIS VUITTON

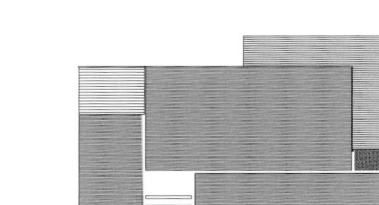

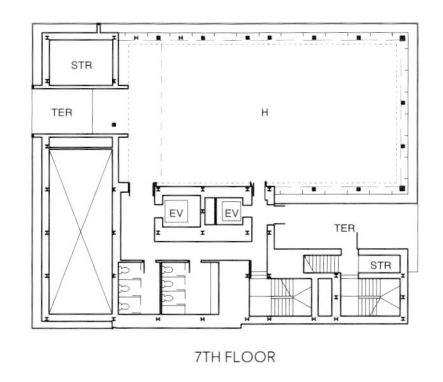

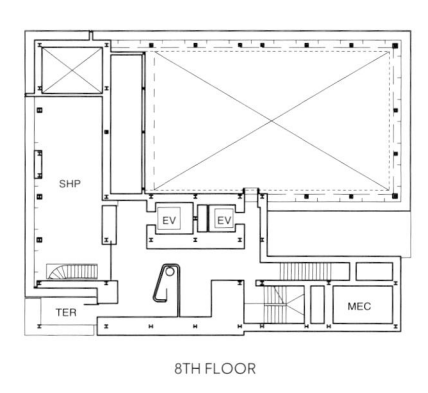

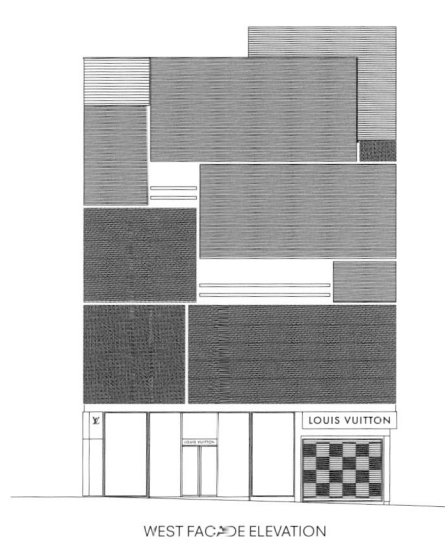

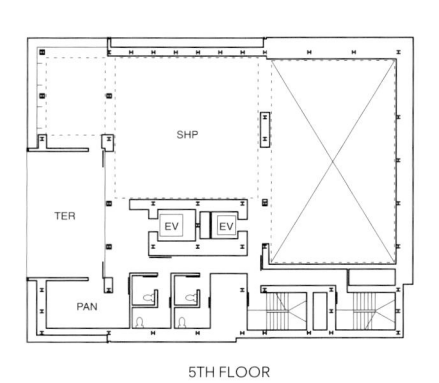

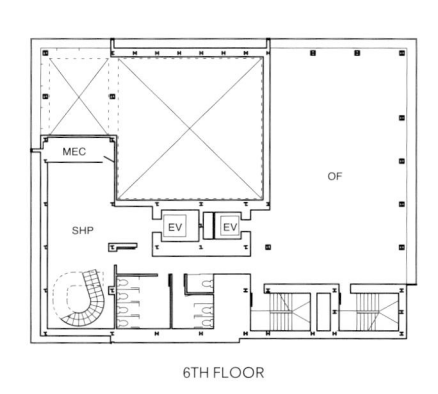

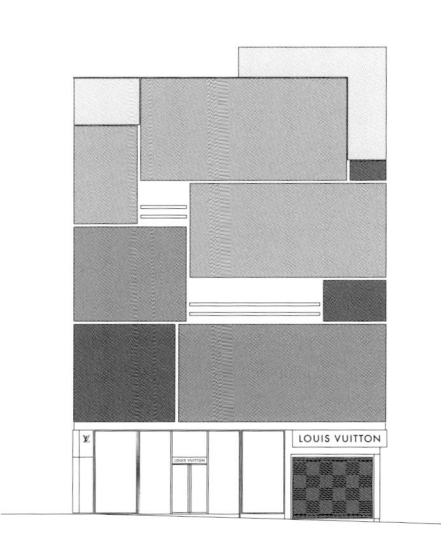

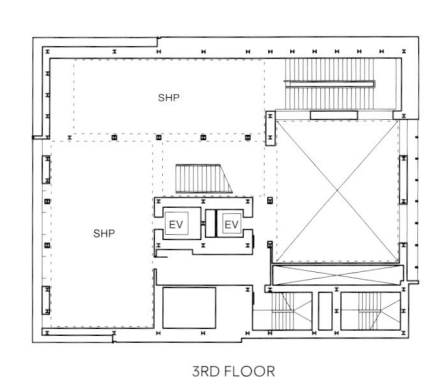

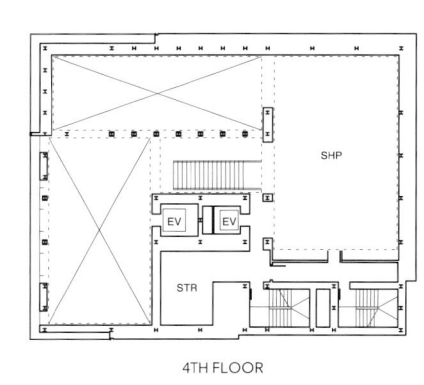

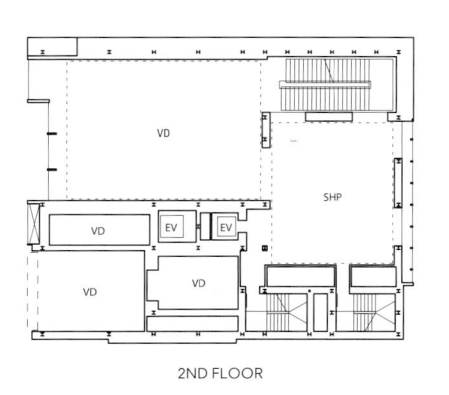

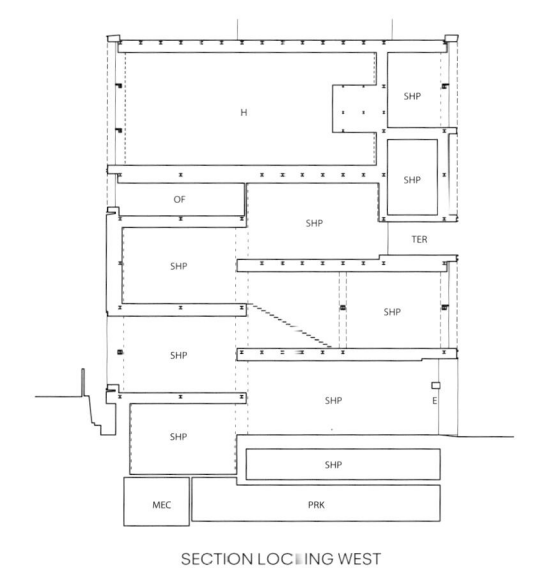

7TH FLOOR	8TH FLOOR	WEST FACADE ELEVATION
5TH FLOOR	6TH FLOOR	
3RD FLOOR	4TH FLOOR	NORTH FACADE ELEVATION
GROUND FLOOR	2ND FLOOR	SECTION LOOKING WEST

ARCHITECTURE AND INTERIORS 33

TOKYO OMOTESANDO

JAPAN

ARCHITECTURE AND INTERIORS 34

TOKYO OMOTESANDO

JAPAN

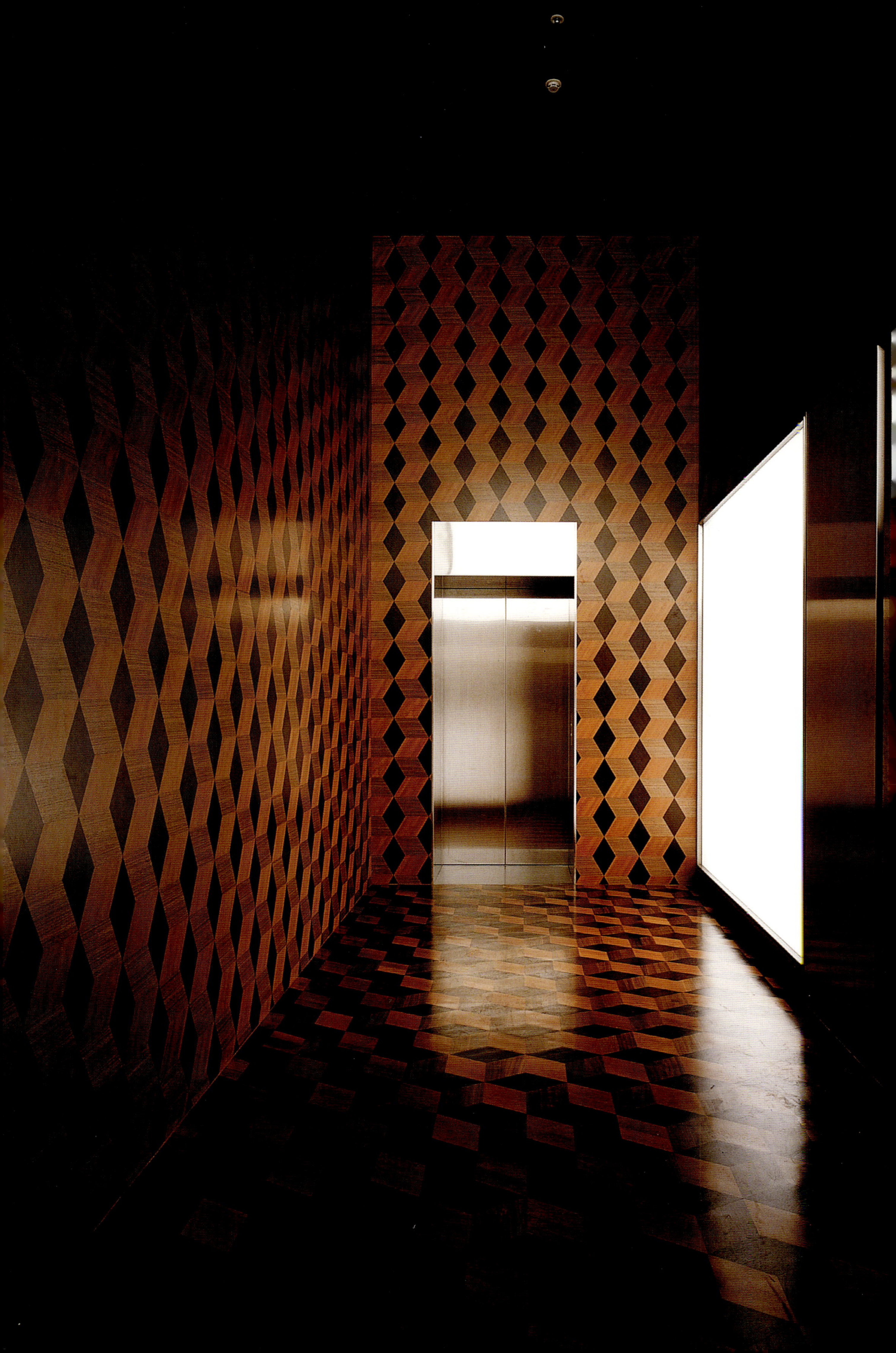

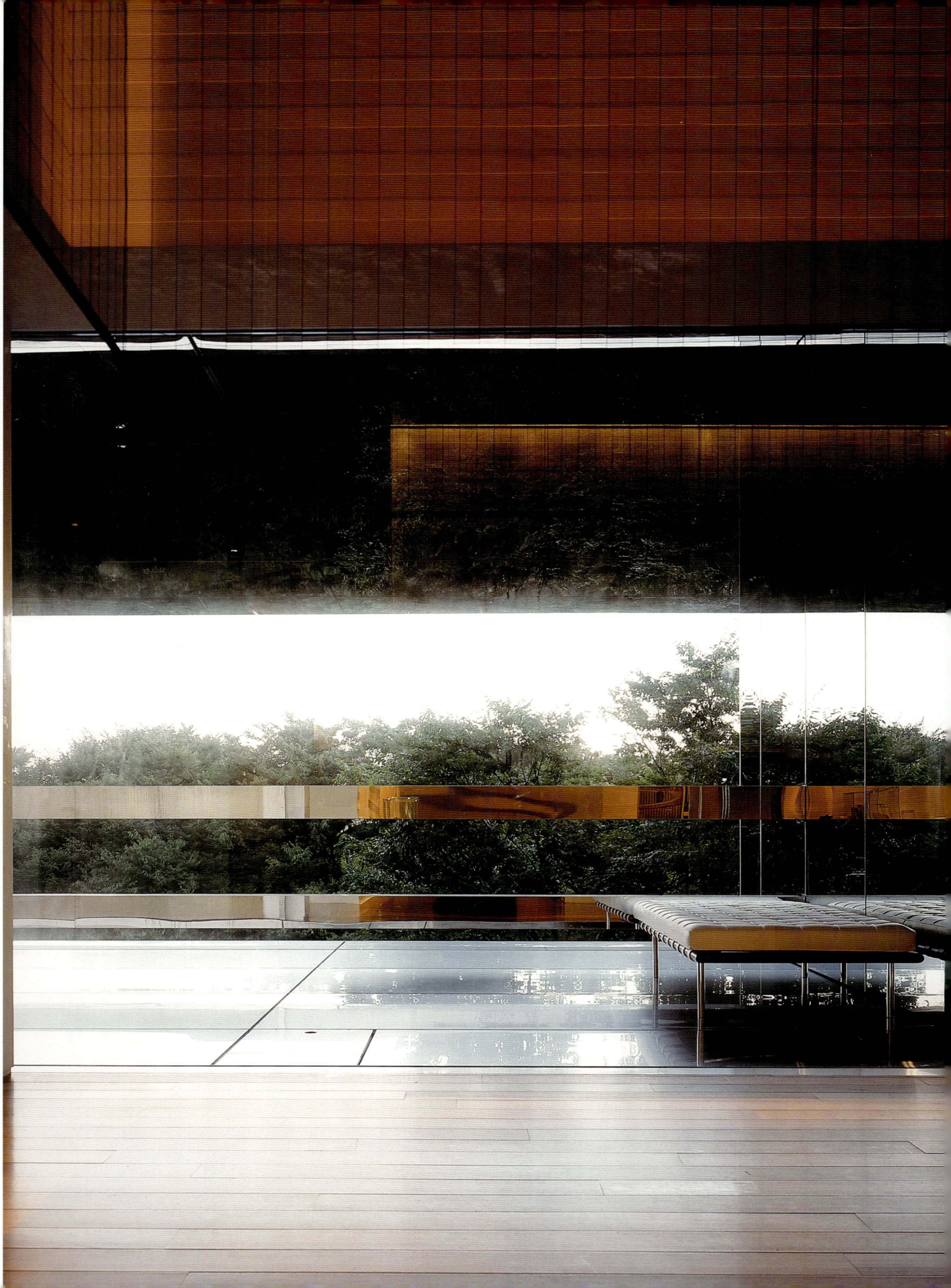

ARCHITECTURE AND INTERIORS 37

TOKYO OMOTESANDO

JAPAN

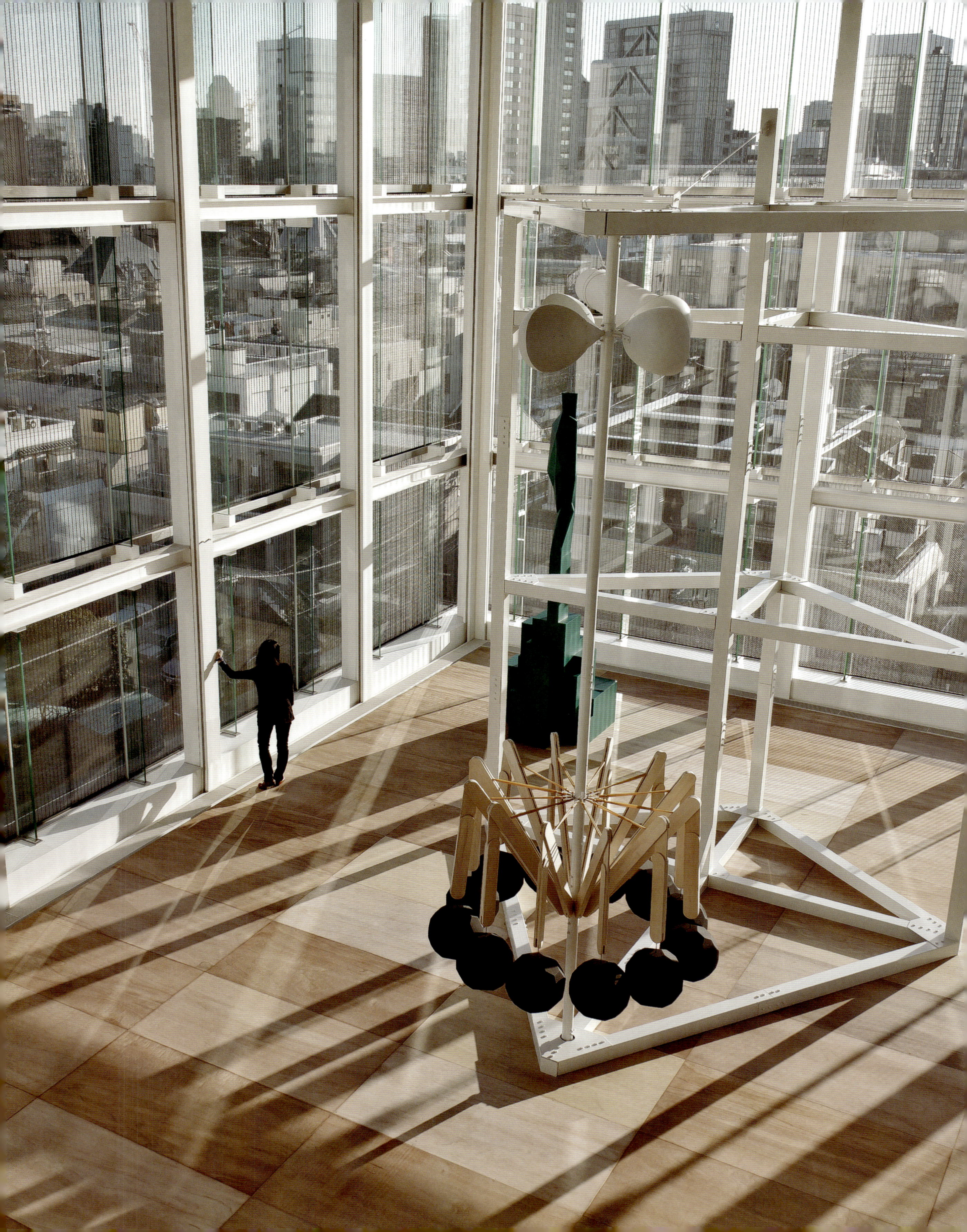

p. 34 top to bottom: watches & jewelry and rare & exceptional product areas on mezzanine level; Bag Bar on ground floor
p. 35 main elevator bank with marquetry done in an abstracted damier pattern
p. 36–37 view of 4th floor terrace overlooking avenue and views of Omotesando
p. 38 and 39 top: view of 7th floor Espace Culturel Louis Vuitton, 2010, with artwork by Xavier Veilhan from his "Free Fall" exhibition, with *Regulator* and *Tokyo Statue* (2010-2011)
p. 39 bottom: detail of the woven fabric screen designed by Yoko Ando in 2002
p. 40 detail of exterior mesh wall
p. 41 nighttime view from the roof

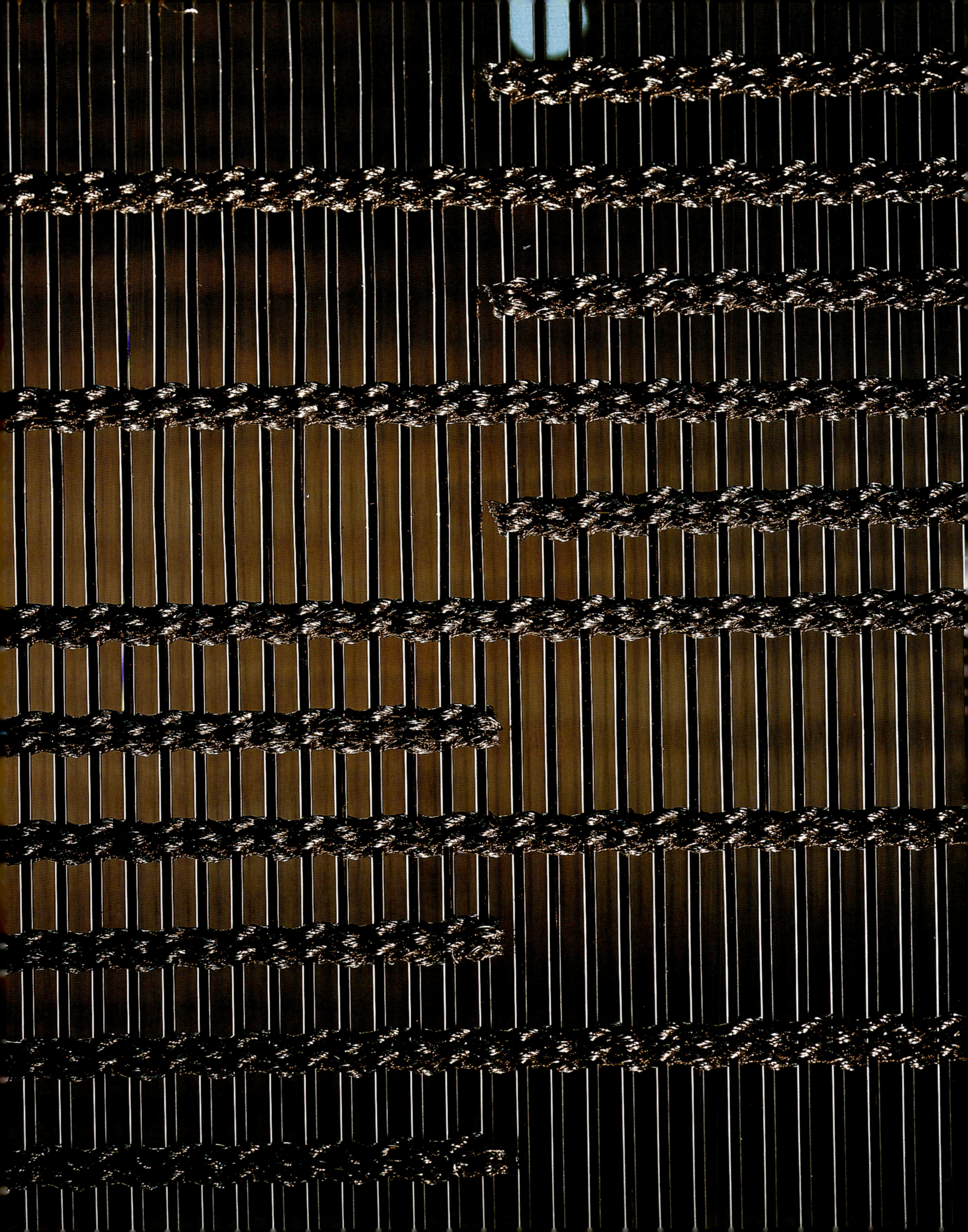

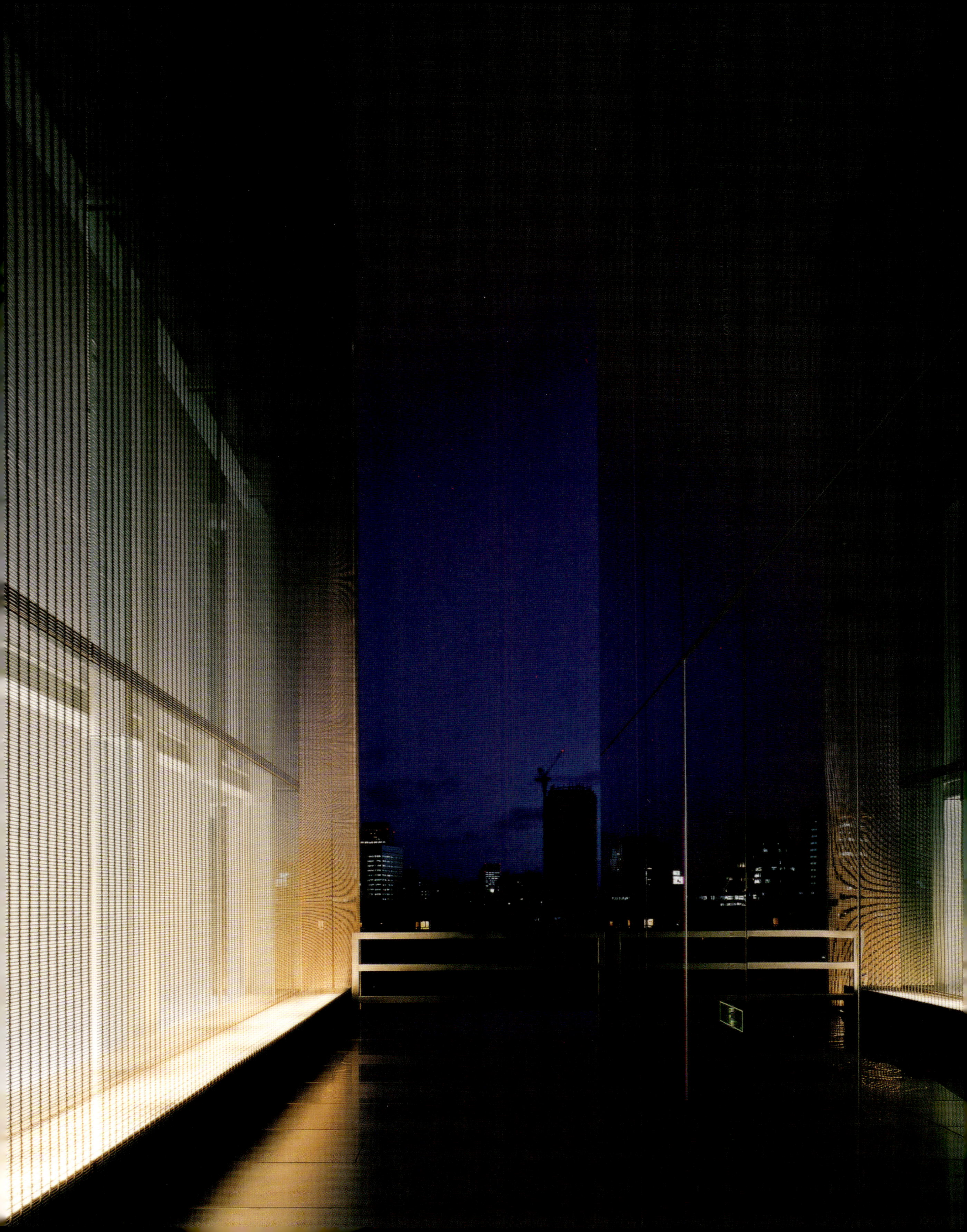

TOKYO ROPPONGI

architects
JUN AOKI & ASSOCIATES;
ERIC CARLSON, AURELIO CLEMENTI;
AND THE LOUIS VUITTON
ARCHITECTURE DEPARTMENT
2003

text by
FRÉDÉRIC EDELMANN

They say Roppongi is Tokyo's most central neighborhood. It's the heart of the Minato district. It's an unverifiable geographical point of view, unless you want to argue with the guards at the Imperial Palace. It still happens to be the liveliest part of the city with its bars, nightclubs, its frenetic nightlife and its offerings of art and luxury during the day. In the late 1980s, Minoru Mori, one of the most powerful Japanese building tycoons decided to develop a monumental tower here, Roppongi Hills, which at 238 meters is not as tall as Tokyo Tower, a communications building a kilometer away. That said, it stands as a kind of imperial palace of modern times.

The American architects from Kohn Pederson Fox Associates (KPF) were entrusted with the design of this sugarloaf filled to the top with good artistic, if not architectural, intentions. The building has nearly 800 apartments and 380 Hyatt hotel rooms. If you include the time it took to acquire the property, 17 years were needed to complete this tower, which was inaugurated in September 2003. It is striking how such an object—which is so present its practically invisible, in the same way that a city can be invisible to itself—has to relate to other more familiar entities in order to get its bearings. One such entity is Tokyo Tower, and another is the Louis Vuitton store, which also bears the emblematic name of the neighborhood: Roppongi. It also opened in 2003.

More about Roppongi. The name signifies the six trees, a metaphor for the six *daimyo*, the six powerful territorial lords who governed there in the shadow of the Tokugawa. In other words, the neighborhood is solidly anchored in history and even if contemporary urban development has partly erased the old markers of the city, there remains an extraordinary urban complexity here that Louis Vuitton and its architects Jun Aoki, with Eric Carlson and Aurelio Clementi, have drawn on quite a bit.

Although in terms of transportation, everything converges on the tower, human activity—you could call it Brownian motion, the crowd is so dense and abundant—naturally spills out into the surrounding neighborhood. From the large terrace, where Minoru Mori's monument is planted, one can clearly see the broad façade down below, which was conceived as a sparkling screen by the three principal architects. There are no images, and no added animation—the neighborhood is already a Tokyo temple of film—just a large, quiet frontage one discovers walking down or up the street. This screen-façade measures 36 meters wide by 14 meters high, resting over a long window that transforms when necessary into an entrance. Composed of thirty thousand glass tubes, 10 cm in diameter and 30 cm long, aligned like honeycomb between two glass panels, it suggests a new manifestation of the Monogram. In fact, it's a pure technical system that traps the outside light and uniformly softens it. From the inside, the view of the city is somewhat obscured in order to draw attention to the store windows. This is for the best: the extremely diverse urban landscape of the neighborhood is contradictory in scale, and can even be disturbing with its combination of "art works" (a heavy footbridge), ungraceful architecture and the cackle of signage and advertising. Rarely does luxury fit in easily with such picturesque situations, as if the horizontality inherited from classic architecture had become a norm. In the façade's depth, one again sees twelve letters softly aligned in a row: "LOUIS VUITTON." They interrupt the feeling of cold abstraction and immobility that this large screen might impart. And, when night falls and the store lights up, they become highly visible to people in the tower.

The space of the store (900 square-meters) is divided by another variation on the circle: circles no longer in glass, but in polished or brushed steel, which overlap to create thousands of flowers, the traditional monogram. They form the material and motifs of tall hanging curtains, allowing one's gaze to pass from one space to another. At once present and light, they help reinforce the specific architecture of the store (this is also true at Omotesando), representing the repetition of norms the company has established under the guidance of Peter Marino. Accidentally, in an attempt at differentiation, it is clear that Jun Aoki met the neighborhood with a kind of polite humor. For example, the entrance—a space that occupies the full height of the store, distinguished by its triangular form—immediately makes one think of a large nightclub, one of those mega clubs that doesn't reveal a thing but invites you to go on the trip. To further drive the point home, the famous Bag Bar faces the door in part of a lower, convivial volume, with a real bar, real stools and rows of bags in the guise of bottles. To the right, a staircase heads toward the sharpest point of the triangle. The client is "accompanied" here by mannequins that could well be him or her.

On the left, a second staircase lets on a bit more about what might be happening on the different floors of Louis Vuitton Roppongi. The nighttime theme can also be felt here and each sales area has a strong identity, with the layout complex enough that it is hard to commit to memory in a single visit. In December 2010, a part of the store was remodeled after only six years of use, as is customary with the company. So much so that it would be risky to want to describe the particularities of the layout: the bars that present scarves, the portholes revealing jewelry, the displays, the recesses, the tables and vitrines, but also the many nuances that, without straying too far from the norms, are rather distinguishable.

Deyan Sudjic wrote in the magazine *Domus*, "Louis Vuitton gives the impression of always having existed, [but] its current success relies on the constant redefinition of its identity and its capacity to find new means of innovation." Here in Roppongi, the transformations are not only necessary to renew the company's image. The neighborhood has also changed. It has become clear that with the arrival of the Roppongi Hills tower and several lavish buildings (one of which housed Louis Vuitton, Roppongi), and the establishment of numerous international luxury brands, that the essence of at least this part of the neighborhood has changed. Clubbers are becoming more rare, or maybe they've gotten a bit older, just like the expats of all nationalities who are another one of Roppongi's specialties.

p. 43 stainless-steel screen viewed from the stair, inspired by Louis Vuitton's flower monogram, which was in turn partly adapted from Japanese *mon* crests
p. 44–45 exterior view along principal façade
p. 46 and 47 bottom: interior views
p. 47 left column: plan locator; right column, top to bottom: 2nd floor plan and ground floor
p. 48 top and 49: watches and jewelry room
p. 48 bottom: Bag Ear
p. 50–51 details of the glass tubes that make up the principal façade

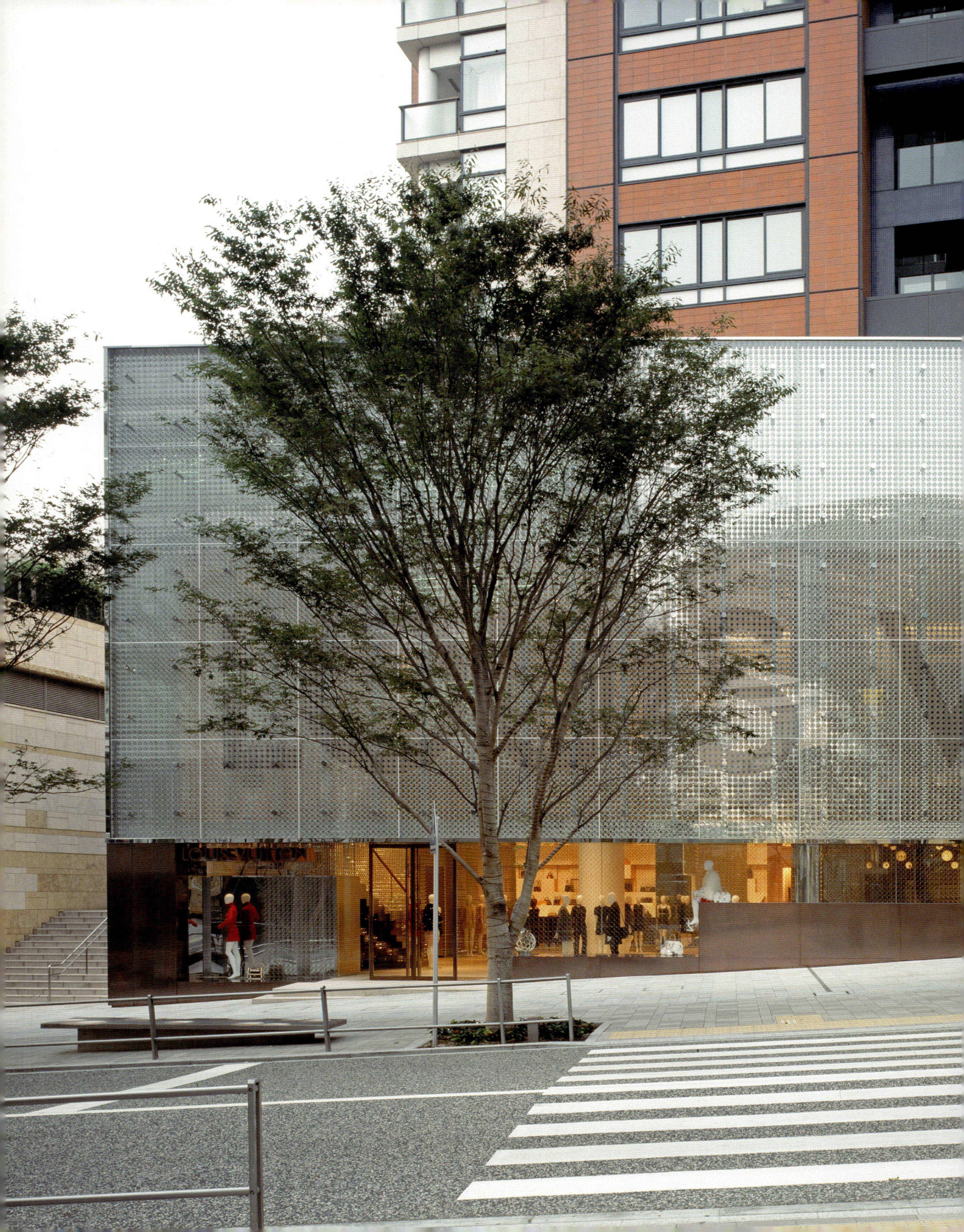
LOUIS VUITTON

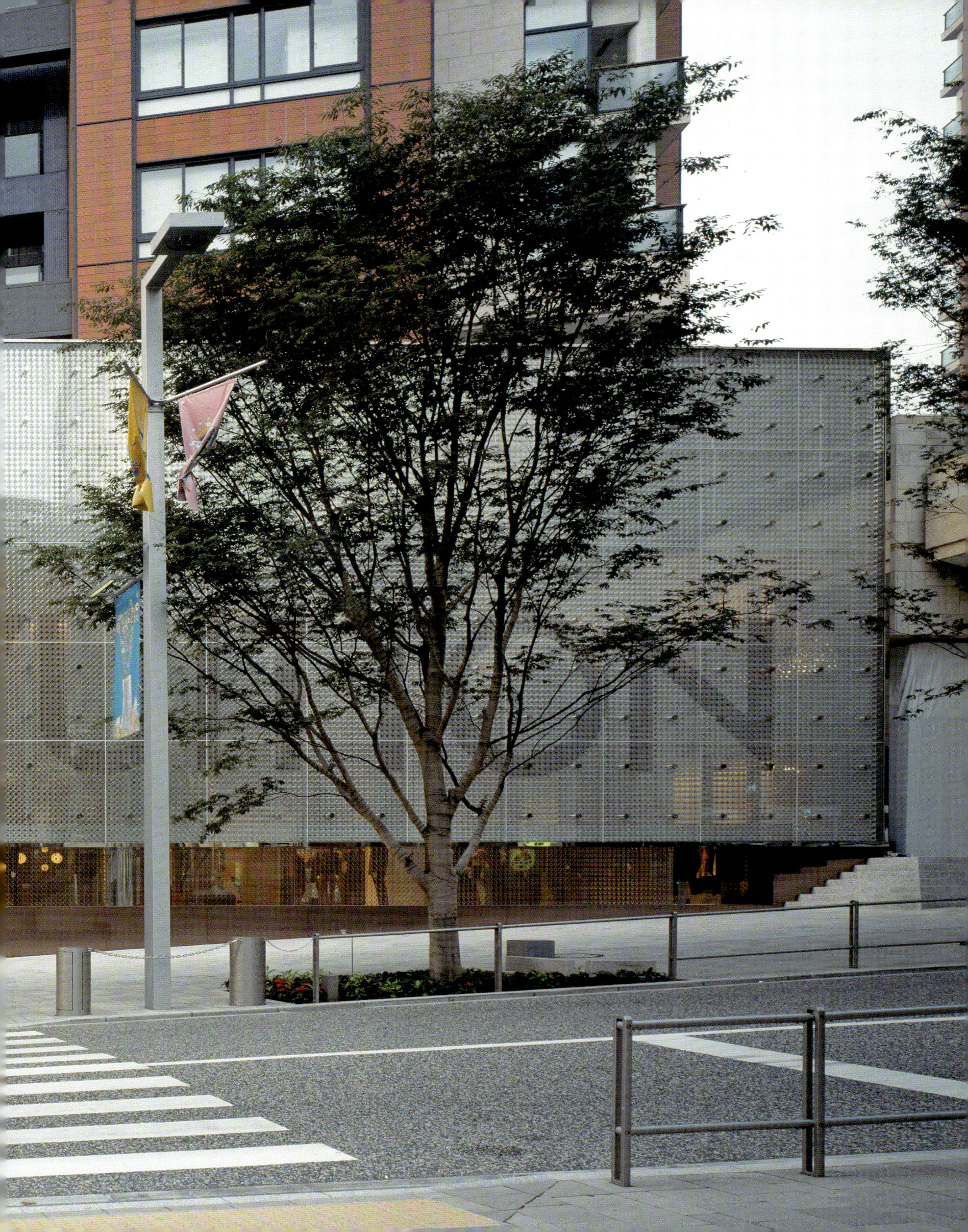

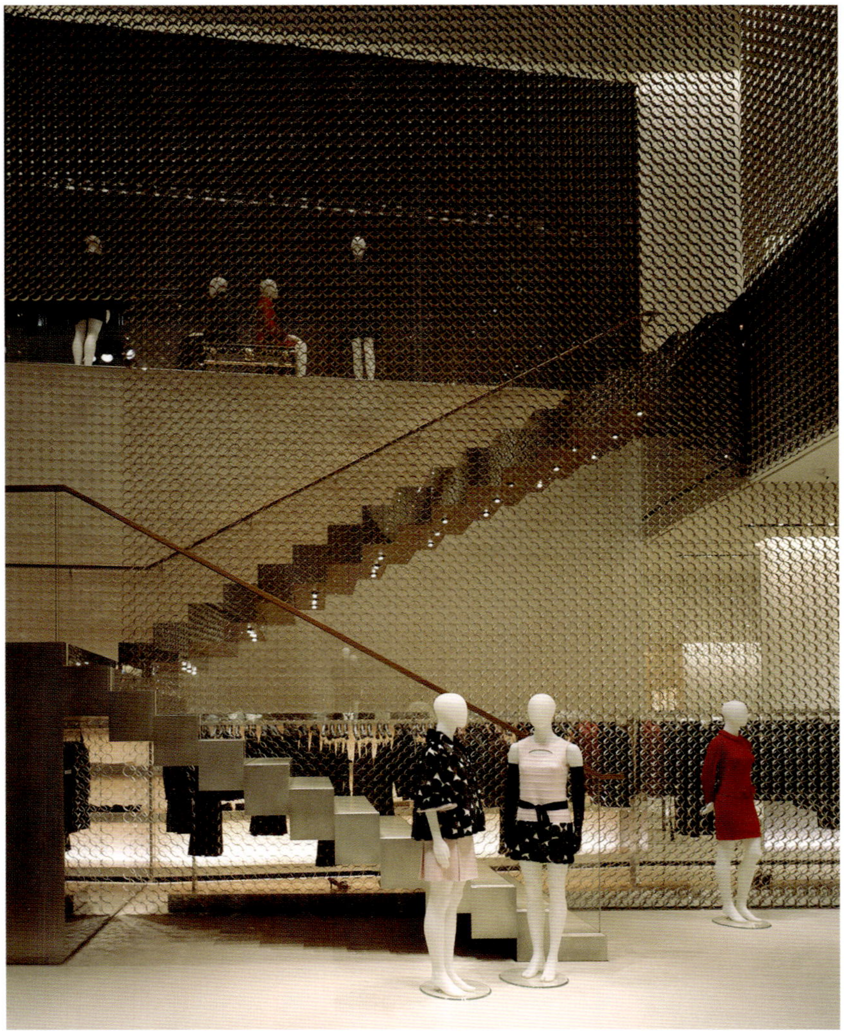

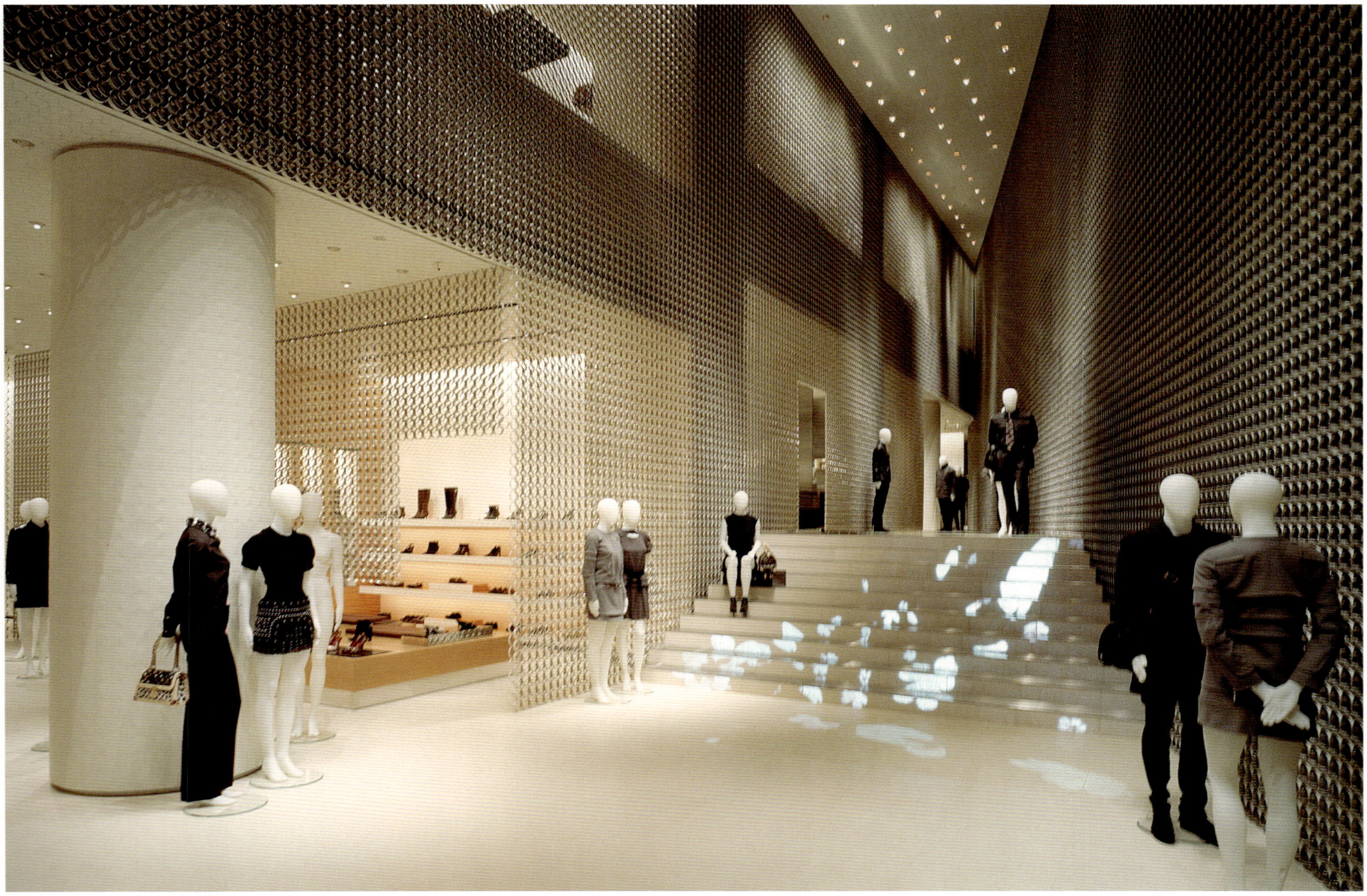

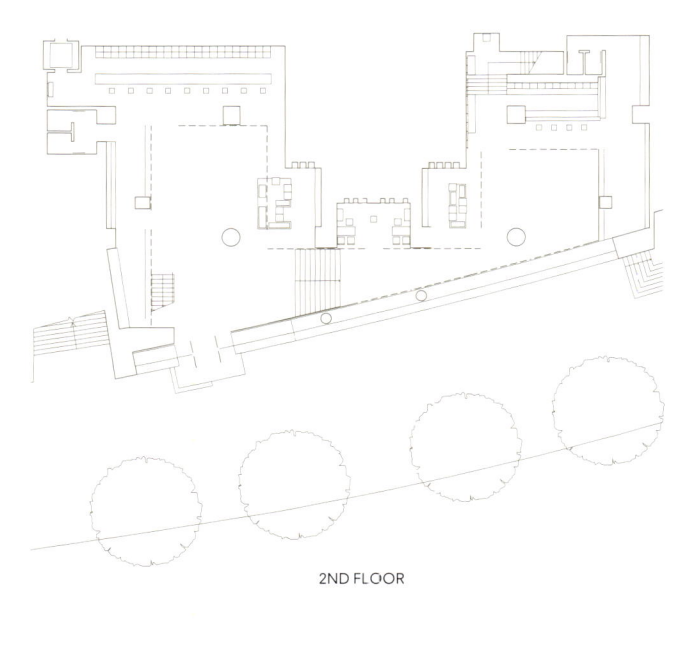

2ND FLOOR

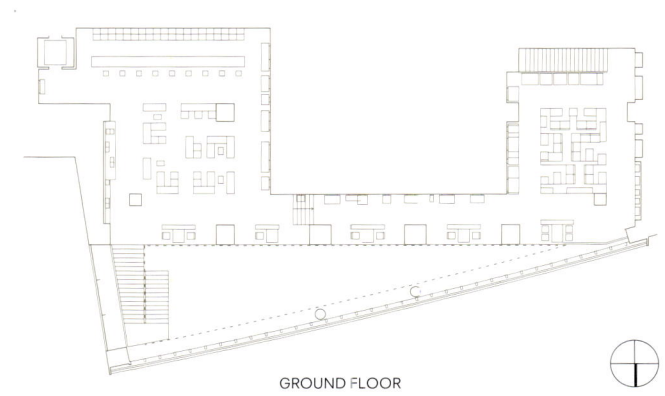

GROUND FLOOR

ARCHITECTURE AND INTERIORS 47

TOKYO ROPPONGI

JAPAN

ARCHITECTURE AND INTERIORS 48

TOKYO ROPPONGI

JAPAN

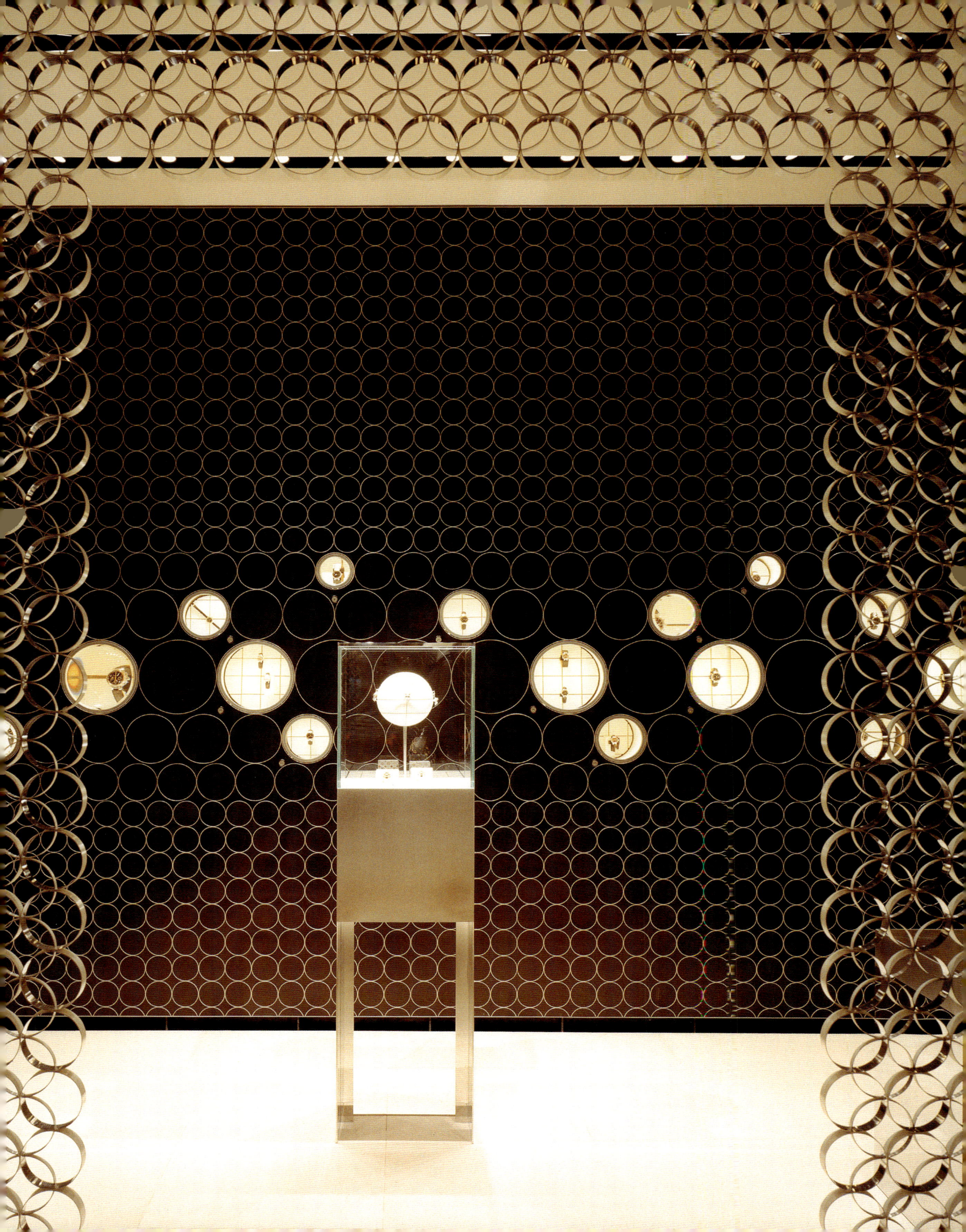

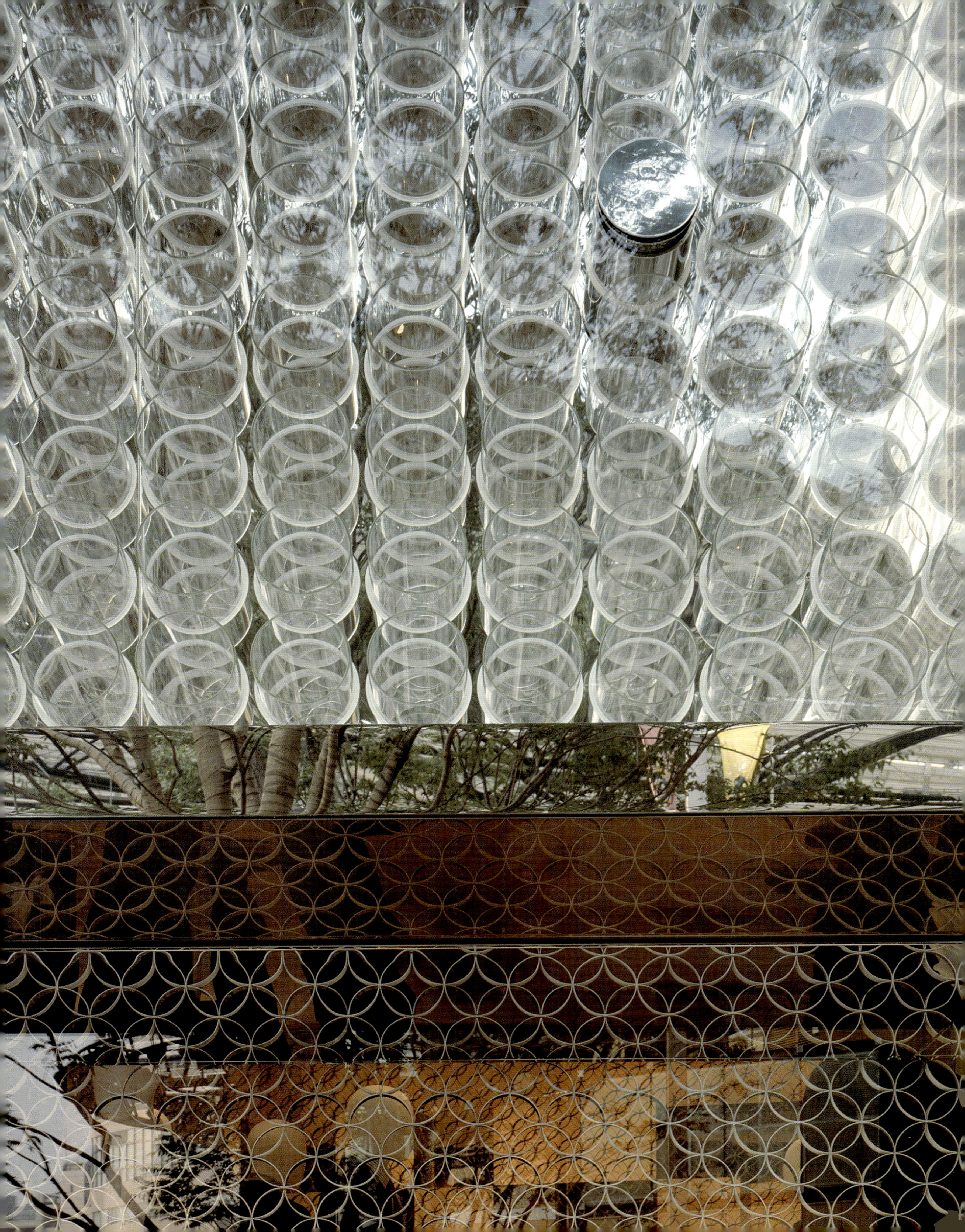

ARCHITECTURE AND INTERIORS 51

TOKYO ROPPONGI

JAPAN

TOKYO NAMIKI DORI

architect
JUN AOKI & ASSOCIATES;
LOUIS VUITTON
ARCHITECTURE DEPARTMENT
2004

text by
RAFAEL MAGROU

As a laboratory of contemporary architecture, Tokyo remains one of the world's most exciting cities. The rapid evolution of building sites and liberal construction standards have opened up a remarkable field of experimentation for architects, offering them great freedom in their creative work. One must be able to compete with billboards and other images that alternate between Japanese calligraphy and advertising, the modern-day equivalent of the signage that once illuminated old Edo. It all forms a vast visual and audio continuum, a maelstrom that forms the heart of the commercial neighborhoods. In the array of these vibrant avenues of lights and *fashionistas*, Ginza has been a pioneer in the use of new, eye-dazzling technologies. Each brand unleashes an arsenal of architectural and lighting mechanisms, always attempting to outdo its neighbor. If Omotesando has become known for its haven of audacious architecture, Ginza clearly has come to embody high-end shopping, devoted body and soul to luxury and elegance. As early as the Meiji period (at the end of the nineteenth century), ancient boutiques made of wood were beginning to be replaced by buildings with brick colonnades and gas lighting. Since then, Ginza has remained the premier area in Tokyo where western products are showcased, synonymous with all things fashionable and chic.

Anticipating these trends, Louis Vuitton embedded itself in the neighborhood as early as 1978—making it the only company to have local headquarters at a time when others were managing their storefronts from abroad. Before it was renovated in 2004, the boutique occupied two floors of a building on the corner of Namiki dori and Ko Junsha dori. This would become the first autonomous Japanese store to distribute Louis Vuitton's manufactured products. Since then, as is the case every twenty years in Japan, the neighborhood has transformed into a nighttime destination dotted with clubs. As such, Ginza dori, only two blocks away, has become the axis on which global luxury brands are leaving their architectural mark. Departing from the hysteria of Ginza, Louis Vuitton decided to remain at the same site at Namiki dori, taking over the whole building that was home to its original boutique.

The transformation, in this case, is spatial. From within the structural corset that is Tokyo real estate, subjected to financial pressure that is unsurpassed worldwide, the architect Jun Aoki reinterpreted the theme of the lantern, paying homage to the history of the city and to its attributes that had been reduced to ashes after the 1923 earthquake and the bombings of WWII. To decorate the cubic volume, the architectural reference of Louis Vuitton involved reinventing rice paper by introducing a fiber-reinforced concrete envelope, approximately one-inch thick. The texture is palpable; although silky, the fibers create the same striations as those of ancestral sheets of paper. There are embedded squares of translucent alabaster in different sizes; the largest among them outline large flat surfaces lit from behind, while constellations of the same geometric form—a sort of bursting checkerboard—explode, spangling this celestial body. Although, by day, the heat differential between the materials is not immediately apparent, the architecture pulsates at night. Not like strident neon, but more like a material glowing red in a subliminal way, seeming to distort the cube and become a breathing thing. A genuine example of "haute architecture," this monolith stands in radical contrast to Ginza's syncopated rhythms, inviting one to penetrate into Louis Vuitton's warm and protective depths. The casing has been transformed into a jewel—a discreet, sophisticated jewel that lets itself be caressed and approached so as to be better adopted as a home.

Upon entering, in an open space rising three floors, there is an exhibition of old trunks, the foundation of every Louis Vuitton boutique. Nowhere but here will you find chests composed of electroluminescent screens that transmit animated images—from an image of the brand's founder to one of the original Paris boutique on Rue Neuve-des-Capucines. Instead of being exhibited on the façade, advertising is here brought inside; as if the brand has no need to deploy seductive techniques, the architecture—not ostentatious, but elegant—is identification enough. A didactic combination of tradition and modernity, a theme dear to the brand, the architecture offers visual communication between the lower level for men, the ground floor for leather goods, and the second floor for women (who also benefit from two floors above, that are more private). Ornate columns, combining reliefs and recessed, Art Deco-style joints, frame this hanging display. The uniformity of the surface treatment between the levels, along with the teak floor and freestanding display cases in metal and glass, create an interior that is very graphic. But, let there be no mistake, these floating segments offset the columns by elongating the framework and supports. Writings evoke the assembly of Japanese constructions, with their spatial, rectilinear overlapping of components, covering the systems of hooks and hangers. What emanates is a kind of minimalism that complements the spirit of the site.

As a counterpoint to the patio, another volume—this one solid—articulates the visitor's movement. This reflective block, which encases the elevator and around which wraps the staircase, offers a material that is dense both to the eye and touch. The detail of the handrail perfectly expresses this substance, like solidified mercury. The rising stairs complement the effect. Both the merchandise and the clients are reflected in the surface, as though they were made for one another. As one climbs, one comes upon the squares from the façade again, but here they are made of Corian (synthetic stones made by combining minerals and pure acrylic resin) palpitating in brilliant colors and revealing their granularity. Inlaid here are single or interlinking display cases, presenting the most recent designs. This sensory spiral leads from the first floor, dedicated to best sellers, up to the fourth floor that presents an original composition for jewelry, like the Landmark store in Hong Kong. The latter space features an alcove that is dark in atmosphere, alternating between checkered and striped patterns of steel and leather. From both sides, large mirrors that seem to be part of the walls, pivot and enclose this case to create a more serene ambiance if the client so prefers. Finally, the fifth floor is reserved for a VIP room furnished with a white horse-hair rug, on top of which reign couches that are hybrids of Mies van der Rohe's Barcelona Chair and Le Corbusier's LC2—upholstered with the checkerboard pattern too.

Squares—always the square, classic and timeless—open like carved windows on the skin of the façade, allowing fine leather goods to be exhibited, and producing a transparency between the street and inside of the boutique, as is the case on the ground floor. Thus, this magic lantern offers a glimpse into its innards, revealing the fire that gives it life. In the intense and exhausting heart of Tokyo, the Namiki dori location is a rejuvenating respite, one that is above all visual—always retaining its identity and integrity. Roland Barthes painted the most handsome portrait of this jubilant city in *Empire of Signs*:

> "This city can only be known through ethnographic activity: one must find their way not by the book or an address, but by walking, by sight, habit, experience; every discovery here is intense and fragile, it can be found only by the memory of the trace it has left in us: to visit a place for the first time is sort of like beginning to write: the address is not being written, it therefore bases itself on its own writing."

Through its architecture, Louis Vuitton was able to reap the benefit of this analysis—in Tokyo in particular, and in the world in general.

ARCHITECTURE AND INTERIORS 54

TOKYO NAMIKI DORI

JAPAN

p. 53 view of façade at night. The glass-reinforced concrete façade of the store is cast with white marble inserts
p. 54 exterior views along Namiki dori. Flush with the wall and appearing opaque to passersby during the day, the translucent membranes modulate the discharge of artificial light from within the store
p. 55 top to bottom: plan locator; nighttime elevation; daytime elevation
p. 56 view of the façade, nighttime
p. 58 views of the watches and jewelry room, and the stationery counter
p. 59 view of the trunks wall in the atrium space

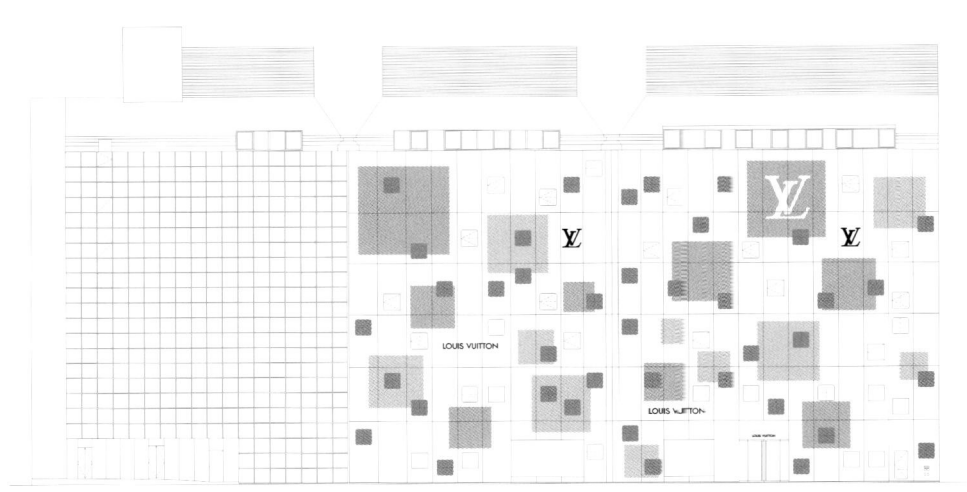

ELEVATION (NIGHTTIME)

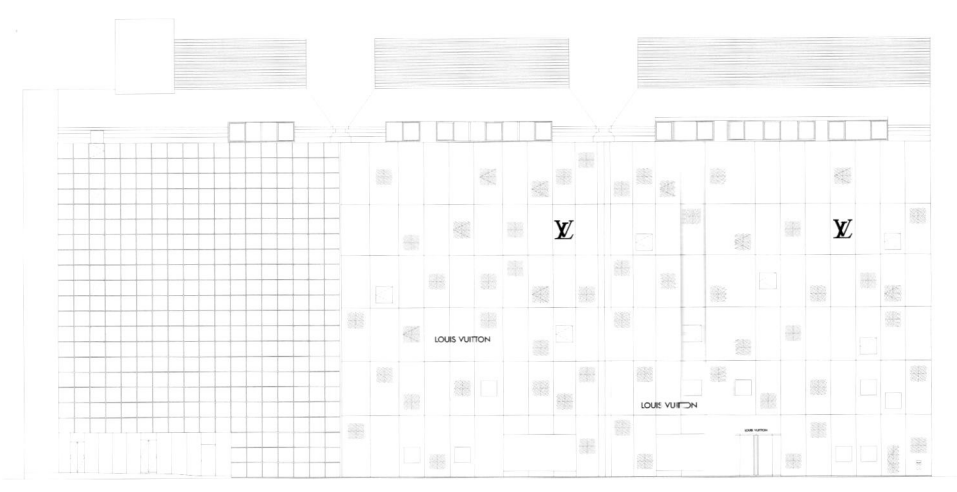

ELEVATION (DAYTIME)

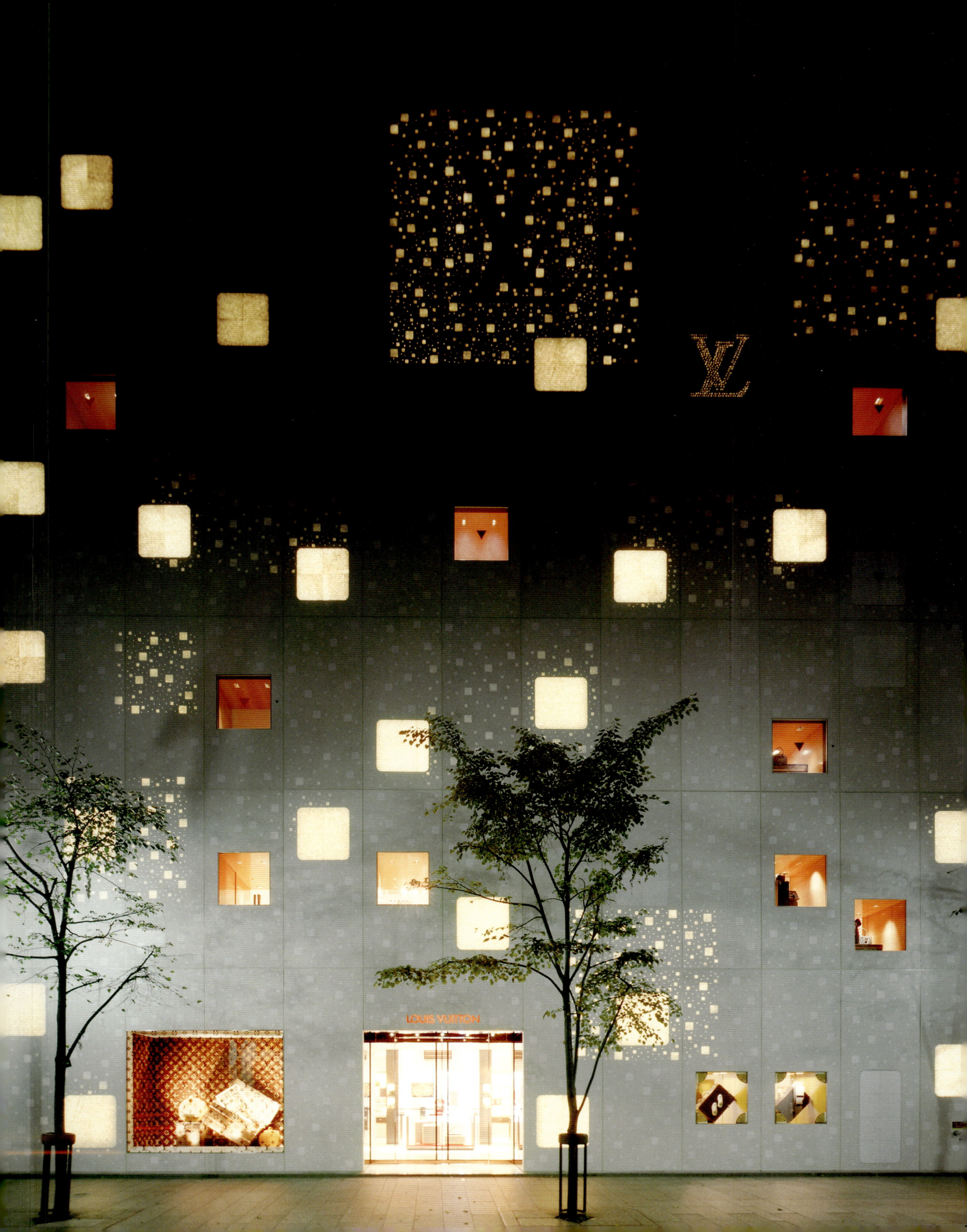
LOUIS VUITTON

6TH FLOOR

7TH FLOOR

4TH FLOOR

5TH FLOOR

2ND FLOOR

3RD FLOOR

BASEMENT FLOOR

1ST FLOOR

ARCHITECTURE AND INTERIORS 58

TOKYO NAMIKI DORI

JAPAN

ARCHITECTURE AND INTERIORS

TOKYO NAMIKI DORI

JAPAN

OSAKA MIDOSUJI PROPOSAL

architects
Scheme 1: JUN AOKI AND ASSOCIATES
Scheme 2: SHIGERU BAN ARCHITECTS
2007

text by
IAN LUNA

Infamously described by the architect Arata Isozaki as "overgrown villages," Tokyo and Osaka present one of the more curious urban rivalries in the developed world. Profoundly modern and with metropolitan populations in the tens of millions, Isozaki overstates things a bit, but ancient, parochial attitudes do undergird the competitive dynamic between these two megacities. As phenomena, Tokyo vs. Osaka/Osaka vs. Tokyo typifies rivalries in national contexts, where large polities united by a common language, culture and identical sociopolitical order do not exactly encourage shared values and intentions. Rio de Janeiro and Sao Paulo, Shanghai and Beijing, New York and Chicago, and St. Petersburg and Moscow provide the most fractious corollaries—and it is telling that either Osaka or Tokyo is officially "sistered" with one or the other city in this list.

The particulars of the Japanese contest are rooted in a violent, feudal history, where eastern and western coalitions organized the country's warring principalities for nearly a millennium. This culminated in a decisive Eastern military victory at the end of the 16th century. With the inexorable shift of political power from the traditional, imperial seat of power in Kyoto (and the larger Kansai region where the cities of Nara and Osaka belong) to the cities of the Kanto region—present-day Tokyo and Yokohama—the rapid commercialization of Japan at the end of the 19th century and the postwar "economic miracle" had recast this East-West divide into a peaceable and largely commercial contest.

Culturally, the transformation of Japan into a unitary and more prosperous state only helped preserve this regional animosity, and its (usually) benign tropes obtain well into the present day. Caricatures were further codified in the media age. Osakans, uncharitably described by their eastern rivals in the 18th-century travelogues as alternately "stingy," "garrulous," "gluttonous," "ostentatious," and generally "lacking in civic spirit," also speak in a unique, emphatic dialect—Osaka-ben—that had for most of the modern period been the drawl of TV and *anime* villains, as most popular media is still generated out of Tokyo. Osaka residents do not chafe easily, and give as good as they get by reducing Kanto residents to insufferable snobs descended from a superficial culture. This mutual stereotyping has relaxed somewhat over time, sublimated to more constructive, if not always complimentary or cooperative pursuits.

The one unifying experience for residents of both East and West is the chaotic nature of urban redevelopment for much of the postwar period. Each city competes in creating iconic gestures to compensate for a perceived lack of urban character. As ever, the constraints of building in the dense fabric of Japan's cities has kept ambitious architectural transformation limited to small doses and discrete areas.

Osaka's more progressive developers and architects, for the most part, had decided to opt out of the hysteria that characterized the explosion of retail typologies in the late 1990s resurgence of Tokyo's Harajuku and Omotesando shopping districts. And not for want of trying. A number of influential figures in modern Japanese architecture either hail or continue to practice from Osaka and its environs (Tadao Ando, Kumiko Inui, Waro Kishi and the late Kenzo Tange), and were crucial in advancing the retail type there from the 1980s onwards—as they most certianly did in Tokyo itself.

The major players in the luxury goods market in Tokyo also dominate the Kansai region. And the desire of consumers for more novelty in label-obsessed Osaka have ensured that the capital projects of the main international fashion combines cater to their conveniences. The spirit of experiment that Louis Vuitton began with Jun Aoki's seminal Nagoya Sakae store (1999) in central Japan developed a conceptual, material and sensory template for all its freestanding stores in the country. Marking a radical break from its approach to retail architecture, the lessons learned in Nagoya advanced novel strategies for building morphology and cladding. These innovations then migrated back up to Tokyo, Paris and New York, and energized the building program of the *malletier* for much of the past decade.

Louis Vuitton's most remarkable intervention in Osaka to date includes a store designed by Kumiko Inui in the northern district of Umeda. Completed in 2004, the two-story façade of the Hilton Plaza store draws sure strength from Aoki's material precedent as it treads a different direction. Like a rainstorm in an aquarium, prismatic shards of steel are barely contained by an outer wall of clear vision glass.

The inauguration of Jun Aoki's Omotesando store in 2002 and the subsequent revamp of Vuitton's Paris flagship introduced the concept of a full-service boutique that has more to do with the prophecies of Rem Koolhaas than it does with modern consumer preferences. As intimated by its name, each of these LV *maisons* is distinguished from retail-only outposts not only by their larger floorplates but by a "domestic" brief. This program manifests itself quite literally in the VIP salons of several stores, or suggested in others, as in the apartment *manqué*-look of the New Bond Street store in London where drawing rooms festooned in LVMH-owned fine art could conceivably be adjoining bedrooms and dining areas. In Japan, the *maison* on Omotesando, with its top-floor "magic room" for special events and other amenities, begged for application elsewhere. And in the heady days preceding the global economic crisis of 2008, these plans included an even bigger structure in Osaka.

An invited competition in 2007 called for a *maison* in central Osaka, on Midosuji Boulevard. Midosuji is the main artery in Osaka, connecting Umeda to the north to the districts of Shinsaibashi and Nanba to the south. A multi-lane highway lined by ginko trees, its character and street-life are a mix of corporate uses and high-end shopping. Showcasing the Chanel and Apple flagships in the city, many stretches of the thoroughfare variously resemble the Marunouchi and Omotesando districts in Tokyo. At a physical and psychic remove from the teeming shopping areas of Shinsaibashi, with its massive *shotengai*—covered shopping galleries common to Japanese cities—the Midosuji store would have exceeded ten floors, making it the largest facility operated by Louis Vuitton in all of Asia.

These programmatic demands, which all told, amount to 6,000 square-meters of retail and ancillary uses, are abetted by a number of thematic requirements. Chief of these was the creation of an Osaka landmark: an "architectural masterpiece" that would resonate beyond its locality and generate international attention.

Formally, it should create a sculptural "rupture" that would set it apart from the orthogonal, cinder-block office structures of the neighborhood. Internally, it should also communicate the idea of an "urban oasis," where shoppers could be seduced into spending more time at the store than the time it takes to buy a bag or a garment. To that end, functions such as a bookstore, café, an art gallery, a spa, a garden and even a swimming pool on the upper floors raises the oasis concept into a full-on *mizu-no-miyako*—a city on the water—organized around a logical and generous circulation plan.

A fitting irony then that the schemes by Japan-based practices were by two men from the Kanto plain with significant experience building in Osaka. Jun Aoki (born in Yokohama) and Shigeru Ban (born in Tokyo) present two very distinct entries.

Jun Aoki & Associates proposes a massing strategy and program redolent of the Hanging Gardens, sheathed in a 70-meter prism of glass plates wedged tightly between highly reflective stainless-steel louvers. At times, this detailing mimics a waterfall, a pleated Vionnet or Fortuny dress, and a billowy sail, puckered in places to provide views from terraces within. The fenestration and the curtain wall abstract both the checkered "Damier" and the striated "Epi" leather trademark patterns.

Arranged on 17 skipped floors, the internal plan benefits from a suspended "hat" structure on the upper floors that allow for the dispersed columns to be suspended from the roof and along the periphery so that large program areas remain free of structural elements. This is advantageous as Aoki puts forward exhibition spaces that could accommodate large-scale installations by Ann Hamilton and Rachel Whiteread and vertical landscaping by Patrick Blanc.

Shigeru Ban, who had previously designed a temporary Papillon Pavilion atop Louis Vuitton's Champs-Élysées in 2006 built in part with hundreds of handbags, put forward a structure that derives its form from traditional Japanese handcrafts, making an explicit link between the artisanship of the *malletier* and these traditional arts. Whereas his recently completed Centre Pompidou Metz (2009) drew its tented roof from a Chinese hat, the same intersecting lattice familiar to bamboo wickerwork are here in his Osaka scheme. The building envelope itself resembles the kind of traditional fish and eel traps once used all over Asia, but also the wicker *kago* totes used by an older generation of Japanese, with its weave of hexagons and triangles providing tensile strength and flexibility. With the elevator cores providing the main gravity and seismic load-carrying systems (as the Kansai area is prone to earthquakes), the frame itself is fabricated in fiber-reinforced polymers (FRP) used in motorsports and aviation, and sheathed in a double skin that is an integral part of the ventilation system and minimizes overall energy use. This sustainable agenda extends to the application of photovoltaic cells on the outer layer of the double skin and a rainwater collection system.

The competition brief also called for the seamless integration of formal signage and other markers of the brand identity onto the façade, which successfully saw application in the translucent aggregate utilized in the Namiki Dori store (2004) by Aoki. A number of important buildings in Osaka, including Paul Andreu's Maritime Museum (2000), Tadao Ando's Suntory Museum (1994) and Aoki's White Chapel (2006) were designed to maximize the visibility of a porous structure at night, and Ban saw the sphere of the *maison* repurposed into a festival lantern. Rather like a 3D billboard with familiar elements of Vuitton's trademark monogram twinkling along an illuminated membrane, a unique lighting design would announce the store's presence on the avenue long after closing time.

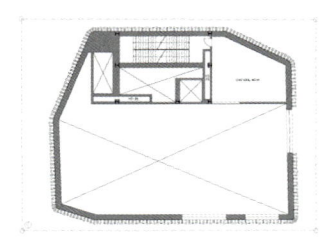

ARCHITECTURE AND INTERIORS

OSAKA MIDOSUJI

17TH FLOOR

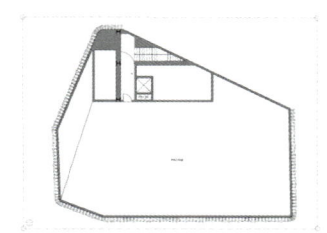

REFUGE FLOOR

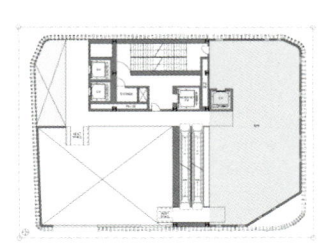

10TH FLOOR

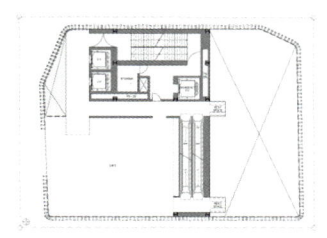

13TH FLOOR

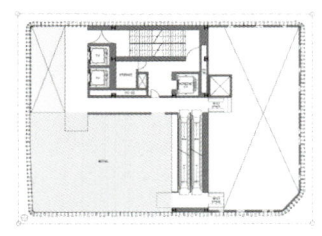

5TH FLOOR

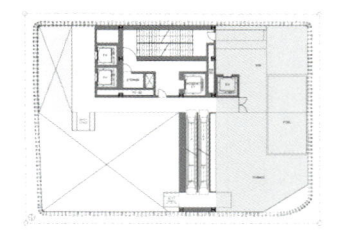

8TH FLOOR

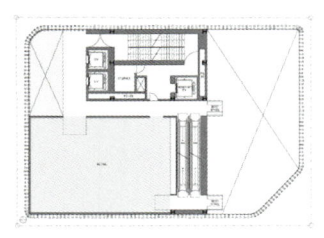

3RD FLOOR

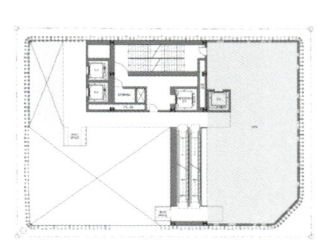

4TH FLOOR

GROUND FLOOR

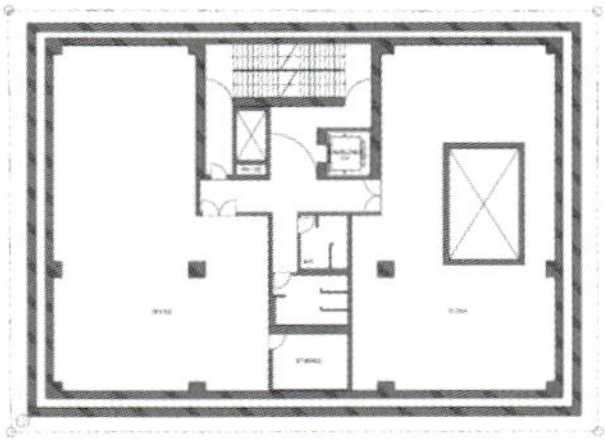

BASEMENT 1ST FLOOR

p. 61 model views of schemes by Jun Aoki (left) and Shigeru Ban (right)
p. 62 All plans and model views on this spread are of the Jun Aoki scheme. Bottom left: view of building at night
p. 63 Jun Aoki scheme: model of East façade on Midosuji Avenue
p. 64 model showing the stainless-steel louvers on the curtain wall
p. 65 interior renderings

JAPAN

ARCHITECTURE AND INTERIORS

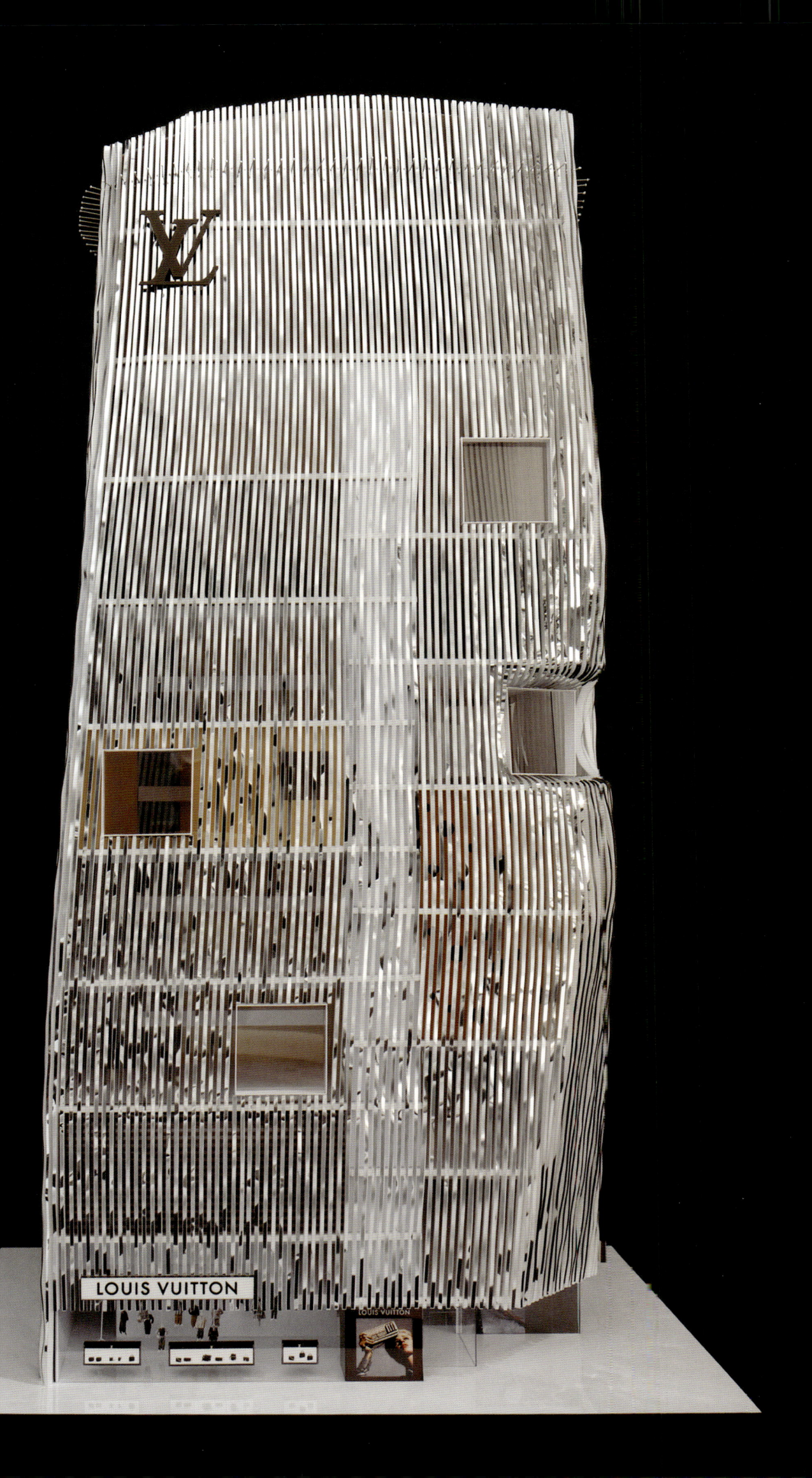

OSAKA MIDOSUJI

JAPAN

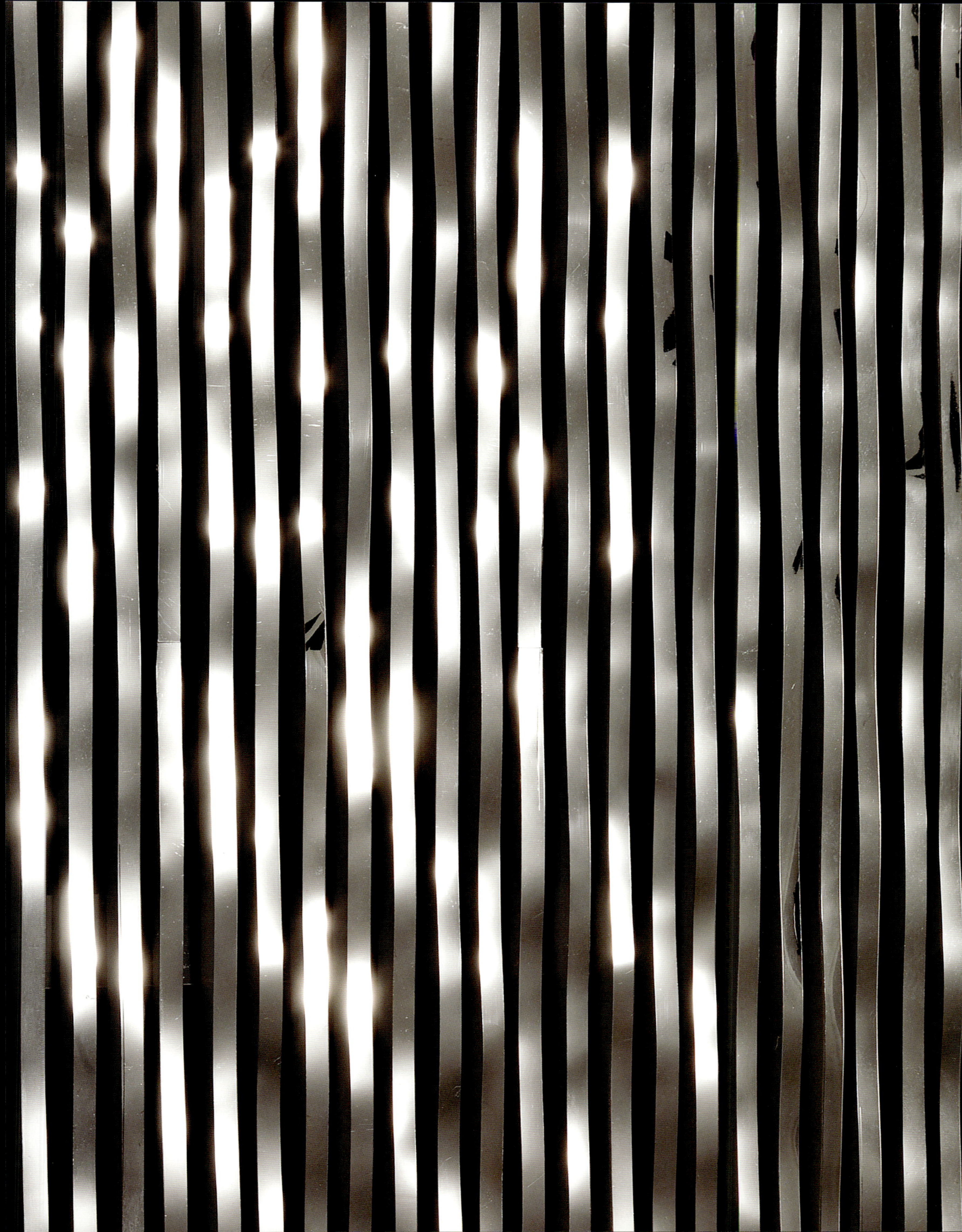

ARCHITECTURE AND INTERIORS

OSAKA MIDOSUJI

JAPAN

ARCHITECTURE AND INTERIORS

OSAKA MIDOSUJI

10TH FLOOR

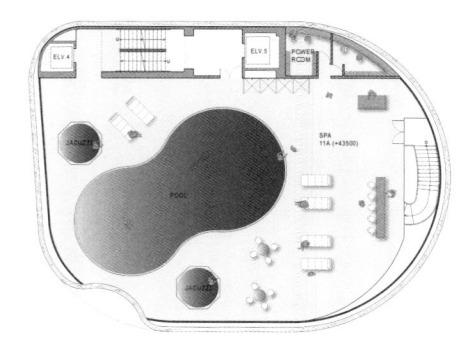

11TH FLOOR SPA

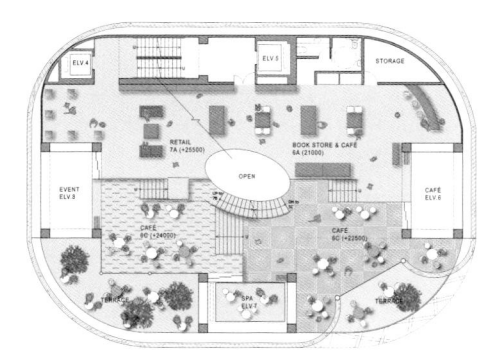

6TH FLOOR

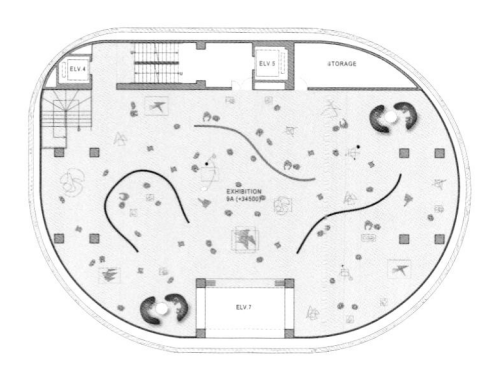

9TH FLOOR

2ND FLOOR

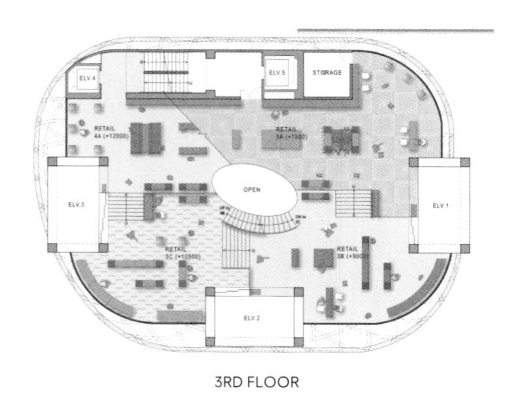

3RD FLOOR

BASEMENT 1ST FLOOR

GROUND FLOOR

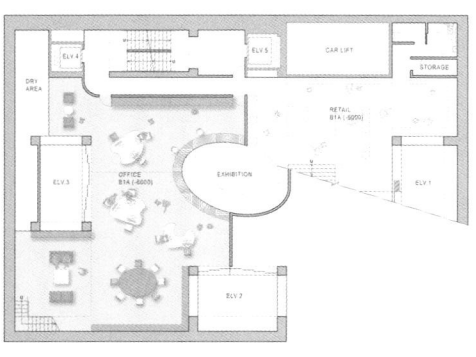

JAPAN

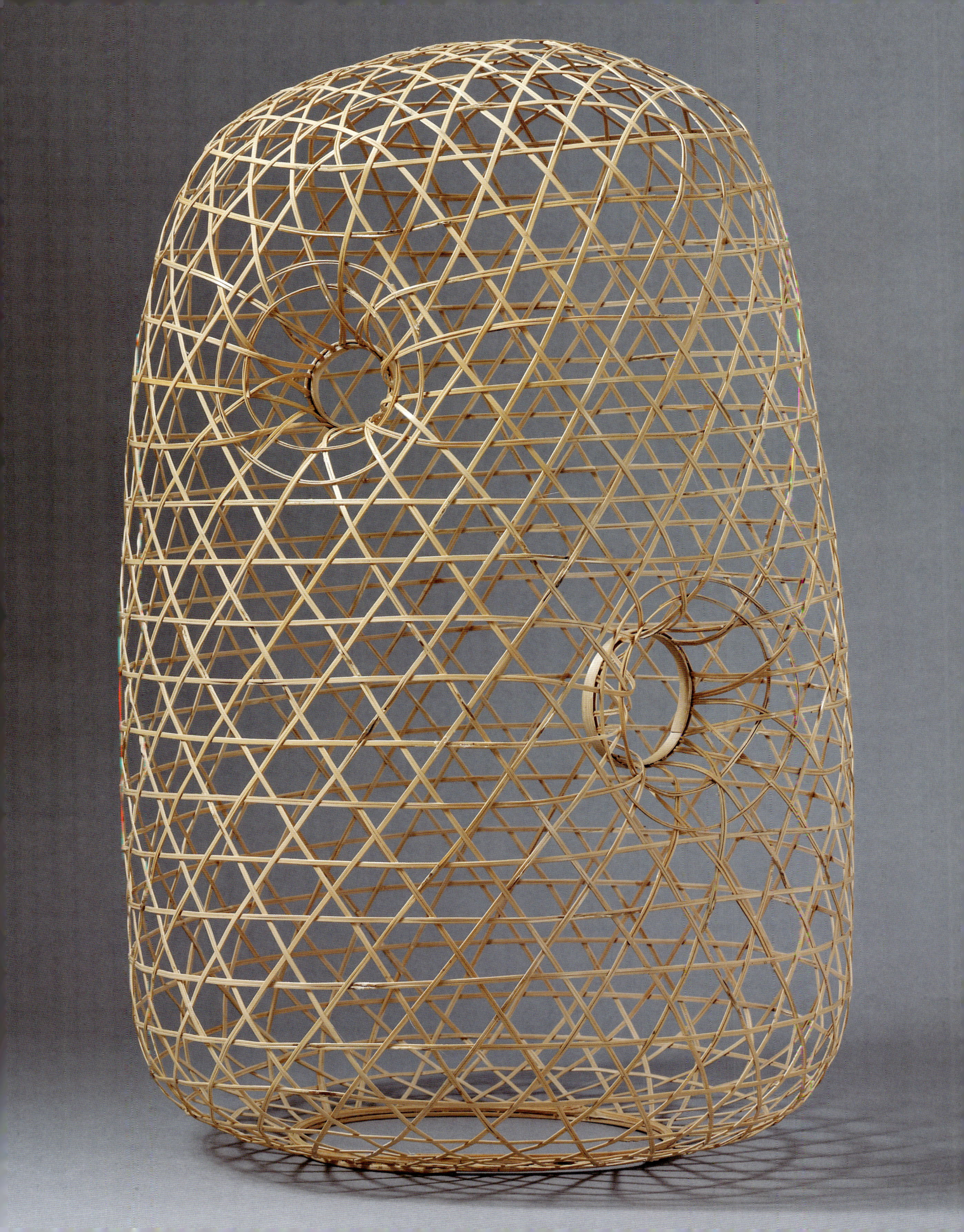

ARCHITECTURE AND INTERIORS 68

OSAKA MIDOSUJI

JAPAN

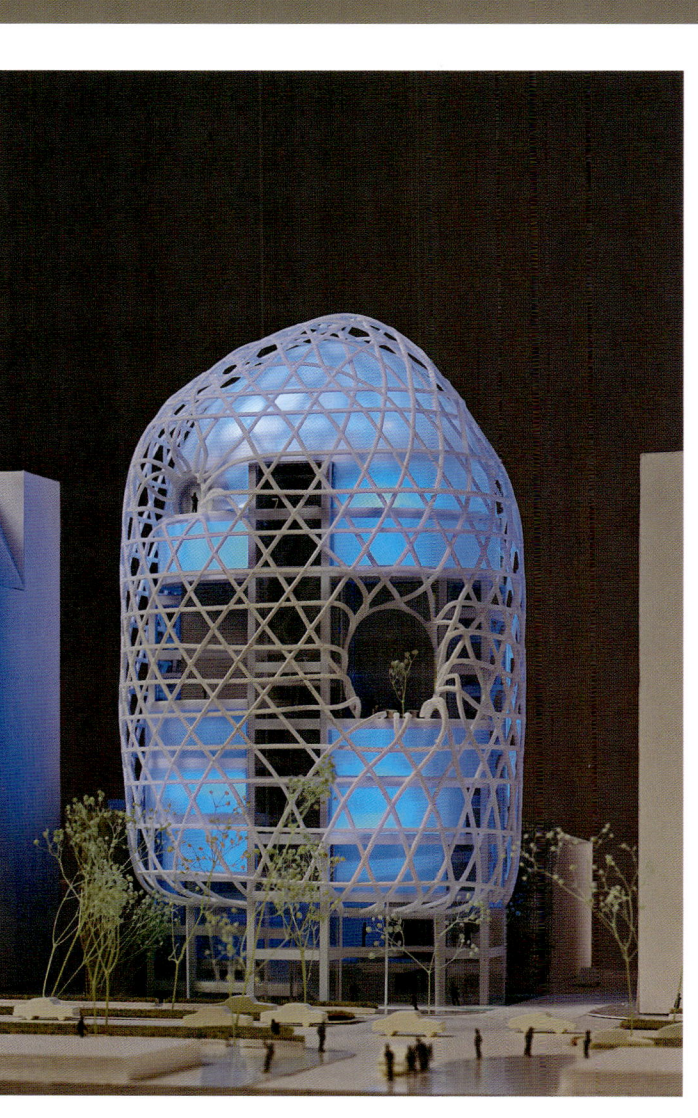

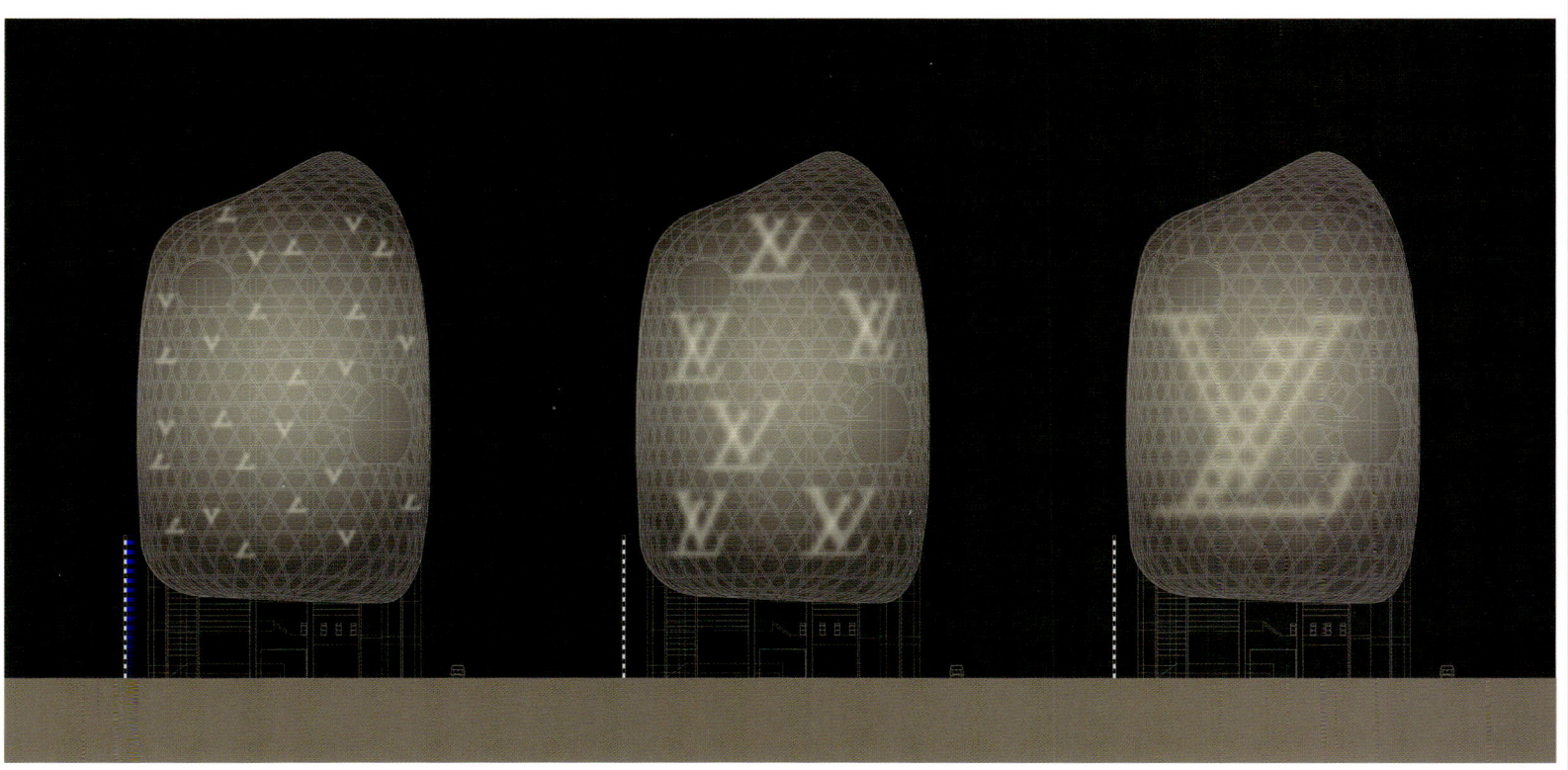

p. 66 All plans and model views on this spread are of the Shigeru Ban scheme.
p. 67 wicker bamboo model of the building envelope
p. 68–69 Shigeru Ban scheme: model and renderings describing the lighting and signage programs at night

A CONVERSATION WITH JUN AOKI AND MOHSEN MOSTAFAVI

MOHSEN MOSTAFAVI: It would be good to start in the beginning. Can you explain how you became involved with LV?
JUN AOKI: It was 1998 and Eric Carlson called me about the possibility of joining the competition project for the Louis Vuitton Nagoya. I participated in the competition and was chosen. This was the first time that I collaborated with LV. Later I asked Eric Carlson why they had selected me as a competitor. In 1998 I was not an established architect. Eric asked his former colleague at OMA, Alejandro Zaera-Polo, who had recommended me. FOA had just won the competition for the Yokohama terminal.

What do you think about the idea of designing for a fashion company and the relationship between architecture and fashion?
In Japan, the major modernist architects almost rejected to design commercial buildings. When I started my own design firm, the focus was on the interior. Both the interior and the structure are really important for me. And the surface of the building was just the result of designing the interior space. But at that time I was pretty afraid to design for fashion groups, and I saw this as a very big challenge to design a building for fashion.

And so when you started with Nagoya, what were some of your thoughts? How did you begin the Nagoya project?
I thought that I could not design the interior space. For me, it is too commercial and I had no idea what kind of space would be efficient for selling. I thought the project needed the exterior design—the shape and appearance of the building. I had to do the design model and felt that this was something negative because it was just a wrapping design idea. For me, the wrapping is a very superficial, perhaps too superficial, idea. So I tried by designing only a surface, but a surface that doesn't just look like a surface: it appears like a volume or the area of the volume, something like that. Even if this feeling is ephemeral—this was my first approach to designing a building for Louis Vuitton.

Where did that come from, your sensibility and decision about the ephemeral?
First I didn't know that every commercial building for fashion changed every five years. I had thought that commercial buildings were more permanent. So the use of materials like stone, or marble would just be out of date in five years and every design and every material would be out of date quite quickly. My solution to this was to make a building that dematerializes. It should have a feeling that can last forever otherwise it would very easily go out of date. My first idea was to reject the use of stone, because stone has a very particular feeling. And other materials also have their own specific feeling. It is only glass that can afford several states, by using the moiré effect, it is not the feeling of glass but this other more abstract more ephemeral quality that is more dominant.

When you started working with LV, did you notice something different about the methods of construction used in the fashion industry compared to your experience with other projects?
No, the methods of construction are essentially the same, except that it must be fast and flexible. Because there is a lot of innovation for the space, it is just these two things that are critical.

How did LV's emphasis on speed of construction and flexibility affect your design process?
One thing is I could not make the building in concrete. I had to use a steel structure. Also every building required some excavation because of the basement. So while the site was being excavated, the structure has to be pre-fabricated in order to optimize the construction time. But in a way that is not so unusual in Japan since every building needs to be constructed as fast as possible.

How about flexibility?
The internal space should be very simple. That is the reason why I proposed just the box.

Presumably simple because at LV, like the rest of the fashion industry the interior will be changed every few years. That is something that must have been unusual for you in designing the building, primarily from the perspective of the building envelope and not the interior.
Yes, this was unusual for me. In my work I had been used to handling the interior space, but this was one of the conditions of working with a fashion group. But even if the space is very simple, just boxes, I still had to decide what to do with it.

So what are some of the specific things you learned from the Nagoya building?
One thing is—this was for me the first occasion to think about the building in the urban landscape. The size, the proportion, and the appearance is quite important for the city. My lesson was that this is not a public building; this is a commercial building, which at the same time is very public. The building can change the environment. Designing this building influences its surroundings. This project made me realize the importance of the design of the exterior.

When you have talked before or written about this question of appearance and about the role of ornament, you have mentioned Roland Barthe's discussion of theatre—how the artifice of theatre is also a form of lie. Do you think the façades you are designing are also playing with this concept? For example, ephemerality is also a form of lying?
For me, the surface doesn't have

the tools of the interior space. But the surface gives you something of the feeling of the internal space. It is a little bit like the use of cosmetics for women. I think that the best cosmetic is the one that doesn't hide a woman's face but enhances the face so the person is still recognizable, and yet the real face is very different.

So that's a kind of enhancement—a way of creating, adding beauty? Is that what you are saying?
Not adding, this is probably a different concept because we always think there is some truth and some lie. But in the cosmetic, it is not this relationship at all. It is not the relationship of truth and lie. The mask or the surface of the building is not just a lie; it is the mixture of truth and lie. This surface gives you some of the very essential concepts of the cosmetic relationship of the inside reality and outside reality.

But given the fact that you're not designing the inside of the building, the relationship between the inside and the outside is not something that you have control over. Your role is focusing more on the outside. I know you have mentioned this idea of the inside is also something that is in some ways empty.
This is the major issue for me, because I sometimes see this internal space as an empty space. But sometimes it needs a body. For example, in the Omotesando building, this occurs in the relationship of the conceptual trunks that make up the interior. It is the proportions, the sizes, and the layout of this three-dimensional construct that is very important to me. Here, I thought that the internal space wasn't completely empty, but that there must be some relationship between the internal space and the external appearance of the building.

Do you consider, for example, the Omotesando project as a kind of critique of modern architecture, in the same way that *Learning from Las Vegas* is a criticism of modern architecture?
This separation of a duck and a decorated shed is for me a very interesting idea. The Omotesando project is a kind of decorated shed building. But it is slightly different from the Venturi idea because the duck and even the decorated shed have some messages to communicate. In the case of a hot dog store, the message is just a hot dog store. Modern architecture has a message too. Modern architecture is the message. Whereas, in the design of the Louis Vuitton store, I think there is no message; of course there is the message, this is a Louis Vuitton store, but it is not a direct message.

Isn't it shifting from a semiotic reading of buildings to an experiential version where you are feeling the building? The experience also conveys a message, but it is about a kind of sensibility—a different kind of sensation. This seems to be a more emotive version of architecture.
That is the message: this is emotion. The movement of sensation is more important for this kind of building.

The LV architecture department said at the beginning that they did not want to work with signature architects. Instead they preferred to develop an architecture that was specifically unique to LV. And with Omotesando, they probably discovered the DNA of that architecture. Even other architects who had been hired by LV have followed some of its qualities. They've almost suppressed their own architectural or stylistic predilections by trying to produce things that are more LV. You have been working with LV for 13 years, so how do you see the future of the stores?
I think there will be change in the future. Now the surfaces of Louis Vuitton buildings are very neutral. But sometimes, like during the Christmas seasons, they put the color monogram pattern on the façade of the neutral surface. This decoration is stronger than the building design itself; my design completely disappears. My design, this neutral design, is a kind of canvas for the decoration.

I think that there are two directions for the future. We can give them a more efficient canvas or we can provide the decoration itself. Sometimes I propose these ideas, but so far they have not been accepted. In the future they will probably choose these types of façades. I'm not sure it is good or not, but every city is getting a similar feeling. Tokyo is a very unique city; it is very instant and susceptible to speedy change. Its decoration, its architecture, is changeable. Now that the speed of things is more accelerated perhaps the whole building can become decoration. This is the real situation for Tokyo. I sometimes wonder if I even want these dreams, to discover or find the next step of decoration, because if architecture becomes decoration it almost signifies the end of architecture. So the most interesting and dangerous challenge to me is what is beyond decoration.

LOUIS VUITTON

ASIA PACIFIC
CHINA, SHANGHAI *PUDONG*
CHINA, HONG KONG *CANTON ROAD*
CHINA, HONG KONG *LANDMARK*
CHINA, MACAO *ONE CENTRAL*
SINGAPORE *MARINA BAY*

SHANGHAI PUDONG

architects
THE LOUIS VUITTON
ARCHITECTURE DEPARTMENT;
PETER MARINO ARCHITECT
2010

text by
FRÉDÉRIC EDELMANN

Two Louis Vuitton shops, categorized as "global stores" opened simultaneously in Shanghai on April 28, 2010. One on Huahai Lu, a long street symbolizing the former French Concession, and the other, in the new neighborhood of Pudong, an impressive new town built in an area that was once filled with truck farms, factories and fishermen. Nothing is insignificant about the emergence of the Global Store of Louis Vuitton in Pudong. Nothing is insignificant about. It overlapped with the Universal Expo 2010, becoming a symbol of the event's optimistic themes. It was an adventure that was masterfully orchestrated throughout China, Shanghai, and even in the French pavilion, for which LVMH was one of four key partners. Number 8 Century Avenue in Shanghai is an address many dream about. But what century is it? And what Shanghai are we talking about? Century Avenue was inaugurated in 1999, at the turn of the 20th century and the start of the 21st century, when the past was left to chance. It is in this past that Louis Vuitton has decided to forge its image, as well as in the future, which it has clearly decided to befriend.

Even before the adventure of the Beijing Olympic Games in 2008 and all the major transformations that took place in the capital, the new development in Shanghai on the east bank of the Huangpu River represented the most impressive urban growth in China after Mao.

In 1999, Century Avenue was still an oddity, cut through with an ax and split diagonally by a bourgeoning new neighborhood. It was a rump of an avenue, meant to serve as an axis for the new neighborhood, symmetrical to the old Shanghai (Puxi) compared to Huangpu, a significant tributary of the vast Yangtze River, which also runs alongside Pudong. It is here that the new Shanghai airport is located, designed by the French architect Paul Andreu, and here as well that the new port of the metropolis is being built.

Zoom in closer! From 2005–2006, the Pudong neighborhood, which overlooks the Bund—the famous embankment of Old Shanghai where the banks and major shipping companies were established—was still as thin as a postcard. The image of the area was dominated by the television tower—a strange vertical object punctuated by three colored balls. Surrounding this was a rather informal panorama from which there emerged a few buildings of note, including the famous Jin Mao Tower (421 meters), which was theoretically completed in 2001 and crowned by Shanghai's first Hyatt Hotel. Shanghai represents China's reconciliation with monumental new politics. Just as the Bund was an emblem of these new policies in the early twentieth century, Pudong will prove to be the second chapter.

In subsequent years, the sector would become denser and the Jin Mao Tower would be rivaled by the Shanghai World Financial Center (WFC), which at 492 meters tall, houses none other than Shanghai's second Hyatt Hotel. Along with the Jin Mao (built by the American firm Skidmore, Owings & Merrill), the WFC (built by the American firm Kohn Pedersen Fox) protects in its shadow the twin towers of the International Financial Center (IFC), the Ritz-Carlton Hotel and a large mall devoted to the pinnacles of luxury. It is here we find ourselves, at the intersection of economic and urban history—and at the gates of Louis Vuitton.

The stage is set, but where's the clientele hiding? Two million square-meters of office, commercial and hotel space have been established in the Lujiazui district, while a growing number of middle class and wealthy residents (19 million inhabitants) have homes nearby. In the months before the Expo, Pudong entered a new phase of urban planning, which included the addition of several subway lines, the construction of numerous institutions for sports, science and culture, and a highway network that inconsistently negotiates the territory.

When Louis Vuitton Pudong opened its doors three days before the Expo, it also made a commercial wager on the urban future of the neighborhood. Here, luxury is high at hand, between the brands of the shopping center that serve the IFC, the Jin Mao Tower and the WFC, the high-end hotels that provide a route for a client-base that is eager for new sensations, and the white-collar employees who have chosen to reside in Lujiazui. The organizers of the Universal Expo 2010 could have never predicted, even if they had a hunch, that the fair would reach a record high of seventy million visitors. The clients came mostly from the region, many from neighboring cities, a few from across Asia, and even fewer from the rest of the world. But this was a clientele that was already sold; the opportunity to visit some of the biggest luxury brands is often part and parcel of the Expo thrill.

When the Expo ended at the end of October 2010, it was not so easy to legitimize its presence in Lujiazui at the foot of China's two tallest skyscrapers, and especially to manifest itself as a leader. As such, the new Louis

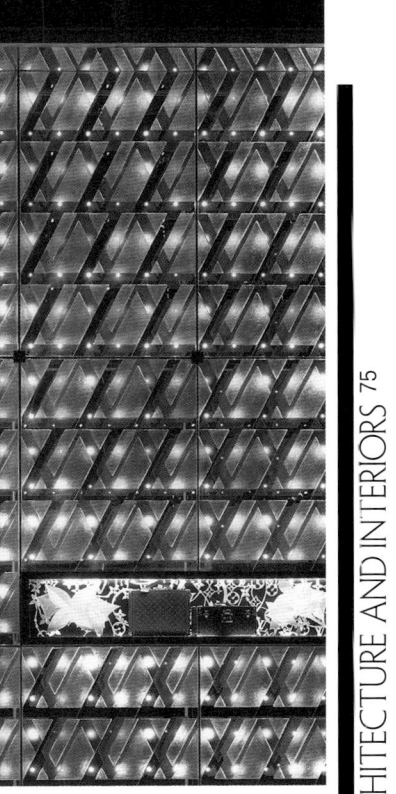

Vuitton store was proactively monitored, as always, but with more good will and a fourfold focus: urban, architectural, decorative and cultural. For this heterogeneous yet changing clientele (no longer the same before and after the Expo), the company needed to simultaneously mark the continuity of the brand and its symbols, and establish itself in a volatile landscape of unfamiliar landmarks. Just a few hundred meters away, construction sites remain open, while the Expo site itself, which was closed in order to be adapted to its new civilian life, has impacted the transportation system as a whole, even though it's located a ways away.

The store, designed by Peter Marino, unfolds over 1,736 square meters, which includes more than 962 square-meters of sales space on one level, a record for the brand. Housed at the main entrance of the IFC mall, it was designed as much to serve as a symbol for the center as it was to signal the presence of Louis Vuitton. Its architecture plays with the verticality of the skyscrapers (the IFC's twin towers and the two larger buildings nearby), but also the horizontal nature of the mall strip, the subway network (lines 2 and 14, the connection with the Maglev bullet train from the airport), the parking garages, and the neat landscape of Lujiazui and its oval-shaped main square.

The building's vertical nature is represented by two major panels that come together to form the corner of the building. Realized in etched glass, within which the famous initials of the brand repeat endlessly, they are illuminated at night by an LED system that signals the presence of Louis Vuitton to the countless windows of surrounding buildings overlooking the IFC. The horizontal nature is expressed by two glass panels that, on a single level, extend and frame the vertical elements. Large windows are integrated into these panels, but instead of being filled with tempting displays, they are used as a way to reinforce the power of this urban landmark. They emit the colors of the Louis Vuitton universe: black, wood, gold, leather—an apparent symmetry that is broken as soon as you enter the store. The main entrance quickly proves to be, if not an illusion, a secondary entrance—an architectural device needed visually, but readily bypassed by customers who prefer to enter through the mall's complex passageways.

This shopping center adheres to an architectural principle that stands entirely in contrast to the strictly geometric and classical vision of Louis Vuitton. Aside from Cartier, which is located across from the store and resumes its formal logic, the IFC is a multi-story atrium of curving forms, offering Baroque and undulating twists and turns to brands that include Dior, Channel, Hermès, Gucci, Armani and Prada on the main floor, while an arsenal of sports stores, computer stores, chocolate stores and smoke shops can be found on the other levels. The inner entrance of Louis Vuitton's was built to comply with this winding world, although it does so with some hesitation, but its sales space gradually recovers from this, readjusting to its own norms.

At the heart of these devices, a large oval area for bags and watches is a courteous nod to the curvatures of the mall. To further distance itself from the surroundings, the store's ceiling, designed by Venezuelan artist Arturo Herrera and titled *Till There Was You*, presents large interlacing designs outlined on the plaster with gold leaf. Westerners might herein perceive the influence of Chinese painting, while the Chinese might find the inspiration harder to detect. The space for shoes, which follows the classical principle of right angles, is embellished by the talents of the German Anselm Reyle, who has created a ceiling inspired by origami using a sophisticated display of folds that echoes the iconic checkerboard of the House of Louis Vuitton.

Around these two volumes follows, in a display of virtuosity, every in-house architectural element: the Bag Bar, which alternates between dark wood luminous leathers, the soft parchment, the supple and mysterious materials, the ever-changing furnishings, the multi-format windows, the meticulously designed tables and display cases, and the warmly colored rugs and deep mirrors framed by lights that absorb the clients' every dream, transporting them into an ever more luxurious world, if one even exists.

p. 72 Louis Vuitton Hong Kong Landmark store, façade view
p. 75 detail of the exterior at night. The curtain wall of glass and metal uses a pattern based on an abstraction of the familiar Louis Vuitton L & V monogram
p. 76 bottom and 77: exterior views
p. 78–79: façade detail
p. 80–81 interior views of Bag Bar, luggage and watches area and women's shoes and leather goods

GROUND FLOOR

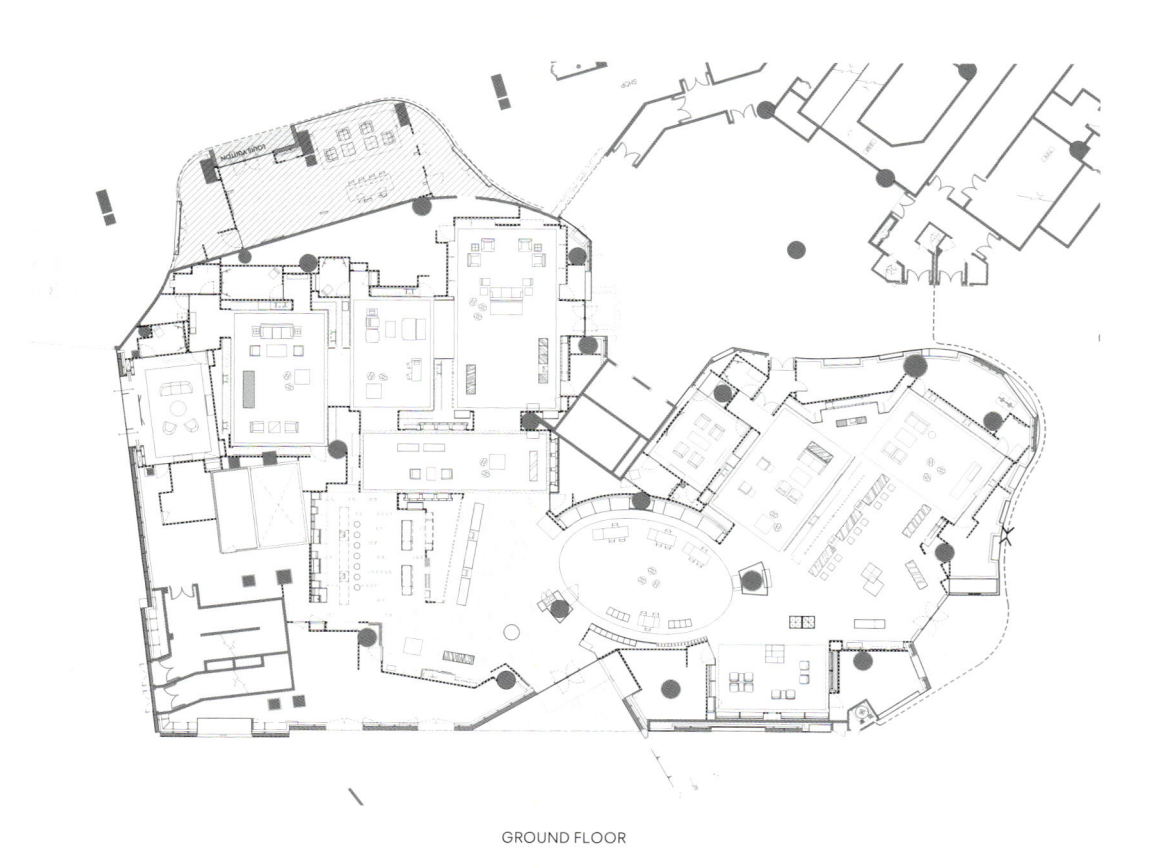

LOUIS VUITTON
LOUIS VUITTON
LOUIS VUITTON
LOUIS VUITTON
LOUIS VUITTON
LOUIS VUITTON

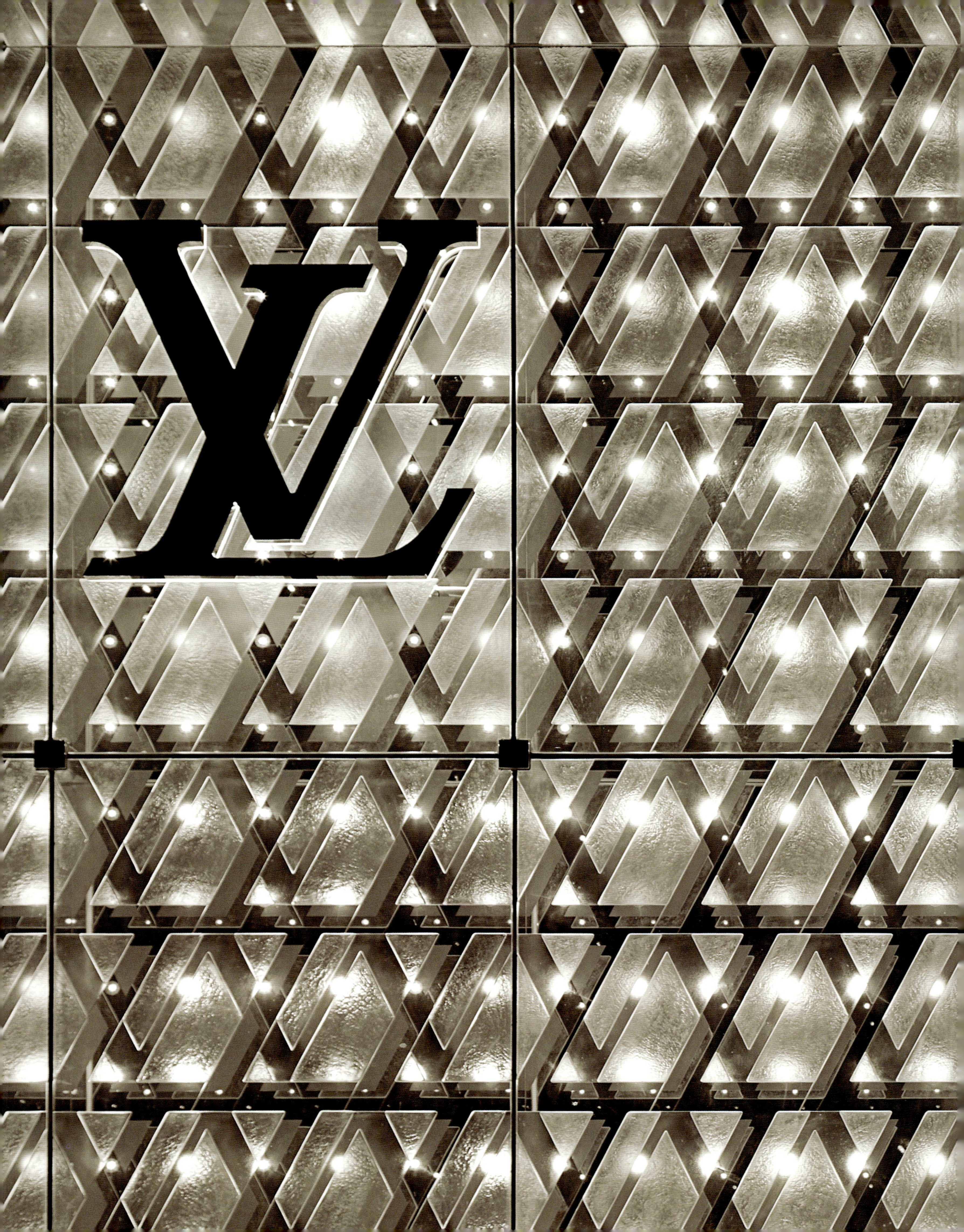

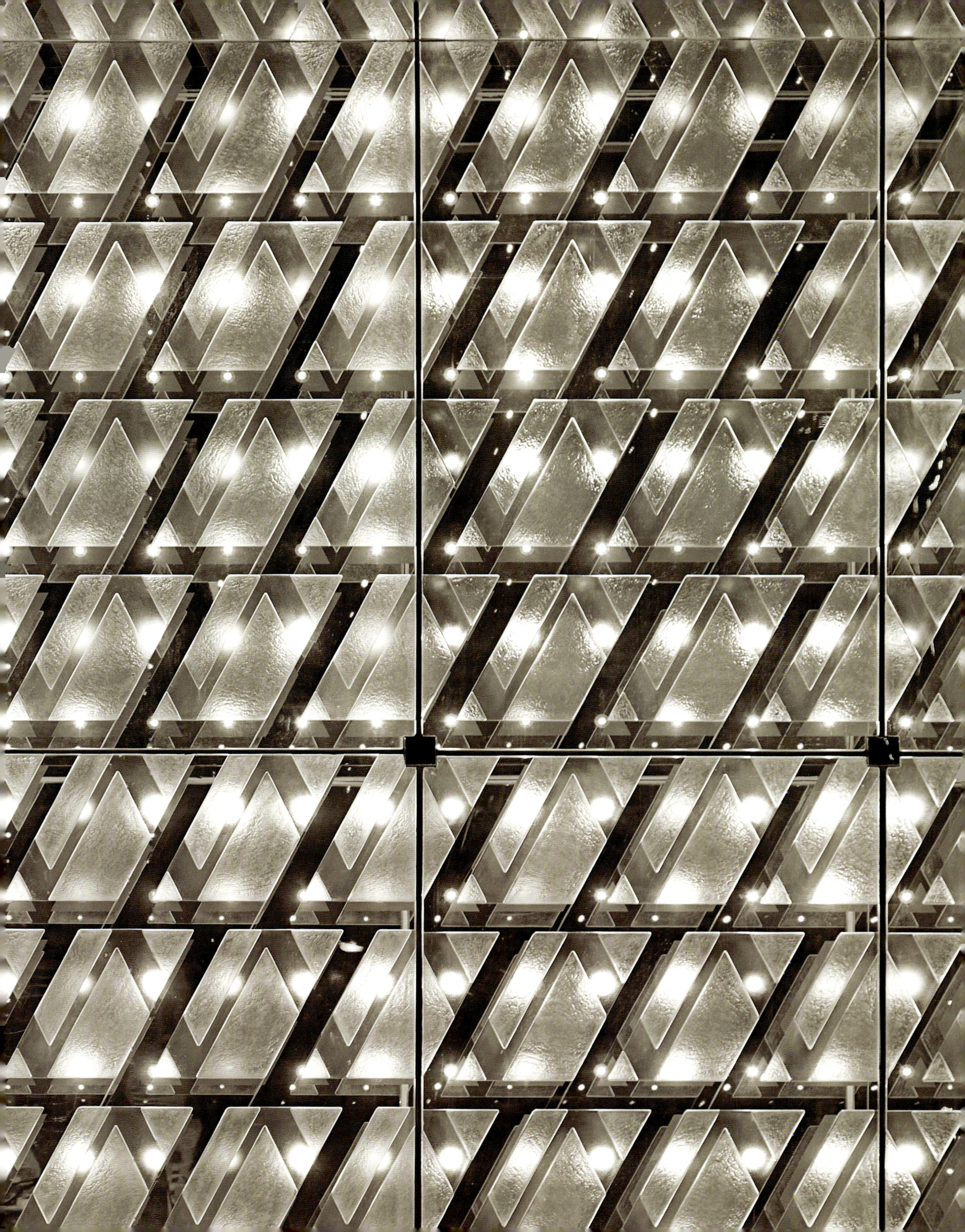

ARCHITECTURE AND INTERIORS 80

SHANGHAI PUDONG

ASIA PACIFIC

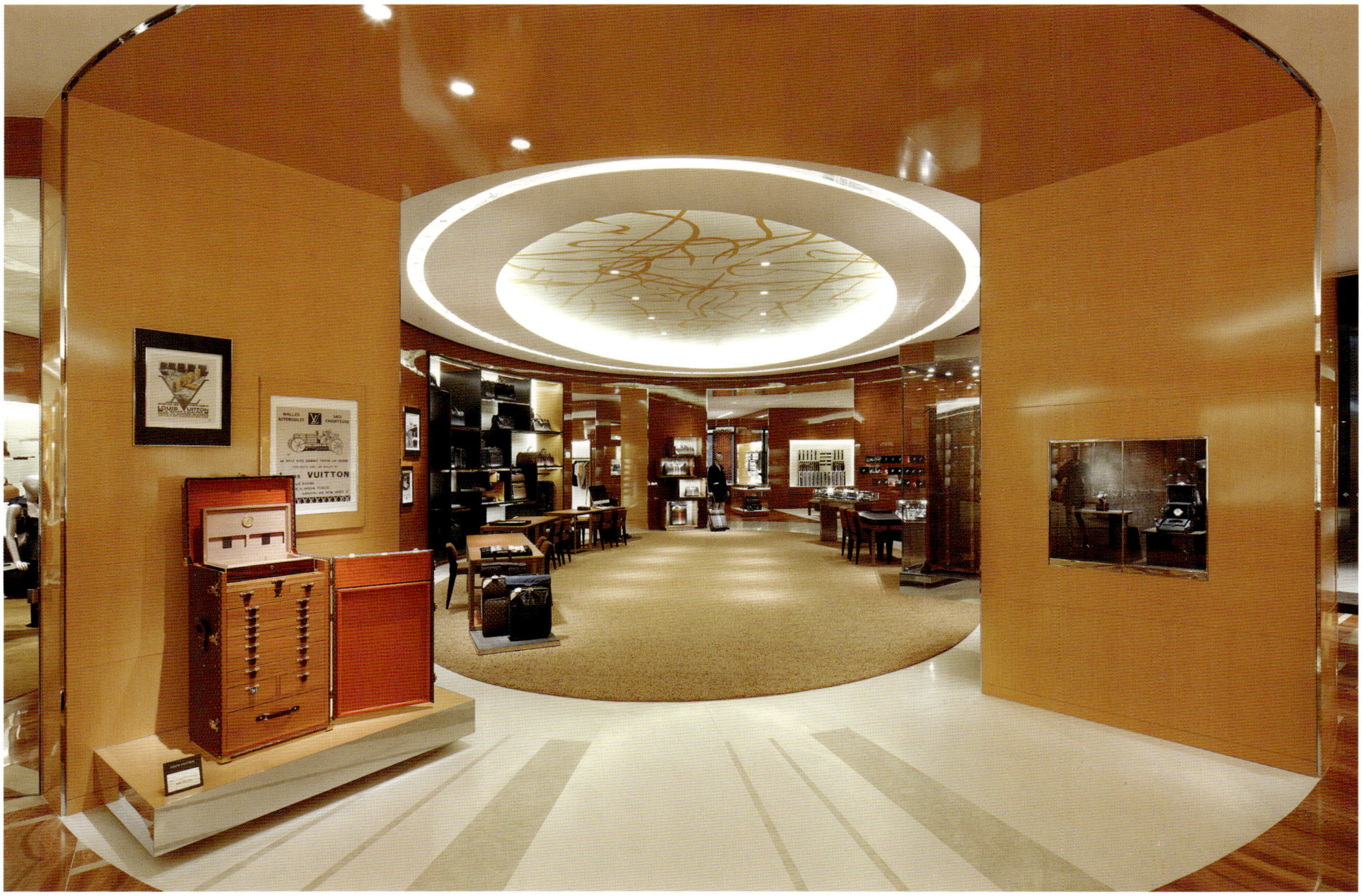
VUITTON

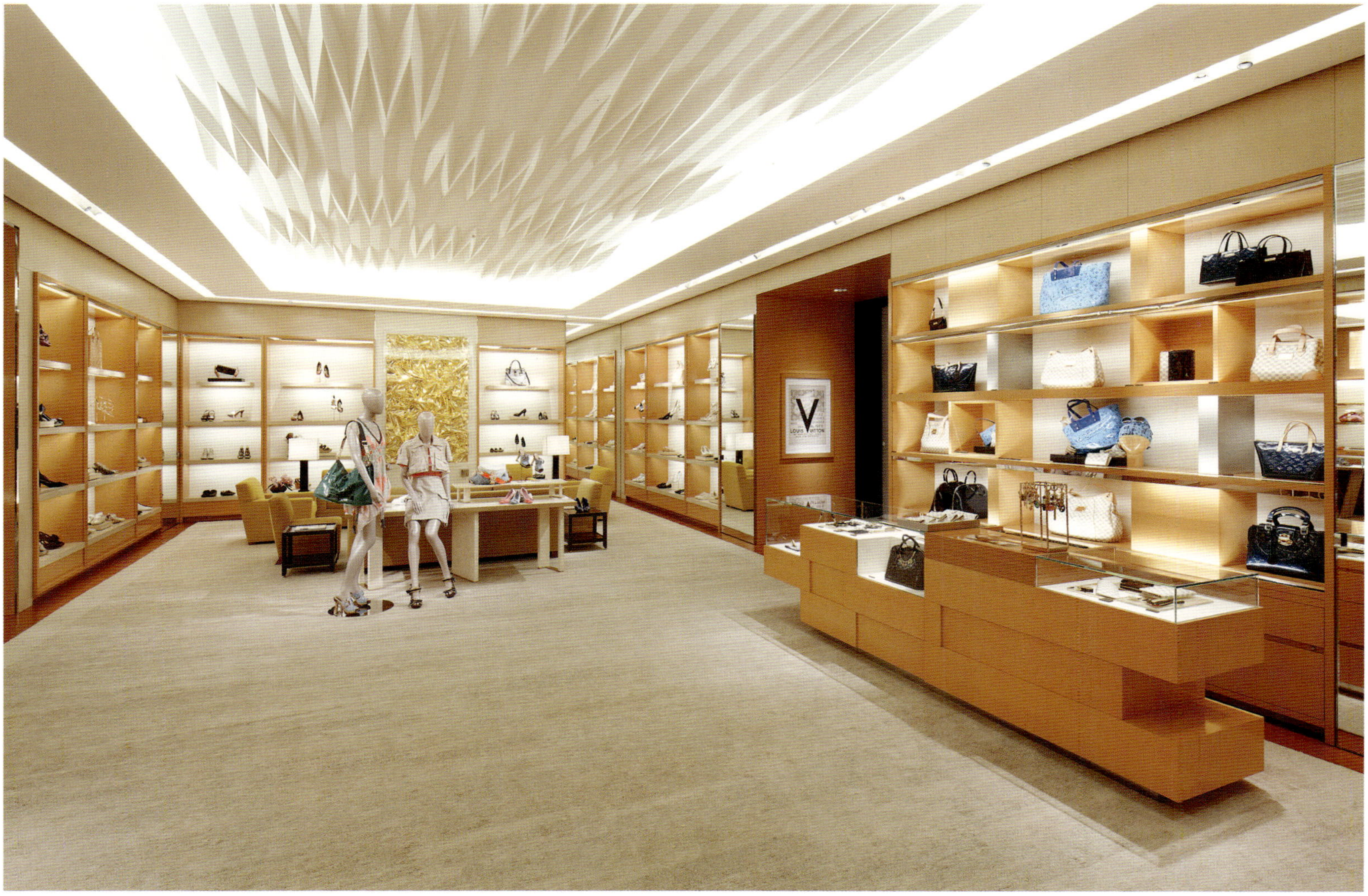

HONG KONG CANTON ROAD

architects
KUMIKO INUI;
THE LOUIS VUITTON
ARCHITECTURE DEPARTMENT
2008

text by
FRÉDÉRIC EDELMANN

When the weekend comes, or a holiday—whether it's the year of the Tiger, the Dog, the Dragon, or any other occasion to celebrate—Canton Road in Hong Kong resembles a huge market with overflowing sidewalks. In fact, these streets are not that broad, and if the population remains as dense as it is in Lille or New York (about 6,500 per square kilometer), it's because we consider the mountains inaccessible and even less habitable than Victoria Peak and the Kowloon Peninsula—which links with the Chinese mainland via Shenzhen, and the fraternal twin of Hong Kong, which has its own Louis Vuitton store and is not easy to get to. In Shenzhen, which was founded and populated by Chinese from the North, they now speak mostly Mandarin (in Hong Kong it's called *Cianggang*), whereas Hong Kong (*Hunggóng*), the "port of perfumes," stubbornly speaks Cantonese and remains a world apart.

Just as Victoria Peak belongs to a tradition of luxury marching silently on, Louis Vuitton's 5 Canton Road, located in Kowloon's Harbor City, bathes in the dynamism that is so loved by *kung fu* filmmakers from the former British colony. In front of the store, the crowd falls into an impressive, well-behaved line: a discipline inherited from the British Empire that remains a feature of inhabitants. This feature only makes the queue of clients—as hooked on Vuitton as museumgoers were to Monet and Basquiat in Paris in early 2011—seem more impressive.

It was on March 14, 2008 that the store opened—then the second largest store (1,749 square meters) after the one on the Champs-Élysées—at 5 Canton Road, giving it the nickname "5CR." The site is not neutral. It's a kind of shopping Mecca, or Rodeo Drive, transplanted from Hollywood but adapted to the rhythm of Hong Kong, which has its own Avenue of Stars. Here the rhythm is *Tsim Sha Tsui*, the name of the neighborhood, a ternary beat that called for an inauguration in which every Asian rock star would join in. The concentration of luxury businesses meant that an event of this kind had to be mind-blowing. As did its architecture: adapted to an urban plan, the building is banal in appearance, but amazingly effective in reality, considering its commercial objective.

Canton Road is in fact the axis of an astonishing business center, its "entrance," facing the ferry terminal and located in the cultural center of Hong Kong Harbor. Asymmetrical, the two sides of the avenue each follow a different urban rhythm. To the east, there's a rapid succession of connecting blocks in which the scansion limits (very relatively) the size of the stores. The store signs blare above the sidewalks. To the west, six, large, identical buildings made of white concrete, expanded south through two longer buildings, all bear the same, relatively insipid architecture. Banks and offices fill the floors. The street architecture is designed according to the succession of stores, their facades, and their signage—all lying flat, parallel to the avenue.

In the background, a second parallel avenue slips beneath the buildings: a shopping center for days of rain or unbearable heat. Here, major luxury brands have found accommodation where they can't be missed by any of their clientele outdoors or indoors. Louis Vuitton has the lion's share. It also has a share that is, at once, the most discreet and the most immediately recognizable, with its "wall" measuring eight hundred square meters, and composed of square screens, or "stones," animated by 90,000 LEDs. This strong composition, designed by the Japanese architect Kumiko Inui, immediately evokes the Louis Vuitton checkerboard pattern. The lower part, divided by the entrance and the windows' golden lights, reveals the supporting structures, as if the materiality of the site needs to be remembered. It's true that a mysterious device of luminous glass makes the Louis Vuitton flower appear, like an otherworldly motif, beyond the mirror. This effect is accepted, but only within the space of the House.

The store entrance along the façade is off-center in order to avoid the load-bearing elements of the structure. It opens right onto an atrium, beyond which lies the Bag Bar, dominated by video art. The first video installation made for the store's opening was by the Italian artist Fabrizio Plessi. Humor? First, second degree? This large piece, titled *Melting Gold*, depicts a gold curtain melting, one to which the melting pot that is the population of Hong Kong will not necessarily have access.

At the outset, once past the entrance—which is distinguished by its ceiling's double-height ceiling and relatively open, if not empty, space—the store promises to be asymmetrical and ruthlessly pull all the stops. The luxury is palpable. Between the woods and coppers, the floors and ceilings, expanses of white and mirrors, the serious solidity of lines of polished steel and the supple material of the rugs, the golden lights caressing artificial white daylight… an extremely varied world reveals itself little by little over the four floors of this stunning ship. Two VIP lounges add to the feeling of imminent departure, unless they're a port of call, since we're in another world.

This universe seems to be telling us that we are indeed in the port of Hong Kong; the theme of travel is palpable. Old collector trunks and posters recall the journeys made by the former British colony. The world of luggage—to buy, to personalize or simply to contemplate—reinforces this feeling, as does the existence of an exhibition gallery (a long, light green wall overlooking the atrium) and a bookstore that caters to the moods of vagabonds. At the end of one of the lounges, in a transitional space, a table offers you three of the seven volumes of the Grand Ricci Dictionary of the Chinese language; consisting of 13,500 words, it was completed at the end of the twentieth century by a group of Jesuit scholars and travelers who occasionally stopped in Hong Kong.

You can exit Louis Vuitton 5CR via the upper deck or, from here, return. This is the universe of a shopping center devoted to luxury; you can stroll here. Empty on days when the weather is nice and fresh, and packed on stormy days, the Louis Vuitton liner dominates amongst a fleet of top labels.

p. 83–85 exterior views along Canton Road, with Kumiko Inui's distinctive application of the trademark damier pattern
p. 86 interior views of the ground floor with video installation *Il lusso è lento* (2008) by Fabrizio Plessi, and luggage area
p. 87 views of the VIP areas
p. 88–89 windows with *Il lusso è lento* video and *Molten* bag installation by Fabrizio Plessi for the opening of the store in 2008

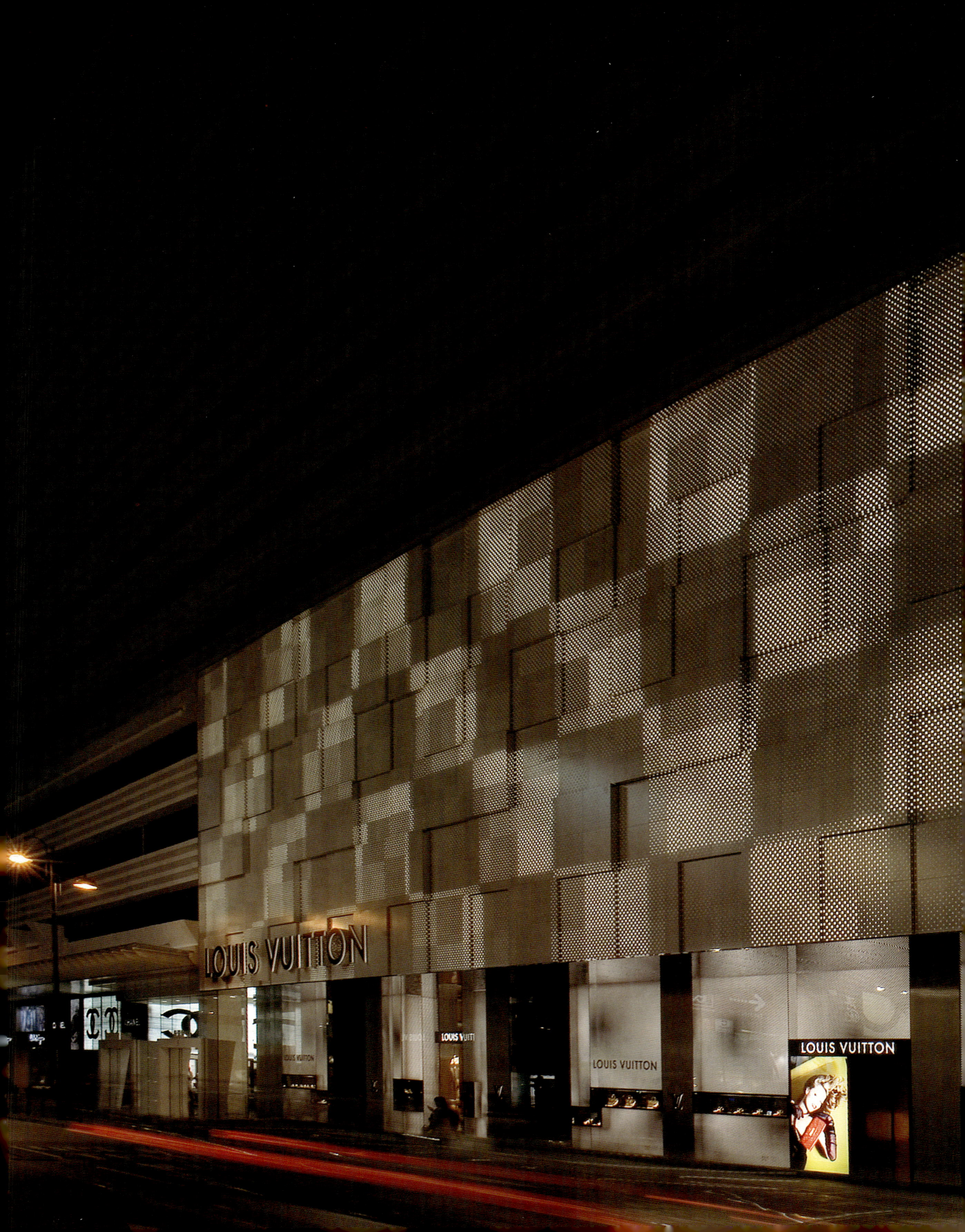
LOUIS VUITTON
LOUIS VUITTON
LOUIS VUITTON

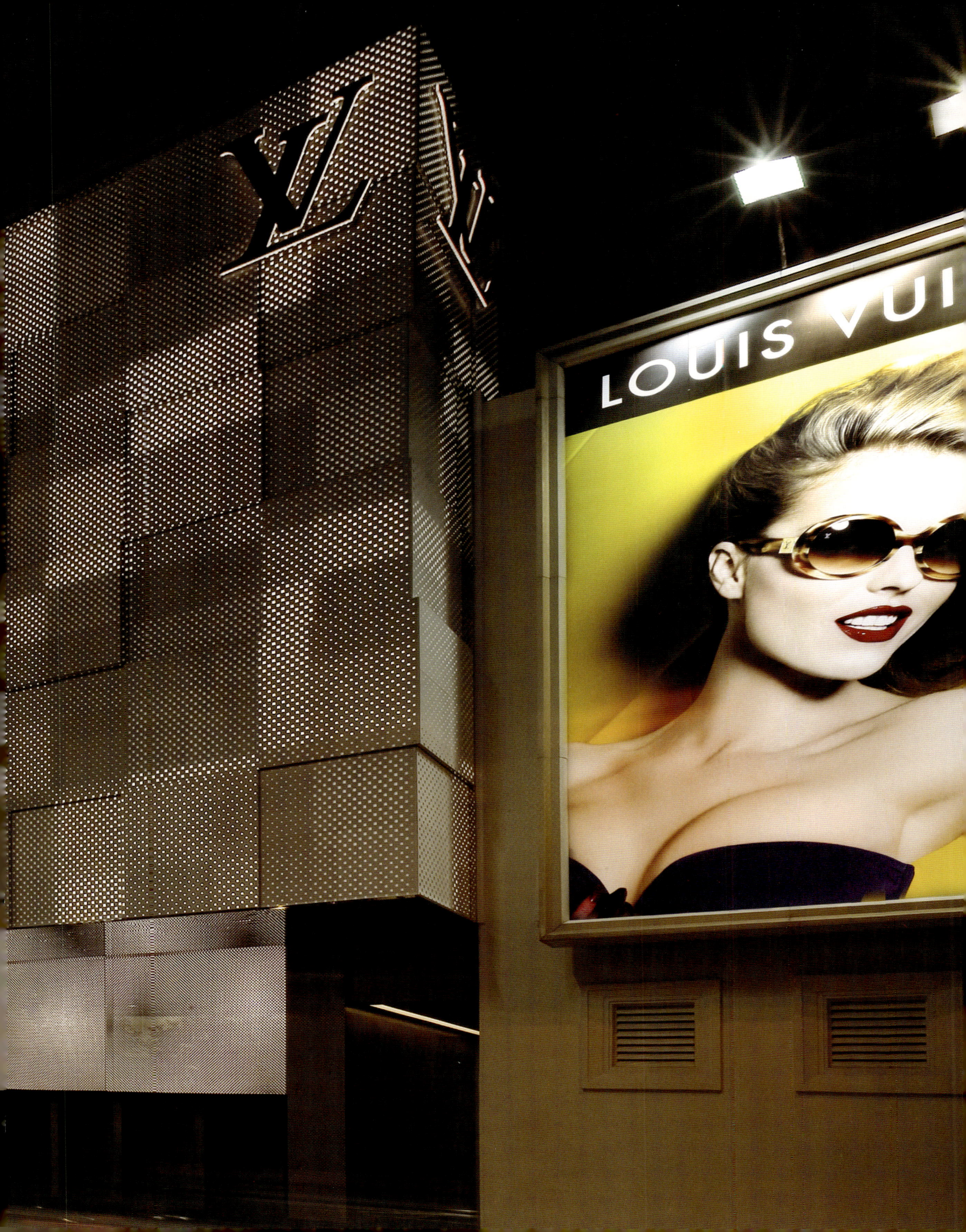
LOUIS VUI

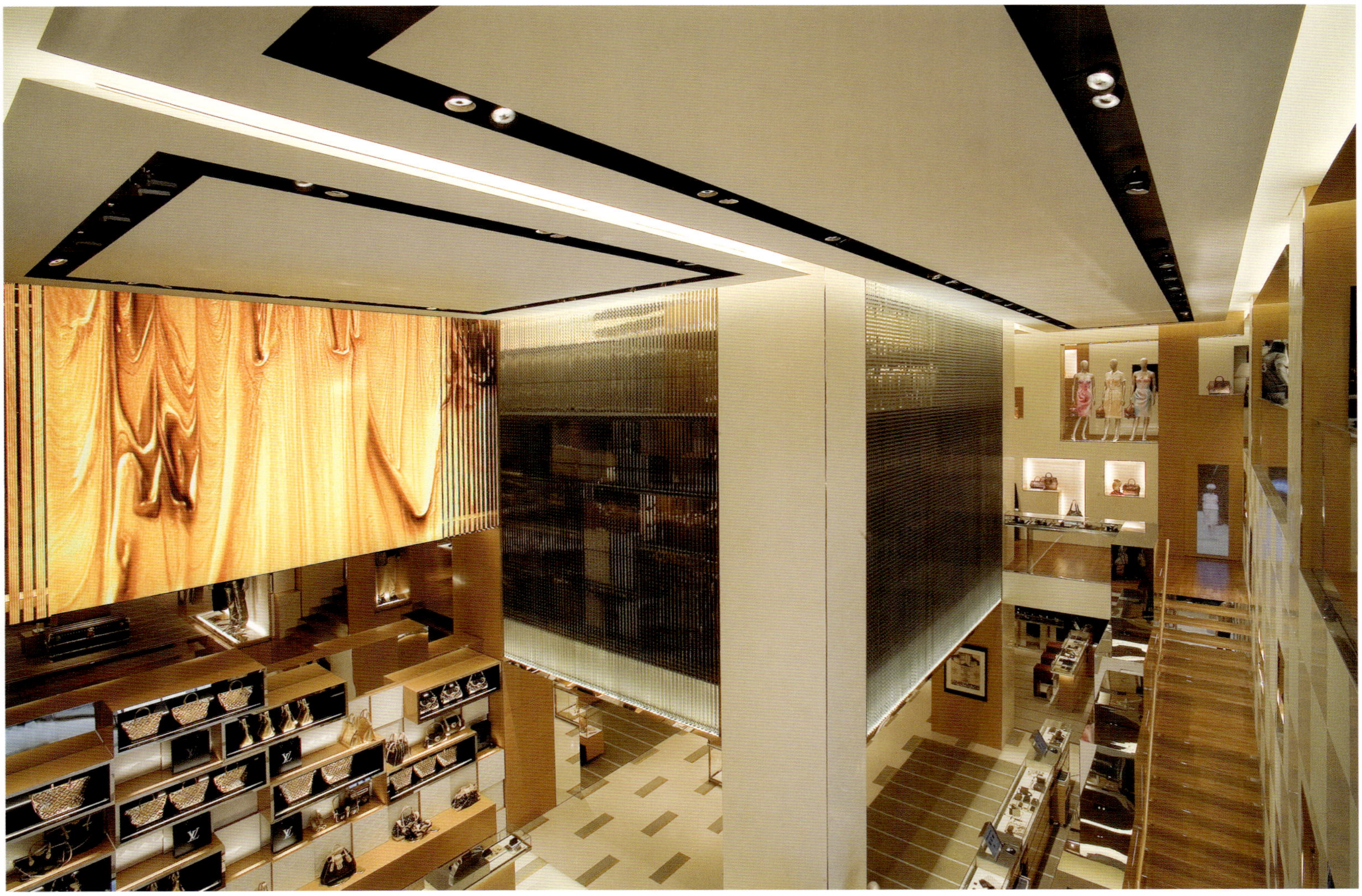

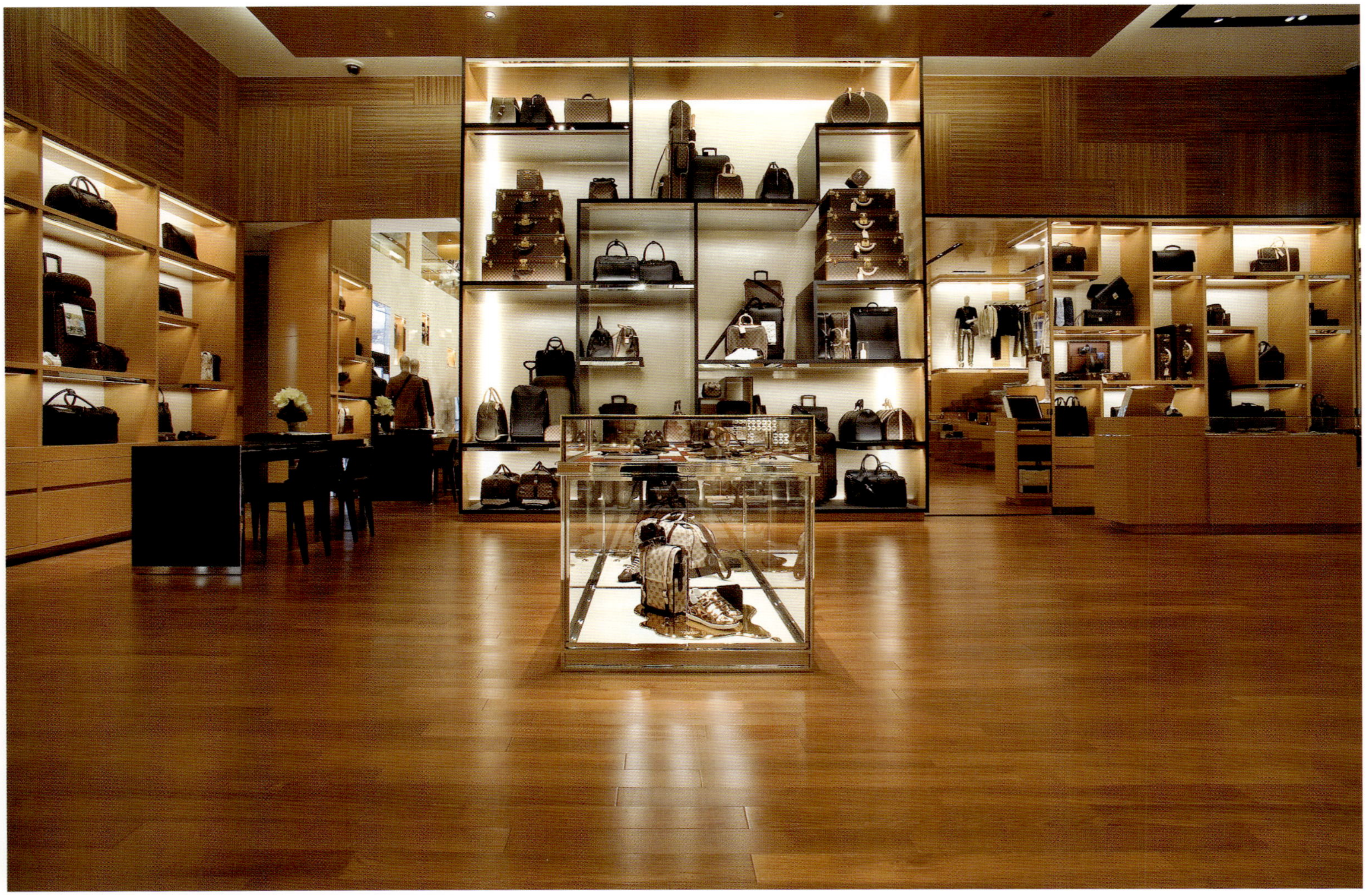

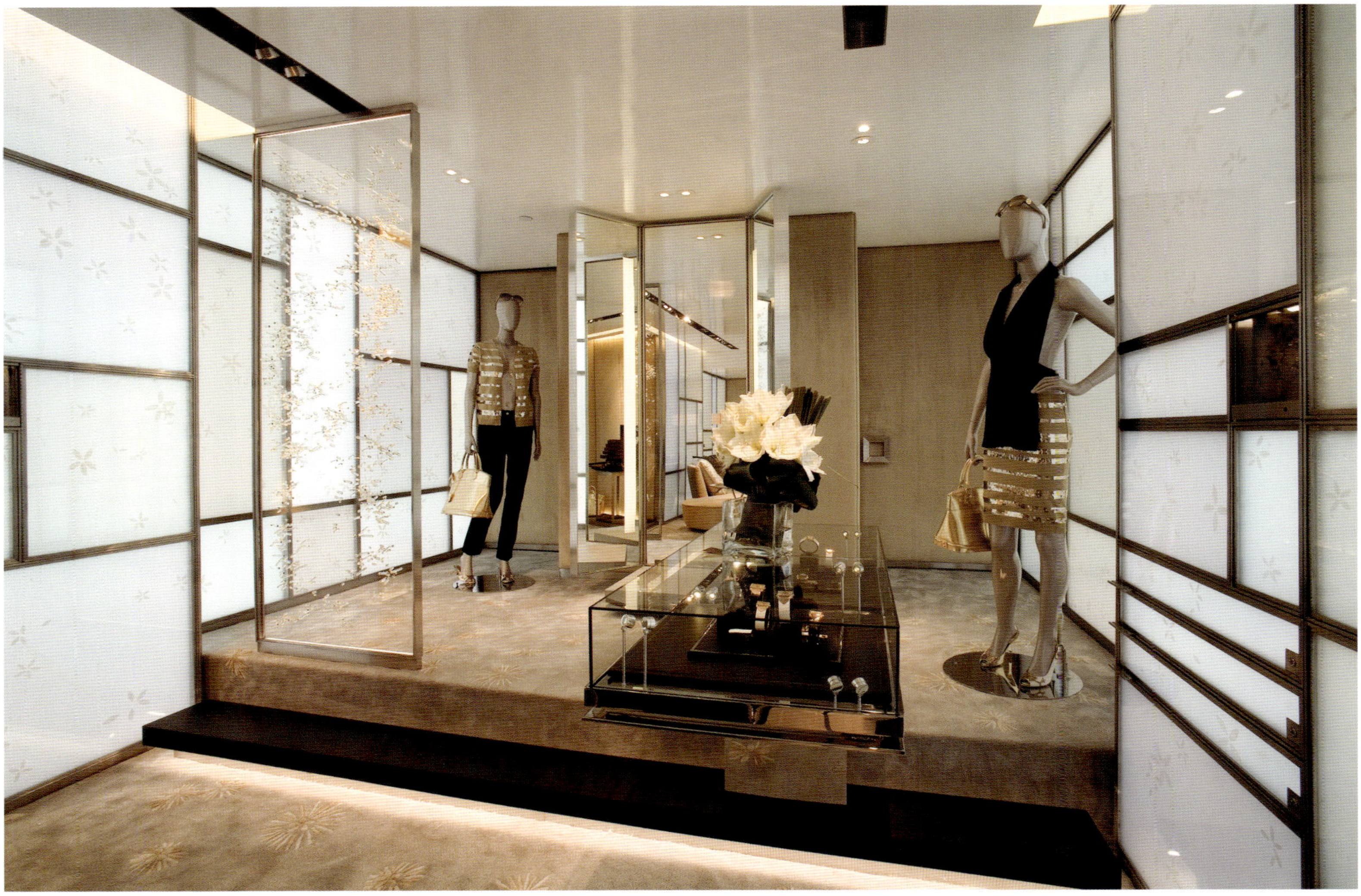

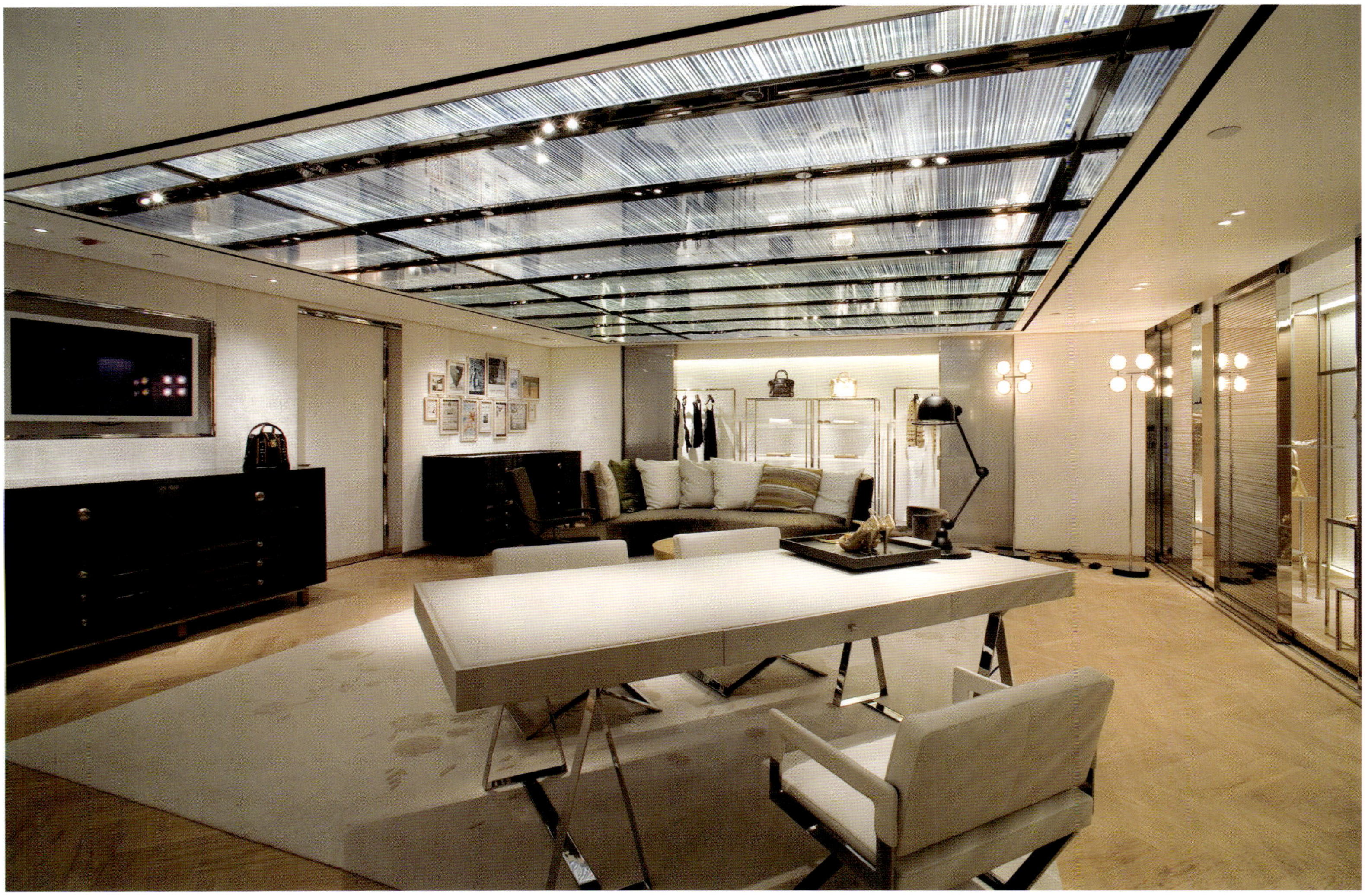

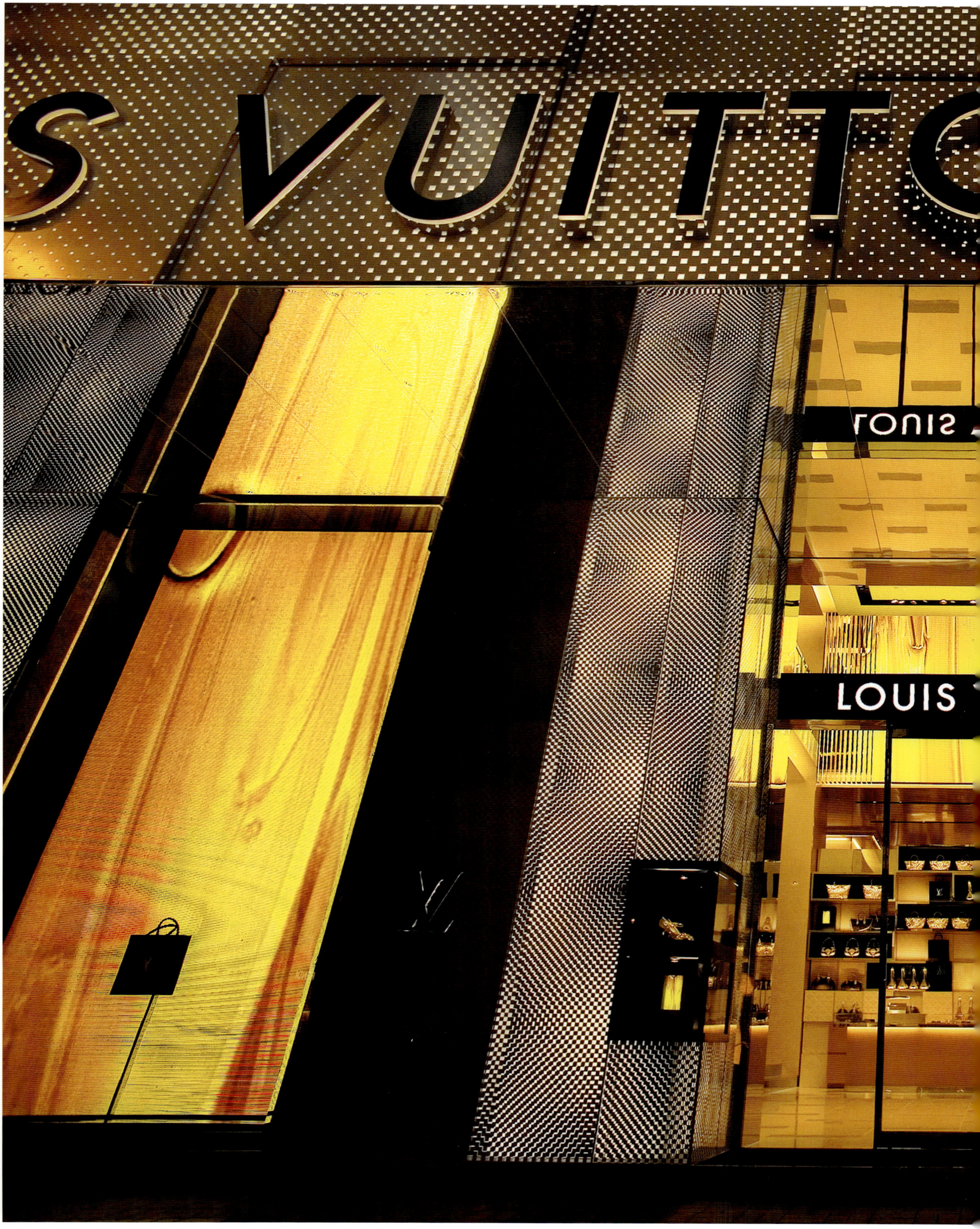
S VUITT
LOUIS
LOUIS

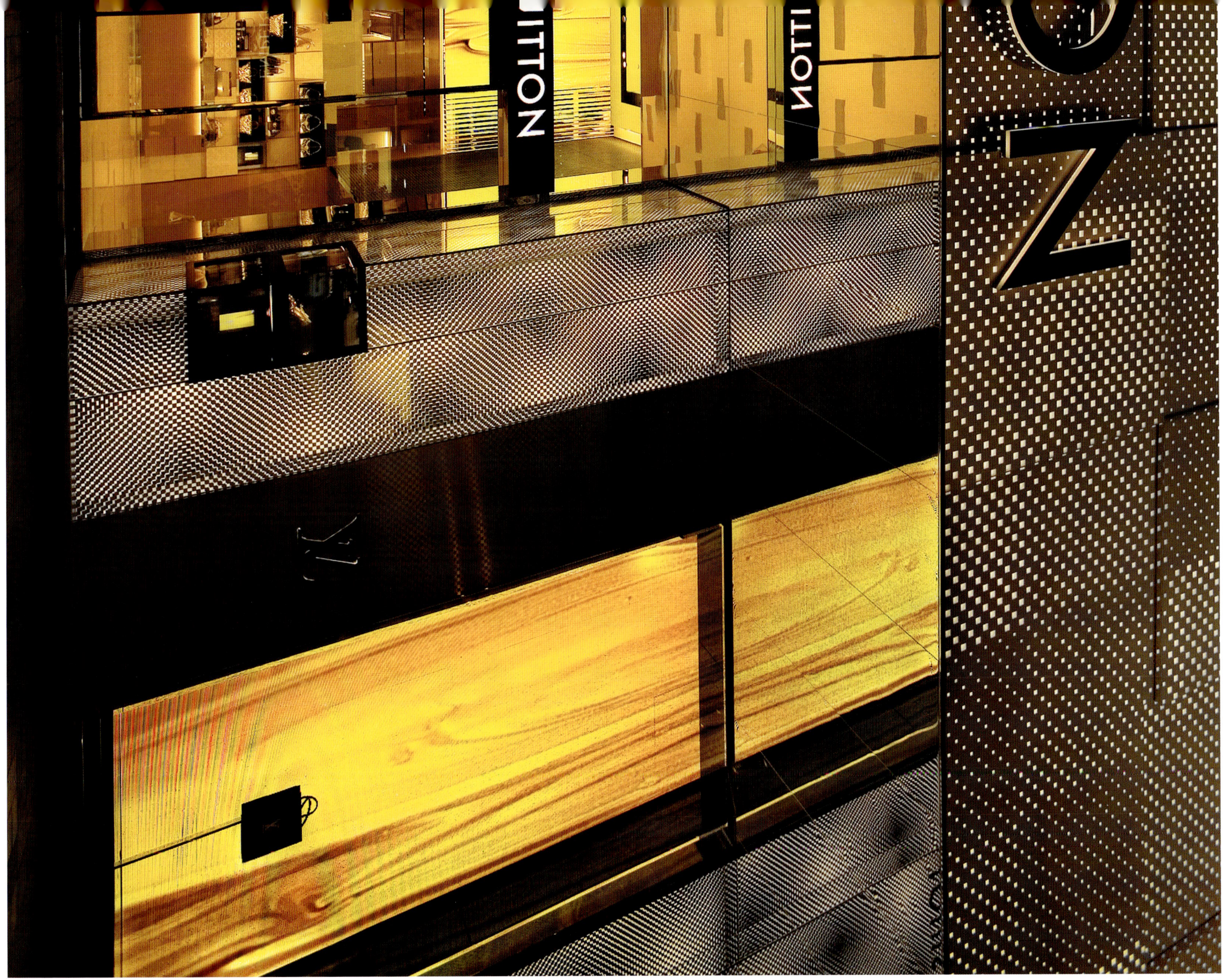

HONG KONG LANDMARK

architects
JUN AOKI & ASSOCIATES;
PETER MARINO ARCHITECT
2005

text by
RAFAEL MAGROU

Hong Kong, the island of a thousand skyscrapers set against lush hills, is a city that has always been familiar with peaks, both in terms of record-building heights and identifiable excess. Always in search of ever-expanding territories, its waterfront offers a unique architectural landscape that is constantly changing. On land, the buzz is incessant, offset by the imperial tramways; the same is true on the water, where the legendary Star Ferry used to rub shoulders with traditional Chinese junks. Louis Vuitton established a relationship with China very early on: first in 1907, for a Paris-Peking expedition equipped with luggage made by the celebrated leather-maker, and again in 1931, with the Yellow Cruise, a journey that followed in the footsteps of Marco Polo. The company has built a lasting relationship with the "Port of Perfumes." In 1982, the mongrammed brand opened its first store near the train station on Des Voeux Road Central, along with the promise of a long-lasting love story.

This street has become a destination for every respected luxury brand. Easily accessed by public transportation, its intersection with Pedder Street articulates The Landmark, a shopping center that assembles the biggest international labels over five floors. One of the first to arrive, Vuitton chose the best location at the corner of the street. This position makes the store immediately perceptible on all sides, taking up no less than 40 meters on Pedder Street and 16 meters on Des Voeux. But in order to stake its ground, the subway entrances in the façades had to be contended with, as did the passageway connecting the street to the covered piazza within this great temple of luxury. Topped by a tower, the base that forms the property is somewhat compressed by dozens of higher levels of concrete grids. From these constraints, Jun Aoki, Vuitton's official alchemist builder, once again transformed metal into gold. More accurately, he succeeded in translating the stirrings of contemporary urban life into a sophisticated casing, displaying a balance of elegance hitherto unknown in this eccentric city.

Depending on your viewpoint, the ground floor and second floor are covered in a kinetic envelope made of some seven thousand stainless steel blades whose sides are brushed, polished, painted white, or set into a ribbon of mirrors, creating drops of silver rain. Not limiting the kaleidoscope to simple bands stretched across the façade, the Japanese inventor developed an indented, vertical silhouette for these parts to be juxtaposed one against the other in a fraction of an inch, reverberating in the void that separates them. In addition to the resulting optical effect, this arrangement evokes a graphic musicality that flickers with the passing of pedestrians, cars and even changes in weather. The climate here is extremely capricious; with the typhoons that sweep across these southern islands, imagine the many mutations of this vibrating skin. This is also why the highest part of the building juts out over the street: to protect pedestrians from the heavy rain that falls on Hong Kong. The alternating surfaces of these strips recreate the brand's beloved checkerboard pattern. In the visual patchwork that is Hong Kong, attempting to build a monolithic envelope for a building is a challenge. As night falls, light-emitting diodes emit natural light, transforming the façade into a sparkling jewel and creating a true, glistening cascade. Then, the silhouettes of clients appear, segmented by these elongated, vertical strips. Their bodies are reflected on the lateral walls, reversing the optical illusion: the relief created by these shades is accentuated, glowing even stronger. This sensation is not diminished by the windows, whose sides create multiple, reflective surfaces in the passages. Nor is it reduced by the glass outer layer that protects this composition, relying on a hidden suspension system, with discreet attachments, always square, connected to glass reinforcements.

Behind the shimmering curtain, eighteen, ancient trunks evoke the expeditions of the Yellow Cruise that linked the West to the East by way of Marco Polo's travels. Floating along the interior façade, metal blinds protect the trunks' leather from the region's harmful sunrays, even though the façades face north. This inside layer stretches along the wall and up to the second floor thanks to the receding flooring. Designed by the architect Peter Marino, the interior layout respects this sensory envelope by incorporating small islands used as displays. Although, through its transparency, you can see the rumbling red and gray taxis that have replaced the rickshaws of the past, the thick glass placed on the outside skin blocks any sound pollution. No additional insulation is needed, which allows for a benevolent transparency to exist between the outside and inside. A doorman invites you to enter this appointed space through a quiet single door. You immediately grasp the scale of the store as you walk in. It is organized into three main sections, with each level punctuated by the shafts of existing columns that support the skyscrapers above.

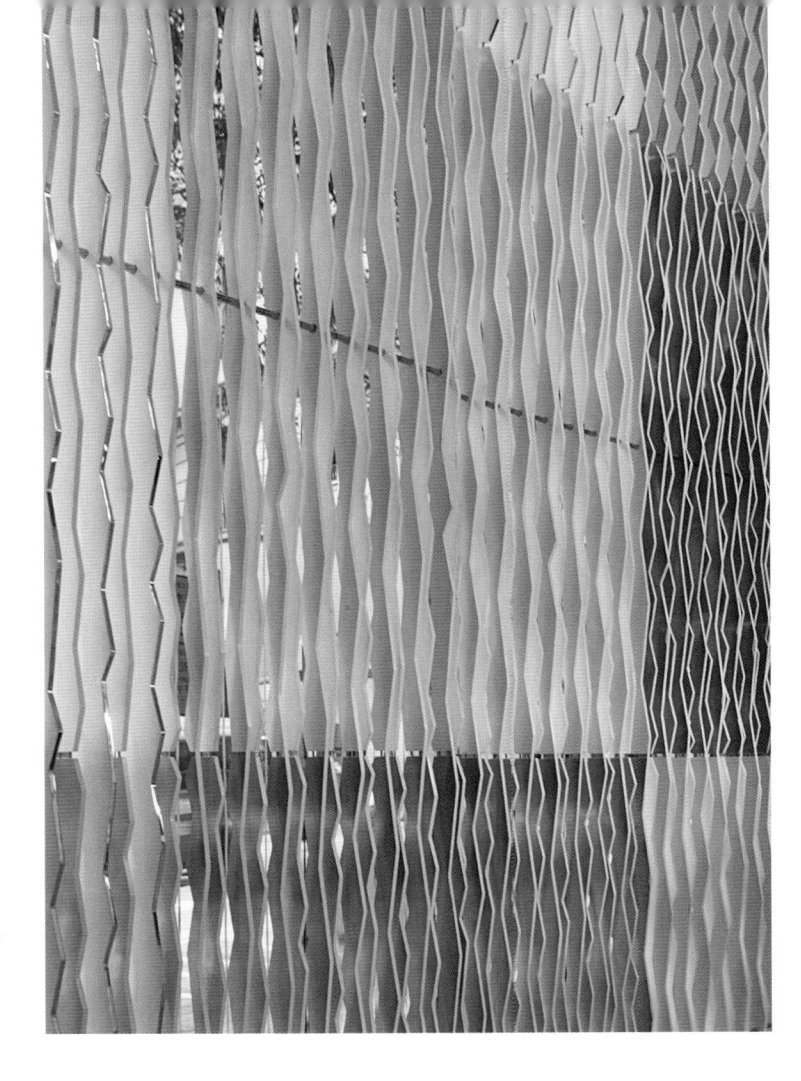

On the ground floor, the universe is of course devoted to leather goods, the company's ancestral expertise. Chinese-inspired shelves, with asymmetrical compartments, lend an oriental air to the leather pieces. The lower level is for men, the upper, for women. A signature, silver rock by Zhan Wang quickly comes into view, the light and surrounding area diffracted in its uneven surface. Next to it, the Bag Bar celebrates the craftsmanship of the company. It is set against a background of white Corian engraved with monograms and paired with stainless steel shelves. Behind this, a second counter, perhaps the largest one ever built for Louis Vuitton, measures thirteen meters and integrates anigre wood instead of gleaming metal. The existing structure and the massive volume of the subway and mall entrance create distinct alcoves; to the right are women's shoes, and to the left, jewelry.

Along with watches, the jewelry section feels like an exclusive area within the store, with its own, separate entrance on Pedder Street. In addition to the House's designs, another jewel—an architectural one—articulates the lofty volume: a reflective, stainless steel spiral that climbs into space. This magnificent piece soaring solidly through the air is a tribute to the top jewelers. Made of precious materials, its strength is surprising, as are its one hundred and twenty, half-inch rods that form its delicate ensemble. At the top is the holiest of holies: a private mezzanine reserved for clients interested in the finest collections. An-other masterpiece, even more spectacular, is the principal stairwell connecting the three levels of the store that is wrapped in LEDs that broadcast moving images on the glass stairs. In total, 18.5 square meters of original graphic artwork can be viewed on one unified surface, without interruption from the stairwell. In contrast to the gray and beige tones of the boutique, the series of scrolling, bright visuals is somewhat dizzying. This transition leads directly to the men's department. At the center of the men's section, a wooden ribbon outlines a podium whose base broadcasts the latest runway show on screens—an enjoyable way, and certainly a rewarding one, to equate model and client. The interior design then relies upon existing columns to create varying heights, not through the furniture but through the delineation of various product displays such as luggage or sunglasses.

Finally, with a special entrance from the shopping center, the second floor is filled with *Taï Taï*, the elegant ladies from Hong Kong who come down from the perch of their homes to shop at the Landmark. The center, which has grown popular for its Western fashions, lies in stark contrast to Canton Road, which is situated across the way in the Kowloon part of the city and remains decidedly Chinese, with a more versatile clientele. They come here especially to try on exotic skins and take in the latest collections from Europe, a fleeting impression that is portrayed in the film *In the Mood for Love*—whose original title *fa yeung ni wa* means "The time of flowers." These same flowers decorate the countless dresses worn by Maggie Cheung, whose presence seems to fill the air of the store.

p. 91 façade detail seen from the interior
p. 92–93 view of the Hong Kong Landmark store on the intersection of Chater Road and Pedder Street. Creating a damier pattern, 7,000 stainless-steel louvers—alternately polished, brushed, mirrored and whitewashed—compose the glazed interlay on the façades

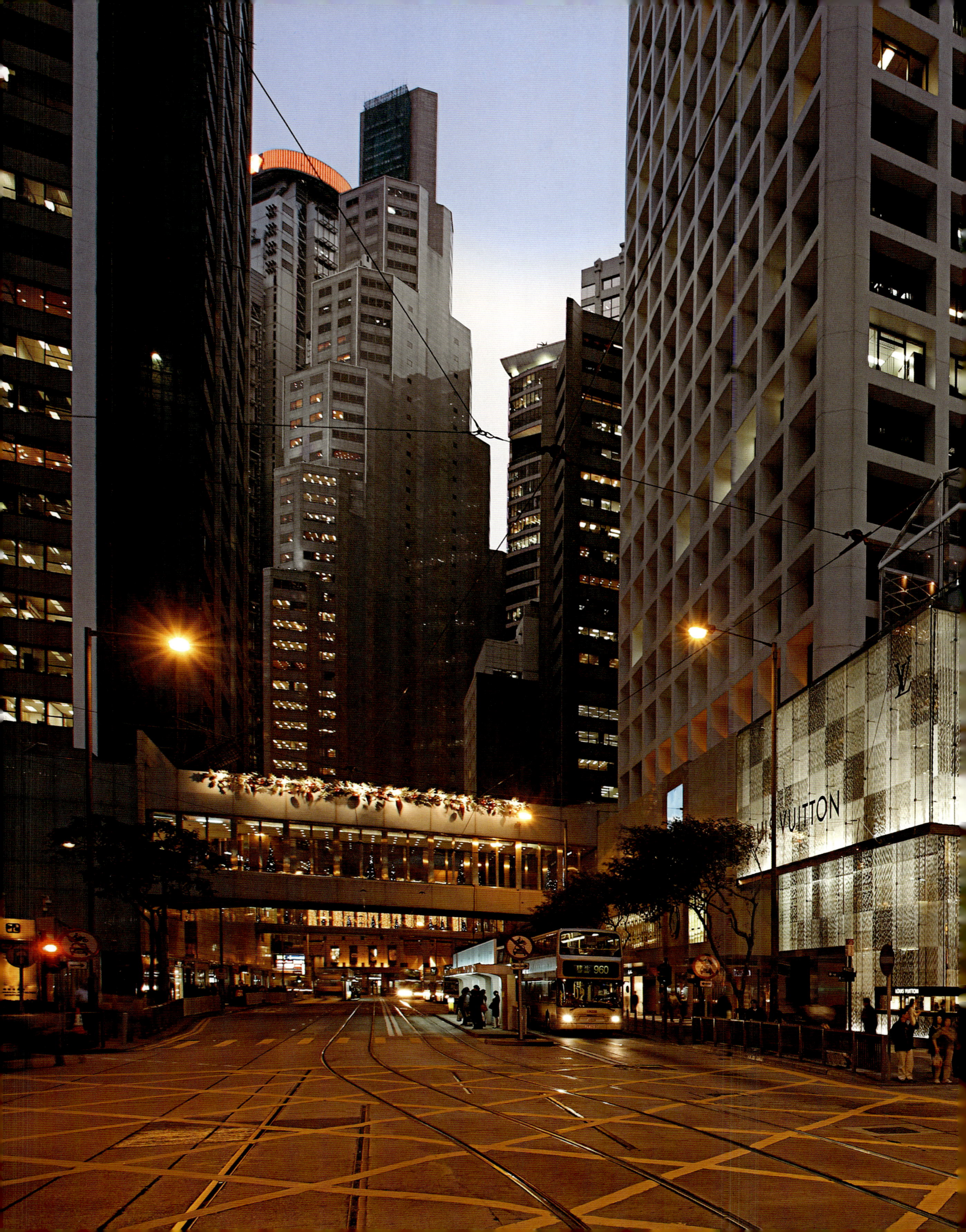
VUITTON
960

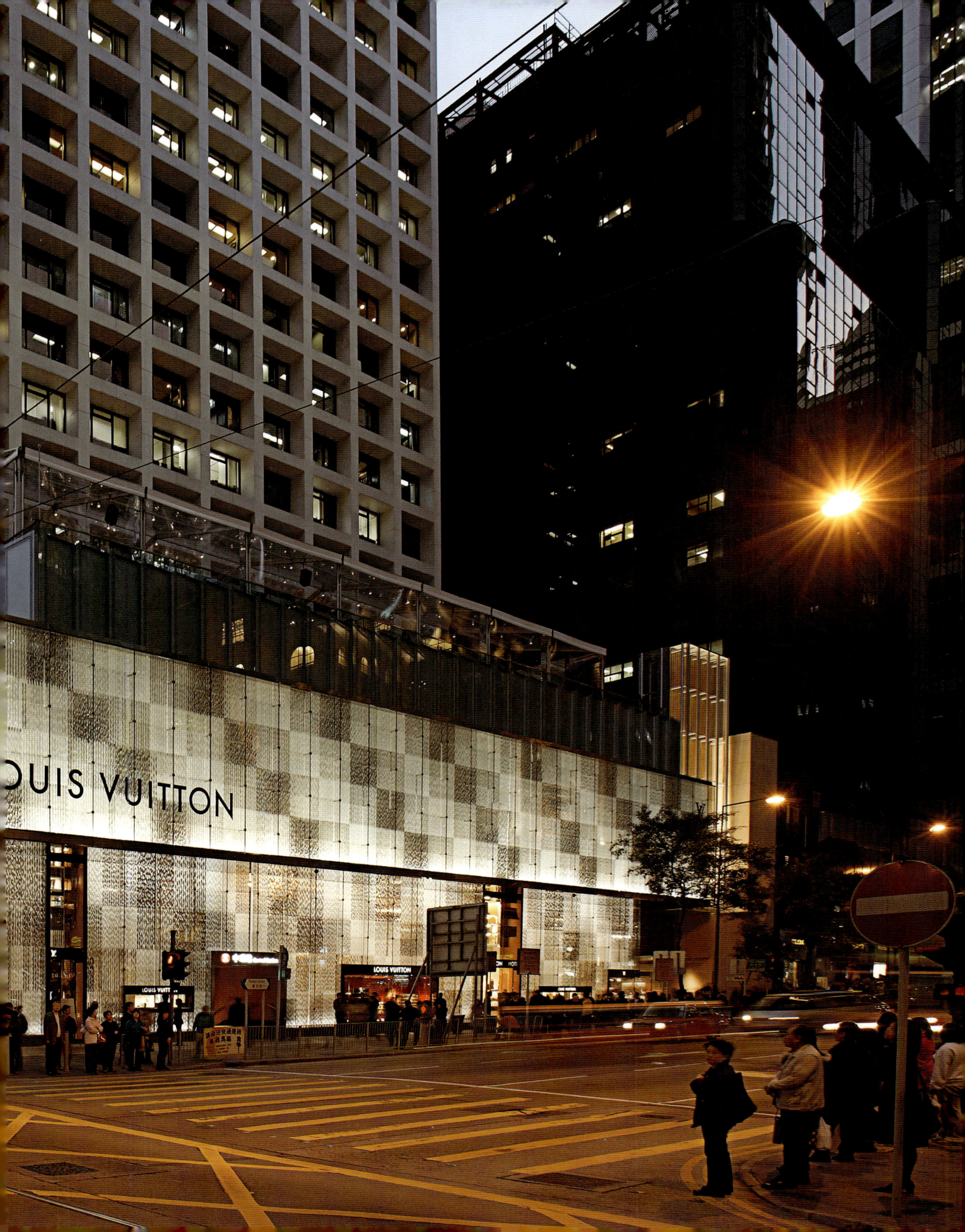
OUIS VUITTON
LOUIS VUITTON

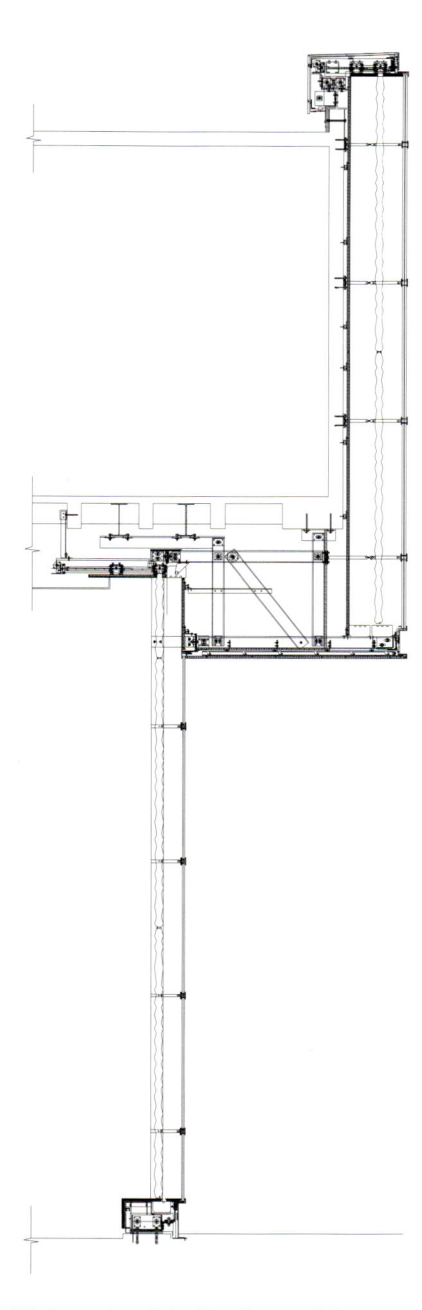

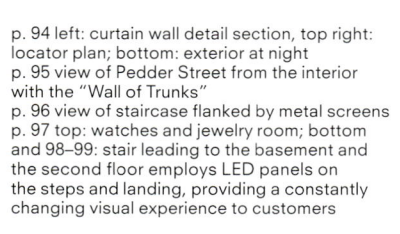

p. 94 left: curtain wall detail section, top right: locator plan; bottom: exterior at night
p. 95 view of Pedder Street from the interior with the "Wall of Trunks"
p. 96 view of staircase flanked by metal screens
p. 97 top: watches and jewelry room; bottom and 98–99: stair leading to the basement and the second floor employs LED panels on the steps and landing, providing a constantly changing visual experience to customers

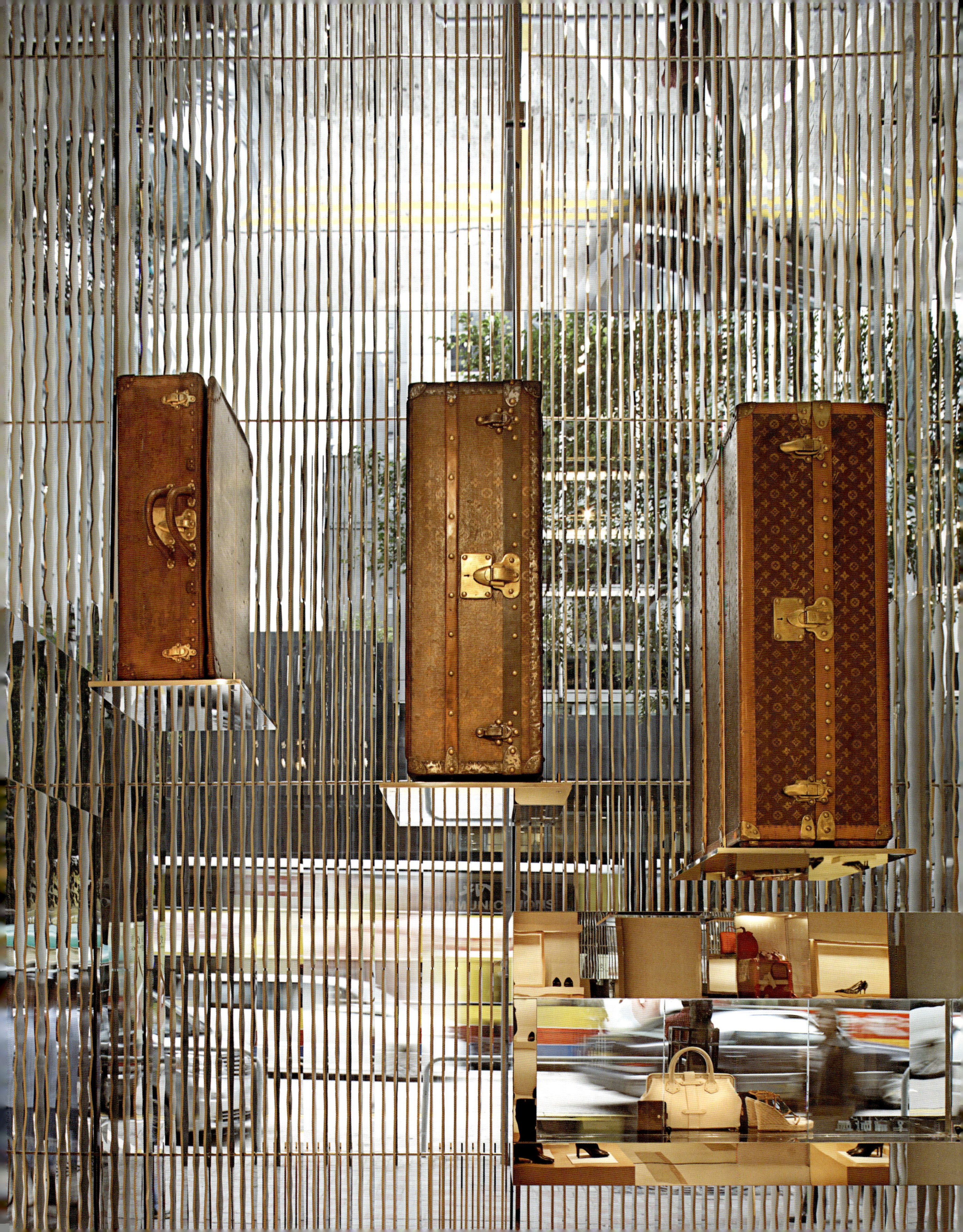

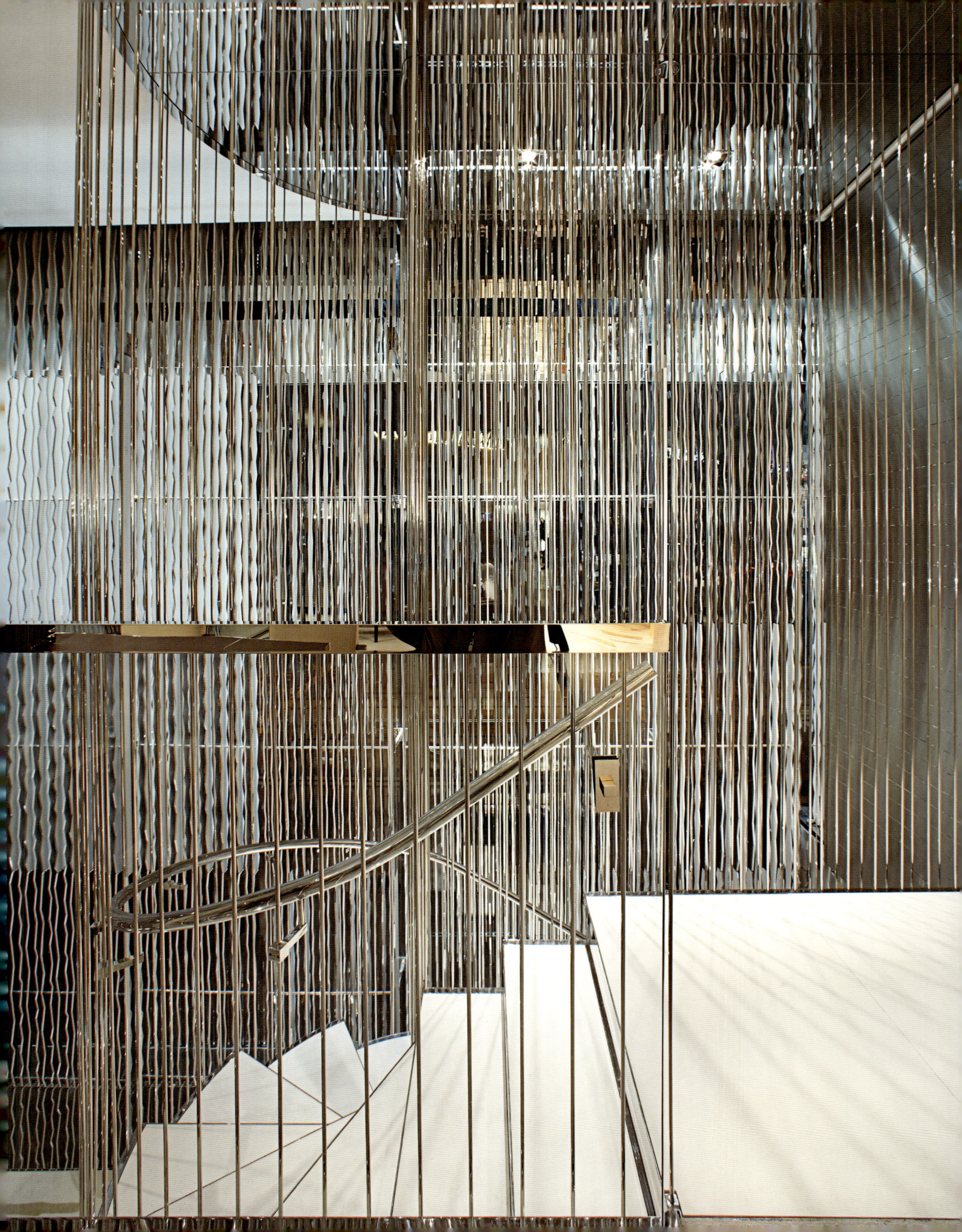

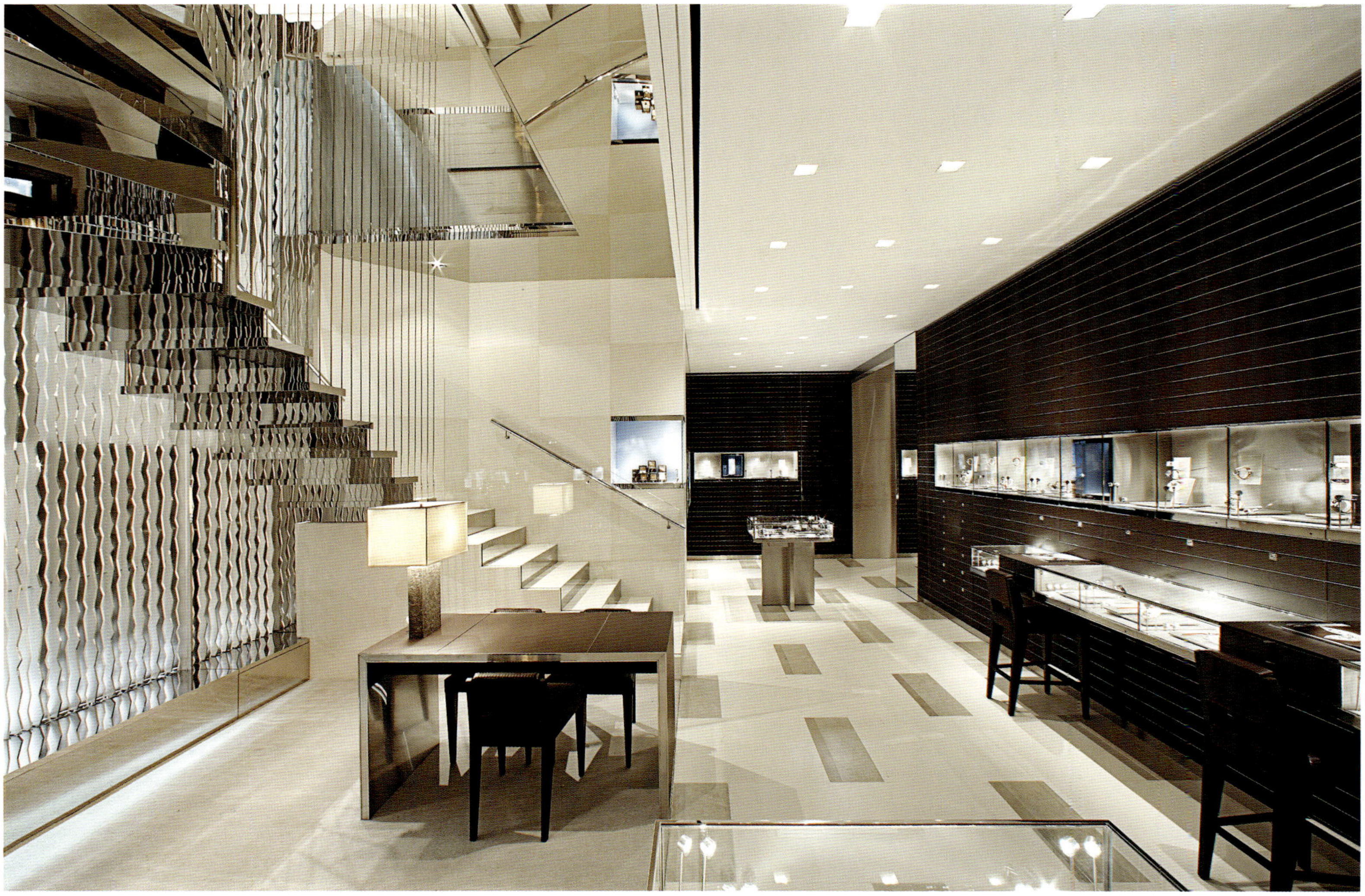

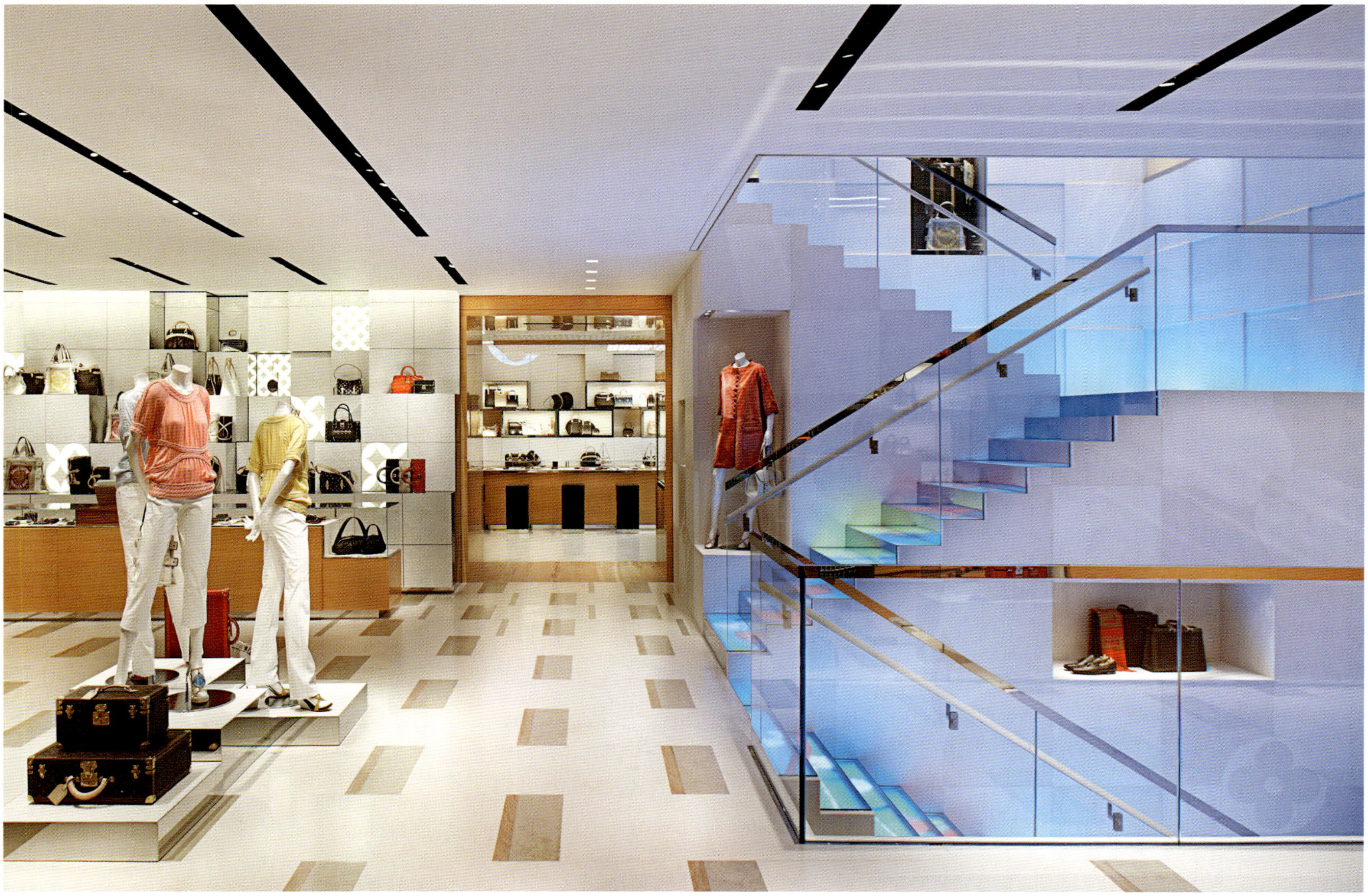

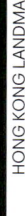

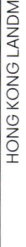

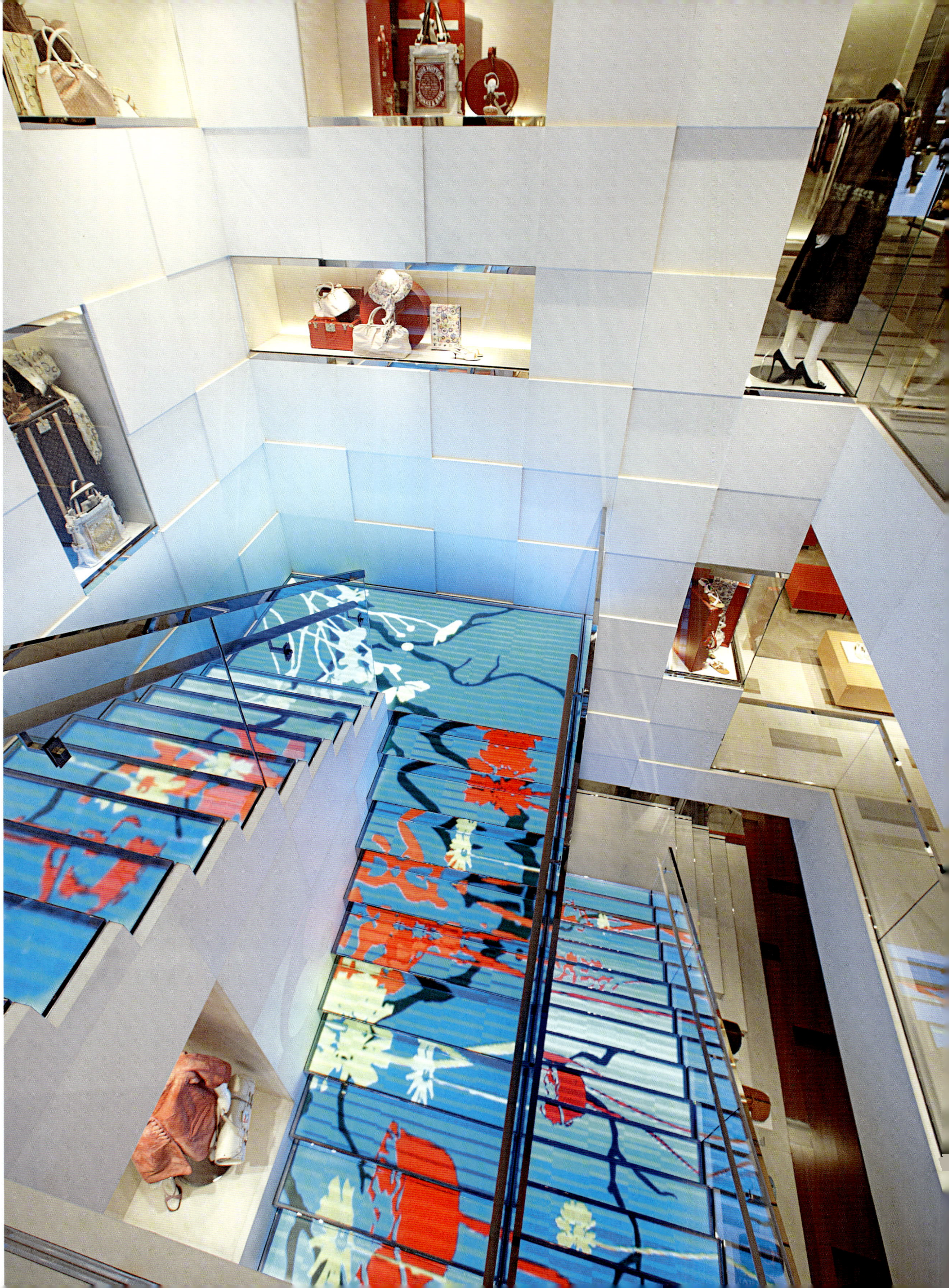

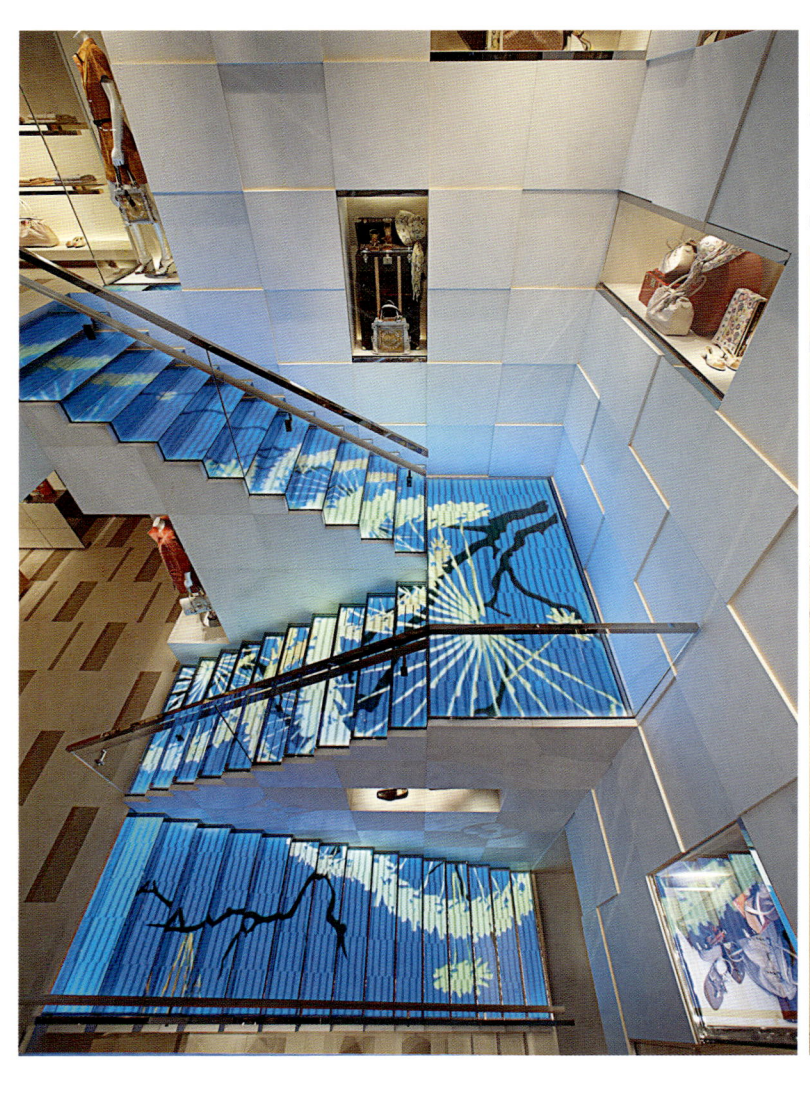

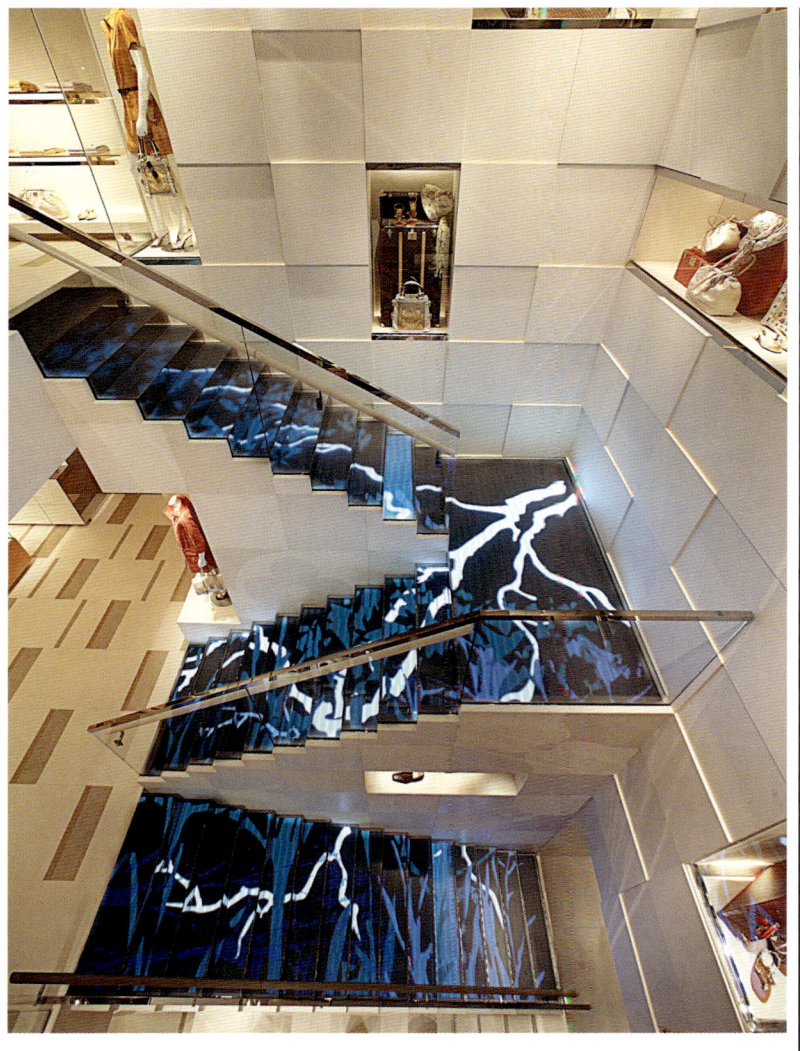

ARCHITECTURE AND INTERIORS 99

ASIA PACIFIC HONG KONG LANDMARK

MACAO ONE CENTRAL

architects
THE LOUIS VUITTON
ARCHITECTURE DEPARTMENT
2009

text by
FRÉDÉRIC EDELMANN

It was in 1557 that the Portuguese founded the oldest continuously occupied European settlement in eastern Asia, to the west of the Pearl River delta, and close to what would become Hong Kong. They called it Macao, a name derived from the Ma Kwok temple built in the 14th century. In 1854, while Louis Vuitton began establishing its business in Paris, the Portuguese were just starting to negotiate the transfer of power of the two islands of Taipa and Coloane, which they had leased from the Celestial Empire in conjunction with the Macao Peninsula. Today, Macao, Taipa and Coloane form a unique, connected entity, similar to Hong Kong's political arrangement with the People's Republic of China. Europeans, other Asians, and non-resident Chinese typically arrive Hong Kong as well as the local airport. They travel to Macao, either to quench a thirst for gambling, to visit the historic town—a magnificent, Portuguese-influenced area that is a UNESCO World Heritage Site—or perhaps to pray before a bone fragment that belonged to the Jesuit Saint Francis Xavier.

Although the Chinese are becoming more and more sensitive to the historic significance of the site—a superb spot for wedding pictures—many do arrive as atavistic gamblers. Many come from the region of Canton through the border town of Zhuhai, a small city of 1.5 million inhabitants that is known for its universities and its gateway to Macao. Sometimes they leave with a smile, a Louis Vuitton bag in hand and a big Mickey Mouse in their arms. Others fall prey to the multitude of shops that will buy back their watches, telephones and glasses—just enough to allow them to return home after their losses.

Since the mid-twentieth century, and especially since its handover to China in 1999, Macao—the "hell of gambling," and, "queen of vice and debauchery," entirely populated by drunken sailors—has become remarkably gentrified. This sterilization was necessary for the city to establish itself as the gambling capital of the world, ahead of even Las Vegas. In 2010, the twenty-two casinos belonging to the former Portuguese colony generated 56.2 billion Patacas, the local currency, or close to 7 billion dollars. The clients of the casinos, which are always coupled with gigantic hotels, have also changed in status. As a result, Macao does everything it can to, "promote the economic diversity of the city," that is, to attract wealthy tourists, amateur golfers and other heavyweights. Once the Asian Las Vegas, it has now become the Monte Carlo of the East.

This was the environment in which Louis Vuitton arrived in 2002 at the first Mandarin Oriental Hotel (that has since become the Mandarin Grand Lapa), a resort at some remove from the city center. On December 1st, 2009, Louis Vuitton reasserted its presence with the opening of a new building attached to the commercial area of the much larger Mandarin downtown, forming a surprising extension to the new luxury neighborhood on the shores of the Nam Van, a semi-artificial lake.

Louis Vuitton Macao One Central *Maison* was given a façade of nearly

1,600 square meters, almost as large as the entire surface area of the store, which is 1,633 square meters. The presence of this facade is no luxury in the overcrowded landscape; from the store, you can see the nearby Governor Nobre de Carvalho Bridge, which leads to the Islands of Taipa and Coloane. Coming back toward Macao, the first thing one sees from the bridge is the House of Louis Vuitton—a geometric, blue prism that stands sharply apart from the pale structures of the Mandarin.

Without this façade, which serves as a sign more so than other stores, one might overlook the site and stare instead at the background of the lake, where one of Macao's most amusing architectural examples stands, and the city isn't stingy. The Grand Lisboa Hotel, at 261 meters, is the highest skyscraper in the city. This building incorporates the motif of the lotus, and was designed by DLN Architects, which came from Hong Kong to correct the issues of *feng shui* that cursed the casino, a plump colorful ball installed at the foot of the hotel. Errors and omissions excepted, One Central should not have to deal with these geomantic problems (*feng shui* is taken very seriously in southern China). The House stands with its back to the "mountain" that is the Mandarin Oriental, is oriented towards the south, and is bordered by the Nam Van Lake, whose waters are refreshed by the sea to which it's connected.

The outside entrance of One Central allows the structure to breathe in the sea air—the least one can expect from this merchant of travelers' dreams. Without a doubt, it was not intended to be widely used by clients, except for those with limousines. Indeed, the traditional Bag Bar—one of the longest in the Vuitton universe—is not only turned away from what is in theory the main entrance, but this area, that spans nearly 9 meters from floor-to-ceiling, seems to have been designed more or less as the center of the store. For other clients, entering from the hotel's shops or even from the MGM casino seems more natural. Here, the blue-tinted tiles on the outside façade, filled with LEDs, turn violet on the interior walls. Another level of this store—there are three, all generous in height—is delimited by another type of façade: tall glass curtains from which emerge an oversized flower motif. Here again, the signature of Vuitton is strongly emphasized, meant perhaps for a clientele that's used to the large retailers within this gambler's paradise. You can't help but think of Robert Venturi's cult book on attention-seeking, *Learning from Las Vegas* (1972). In this great labyrinth, a homothetic transformation of casino circuits, there are rather humorous nods to the world of gambling everywhere. The space, dedicated to the art of travel with various displays and Louis Vuitton archives, presents picturesque trunks for inveterate gamblers—preferably the insomniacs among them. The floor that the gallery is on is also devoted to the world of casinos. As its centerpiece rests Liu Jianhua's *Unreal Scene* (2009), a map of Macao and its islands made from casino chips and dice. Other works are less about parody, such as Chen Wenbo's *Chance*, or *Surreal*, a photograph by Jean Larivière that depicts bathing chess players.

A large terrace overlooking Nam Van Lake catches gamblers off-guard, confronting their willingness to be shut in night and day between the roulette tables, the slot machines and their beds. An unspoken rule in Las Vegas hotels enforces this habit by placing the heads of beds in front of the curtains, thereby preventing any daylight from seeping in. Similar care and attention is given to the particular preferences of the Macao customer visiting One Central, as it fulfils an expectation of grandeur and refinement.

p. 100 detail of exterior at night
p. 103 views of the gallery
p. 104–105 exterior view along the waterfront
p. 106 views of VIP areas
p. 107 views of terrace overlooking Nam Van Lake

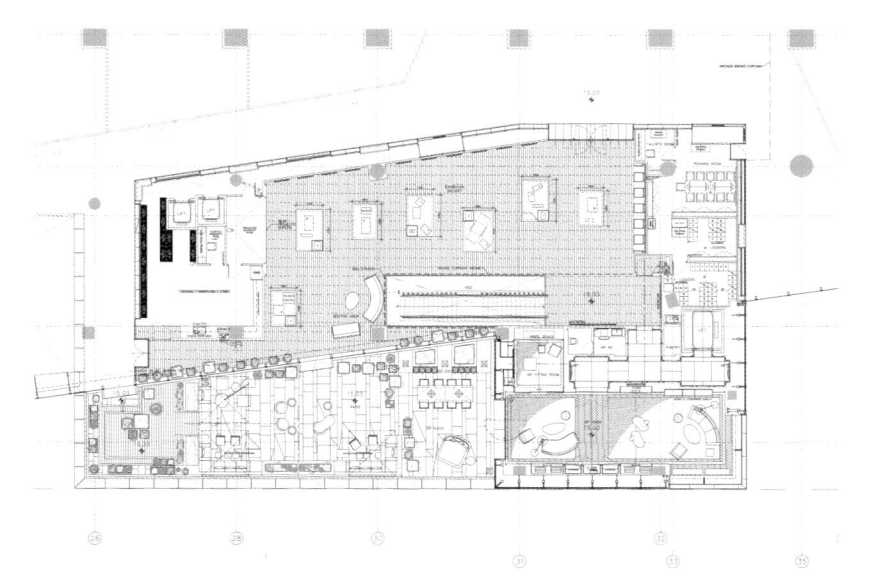

3RD FLOOR

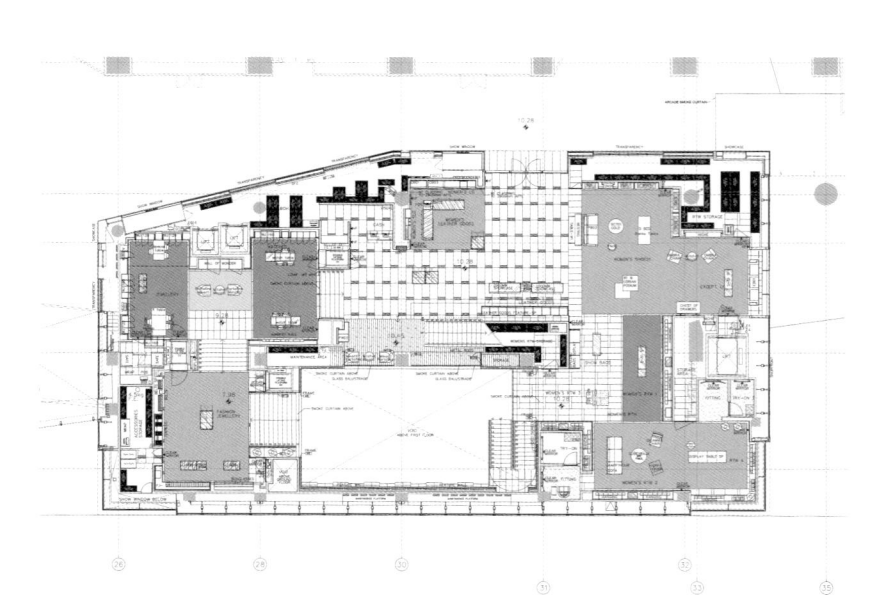

2ND FLOOR

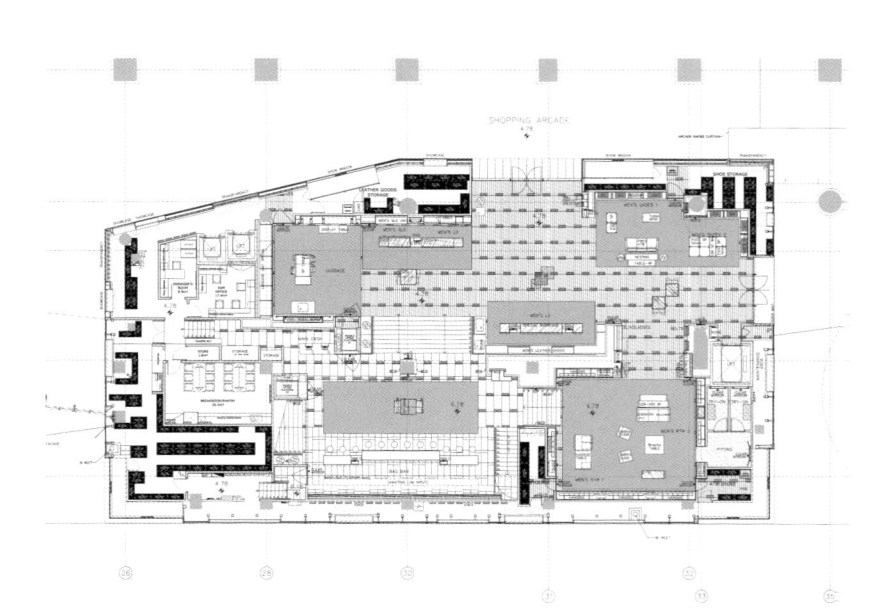

GROUND FLOOR

ARCHITECTURE AND INTERIORS 103

MACAO ONE CENTRAL

ASIA PACIFIC

ARCHITECTURE AND INTERIORS 104

MACAO ONE CENTRAL

ASIA PACIFIC

MACAO ONE CENTRAL

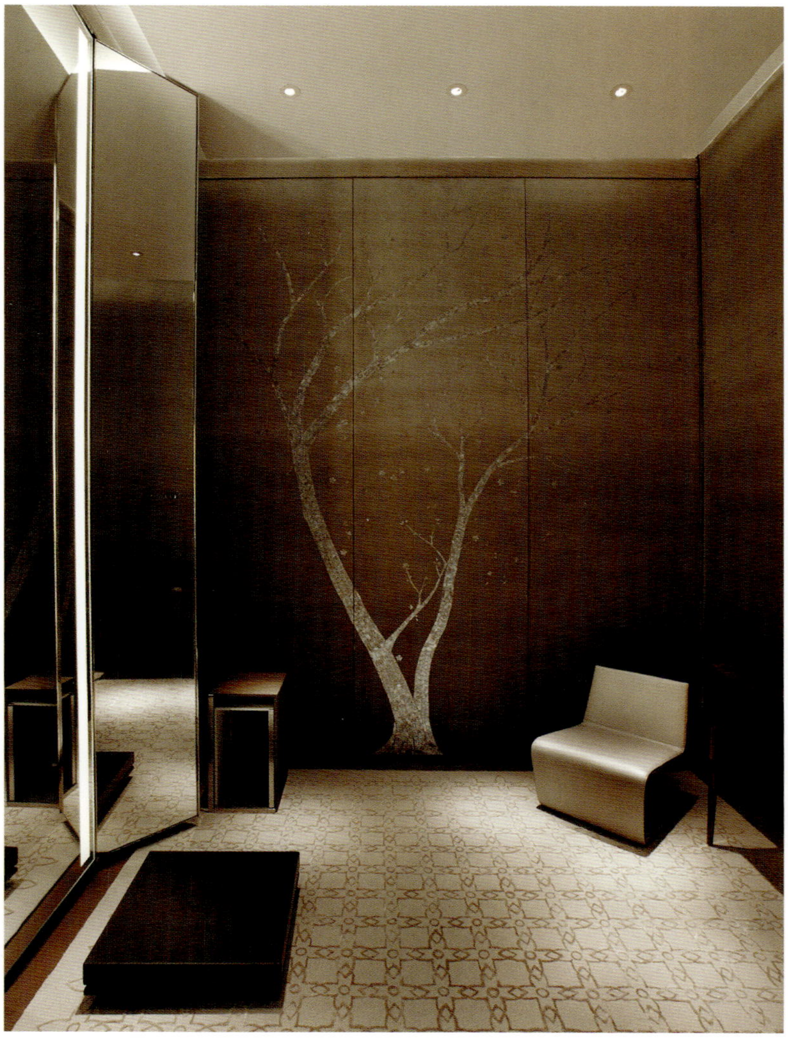

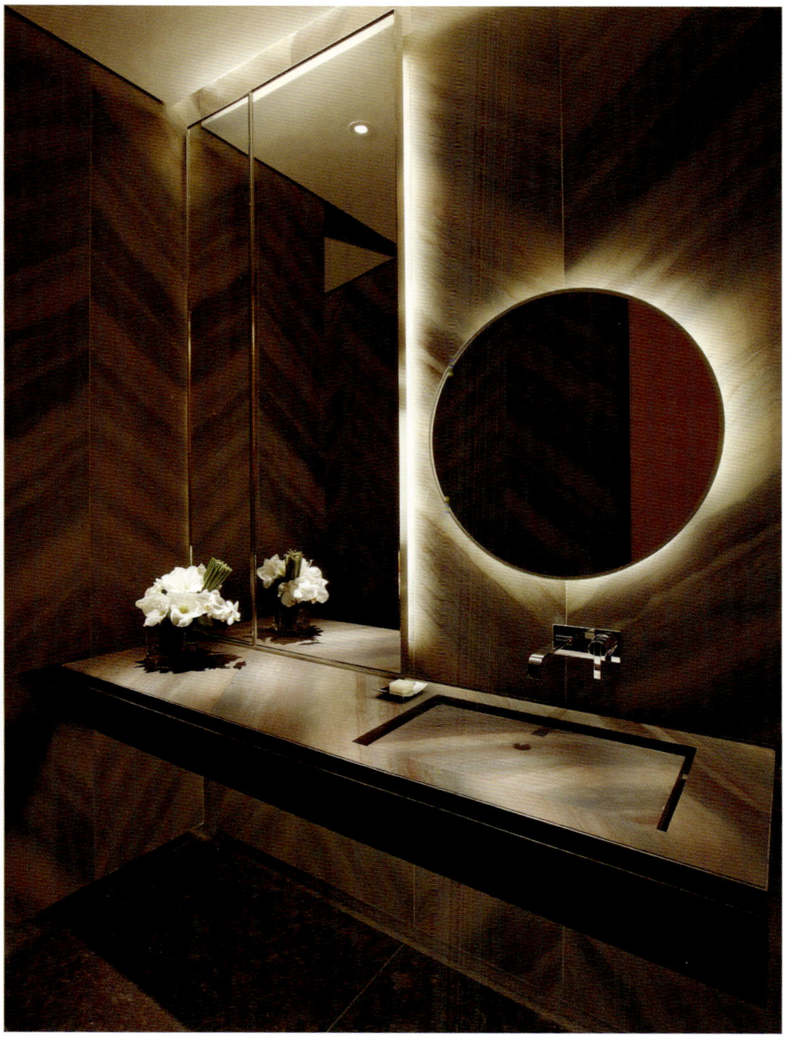

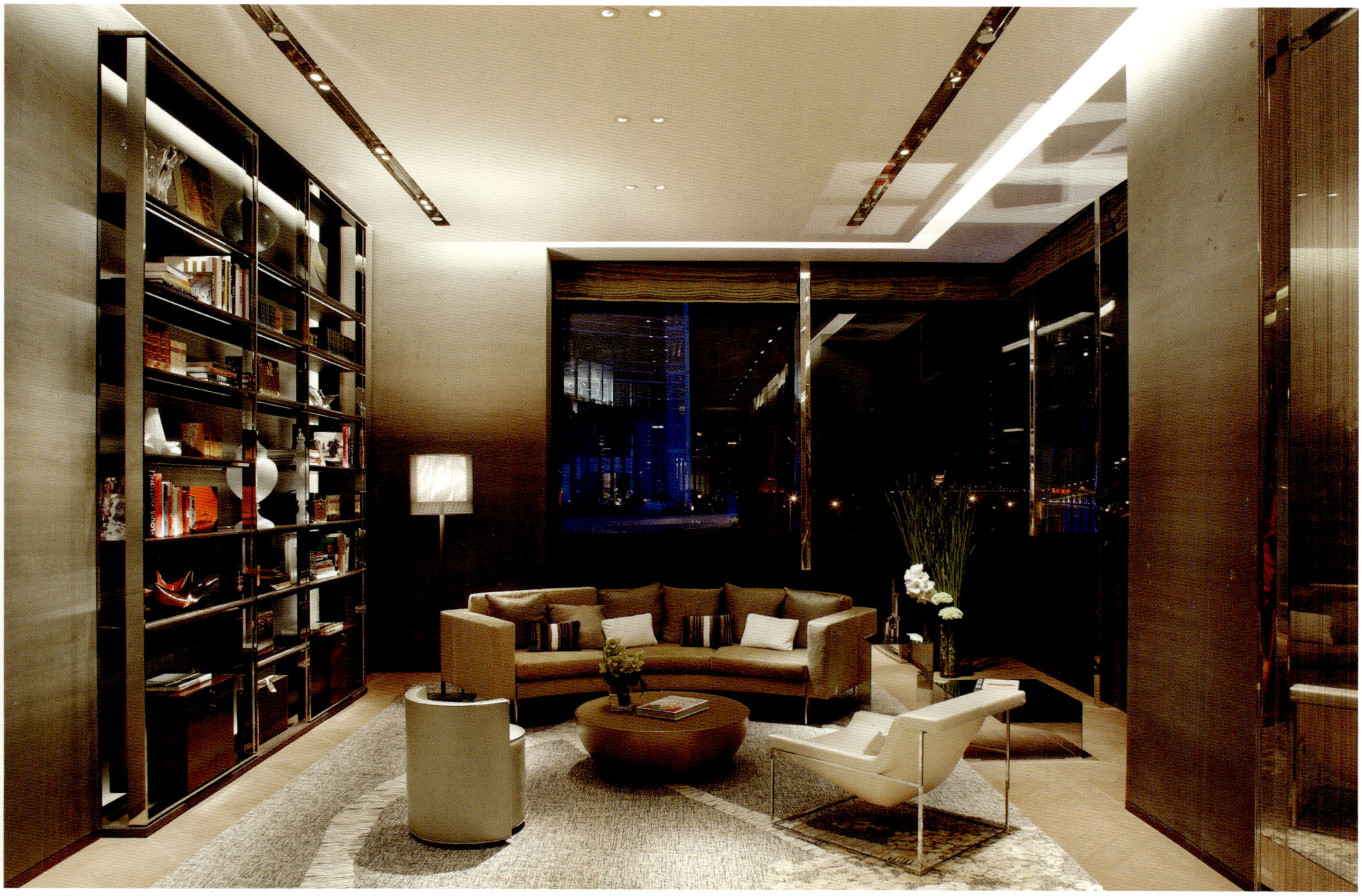

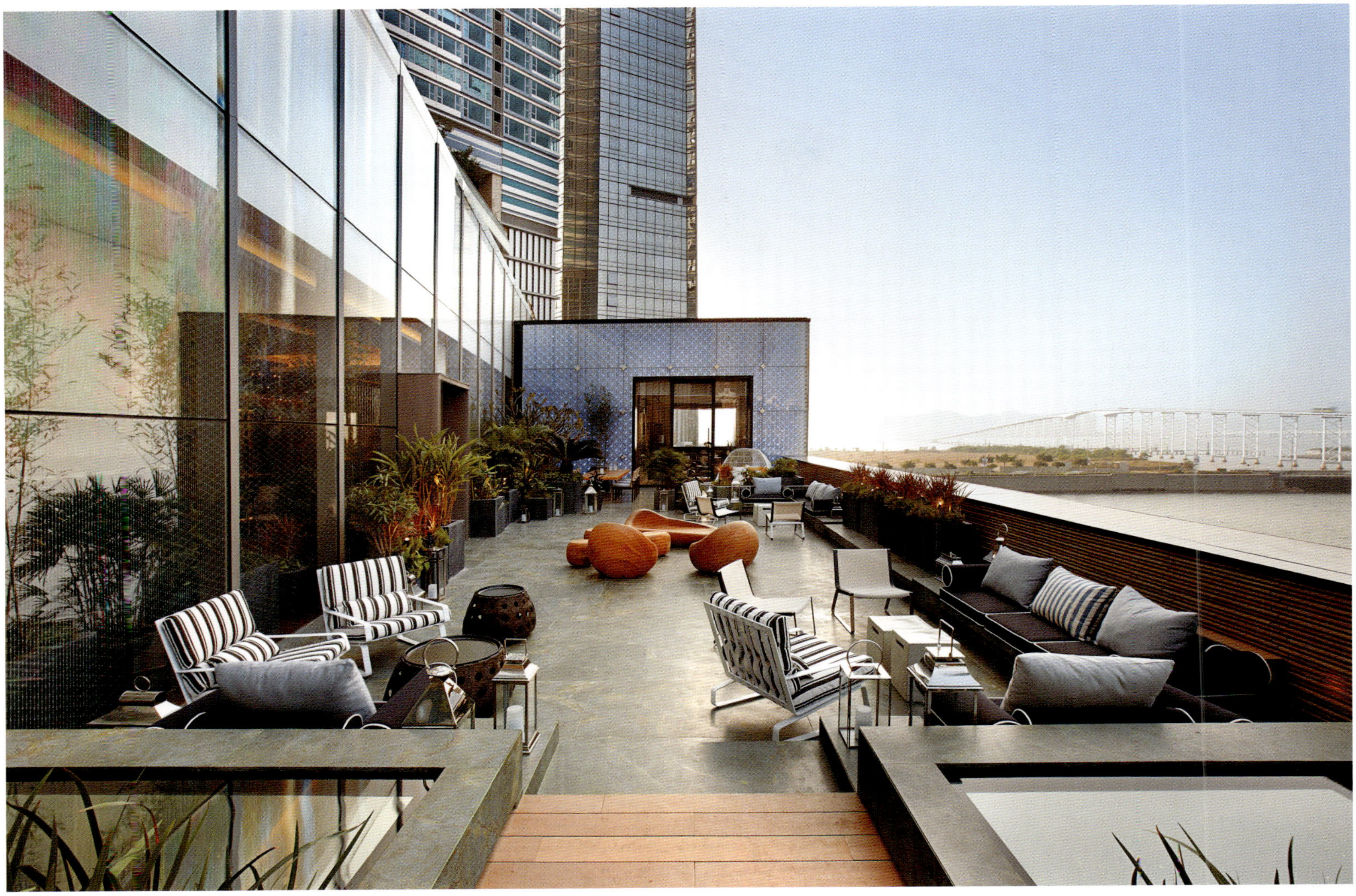

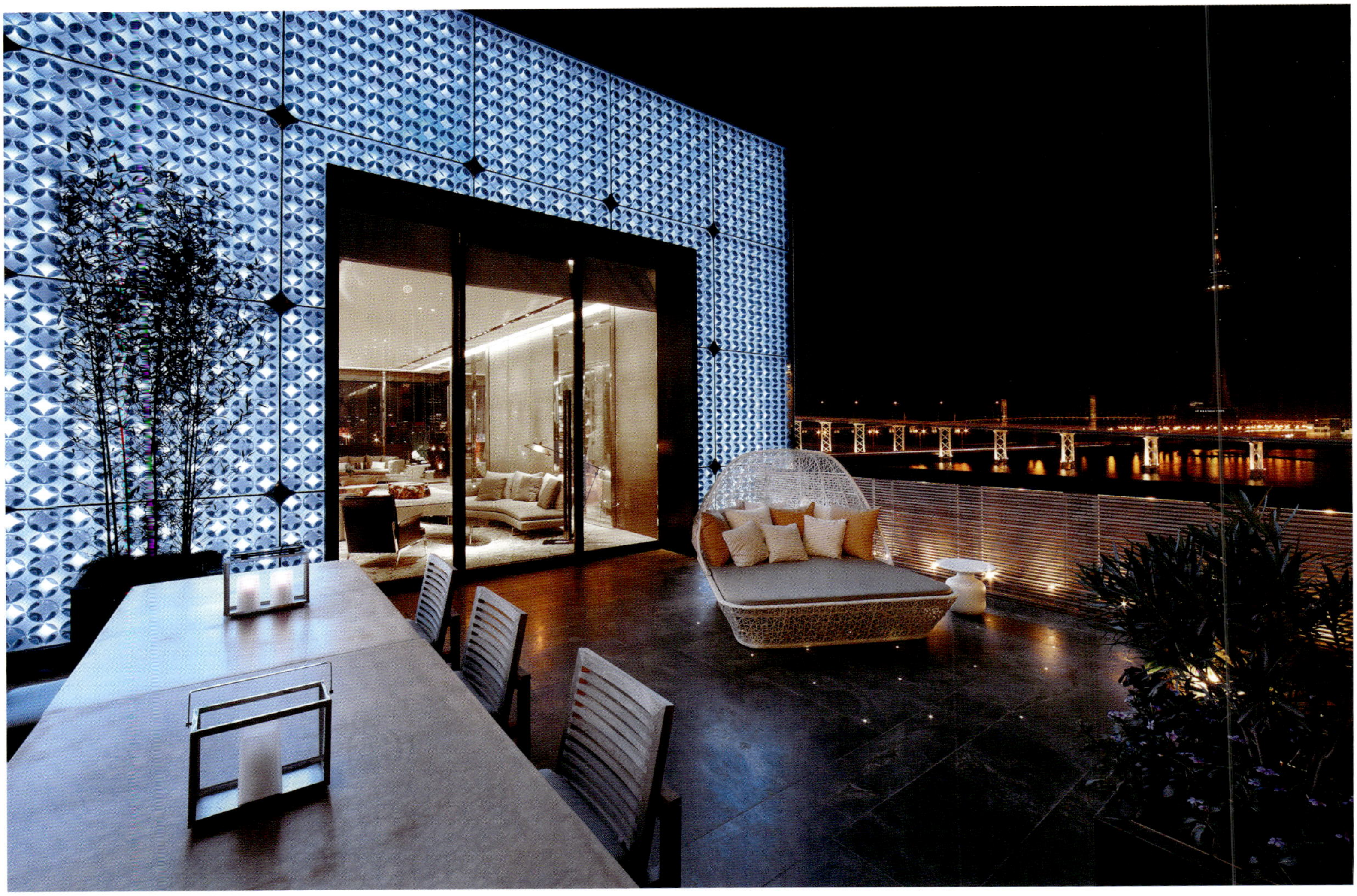

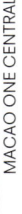

MACAO ONE CENTRAL PROPOSAL

architects
ZAHA HADID ARCHITECTS

text by
IAN LUNA

The Macanese—those intrepid and hardy descendants of Portugal's unlikely colonial adventure in 16th-century Canton—speak a curious dialect, melding Malay, Cantonese, Sinhalese and Portuguese. This *patuá* draws much of its structure and energy from peculiar syntax and noun usage of Malay languages, especially its propensity for repeating words for emphasis or quantity. In common usage, key Portuguese words are often drafted. The singular *casa*, when elevated to the creole *casa-casa*, can denote either the plural form or an order of magnitude.

In 2007, Zaha Hadid submitted a preliminary design study for Louis Vuitton's One Central *maison* (or more appropriately, *casa das casas*) in Macao, as it forms the centerpiece of nearly 37,000 square-meters of luxury *casa-casa* arranged on the plinth of the Mandarin Oriental Hotel. In what would have been her first retail commission for the house, the Pritzker Prize-winning architect envisioned some serious *bling-bling*.

Projecting from a ledge overlooking the man-made Nam Van Lake to the West, and set forward from the glazed wall of its corporate-modernist parent, this jeweled object was designed to be visible from a great distance, particularly to the would-be promenaders along the generous waterfront park up and down from the development.

With a total area of 2,400 square meters distributed on three floors, Hadid proposes a unique structural carapace for what is basically an extruded cube. With elevations on three sides, a contiguous envelope resembling a massive honeycomb provides the design's principal architectural gesture. Lit from within at night, this textural effect distorts the ordered delicacy of Jun Aoki's storefront of hollow glass tubes for Louis Vuitton's Roppongi Hills store in Tokyo into a muscular, even menacing, array of telescoping and skewed cylinders, capped by a skylight membrane.

In conflict with the orthogonal shapes and the right angles of its immediate surround, the store appears to grow organically out of its host, the 42-story Mandarin hotel tower on Avenida Dr. Sun Yat Sen, designed by the American firm Kohn Pedersen Fox. But it is a parasite in the way orchids are in their natural environment. A beacon to shoppers, its skin—framed either in concrete, or clad in stainless-steel or anodized aluminum—further amplifies this biological allusion, with the familiar icons of Louis Vuitton's flower monogram stamped strategically in places (although to local residents, it may very well resemble the texture of the stewed beef tripe that is a favorite *dim sum* in these parts).

The experience of this fenestration is heightened in the interior, where the play of light and shadow initiated by these irregular forms are seen through glazing set deep into this matrix, applied directly atop, or projecting from their frames. The windows themselves vary in size, providing uninterrupted floor-height views, to panoramic vistas from the corners, to framed glimpses of Nam Van Lake. Illuminated from within at night, some of these apertures could double as niches or illuminated billboards, adding potential to the internal layout as it activates the street.

In a nod to the tropes of traditional Chinese cosmology, the integration of these rounded apertures with a four-sided plan unite the pure, uninterrupted form of the circle—that represents the sky—with the square—symbolic of the earth and the abode of men. In traditional Chinese architecture, this is expressed formally in the "moon gate" used in both sacred and secular typologies.

Developed with the London office of the structural engineering firm Ove Arup, this scheme can also be likened to an elaborate curio box or *to-pao ko*—the kind of ornately carved, wooden reliquary seen in every house in China and in the mantelpieces of homes in far-flung diasporic communities. Coupled with the symbolism of the circle-in-the-square, this conception of a container imbues Hadid's design with properties both sensory and metaphysical, with resonances specific to its intended end-users. Used for objects both precious and mundane, the curio box trickled down to popular use from imperial precedents, and is the essence of luxury, as it addresses a variety of practical needs while remaining an indisputable object of beauty. This beauty is often not easily apprehended; some boxes come as interlocking wood puzzles or nested boxes, challenging their users while engaging them in the very work of creation.

Hadid's scheme remains unrealized and Louis Vuitton's in-house team completed Macao One Central in 2009. Like the inveterate gamblers of Macao, architects—even those at the height of their powers—know a little something about the throw of the dice, of opportunities wagered and lost, and the caprices of fashion.

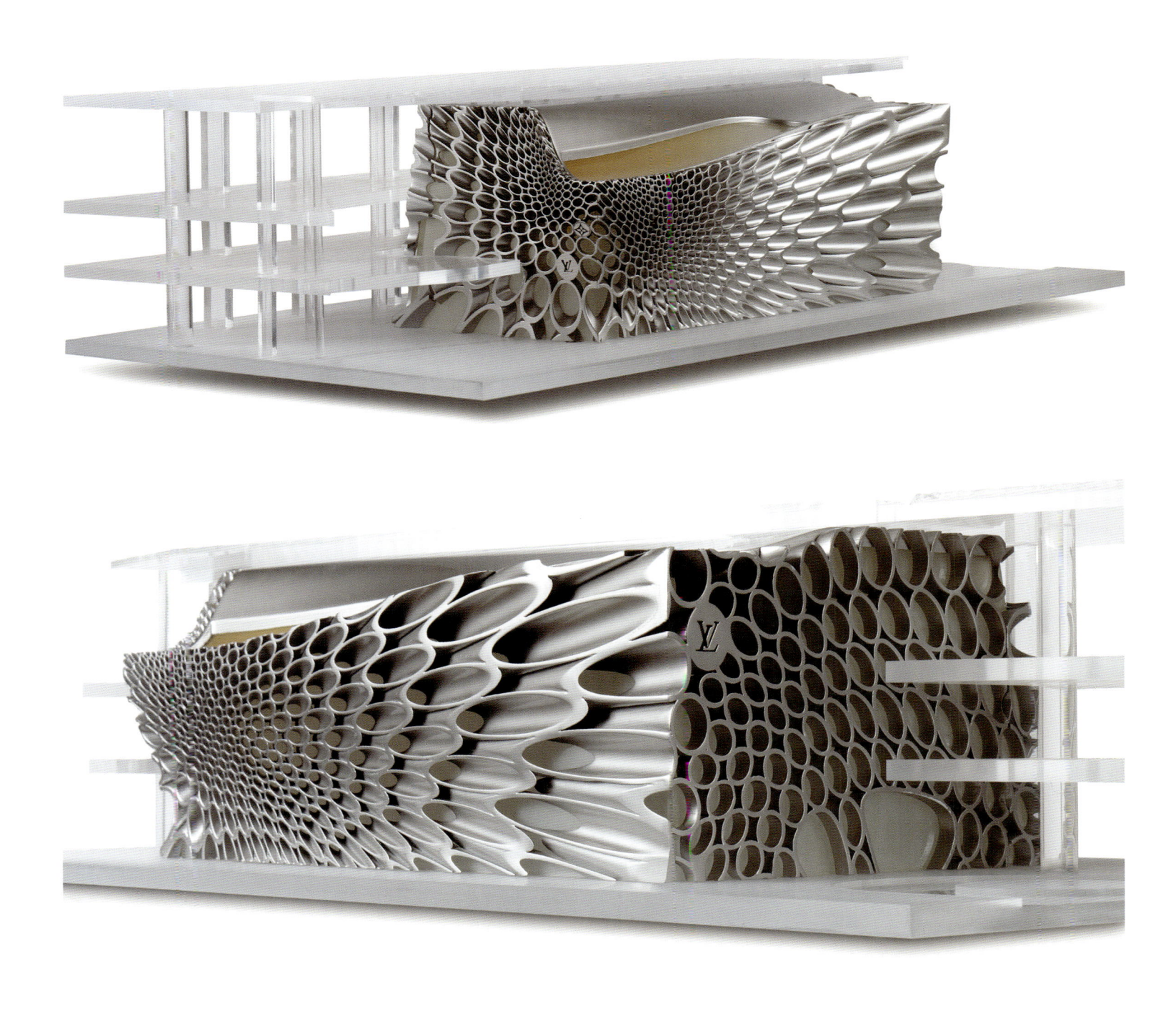

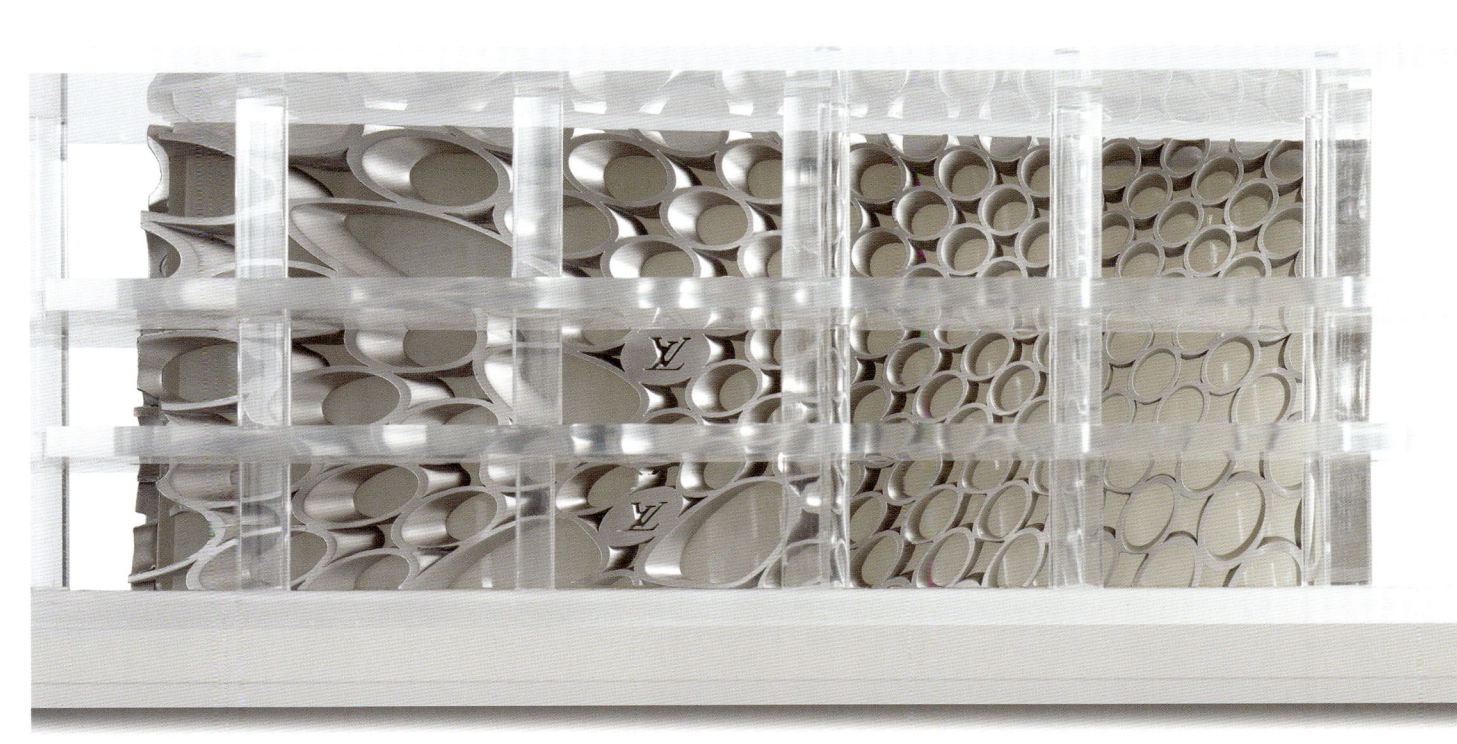

ARCHITECTURE AND INTERIORS 109

MACAO ONE CENTRAL

ASIA PACIFIC

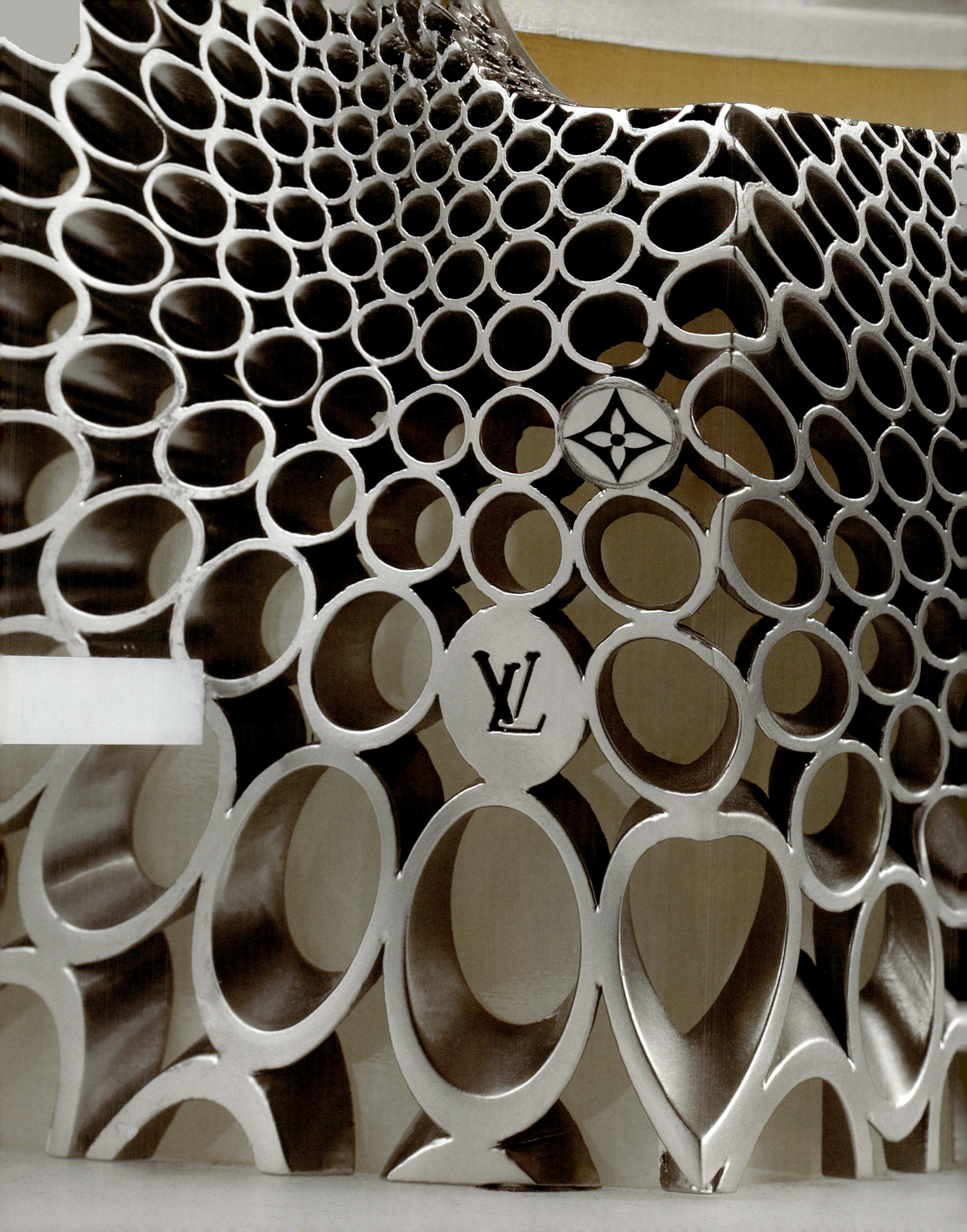

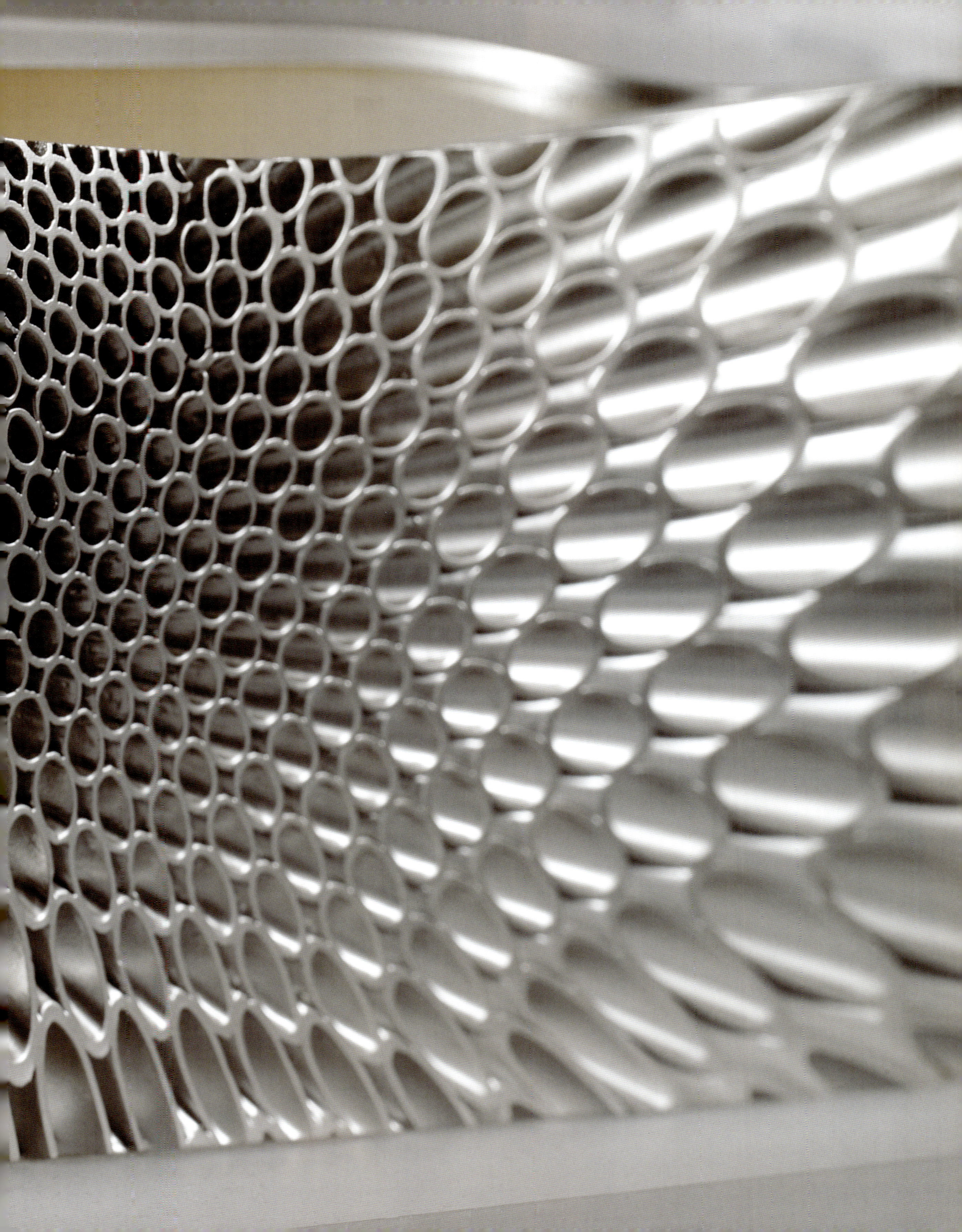

p. 109–111 model views
p. 112–113 exterior renderings

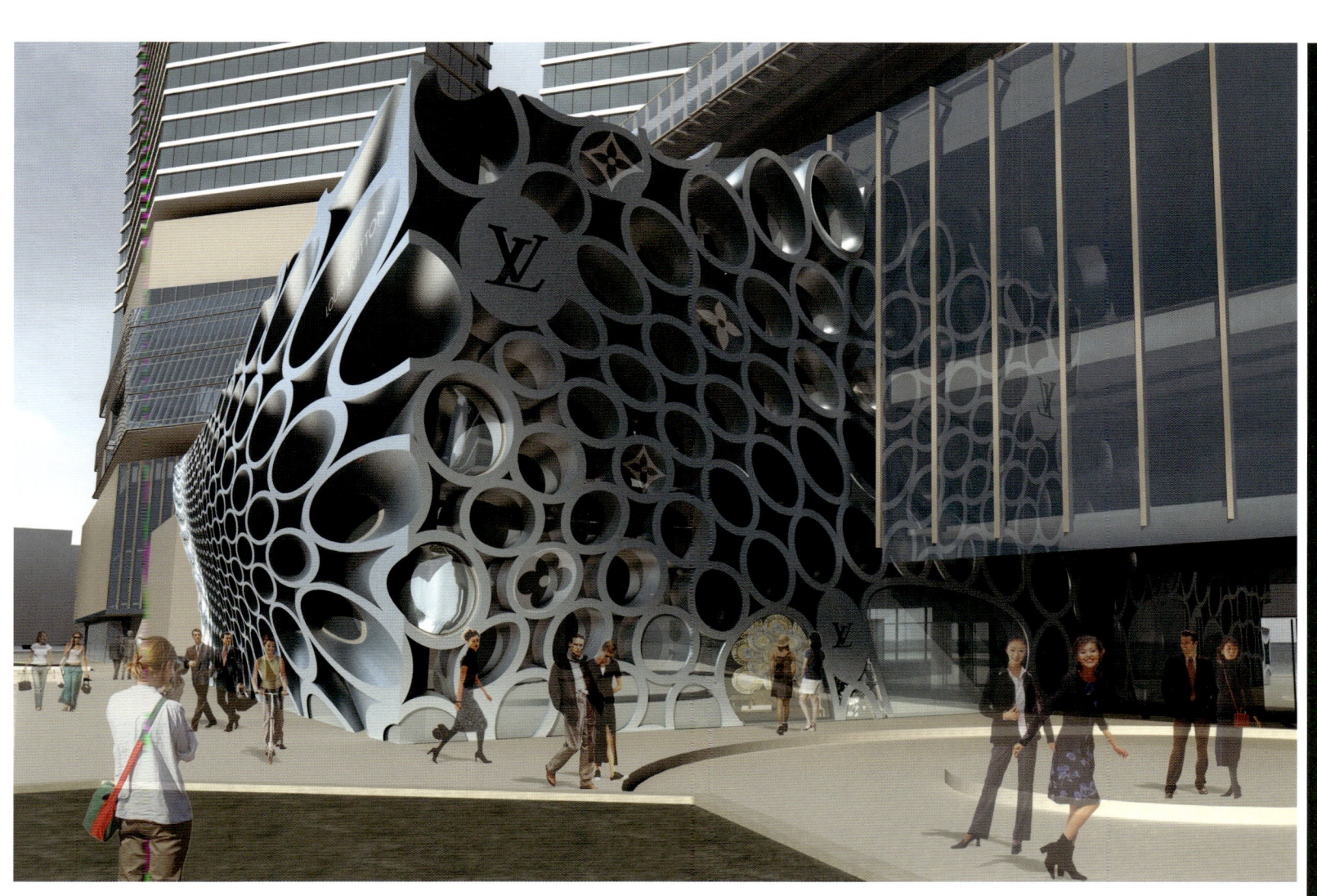

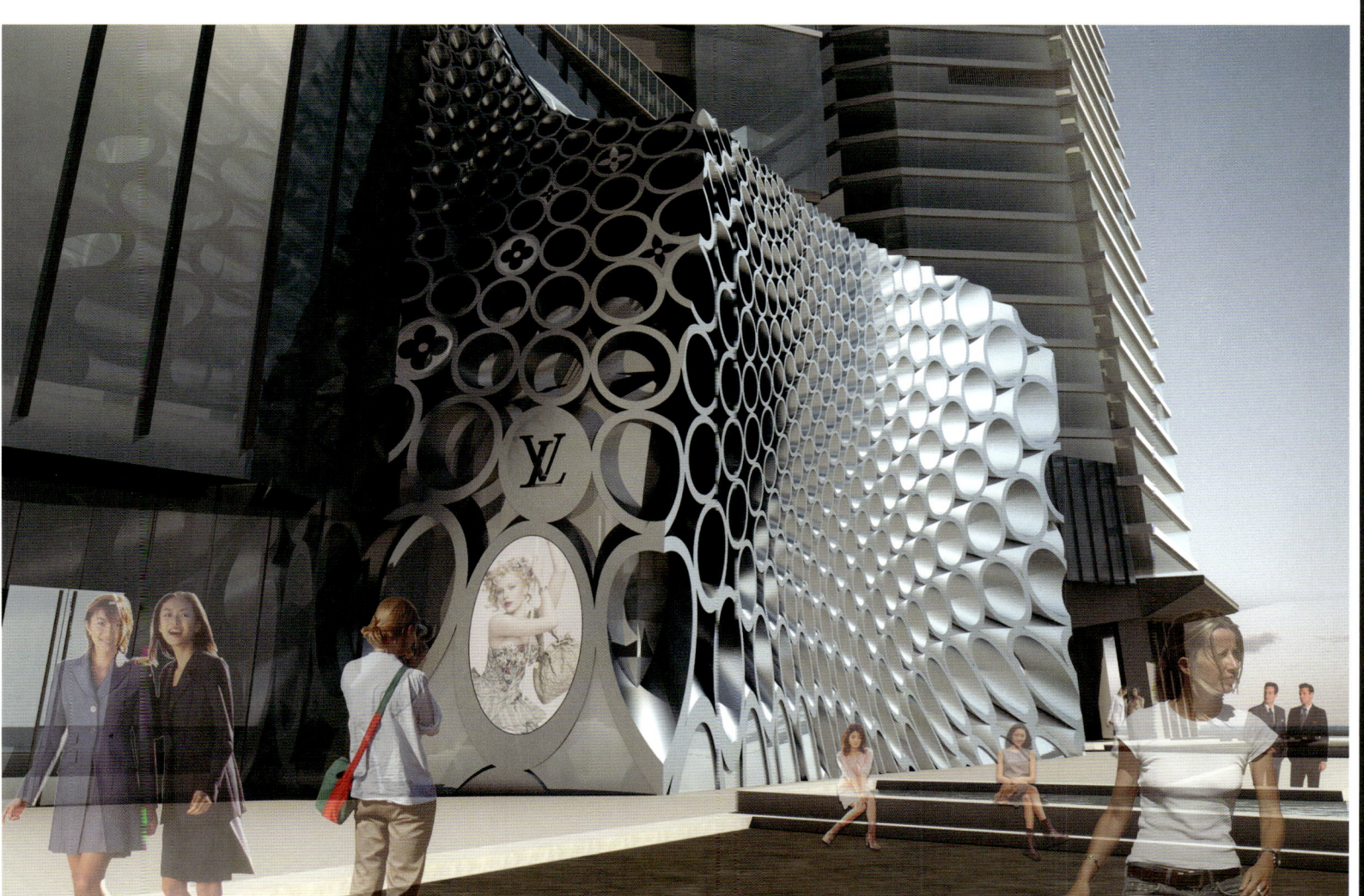

ARCHITECTURE AND INTERIORS 113

MACAO ONE CENTRAL

ASIA PACIFIC

SINGAPORE MARINA BAY

architects
PETER MARINO ARCHITECT
2011

text by
FRÉDÉRIC EDELMANN

It is said that in Singapore, anything that's fun is prohibited. While this tourist guide cliché makes no mention of what might be considered "fun," it's no crime to remind yourself what is authorized in this small republic, which is as small (with nearly 650 square kilometers for five million inhabitants) as it is strong (the second busiest port in the world, with the fourth highest GDP per capita worldwide). Anchored off the tip of the Malay Peninsula and run by the firm but paternal Lee Kuan Yew and his family, this is a place where you can make your fortune off of sea trading or real estate, build the world's most whimsical architectural projects (on a territory that's devoid of almost any pure patrimony), replicate golf courses and casinos, collect yachts and enjoy them between typhoons, and, most recently, participate in cultural events that constitute the glory of prosperous nations. The inevitable corollary of every lawful activity: a passion for luxury brands.

Louis Vuitton decided to stake ground for its most recent store at the recently completed Marina Bay Sands, a site where every retail business with a Singaporean "license" to operate has come together. Strangely enough, despite the size of the project, this location is not yet classified as a maison. Like a sphinx at the foot of the pyramids, it stands on the tranquil Marina reservoir that is created by a large artificial island and an impressive barrage at the mouth of the Singapore and Kallang Rivers that bisect structure and refresh the city. Once again using a proven technique of the firm, it is the urban and social context that provide the rationale for the new flagship: the principal store, which opened in 2009 and exhibited an entirely curvilinear design, could be found until recently on Orchard Road. The first of its kind for Vuitton, the structure presents itself as an isolated pavilion, apparently independent of any other structure, but also appears as though it is an edifice floating in water. This metaphor of a ship is reminiscent of—by principle, if not by style—the boat of Purity and Ease (*Qing Yan Fang*), built in marble on the grounds of the Summer Palace in Peking in 1860 for Cixi, the last Empress of China. The reference does not go unnoticed in Singapore, which is more than 76% populated by Chinese who came largely from mainland China and have become powerful investors since Mao's death.

The Crystal Pavilion was the first name given to the building by its American developers, the Las Vegas Sands, whose chosen initials, LVS, bear no relation to Vuitton's parent luxury group. This pavilion, which has an asymmetrical, younger brother lying upstream on the same lake, is anchored in front of an urban mountain whose first foothills, along the bank, are formed by a huge shopping arcade that stretches over several hundred meters. Three of its subdivisions frame three large volumes whose primary functions are to attract tourism. One such volume is home to two theaters; the second, a mega-casino ready for action with 500 gaming tables and 1,600 slot machines, rumbles beneath a gold vaulted ceiling; the third is a convention center classified as MICE (meetings/ incentives/ conventions/ events), one of the largest in the world. Lined up behind the casino is the inevitable hotel, arranged in three identical towers shaped like clothespins. These climb nearly 200 meters high, a banal feat in and of itself, if it weren't for the long platform connecting them at the top. The vocabulary of this element is borrowed from surfboards, but is long enough (340 meters) to accommodate a pool (three times the length of an Olympic one), and sure to induce vertigo. The landscape is finally complemented by a large museum dedicated to science whose shape, inspired by a flower in bloom, allows one to imagine Marina Bays Sands as an assemblage of eclectic architectural styles.

Although disparate, behind this diversity—a quality that was in fact sought after by the developer—there is but one single architect behind this absolutely stunning effect: Moshe Safdie. Born in Haifa, Israel in 1939, raised in Canada and currently residing in the United States near Boston, Safdie is celebrated as the artist behind the Yad Vashem Holocaust History Museum in Jerusalem, and his firm is known for a number of impressive and large-scale projects.

Hovering in the limelight of this urban monument, the new Louis Vuitton store will prove to be an excellent flagship for the group. Of the entire ensemble, it's the only one that possesses a relatively simple form. Architecture theorists will surely read into it as a vessel that has been passed into the hands of a master of Deconstructivism. The building seems to burst visibly into two identical elements attached head to tail, each some 40 meters long, sparing it from the random curves that dominate the ensemble of Marina Bay Sands. The heavy steel structures, characteristic to earthquake-prone regions and here covered in glass—rendering them oblivious to the strength of the region's sun and the inevitable greenhouse effect—seem to designate a construction that was designed as a signal with no specific function. Although this presented a great opportunity for the brand, it was also a challenge for the architecture teams at Louis Vuitton who were faced with the mission of marrying Moshe Safdie's creativity with Peter Marino's meticulous sense of design.

Initially accessible from the hotel and casino via a wide, underwater corridor considered to be an extension of the store, the new flagship now is connected by an attractive footbridge that, passing over the water of the bay, reinforces the nautical nature of the project. For it's clearly around the theme of the boat, inextricably linked to Louis Vuitton, that this project was conceived and ultimately found its shape. The ship reference is subtle, only suggested by the shape and location of the small island, and the railing of the footbridge. The theme becomes more apparent inside, where the brand—straying from Safdie's architecture—returns to the simple model of a ship: a large room at the bow, two decks or levels at the stern, and a beautiful, wide staircase connecting them all. Three main volumes are created in which one will find all of Peter Marino's recognizable codes, volumes and furnishings. At the end of this succession of scales, which stem from Safdie's massive creation, are the accessories—polished and cured in the factories of the legendary trunk maker.

The inclement weather of the region cannot be ruled out. But the thunderstorms that batter the terrace of the upper deck in the evening give way to the blessings of a view over the bay in the morning. The mechanics of the premises and the placement of the Louis Vuitton flagship at the end of the chain, like the requisite grand finale, should guarantee a few wonderful years of service for a clientele that Singapore's famous prohibitions cannot keep away.

p. 115 exterior rendering
p. 117 section through podium and pavilion and model views

PAVILION LEVEL 3

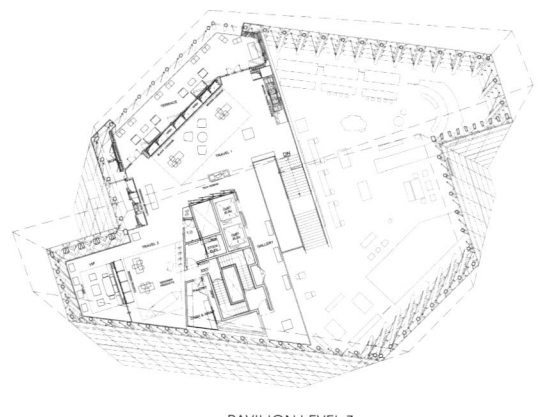

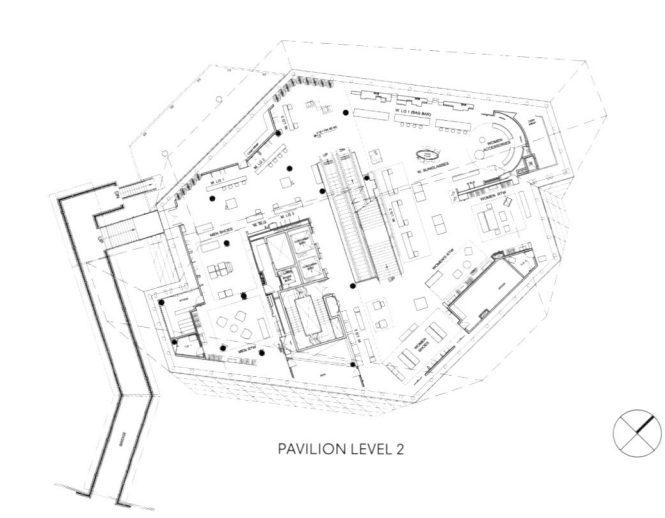

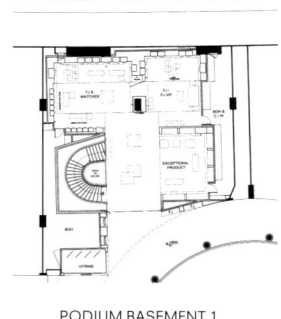

PAVILION LEVEL 2

PODIUM BASEMENT 1

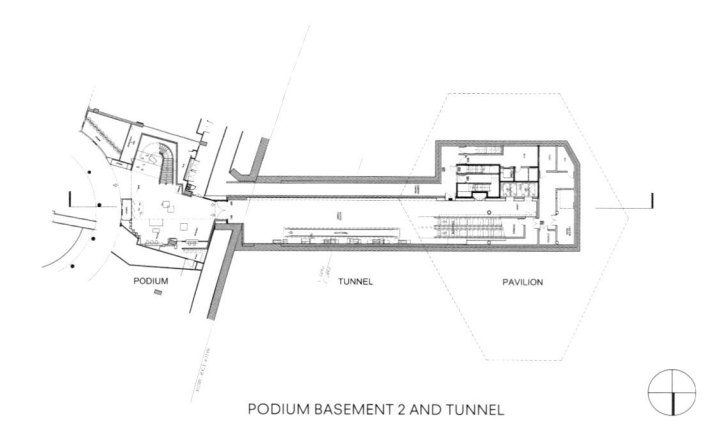

PODIUM | TUNNEL | PAVILION

PODIUM BASEMENT 2 AND TUNNEL

PODIUM　　　TUNNEL　　　PAVILION

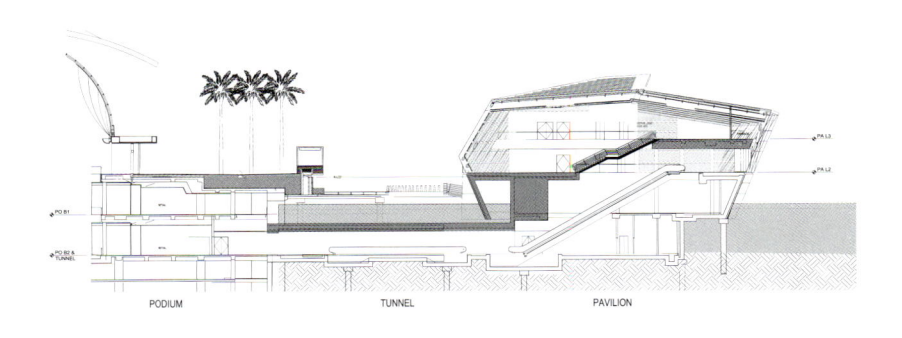

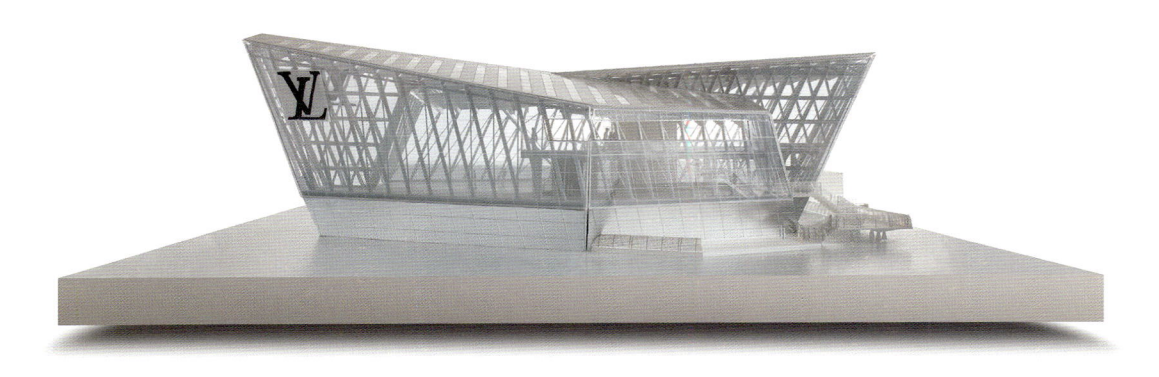

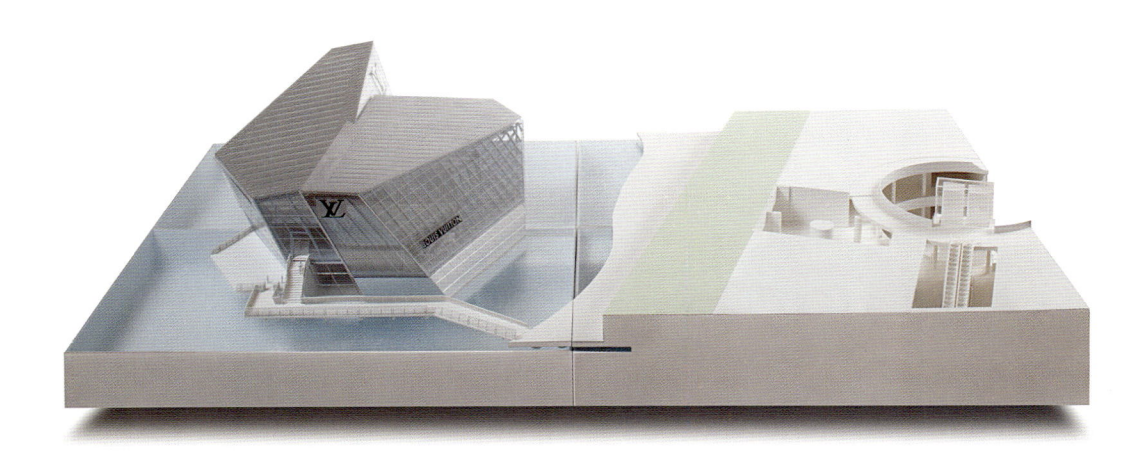

ARCHITECTURE AND INTERIORS 117

SINGAPORE MARINA BAY

ASIA PACIFIC

A CONVERSATION WITH
PETER MARINO
AND
MOHSEN MOSTAFAVI

MOHSEN MOSTAFAVI: You've had a long collaboration with LV and over the years your interiors have become synonymous with the brand. How did it all begin? Why do you think they came to you? And how did you start developing some specific thoughts as far as the LV brand is concerned?
PETER MARINO: We started with being hired by Christian Dior in 1995. The company had me flown over to Paris to interview me for the renovation of Dior on Avenue Montaigne because it had this horrible 1979 renovation with really silly things inside. It was a 1970's version of what ought to be French, and it was a mess. So we really started with Dior. In 6 to 9 months, I was interviewed a few times by Yves Carcelle because he was there at the beginning, and he hired me to do the Champs-Élysées in Paris, which was then considered the flagship of the company. It was going to have a wonderful new look. It's very interesting, historically, before me they had hired Anouska Hempel. Do you know this designer, because you're familiar with the scene in London?

Yes, of course, she had a very specific style. She did the Blakes Hotel and later the Hempel Hotel.
Well, she did a Louis Vuitton, which is still there, and is very beautiful, on the left bank, around the corner from Café de Flore, Les Deux Magots et tout ça. And she did a one-off store and it was more— let's say it was totally in her style, which was very, very dark, Asiatic lighting. It was exotic and beautiful as a one-off. Yves Carcelle and Bernard Arnault, when they analyzed it, said: "This is really a beautiful one-off store—we love it. But we've got 450 stores in the network." So they didn't think it was going to work having 450 stores with Asiatic lighting. Their charge to me was not to do a one-off; we refer to it as the everyman store. It's very interesting. I always get: "Give me the customer profile." Is it, you know, just for rich people? Is it just for middle-class people? You know, who's the profile? Who's shopping here? And the Vuitton brand, as opposed to most of the other brands I work for, went: "This is an every-man store." And I said: "Oh, that's quite jolly." And they said it's part of that overwhelmingly democratic approach.

Did that present a particular challenge?
I think that it's very hard to do the every-man store. Very hard. It is *much* easier to position a brand like Chanel or Dior and say: "This is for the very well-heeled lady customer who needs to feel that she's home in her own salon." It's easier to narrow your focus than to say, "I need a store that a wide range of clients feel comfortable in at the same time." That's not so easy. And the reason it's not so easy is, if it were, department stores would be a lot different from the way they are today. Department stores make what I call that fatal mistake of going for the middle ground because they want to appeal to everyone. They say, "Let's put the taste right in the middle. We don't want to be too low and we don't want to be too high. Let's put it in the middle because the middle is generally perceived as bigger." So the brief to me was: people who have the lowest minimal wage should be happy there and the very wealthy people should be happy too. We want an every-man store. It's a very upbeat brand.

How did you carry this idea forward in the Champs-Élysées store?
It was almost 20,000 square feet. At that time, as a boutique chain, none of the stores in the line was more than 10,000 feet. So this was a big leap in 1996, and it was the beginning. When I started working for them, they had less than 800 million dollars a year in sales, and now they're over 6 billion. So in the 15 years I've worked for them, you can see there's growth. And I'm really proud of being part of that growth story.

I realize that Mr. Arnault is unbelievably committed to you. So from the perspective of practice, how did you develop what is now a very distinct look for LV compared to some of the other brands?
Remember I had the background. I had seven years of doing Barneys. And that was a big challenge—to create a new look in this kind of branding, and I was a lot younger back then. And so this was, for me, challenge number two. The Champs-Elysées store has every single category of merchandise: it has clothing, it has leather goods, it has shoes, it has belts, even watches. That's always the hardest thing to do because it's got everything. We had to spend an incredible number of hours designing different settings. But Vuitton is no different than the other clients in that I always begin with materials. In our office we have a wall room for every individual client. And we have a very large wall room for Vuitton. Every architect starts differently; maybe some start with volumes, some with elevations, and others sketch something. I have a different approach. Even if I am doing a building I don't start with the volume, I start with materials. A lot of architects apply materials to their drawings later—they will draw a cube and think it can be white marble. I am the reverse. I put hundreds of sample of things on a giant table and surround the room with Vuitton products. I remember at one point I made them send me over 20 Vuitton hand bags and large selection of trunks and we put them all around the room with the table in the middle. We reorganized the materials until they felt like the brand. I don't let them start drawing things up until we have the relationship between the materials and the products worked out.

What you're saying is very interesting and quite important. It is true that many architects aspire to a certain

recognizable look—they have a particular style. But this approach to materials makes everything more contingent or relational. At the same time, there has evolved a particular and identifiable LV look as well. Are you comfortable with this idea of producing a different look for each brand?

I'm super comfortable with it. I honestly believe that when an architect has a look, it's a bit, may I just say, simplistic? Selling their look to you and applying it to everything? I'll just give you my opinion in architecture. I think that Herzog & de Meuron—who don't have a look and every project looks different—are infinitely more creative and greater artists than, may I say, a Frank Gehry, where all the buildings are immediately recognizable. Sorry to put it that way, but that's my general impression. For some of them it's because they are artists like Frank, and that's just his look in paintings, and it's going to be that way no matter what. Others, like SOM, have a look for commercial reasons. They've got a very large staff and they've got to produce. Corporations come to them because they liked the look of the last project. And between you and me, to have a different look for every single project is so time-consuming. I mean, it's hell on Earth what I do.

But do you feel that the variations amongst the brands still have a consistency across them as projects? For example, by focusing on materials at the beginning? Are there certain things that remain part of the consistency of your process?

Yes. The way I work is constant. It's just that the end product will be varied and responds to something as seemingly ephemeral as the new design direction that Marc Jacobs is giving to dresses this year.

So how has your design responded to these fleeting changes in fashion?

Marc came out with a whole new sexy look this time. With this new look we had to throw in something a little edgier with the materials. I'm getting a little bit sexier voice here—it is a lot more feminine. I have to move away from this kind of khaki jacket that we started with 15 years ago. I try to create something new based on distilling the message that the clients give. But what makes LV so special and Yves Carcelle such a tactician is the fact that he doesn't want to have each store be so radically different from the others in the network. So we have to push the brand, but know that we are dealing with 450 stores and to make sure that the message is clear. We can make changes, but perhaps only 20 percent.

Earlier you mentioned the shift from sales of 800 million to 6 billion dollars a year. You've emphasized the value of continuity over the years in relation to the evolution of a concept that can apply to 450 stores. The concept can't be singular, but it has to be identifiable. And it has to change. What are some of the key elements of the evolution of the brand over the years? What are some of the things that have been constant? And what are some of the key issues that are important to you in terms of change?

The main focus is always going to be in terms of materiality and lighting. For example, the stores can't be too dark. I said from the beginning that if you want an everyman brand then the lighting has to be at daylight levels. At the time that was a bit of a revolution. A lot of stores had used dark dramatic theatrical lighting. Also because the nature of their product was mainly luggage, I felt we had to go with the route of natural materials. We came up with wood and stone and a color palette that was very pleasing to everybody. We did not do anything too dark, and we did not do anything too light. There were no whites or blacks allowed in our Vuitton designs. It was all going to be in beige stone floors and going up to the darkest brown wood that matched their trunks. That was our coloring. And we decided to keep it in this range of beige, coffee, and brown over the past 15 years. We make changes within the spectrum of materials and colors. Fashion changes very, very quickly and for a while in Japan the stores were at the very light end of the beige. Now, for instance, in the London boutique everyone says, "Oh, I love all the wood in the store!" And I go: "It's not wood, it's composite, we don't use wood any more in Vuitton." We are as green as the next guy.

It seems that many companies, including LV, are rethinking the nature of the shopping experience. Sometimes the settings are more domestic, and in other instances more akin to an art gallery. I know art has been an important part of your métier as an architect. How do you see the store experience changing in the future?

I was an art student before I went to architecture school. Andy Warhol put me into business. And I did Andy's house and my first three clients were all artists. That's my background, that's me. I think artists have a vision and a voice. Why am I close to them? Why do I bring them in very early, and why do I commission them rather than buying artworks? Because if I want to really be ahead of the game, that's who's got the vision. Architects—between you and me—are a lagging indicator. By the time we get this stuff built, that idea is two years old. Artists can pump out the new idea overnight. I really like involving artists because they can do it fast, and they're ahead of the game, and that's the reason they are artists. They're interpretive bodies. So I feel very close to the way they work; I'm the same. Like, my eyes—this is the interpretive approach.

So do you see the stores shifting in a way? I don't mean to be like galleries with art on the wall, but the way in which the collaboration with certain artists will create a different ambiance, an interior that will complement what you are doing with regards to materiality. The point, for example, about lighting and the mood of a place is quite apt.

I have a complex approach towards art. I don't know why—I mean, I do view artists as interpretive people. And I consider art to be some of the strongest propaganda that exists. And I use that word 'propaganda' because… How would you describe Michelangelo's ceiling in the Sistine Chapel? That's pure propaganda for the Church. Pure and simple. It's great art. And I always give that example when I get artists in here. Apart from artists I feel very close to Marc Jacobs, not just philosophically but visually. My coordination with him on the brand is very strong and very positive because he really gets it. He's enhanced the brand, he's enhanced the artists' careers, and he's enhanced the public's enjoyment. It's a very, very strong team that I think they've got there.

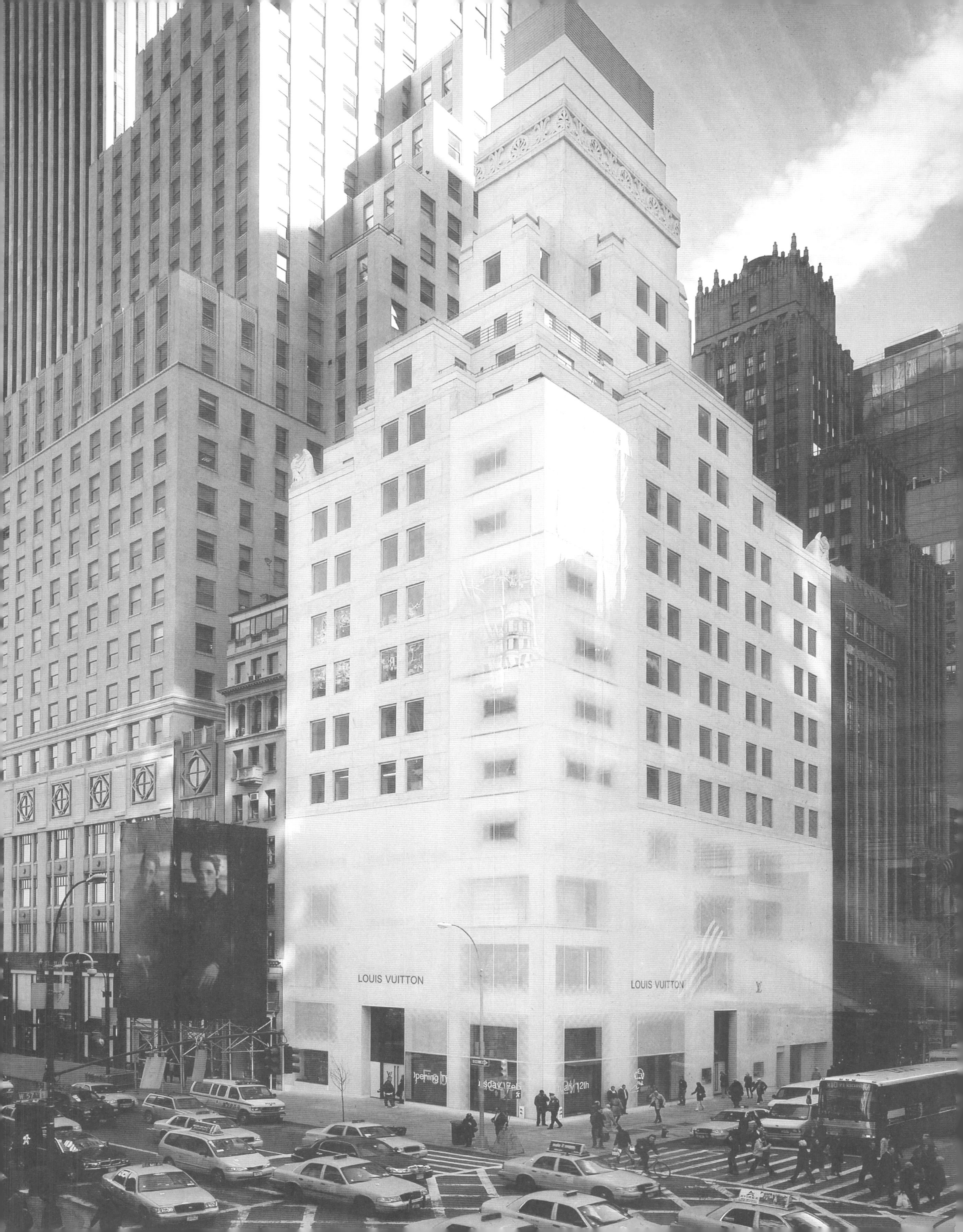
LOUIS VUITTON
LOUIS VUITTON

UNITED STATES
LAS VEGAS, CITY CENTER
NEW YORK, NEW YORK
FIFTH AVENUE

LAS VEGAS CITY CENTER

architects
THE LOUIS VUITTON
ARCHITECTURE DEPARTMENT
2009

Text by
RAFAEL MAGROU

Along with Macao, its twin in Asia, Las Vegas is the embodiment of all the potential excesses intertwined in gambling, shopping and entertainment. The Strip, the boulevard that has been filmed endlessly for its cinematographic allure, strings together the city's various periods like pearls, from the 1940s to today—with the legendary Flamingo, Tropicana and Mirage hotels, whose stages have welcomed the likes of Frank Sinatra and Elvis Presley. A bastion of freedom in the heart of the United States, these "fertile valleys" offer an array of architectural objects, a topic on which Robert Venturi and Denise Scott-Brown developed a critical understanding in *Learning from Las Vegas* (a manifesto on Las Vegas), promoting the principle of the "decorated shed." Thankfully, the latest generation of buildings erected by the City Center revives spatial inventiveness, drawing on an architectural vocabulary that departs from small-scale copies of international monuments. Across from the miniature Eiffel Tower and a few blocks from the condensed New York City, Statue of Liberty included, this 8.5 billion dollar architectural wager presents a series of towers that sparkle day and night, serving as a magnetic pole for tourists who've come to spend their money at slot machines and card tables. On the street level, a shopping center connects the steel and glass giants and brings together every luxury brand within its metallic shell. Located directly next to the Strip and the Aria, the hotel-casino that's an explosion of architectural materials and slot machines, Crystals—the name of Vegas's newest jewel—was designed by Daniel Libeskind, the artist behind the Freedom Tower at Ground Zero in New York, who's known for his complex forms that, on occasion, make them difficult to use. Com-pleted by MGM Mirage and Dubai World in the midst of an economic crisis, this 46,000 square-meter devoted shopping area is home to the largest Louis Vuitton boutique in North America, with close to 1,600 square meters of retail space, or double the usual size. It's in fact the sixth store within the giant casino that constitutes Las Vegas, because each hotel really comprises its own separate city. As such, that of Crystals best reflects the local spirit—supremely centralized and considered an attraction in the noblest sense of the word—for the thousands of travelers who come here to make their dreams come true.

Since it was the first store to open at Crystals—followed months later by other luxury contemporary brands—Louis Vuitton benefits from having the best location. Despite trying times, and having suffered the full brunt of the last three years of financial crisis, the brand wanted to maintain its course at any cost. And for good reason—it's a given that the largest of Louis Vuitton's North American stores is the buzz on the Strip, even with its competition of endlessly flashing signs. With its 3,000 square meter façade, the New York research department, which oversees the visual aspects of the North American boutiques, wanted to seize the opportunity to create a sensational surface. No less than 4,600 LEDs are embedded into the metallic skin, propagating an animated, visual dynamic that is at once sensual and poetic, revolving around the French brand's logos. The show lasts almost a half-hour and is looped at night, controlled from behind by computers straight out of the *Matrix* that take turns vibrating the surface. Artful and stylish, these rich ideas identify the brand as being at the height of current technology and graphic elegance, a standout in the crowded visual laboratory that is Las Vegas. By day, the stainless steel envelope stamped with endlessly repeating and overlapping L and V letters (the initials of both the city and the brand) forms a protective texture for the sloping wall. The equation between material and logo scrupulously respects the vocabulary of Libeskind, with its shifting metal siding and diagonal tiles that accentuate the geometric dynamic. Through this combination of effects, the Louis Vuitton boutique seems to be cushioned in a shining framework, transmitting a special sophistication amid the triviality that predominates over Las Vegas.

In fact, one accesses the store mostly from inside the complex, because the sun on the Strip is so oppressive. Passageways for foot traffic skirt the eight-lane avenues and penetrate into the belly of each gambling universe, while the monorail links the different hotels, avoiding the melted asphalt of the major routes—temperatures hover around 50°C (122°F) throughout the year, without a drop of rain. The logo repeated on the façade is reintegrated here, in a medium painted in the warmer tone of "champagne gold" and highlighted by a retro backlit sign that can be seen from every corner of the shopping center. The window displays take center stage. They're inviting but don't need to convince visitors to enter; they've already been enticed by the array of products set against thematic backdrops developed each season with increasing inventiveness. At Louis Vuitton, more than anywhere else, it must be noted that the windows create an event in and of itself as the brand imagines its own singular universe, inviting artists from across the world to meditate on the theme of travel and its multiple dimensions.

Inside, the store benefits from several entrance points—from the outside boulevard and from upper and lower galleries that unfurl in Crystals' immense shopping center. The lower level crosses Libeskind's sculpture from side to side, presenting bags and leather goods for men and women. The mezzanine is home to the most precious products, including jewelry, watches, special bags and exotic leathers, as well as personalization services. Finally, the upper level is reserved for women and incorporates private areas for trying on ready-to-wear items.

The brainchild of Peter Marino, the whole space centers around a hollow ring that articulates the areas both visually and physically, through the placement of a suspended staircase. In a clever game of reflections created by dematerialized, mirrored stairs, the stairwell is a floating cross that contributes to the general impression of weightlessness on this peaceful island amid the constant solicitation presented by Vegas and its attributes. An ascending escalator carries clients upstairs, an inevitable feature for a population that allows itself to be transported through a sea of signs to slot machines. The elliptical cavity is magnified by a giant chandelier, inspired by the one at the GUM department store in Moscow, with stylized glass, titanium and wood flowers dangling from the suspended ceiling, the beveled panels of which forge theappearance of a simple sheet of stucco. The walls wind and unwind at the discretion of the gold metallic mesh, the unifying wall relief that clearly identifies Louis Vuitton's fine craftsmanship. In addition, the Bag Bar here is stationed at a rounded counter in order to better accommodate the uniquely versatile clientele.

The range of materials now recorded in the last testament of LV, conceived of by Marino, was also deployed here, using essences of Cumaru and Zebrono wood, lacquer, and also travertine and granite, with accents of tufted carpets and knotted rugs, used to create a masculine or feminine ambiance. *Lucky colors*, hanging Plexiglas cubes made by Lionel Estève, add a touch of life in a suspended mobile above the men's accessories, while photographs by Jean Larivière open distant horizons in ochre tones. Two special editions of the "Casino Trunk" incorporate everything you need to win—and lose—with roulette on top and a game table incorporated in the silhouette, accommodating this destination frequented by gamblers from around the world. Through a system of mechanical blinds, the VIP lounge unveils the latest collections to the most demanding clients, creating an element of surprise in the same way that the curtains rise at the many theaters that dot the city. This is, after all, the ever-sparkling city of entertainment.

An ongoing city-spectacle, Las Vegas is open to projects straight out of your wildest dreams in terms of technique, size and magic. As part of this extraordinary architectural program, outside of the undisputed luxury of its merchandise, Louis Vuitton contributes to the sensational effect of this city that is undoubtedly undergoing an architectural renaissance.

p. 120 Maison Louis Vuitton New York Fifth Avenue, façade on the corner of Fifth Avenue and 57th Street
p. 123 aerial view of store at night with signage patterns
p. 124 view of The Strip at night
p. 125 detail of façade with embossed metallic panels and LEDs
p. 126 interior, view of atrium
p. 127 top left: 2nd floor interior; top right: view from the street plaza
p. 128–129 view of patterns on the principal façades showing the application of abstracted Louis Vuitton iconography

2ND FLOOR

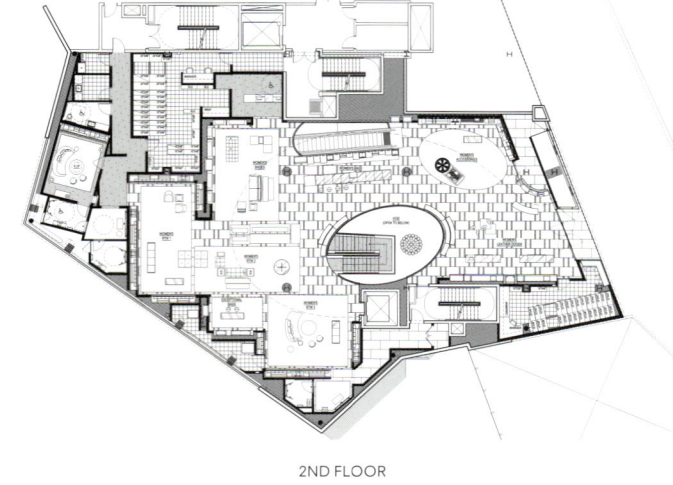

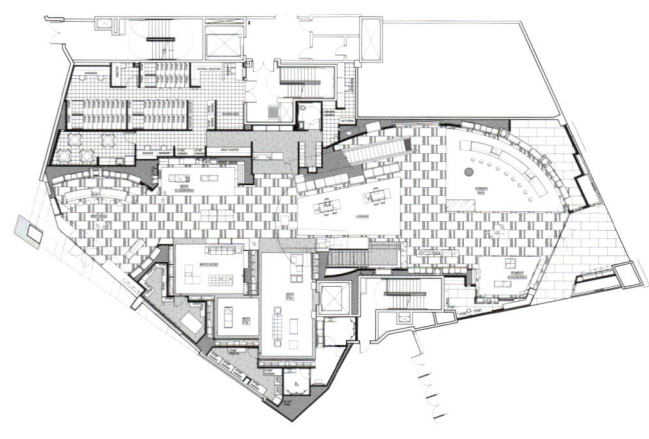

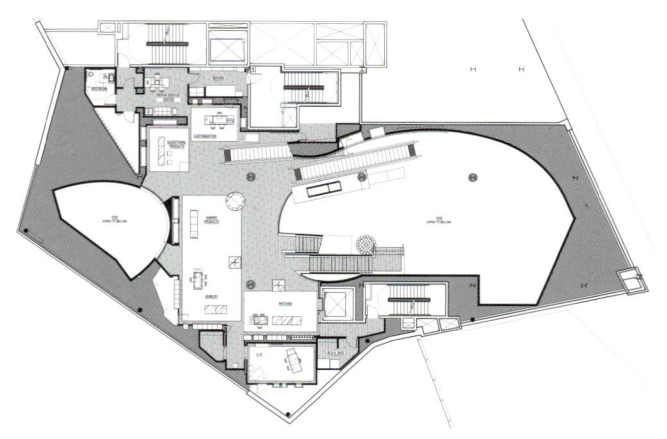

GROUND FLOOR

MEZZANINE (BETWEEN GROUND AND 2ND FLOOR)

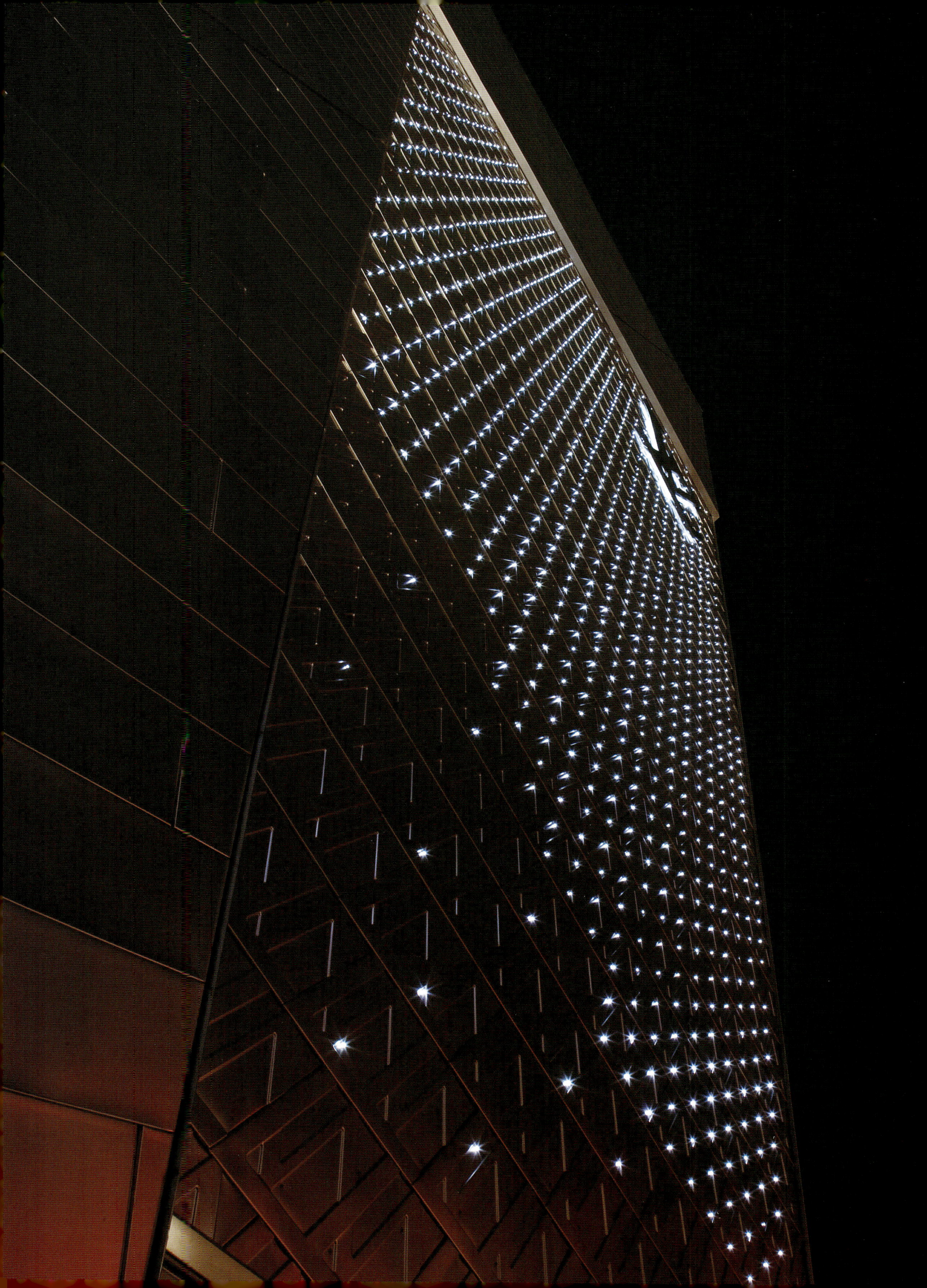

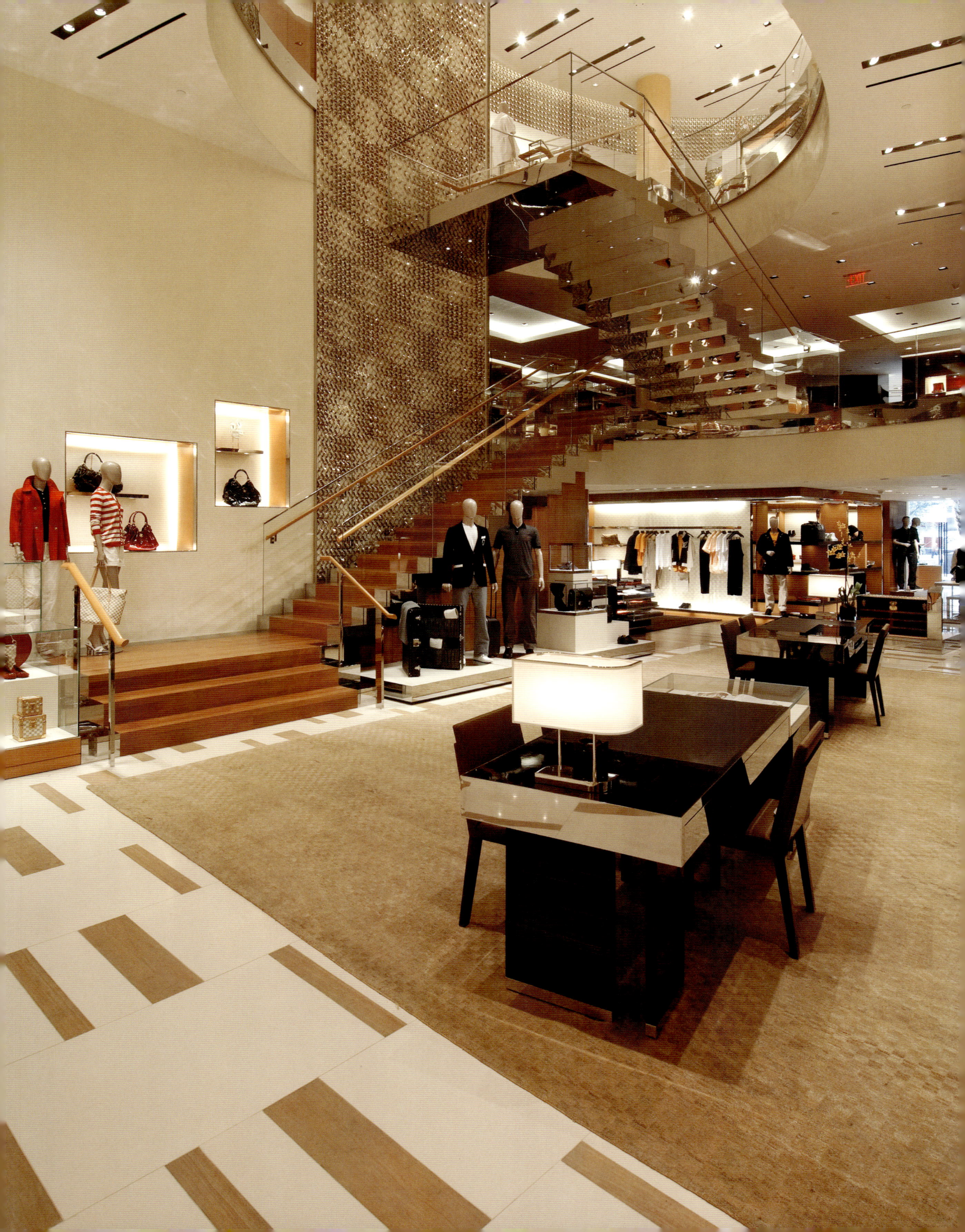
EXIT

ARCHITECTURE AND INTERIORS 127

LAS VEGAS CITY CENTER

UNITED STATES

ARCHITECTURE AND INTERIORS 128

LAS VEGAS CITY CENTER

UNITED STATES

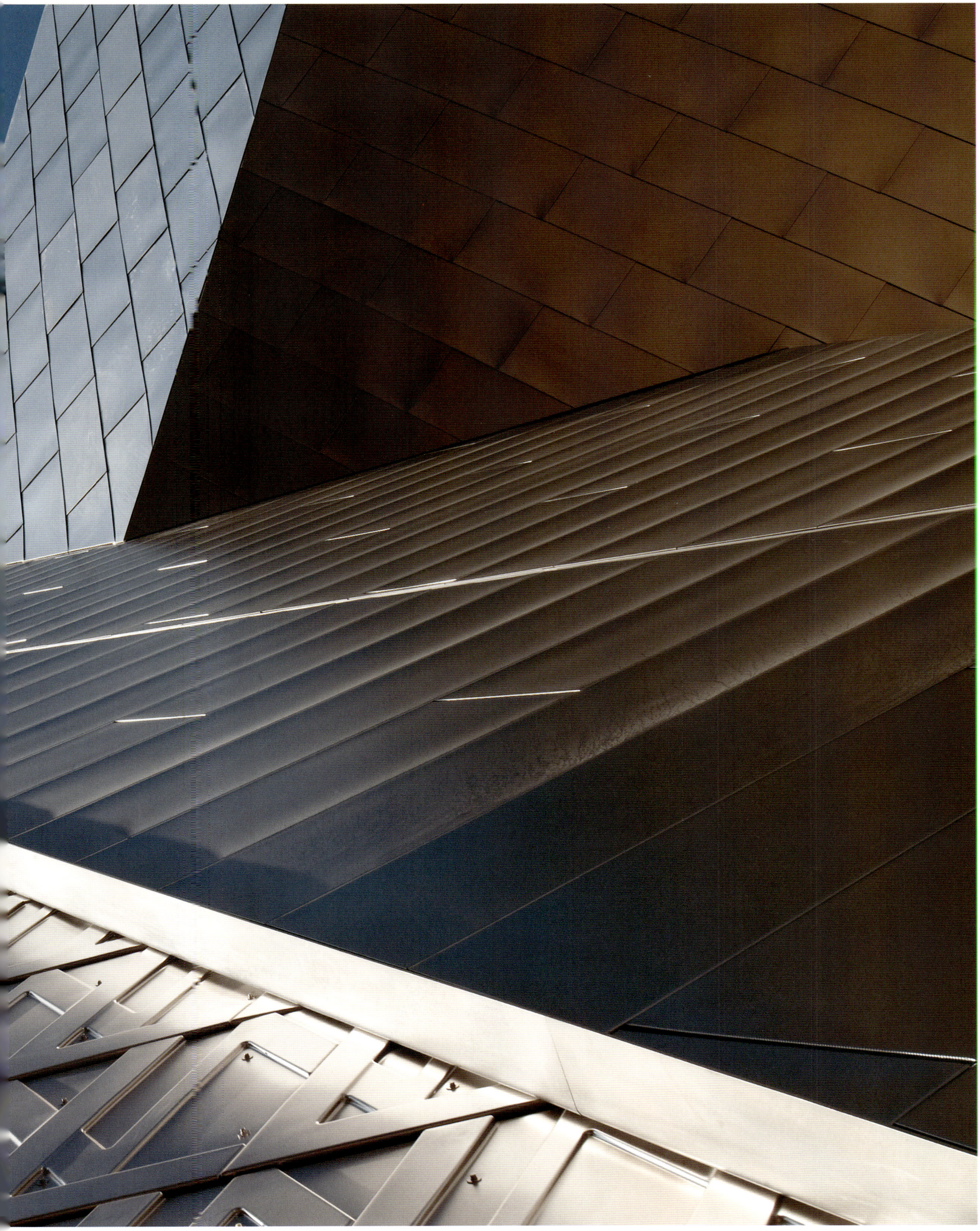

NEW YORK
FIFTH AVENUE

architects
JUN AOKI & ASSOCIATES;
PETER MARINO ARCHITECT
2004

text by
RAFAEL MAGROU

New York, New York! The city of possibilities is as dazzling as an ensemble, but its individual buildings would seem pale-faced without the others that surround them, scraping against the changing sky of the city that never sleeps. Naturally, Louis Vuitton wanted to share in its galvanizing energy— "to be a part of it," as Liza Minnelli sang in Martin Scorsese's film. To be king of the hill, the company had to have a significant presence for their new venture: a solid address on "Fifth," whose reputation is as renowned in New York as the Champs-Élysées' is in Paris. The blocks between 34th street—with the Empire State Building—and 59th street—marking the southern border of Central Park— are known for housing the most famous luxury stores. And the intersection at the corner of 57th is the most prestigious in the city, with the Crown Building (easily recognizable from its gilded pyramidal roof in the "French château" style) and Bergdorf Goodman (in the Mansard style), hosting the most celebrated jewelers. It could be called a "little France," and Louis Vuitton occupies a strategic spot there in the Northeast corner, at number 1 East 57th Street. Vuitton's move was a radical change of usage and décor for this address, which formerly housed the Warner Brothers store. In both style and spirit, it was a bit like switching from Pepsi-Cola to the finest champagne.

The white marble of the existing edifice is divided into fourteen levels of sequential geometric windows, somewhat gloomy in their rigor. Here, the Japanese architect Jun Aoki plays with the card of timelessness. He refreshes the ensemble by enveloping the first four levels with a second skin of glass, the sensuality of which transcends the intersection. Following the metaphor of New York as a mountain range with its tall peaks, the designer of the Louis Vuitton facades in Namiki dori and Omotesando in Tokyo, as well as the Landmark in Hong Kong, develops a shining crystal surface for the Fifth Avenue store, visually suggesting a silky touch, especially in relationship to the ambient grayness of the other façades on the Eastern side. Aoki accentuates this effect by carrying the glazing all the way to the eleventh floor, just at the corner of the building, creating a beacon visible from several blocks away; he knows that for a retail space, the façade offers the best interface between exterior and interior. Like Superman's kryptonite palace, the corner of the 1930s edifice raises up its mutant epidermis, its diaphanous aspect subtly created by two layers, front and back, of white checkerboard patterning. The gradations in size of this cubist puzzle create a clear opening in front of the existing windows, with neither a change in material nor a shift in the façade's layout. Integral to the design, this audacious choice reverses the laws of weightlessness, forming an evanescent section at the base, while the edifice rests on this ether, hoisting itself up level-by-level to its summit. At nightfall, the opalescence takes leave of its satin robes and melts into the inner wall, revealing the relative intimacy of the store. The frames in the back-ground of the glass wall seem to trace so many boxes, evocative of Vuitton's timeless trunks. In a play of light in blond and golden tones, this stacking is reinforced by the slightly offset openings that are wider than they are high. The two glass sides create a giant, L-shaped surface for visual communication events, such as the advertising campaign featuring Buzz Aldrin, Jim Lovell and Sally Ride to celebrate the 40th anniversary of the moon landing, or the emblems from Ruben Toledo's city guides designed for the 2009 holiday season. The building becomes a complete vitrine, in the American tradition of grand-scale spaces.

At the heart of the urban agitation that characterizes New York, with its permanent flotilla of cars and coffee-laden, sneaker-shod pedestrians, Louis Vuitton's new location seems like an enigmatic monolith, at once reflective of its infernal cadences and protective of this perpetual movement. According to the season, the angle of the sun, and the mood of the sky, the edifice participates in this dynamic, while sheltering the clientele from its discomforts. Nevertheless, the ballet of yellow taxis is still perceptible from inside as mobile pigments that dissolve in the imprint at the base of the façade. But most surprising is the ample space in the store, with its 1,200 square meters. As in Tokyo, space is a luxury here. And Louis Vuitton doesn't hesitate to demonstrate that it can offer this pleasure to both loyal customers and one-off visitors alike. Vertiginous when viewed from below, the interior architecture seems to have been hollowed out, as if the empty space had generated the staggered structures and planes respectively dedicated to the various departments. The design echoes the giant, covered patio of the MoMA, located on 54th street, conceived by another Japanese architect, Yoshio Taniguchi. While the display of ingenious creations by Vuitton and his descendants marks the street view, the structural columns are deconstructed by the application of video screens projecting runway shows and other aspects of the brand's *savoir-faire*. Thrusting upwards towards a ceiling no less than four floors above, they support overhanging terraces that structure the organization of the collections and the stack of empty, thematic spaces.

Assuming the role of the experienced neighbor, Peter Marino intervenes brilliantly in the boutique's design. He masters the thickness of the New York air to perfection, explaining, "the secret of luxury is space." Having grown up in the pulsing rhythm of New York in the sixties, and moving in circles with Andy Warhol—whose new studio on Broadway, and private apartment, he created—the young Marino was thrust into the world of architecture thanks to the Pop Art master, never losing sight of the artistic dimension that comes to the fore in his interiors. On Fifth Avenue, where the landlords flirt with ridiculous sums of money, Louis Vuitton nevertheless takes the opportunity to express this spatial expansiveness—a necessary feature for clientele constantly on the quest for exhilarating experiences. We are in New York; anything is possible if we can pay the price. By this articulation of empty spaces, Peter Marino succeeds in optimizing the visual impact of the articles on display, as if they were in an art gallery—the credo of all his projects for the brand. Louis Vuitton's *maisons* integrate works of contemporary art into their spaces—an ingenious idea that reinforces their attractive power. In the words of Marino, "In a boutique, everything is a question of desire. The clients have to want to buy everything."

Around a tall, three-dimensional, central wall in a checkerboard of illuminated, colored retro glass, a wooden staircase unfurls. Without touching the wall, it is held in place by a thread, or more precisely a shaft, which, if examined closely, is a feat of technical prowess comprising cantilevers in three dimensions. The wall, which palpitates with a soft, changing light, includes windows in its glass encasing; around it, several plateaus are staggered perpendicularly to accentuate the spatial experience. Between its lacquered walls, jewelry and Tambour watches have descended from the floor above in order to be at the same level as the competitors across the street, and to set the chic, sparkling tone of the ensemble, composed here at this iconic intersection. Remarkably arranged on the mezzanine, stretching over the entire width of the store, the Bag Bar takes advantage of the natural light, so rare in New York's commercial spaces. This light is cleverly filtered through a geometric film that covers the windows, protecting the leather products from the sun. The immense atrium also demonstrates this intention to maximize sunlight, at the same time offering the visitor an all-encompassing view of the store's offerings in a single glimpse. Similarly, the hall dedicated to top-of-the-line products creates a perspective drawing the gaze towards the street. The display furniture is conceived as a collection of independent islands that allow for the free flow of movement through the space—an important consideration, with two million visitors per year—and also offers clientele the high quality of presentation and service they expect from the brand. These are amongst the most fundamental rules of design for the very closed circle of Louis Vuitton *maisons* which include the stores on the Champs-Élysées, New Bond Street, Hong Kong Landmark, and Namiki dori and Omotesando in Tokyo.

If time is suspended in this North American niche—which celebrated the brand's 150th anniversary at its opening—then its architectural volumes also represent this state of erudite equilibrium, where every detail counts. The ladies' dressing room on the second floor is made up of a horizontally striped, textile lantern, stamped with the manufacturer's flower, which seems to rest on the ambient air, infused with the leathery scent of the items for sale. Here, a ceiling mirror inverts the way we read the space, all the way to the upside-down street. The glazed balustrades, topped with metallic handrails, help us grasp both the spatial environment and the commercial offerings. The fields of darkened, hollow-jointed floors accentuate this sensation, diminishing the structural and technical thickness of the slabs. The mobile by the French artist Xavier Veilhan, who showed his work at a monographic exhibition in Versailles, also contributes to the ambiance of celestial magic with his twenty spheres in intense purple, complementing the amber-colored walls that combine Zebrano wood and large-format photographs overlaid with metallic mesh in alternating bands. On the fourth floor, a VIP salon—the precursor to what would be established in all the Louis Vuitton *maisons*, as well as in the collector's apartment on New Bond Street in London six years later—dominates the area. It is introduced by a limited-edition collection of pieces created by guest designers such as Vivianne Westwood and Azzedine Alaïa.

The building grows higher still; by transferring the offices previously occupied by Dior to Christian de Portzamparc's tower in a few months, Louis Vuitton's total occupation of the building will make it their first single, coherent edifice since the original New York boutique in 1980. This is an exceptional situation in New York—a haughty position conquered over the years, when we consider that at the end of the 19th century, Louis Vuitton was already selling his wares through John Wanamaker, owner of several luxury department stores. Even then, orders were pouring in from all sides for the adventurers of the day: passengers traveling on transatlantic ocean liners and followers of Charles Lindbergh in their stratocruisers—back when airplane interiors resembled hotel salons and the journey was reserved only for the elite. Legend even has it that, in 1912, Louis Vuitton trunks were the only baggage that survived the sinking of the Titanic!

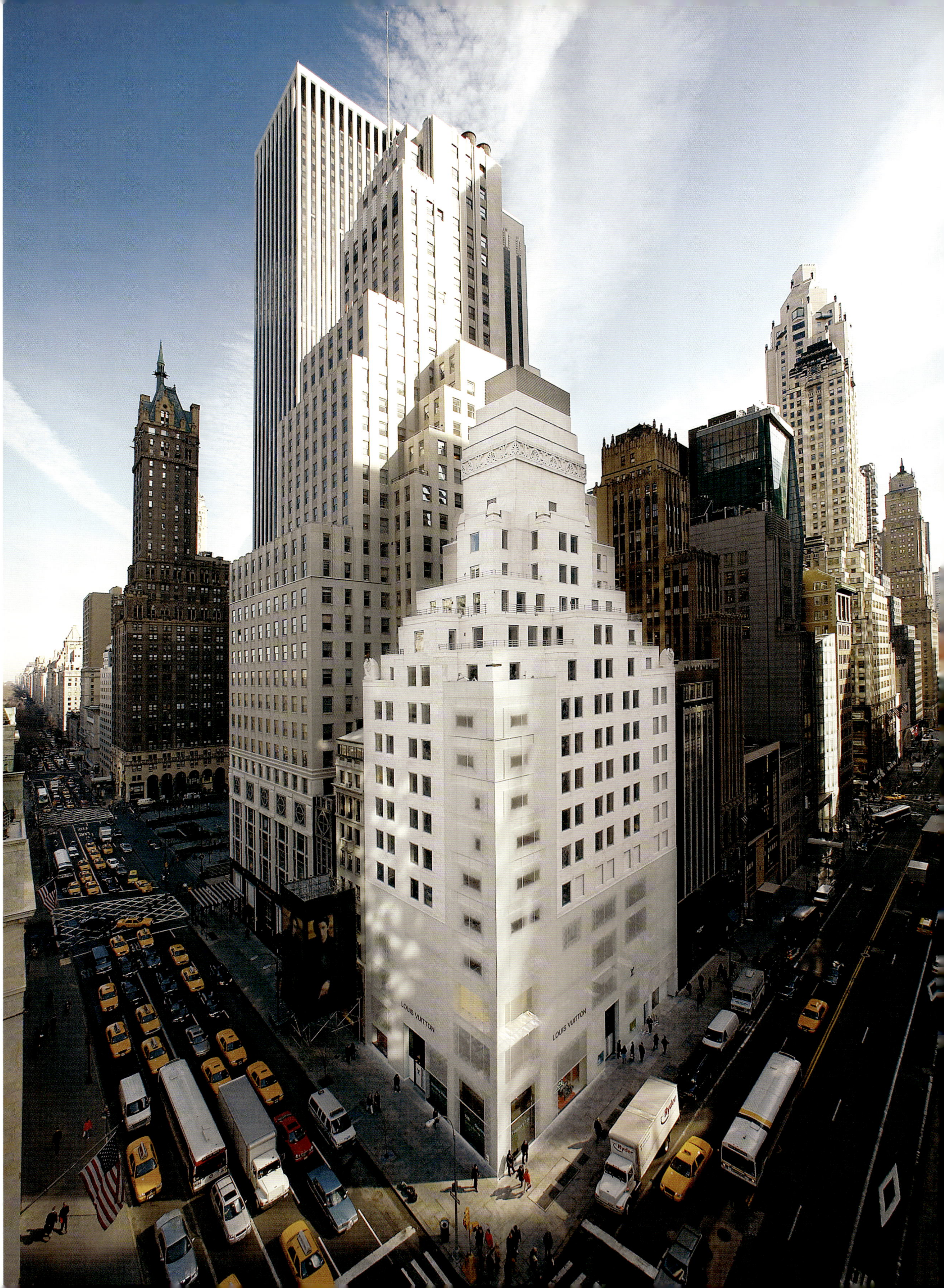

NEW YORK FIFTH AVENUE

UNITED STATES

p. 131 interior detail, staircase
p. 132 façade on the corner of Fifth Avenue and 57th Street
p. 134 ground floor atrium
p. 135 top: illuminated wall along staircase; bottom: watches and jewelry room
p. 136–137 view of atrium with artwork by Xavier Veilhan *Mobile* (2009)
p. 138 view of Bag Bar
p. 139 aerial view of Fifth Avenue at night

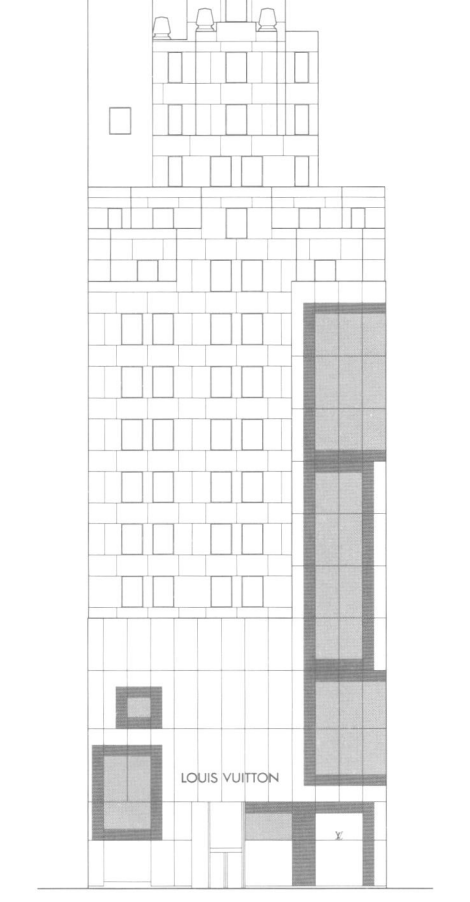

SOUTH ELEVATION

WEST ELEVATION

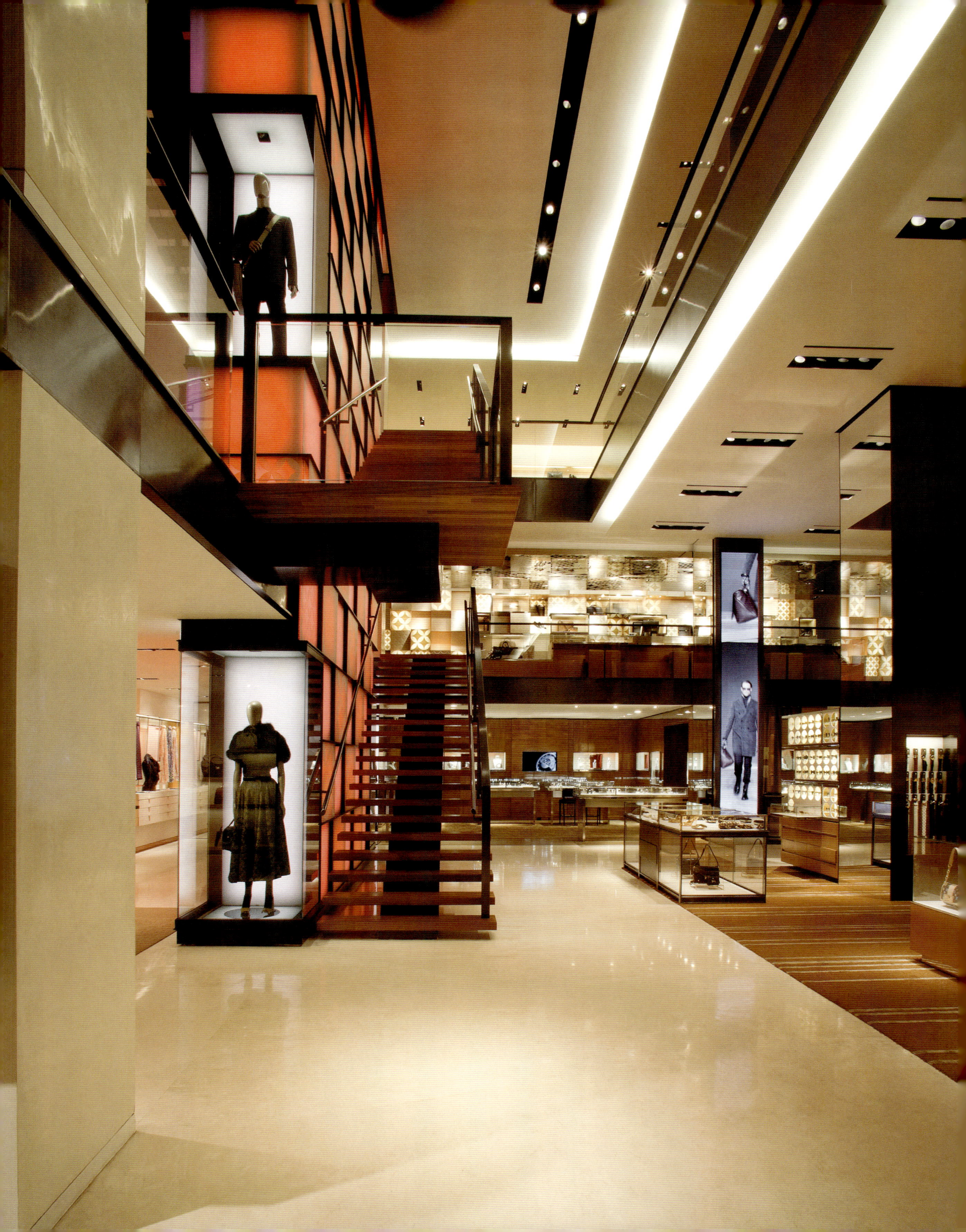

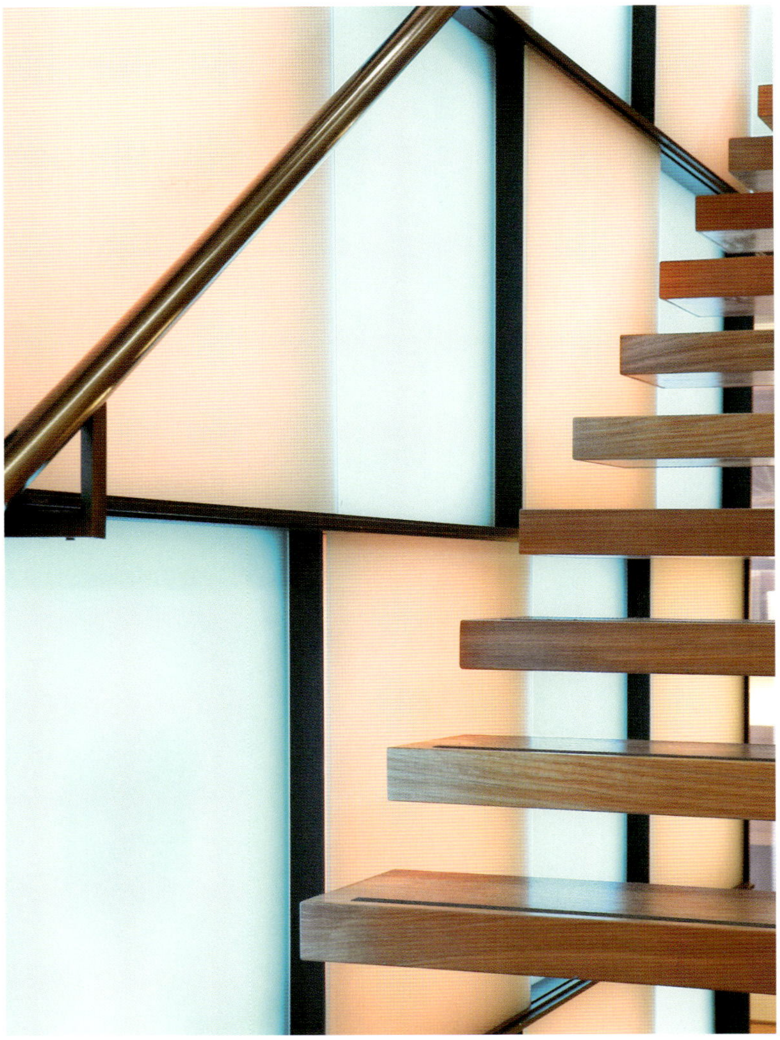

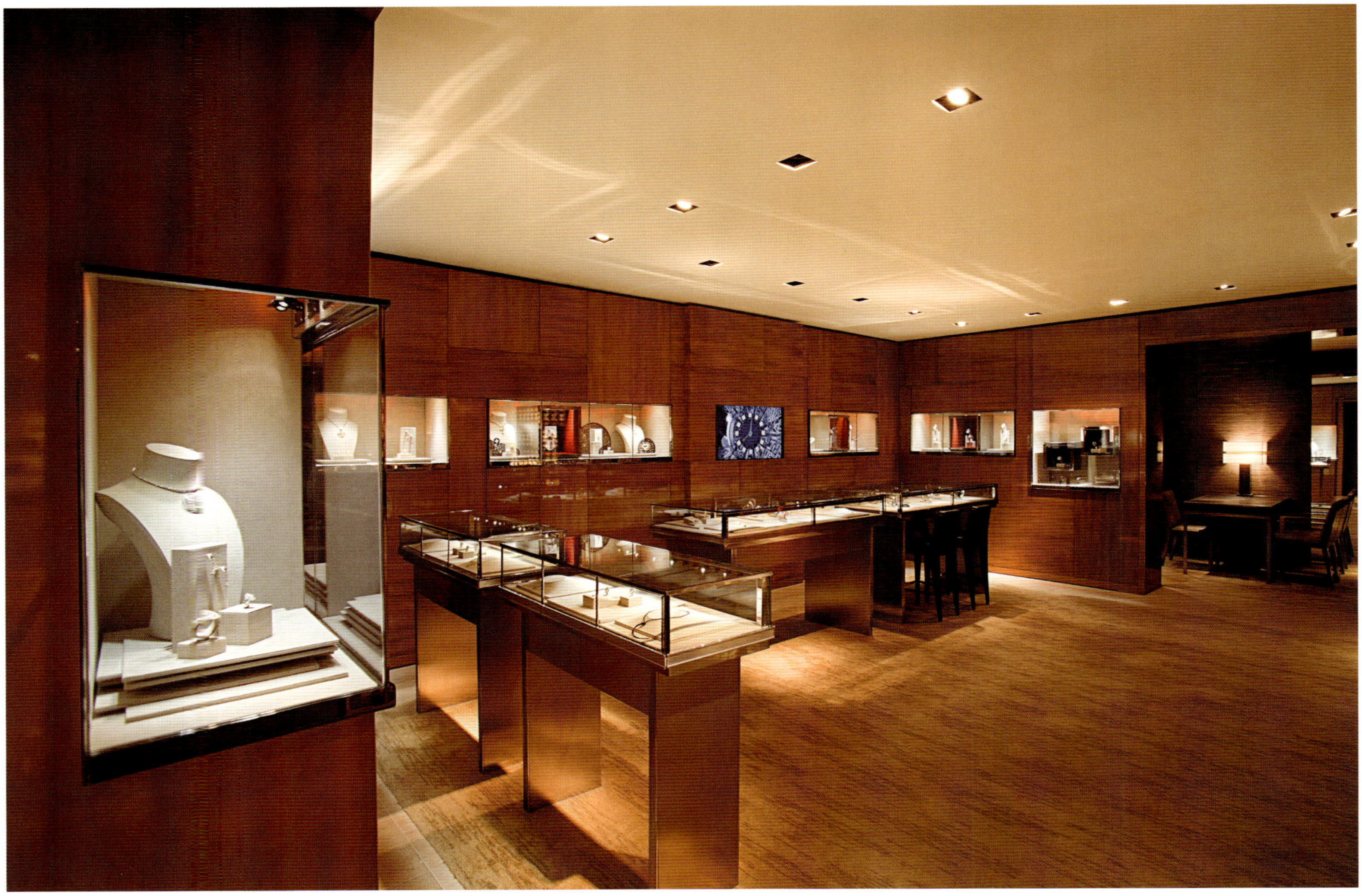

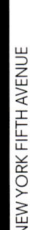

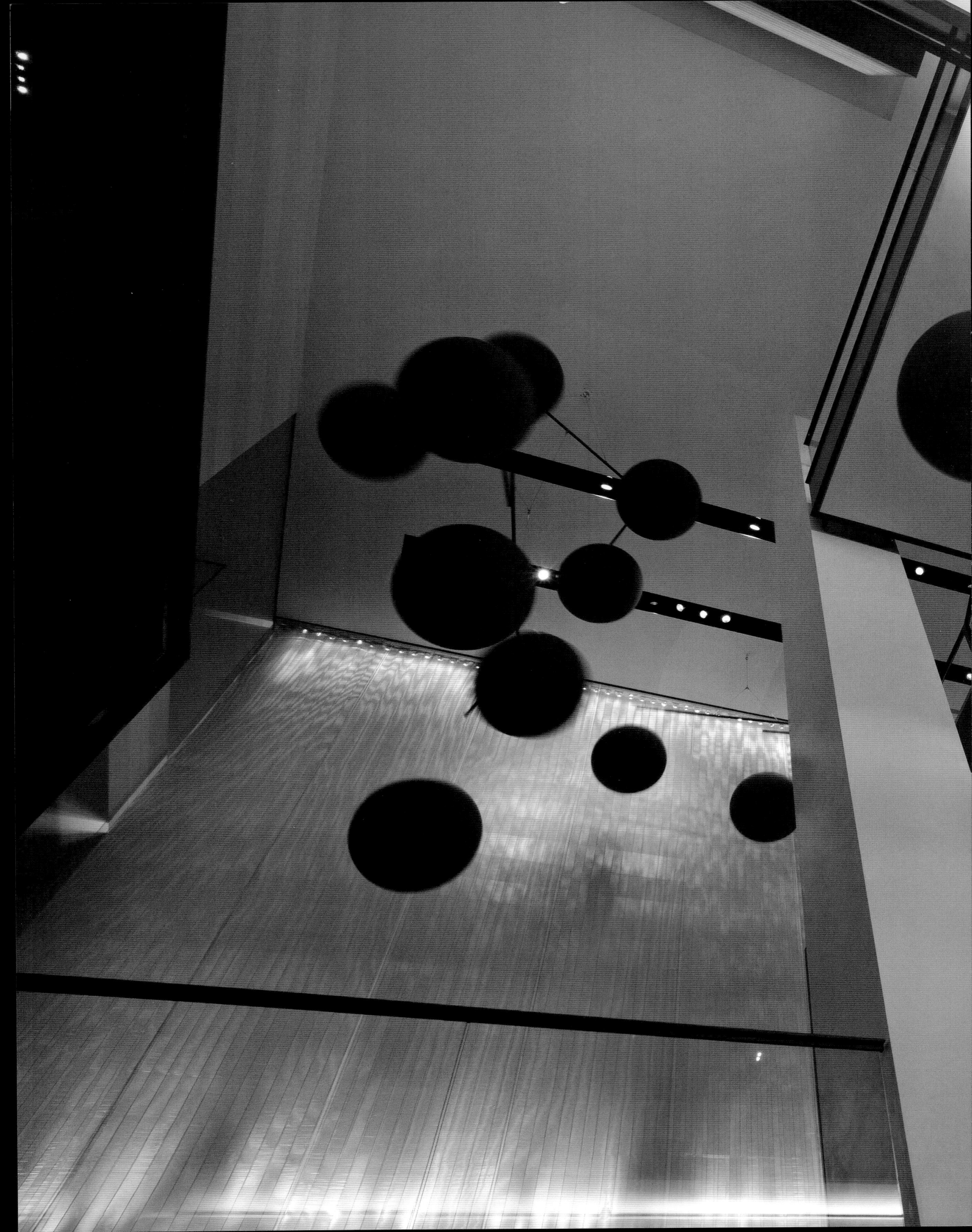

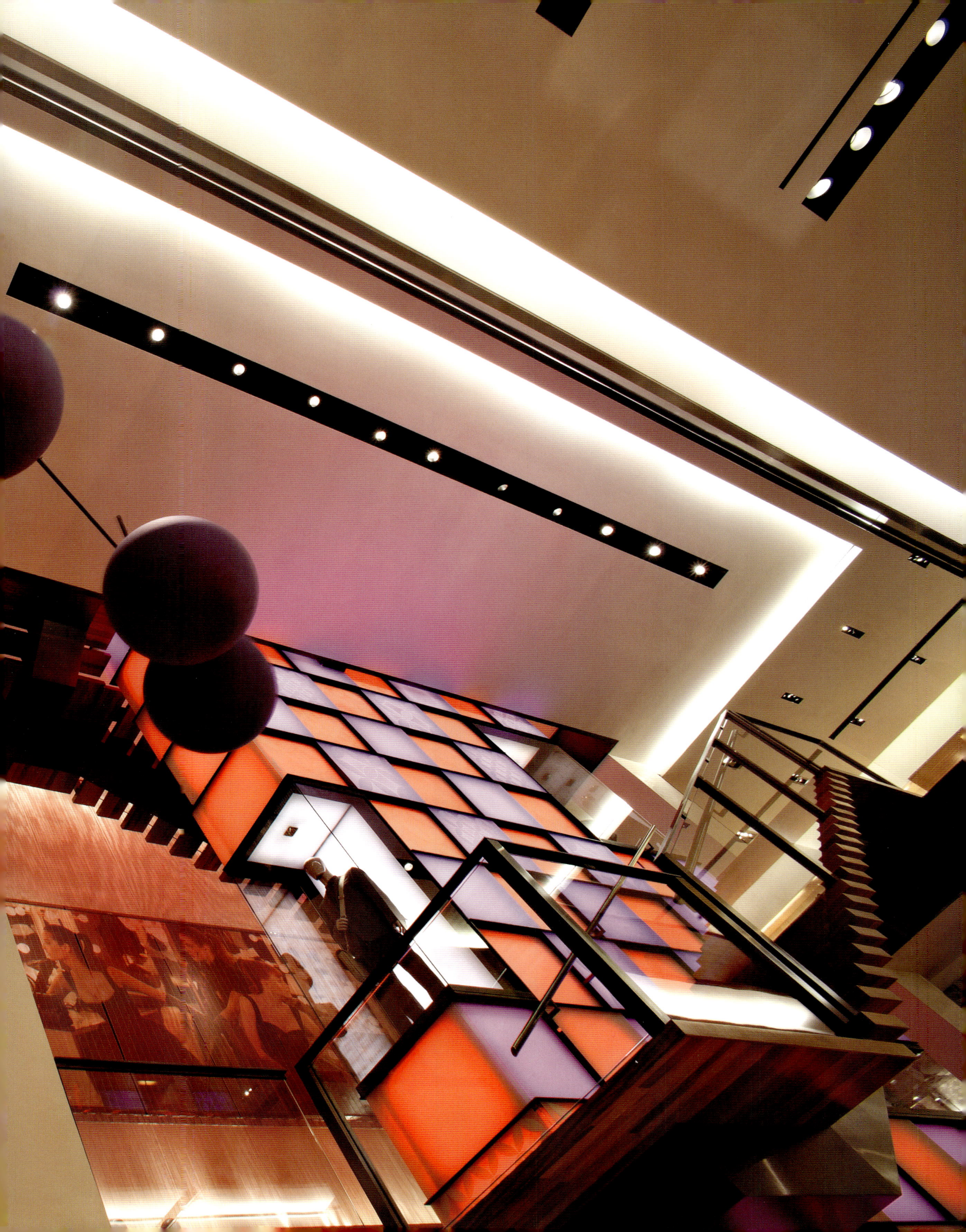

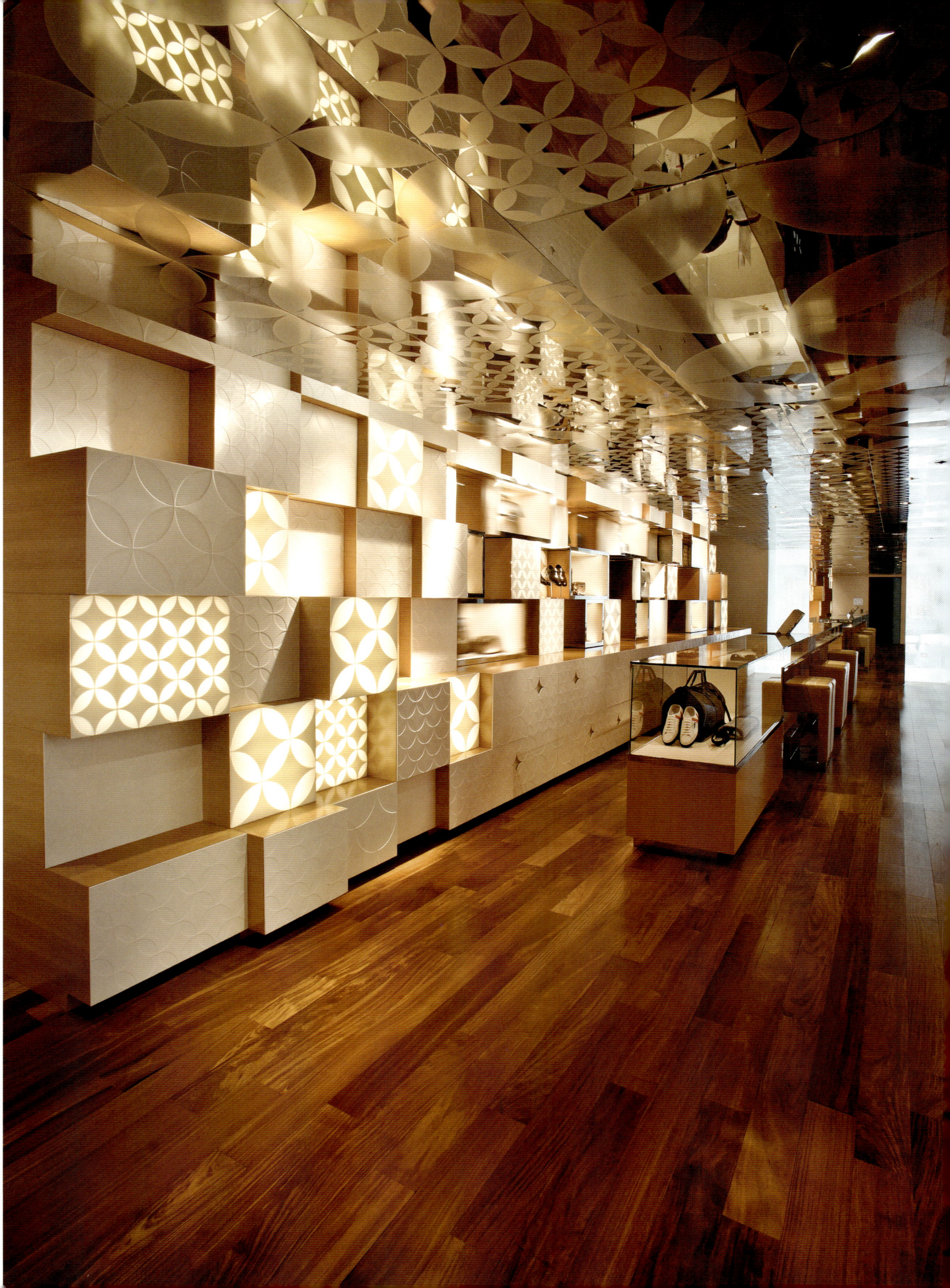

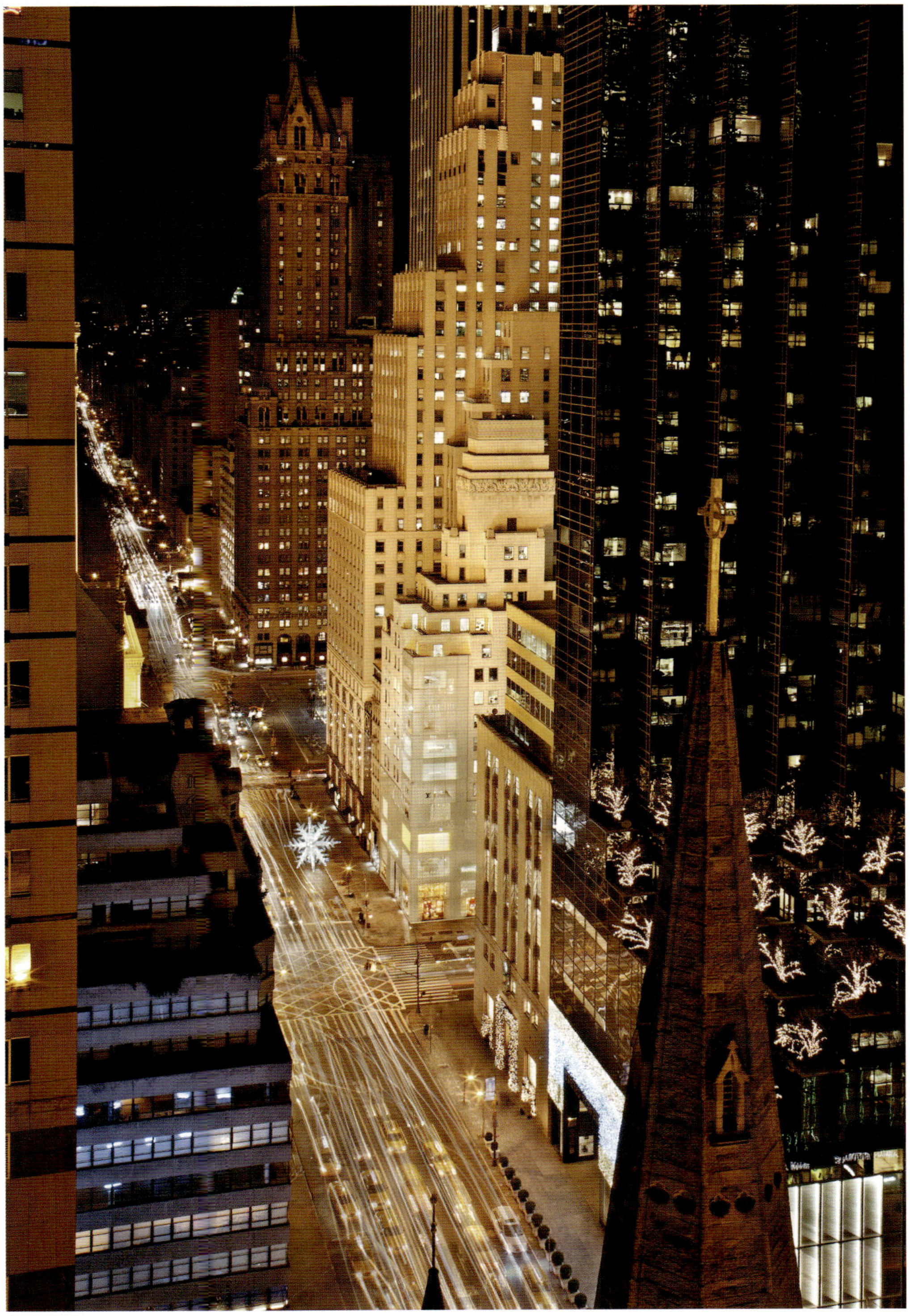

A CONVERSATION WITH DAVID MCNULTY AND MOHSEN MOSTAFAVI

MOHSEN MOSTAFAVI: Can you talk about the evolution of the architecture of Louis Vuitton? What are some of the key changes that have occurred since you joined the company?
DAVID MCNULTY: I started in 1996, which was a little time before Louis Vuitton enlarged its product offering. It was essentially a company selling goods for travelling—bags and suitcases. From 1997, when Marc Jacobs was hired to bring in a line of ready-to-wear and shoes into the company's product mix, it quickly became clear that the stores needed to be bigger because for years and years the stores were what used to be called "bowling alleys." They were the 1,000 sq. ft. store in a lot of shopping malls across America, quite a few in Japan at that stage, and several in South East Asia. The walls of these "bowling alleys" were lined with leather goods on each side and the customer would walk to the end and walk back out again and get involved across counters with the merchandise. Usually at the end of the store there would be a table to buy the more expensive items, such as the suitcases or luggage items. So with all these new products, as well as the rise of Japanese travel retail in the 1990s, the stores had to get bigger. Our business really exploded with the Japanese public in the late 1990s—that is why we expanded our network of stores there. The idea of having bigger stores, what we called "global stores" at the time became the challenge for us.

How did the architecture of the "global store" come about?
In the late 1990s we organized a competition for a project of a free-standing building in Japan. This is something we had never done before. It was a proposal that Eric Carlson and I made to the management in order to identify an architect with whom we could work not just on this project but potentially on others also. We knew then that we would need several stores in various locations. The competition was organized among five architecture firms, four Japanese and one French because our intention was to identify a Japanese architect for projects locally. And all but one did very classical schemes in stone with columns and pediments. They must have all expected that we were looking for a French building in Japan. But Jun Aoki was the only one to present us with something different—a very simple model of a double-layered system with a checkerboard pattern on both layers; one layer in glass and transparent, the other opaque. And by simply moving the little model he revealed the interest of this type of magical façade. He quickly transposed that idea into a building with vitrines, entrances, signage and so on. That became a real driving idea, not just for Nagoya, but for many other projects after that.

What was the nature of the subsequent collaboration between the Paris design office and Jun Aoki in Tokyo?
From that point we worked with Jun on a couple of projects and then developed a new idea ourselves. This in-house project was to translate the double-layer made of glass, which was very smooth and clean in appearance, into something more textured. The concept of texture was first explored in a building in Seoul, where we used metal mesh. This material reminded us, in an architectural way, of how the bags were originally woven. It wasn't a very flat and clean surface like glass but, like a weave, it was woven tightly. We collaborated on the fabrication of metal fabrics to allow us to create both a double-skin and the notion of texture. Jun took that idea into his projects, such as the Omotesando. But we still use glass and in New York, for example, we went back to the very smooth surface that Jun really wanted so that the surface of the Fifth Avenue building could align with the marble of the 1930s facade, which was very successful.

So it seems you go back and forth—there is an oscillation of the ideas depending on the specificity of the location.
At every stage we've tried to explore a new facet of how we exploit the idea of patterns and pattern making, how we exploit the idea of depth, and how we exploit the separation between the inside and outside. One criteria of our thinking was that as a commercial entity we need to make the interior attractive and to draw people in. We also aim to create a certain ambiance and a certain sense of being protected once inside. And that means protection from the noise of the street, the pollution, and the crowds outside. In order to achieve this sense of being protected, we developed the notion of a lining to the interior. This lining could be a treatment on a glass or a textured material or a physical construct such as the "skin" in Roppongi. The skin then became a device for pattern-making to reflect the brand itself. Trying to inspire ourselves from the history of the brand and its patterns has played an important part in our architecture.

So what are some of your current preoccupations?
Recently we've been more interested, through projects in Singapore and China, in developing and exploring ideas to do with the texturing of glass. Because I think it is all very well to make a metal mesh façade but, at the same time, we were very interested in introducing texture into glass instead of focusing solely on patterns. We'd like to explore the nature of glass in more detail, in particular that of molded glass. We have been working with the architecture firm Front Inc. in Singapore, for example, where they proposed a project with curved or folded glass like a curtain. The "curtain" was also

treated in a very physical way to transform the surface and in some ways modulates the condition between the outside and the inside. We have also explored at Chengdu and Shanghai IFC using texture to make patterns and create a pixel field that is readable at different scales and distances. This is different from the idea of glass façade as you would expect in a shop front. But rather we use glass as a building material to define opacity, which can be completely opaque or semi-opaque. This is where we are, at the moment, in maintaining our research with a greater sense of focus on the protection of the interior. I mention this in the book *Logique Visuelle* where in the movie *Breakfast at Tiffany's*, Holly Golightly, played by Audrey Hepburn says, "The reason I like Tiffany's is that once you are inside you feel no harm can come to you." And really this is the world of luxury that Vuitton is part of. Somehow, once you are inside a Louis Vuitton store, you can expect a certain security—a certain level of luxury and a sense of belonging. More and more our stores are giving us opportunities to create an emotion—not just the emotion of buying a beautiful object and having something you will treasure and pass to the next generation, but also an emotion where the experience of the visit is more than just a customer going into a store.

What are some of the examples of ways in which you are developing strategies for creating the appropriate ambiance for creating the desired emotional response?
The experience should be more like going into a space the visitor can discover artwork and be excited by other creative works that have been commissioned for that space. We've had James Turrell at the Champs Élysées store designing a work that is specifically made for that space. We are already looking to the possibility of working with James again in another space. The ideas could also be simple, like hanging a piece of art or placing another in a space as an additional level of excitement and in a way distraction. We've of course also been working with Murakami and with artists like Tim White who has designed a video wall. We would love to do an art space in China because we feel there is a world of Chinese artists to explore. The opportunity to provide our visitors the sensations and emotions that the art world can create is really fantastic. There are not a lot of companies which can do that.

It seems that one of the developments within LV has been the one between the visual identity of the brand and its relationship to the visual experience of the visitor. From the beginning it has always been the movement of the body that helps animate the building as a sign.
Well, the very first real project that attracted us was the kinetic effect of the optical illusion, or the optical transformation, that took place with the double-layer system of patterns. And of course that can be done in many ways, but in our case was done with a checkerboard pattern superimposed on the second layer. That was the first contact with the audience. This idea was transposed a little bit into what would happen if we created a see-through effect and tried to keep some layer or opacity or effect ongoing. For example, what would happen if we played with a mirror? What would happen if we lit the façade in a different way? Then somebody said, well, why don't we introduce one-way mirrors and try different tricks? Polarizing glass was another idea. So the process had involved many small experiments. In one of our recent stores in Shanghai, which we opened recently, it was the incredible experience of light that helped define the finely decorated space, because we had a lot of beautiful furniture and other furnishings which were really quite richly done.

By now you have been working with a fashion company for a long time; what are some of the key issues for you in terms of the reciprocities between fashion and architecture?
I think architecture can be very good for fashion insofar as it is a way of expression—giving fashion the means to express its identity. Fashion creators, like Marc Jacobs, can really reinforce their own identity through architecture. Fashion can be very useful for architecture as well. I think fashion can put architecture back in the public spotlight, give it a space to exist in the minds of people. It's something that is very positive. But it should not come as a surprise, there has always been an important and fruitful relationship between merchants and architects. It is about creating something new in the world which is entirely about fashion, entirely about something that is ephemeral. And we'd like to think that we do something similar—that our architects benefit from the world of fashion. These large flagship stores in key cities are becoming a little bit like the way people used to go to museums or galleries. I think the retail world in general and fashion houses in particular can use architecture, and architects can use them, so it is a great mix.

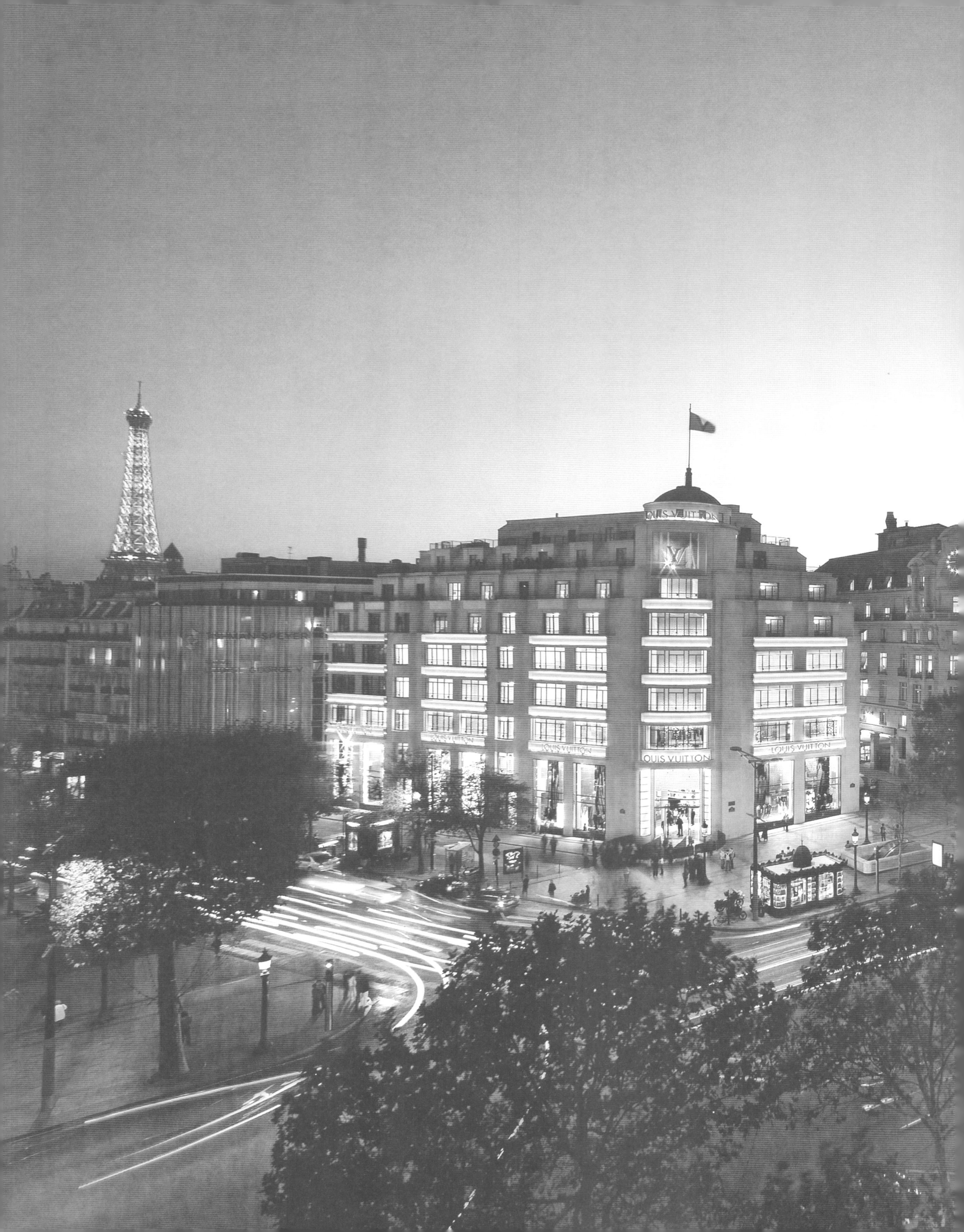
LOUIS VUITTON
LOUIS VUITTON
LOUIS VUITTON

EUROPE
UNITED KINGDOM, LONDON *NEW BOND STREET*
FRANCE, PARIS *CHAMPS-ELYSÉES*
FRANCE, *SAINT-TROPEZ*
ITALY, ROME *ETOILE*
RUSSIA, MOSCOW *GUM*

LONDON NEW BOND STREET

architects
LOUIS VUITTON
ARCHITECTURE DEPARTMENT;
PETER MARINO ARCHITECT
2010

text by
RAFAEL MAGROU

For two centuries, between Piccadilly Circus and Oxford Street, the Mayfair area has housed London's most elegant boutiques. Its principle artery, New and Old Bond Street, reserves the best locations for luxury brands; it is a veritable thoroughfare of honor where London taxis line up alongside sports cars. The luxury houses are all represented here, their logo-emblazoned flags announcing their presence above vitrines displaying bowler hats and leather boots, rivaling each other in chic. All but one—which has no need to unfurl a Union Jack like its neighbor, nor to deploy an ensign bearing its own coat of arms to hail the passers-by. Intimately linked to the British capital since 1885 (the first of its stores to open abroad was located on Oxford Street), Louis Vuitton's architecture concentrates all the necessary ingredients for affirming its identity within its form.

It was in 1998 that the brand opened the New Bond Street store; having quickly outgrown this space following the success associated with Marc Jacobs' arrival, the brand decided to expand and invest in the neighboring building. But how, on two anachronistic and untouchable façades, could they present the colors and monogram of their brand's identity? Opening at the end of May 2010, the House occupies two radically different edifices: one, on the corner of New Bond Street and Clifford Street, is in the Art Deco style and was already occupied by Louis Vuitton, while the other, a recent extension, is classical in its details, in an Edwardian style dating from the end of the 19th century. "The great difficulty was to unite the two façades in one single unified element, identifiable as such, while still respecting the specific characteristics of their heritage," explains David McNulty, the director of the Architectural Department at Louis Vuitton in Paris. A subtle graphic banner of interlacing monograms on the upper lintel creates the union between the two buildings. But the essential, seamless stitching together of the spaces occurs in the interior. Like the brand's leather products, the lining is as important as the visible outer layers.

Respecting the precedent of the work executed for the Champs-Élysées store, the architect Peter Marino performed a sort of surgical operation, both complex and sensitive, creating a universe that preserves the sense of scale and meaning. A giant, ten-meter-tall gauze of metallic flowers stitches the two buildings together across the length of each floor. After several months of work, no scars remained; the graft was a perfect success. The brass discs can be seen on the outside through the multiple storefront windows—now linked—like a shimmering, interior skin that forms the background for the display, giving it an iridescent quality. The azure sky makes the light seem closed inside; as it passes it enchants the ensemble, making it incredibly attractive. The effect is poetic; the parts, alternately shedding their petals, seem to say: "she loves me, she loves me not…" After the Parisian address, which is already very expressive in its textures, New Bond Street exponentially multiplies the range of materials, making this boutique the most luxurious Louis Vuitton store in the world to date. The composition employs all the superlatives where obsession, temptation and accumulation are concerned. The 1,520 square meters exhibit an incredible—almost shocking—collection of wood, stones, and textiles. Peter Marino's dexterity succeeds in combining this assortment to create a sort of cabinet of curiosities without slipping into bad taste or overindulgence; it is simply opulence operating as a synonym for luxury. Nevertheless, he obliges us from time to time with the odd note of British kitsch.

A veritable laboratory of the senses is deployed here: Turkish marble floors with marquetry in anigre wood, white Portland stone, Limra sandstone or Tivoli stone, cumaru, afromosia and other exotic woods, Corian ceilings forming the Louis Vuitton monogram, display shelves clothed in leather, lacquered wood and silk carpeting… and everything in the right dosage. Luxury is combined here with space and rarity. On one side, the seven windows installed in the existing frames benefit from this double height, with giraffes or long-necked ostriches stretching from one floor to the other. On the other, it is the impressive compartments that have accompanied modernity throughout the company's 150 years: suspended by cables, gilded titanium plates hold the famous trunks in this inspired emptiness. Coupled with more recent pieces, they offer a sort of historical shortcut—a tongue in cheek touch that gives the experience of shopping a lighter note. As the New York architect, dressed entirely in leather with his Cuban cap and sunglasses, explains: "while certain stores take themselves too seriously, we want to make our clients smile." Permission is granted in Queen Elizabeth's country, where humor is second nature. Something falsely frivolous emanates from this transformed address.

Surprising effects appear one after another at the London *maison*. The sense of depth, for

example, is impressive. These linking sequences enthrall the visitor, each one differentiated in their format, their form, their texture, and, of course, in their collection of products. It is enough to make heads spin, and hearts break. On the ground floor, we find women's leather goods near the entrance, then pass by the jewelry and watches whose treasured arrangements give Louis Vuitton its noble ranking in this competitive market, finally arriving at the brand's outstanding bags. The space curves around to receive accessories and sunglasses, framing the Bag Bar. These units create visual spirals, with one composing a whirling planetary system, and the other creating a ceiling in slats that evoke the eye's iris.
In the interstitial space between the shining façade and the three levels, a videographic staircase forms a vector transitioning towards the men's section in the courtyard area, or the women's section upstairs. The descending and ascending views each offer a tonal range associated with their respective characters: the lower level creates its ambience with leather club chairs on dark oak flooring, and the second floor is blond and ivory with a silky, slightly golden essence, finished with pale anigre wood. As for the library, it occupies an autonomous space on the first floor. Tented by illuminated vaulting, the intensity of which is adjustable for events, it exhibits the featured works to their best advantage as their covers compose thematic and stylistic arrangements. Two, large, horizontal vitrines display reading stands and, under the glass, limited edition copies. Again, there is a persistent visual quality that evokes the blurred colors of a Turner painting.

The concept for the second floor is the collector's apartment, with several salons and dressing rooms, transcending the status of a VIP room. The space is a first in the history of Louis Vuitton; it has inspired a furious desire to repeat the experience in their other *maisons*.

Here, the client is the host; better yet, he feels at home. Comfortably installed in the soft sofas with a bird's eye view of the street, protected by textile coverings and surrounded by walls enrobed in silk and gold, he is in close contact with the pieces from the Vuitton collection as they invite him on multidimensional journeys. The walls exhibit art by Hans Hartung (*T1985 H12*), Bertrand Lavier (*Atomium détail n°10 and IBO*), Richard Prince (*The Blue Cowboys*), Jean-Michel Basquiat (*Napoleonic stereotype circa 44*) and the couple Gilbert & George (*NET*). Similarly, other works grace the other floors—albeit more publicly—such as *KIKI* by Takashi Murakami or the Medical Cabinet by Damien Hirst, in black Nomad leather with deep blue microfiber lining, created with Louis Vuitton as a charitable work benefiting the British Red Cross. This art collection is not a whim, but rather a historical anchor with the founder's interest in contemporary art; in fact, in 1874, he took his son, Georges, to visit Félix Nadar's studio, where the photographer was showing the works of Monet, Renoir, Cézanne and Degas, who were banished from the official Salon. One hundred thirty-five years later, it is London that boasts the liveliest artistic scene in the world. With its numerous galleries and artists of international renown, London offers the ideal environment for developing the Louis Vuitton Young Art Project. This communal initiative unites five of the city's galleries and museums (Hayward Gallery, Royal Academy of Arts, South London Gallery, Tate Britain and Whitechapel Gallery) with the aim of encouraging artistic vocations, under the leadership of British artists like Tracey Emin, Anish Kapoor, and Gary Hume. Here, they have all they need to maintain this intimate, necessary—and sometimes hysterical—state of panic in the streets of London, and more precisely on New Bond Street, where the new Louis Vuitton *maison* has made its mark.

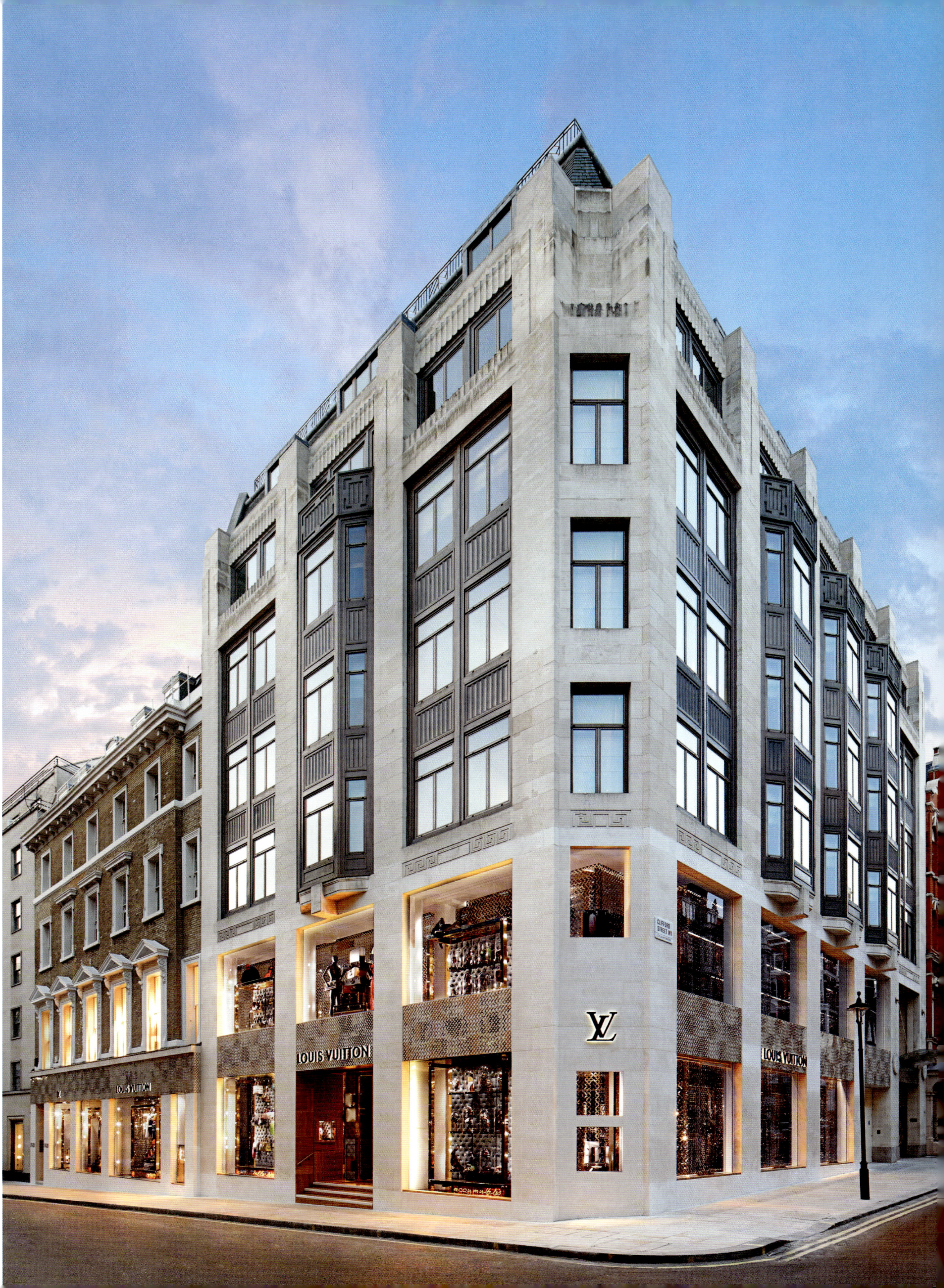
LOUIS VUITTON
LOUIS VUITTON
LOUIS VUITTON

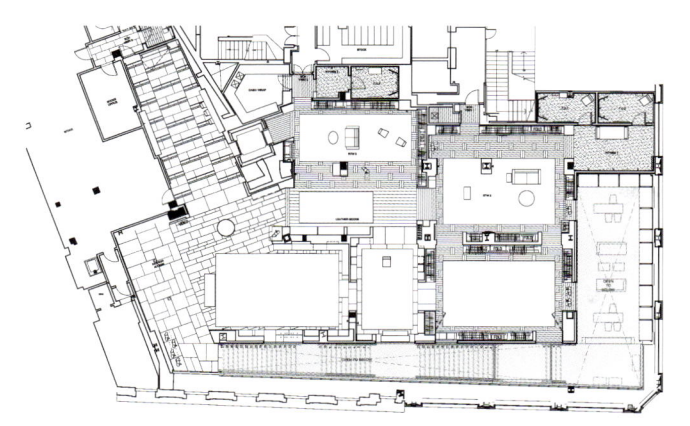

2ND FLOOR

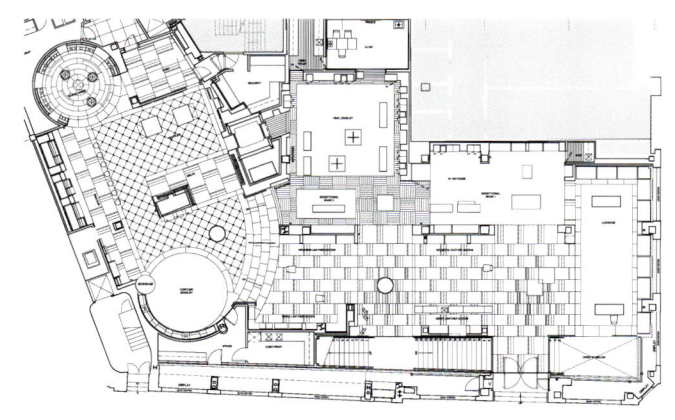

GROUND FLOOR

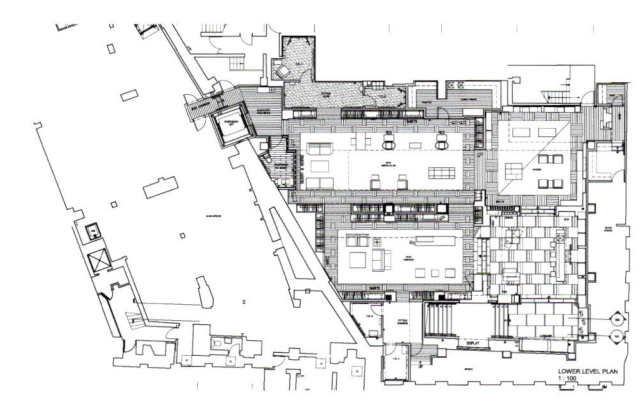

BASEMENT FLOOR

p. 142 Maison Louis Vuitton Champs-Élysées
p. 145 view of façade on New Bond Street
p. 146 view of exterior from the corner of New Bond Street & Clifford Street
p. 148 interior view of the luggage area and wall of trunks
p. 149 sunglasses room
p. 150 main staircase from 2nd floor plan to basement
p. 151 top: VIP apartment view with artwork by Hans Hartung, *T1985H12* (1985)
p. 151 bottom: watches and jewelry area
p. 152 mens collections with artwork by Gilbert and George, *Paws* (2005)
p. 153 top: bookstore
p. 153 bottom: interior detail with artwork by Takashi Murakami, *Kiki* (2000)
p. 154 interior view with detail of mesh screen
p. 155 women's changing area

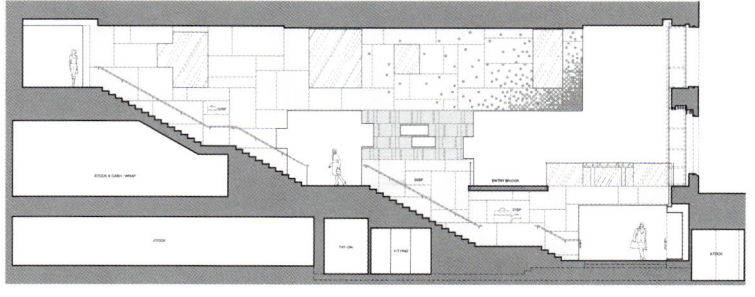

SECTION LOOKING EAST

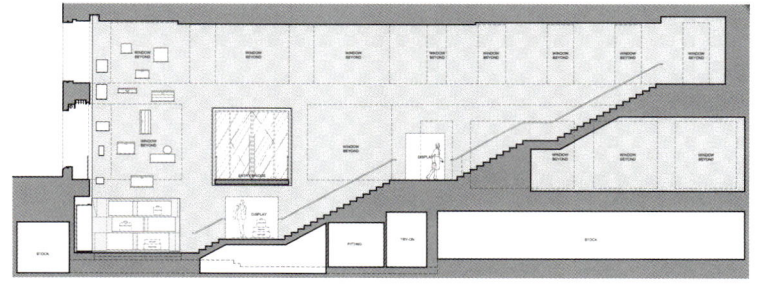

SECTION LOOKING WEST

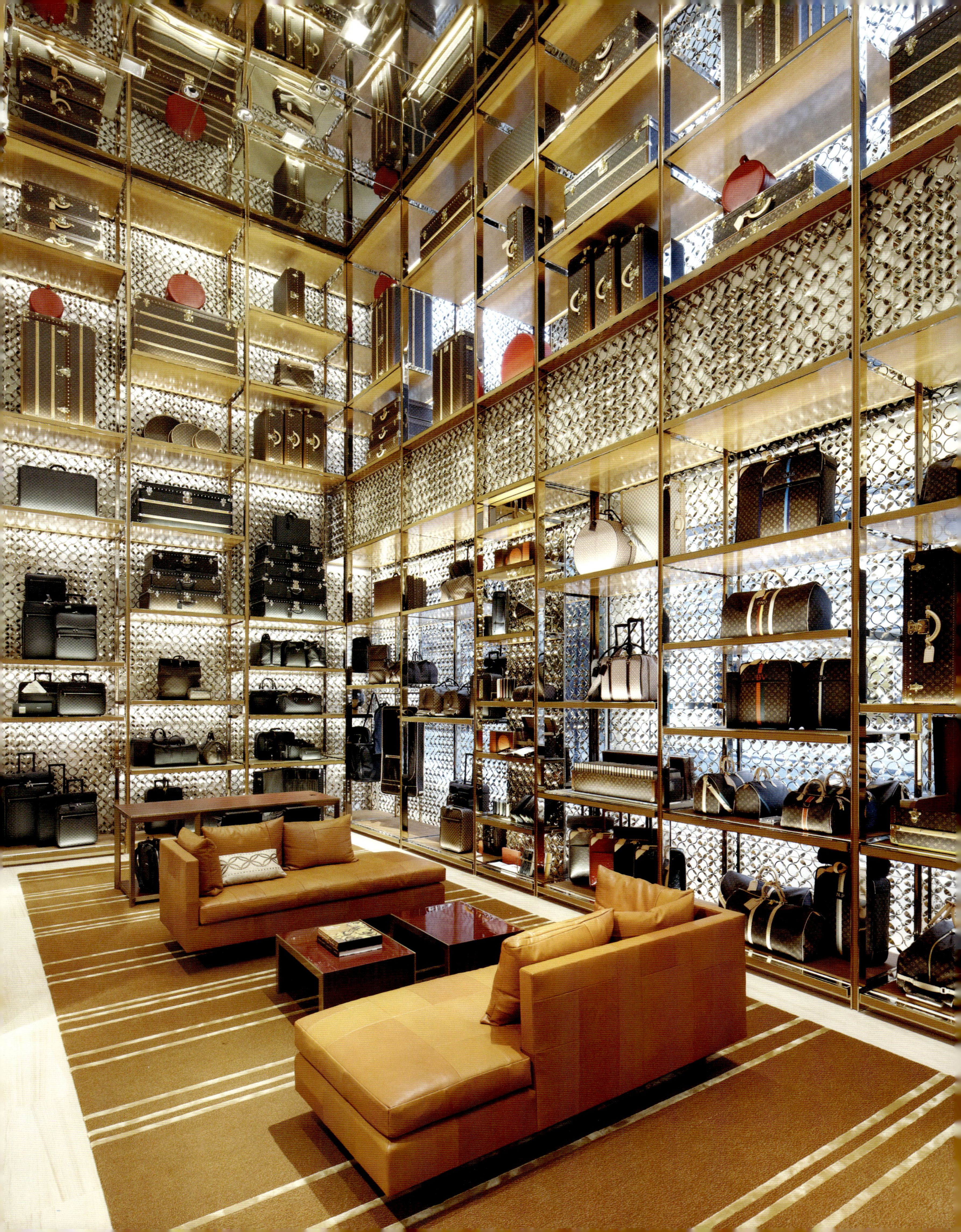

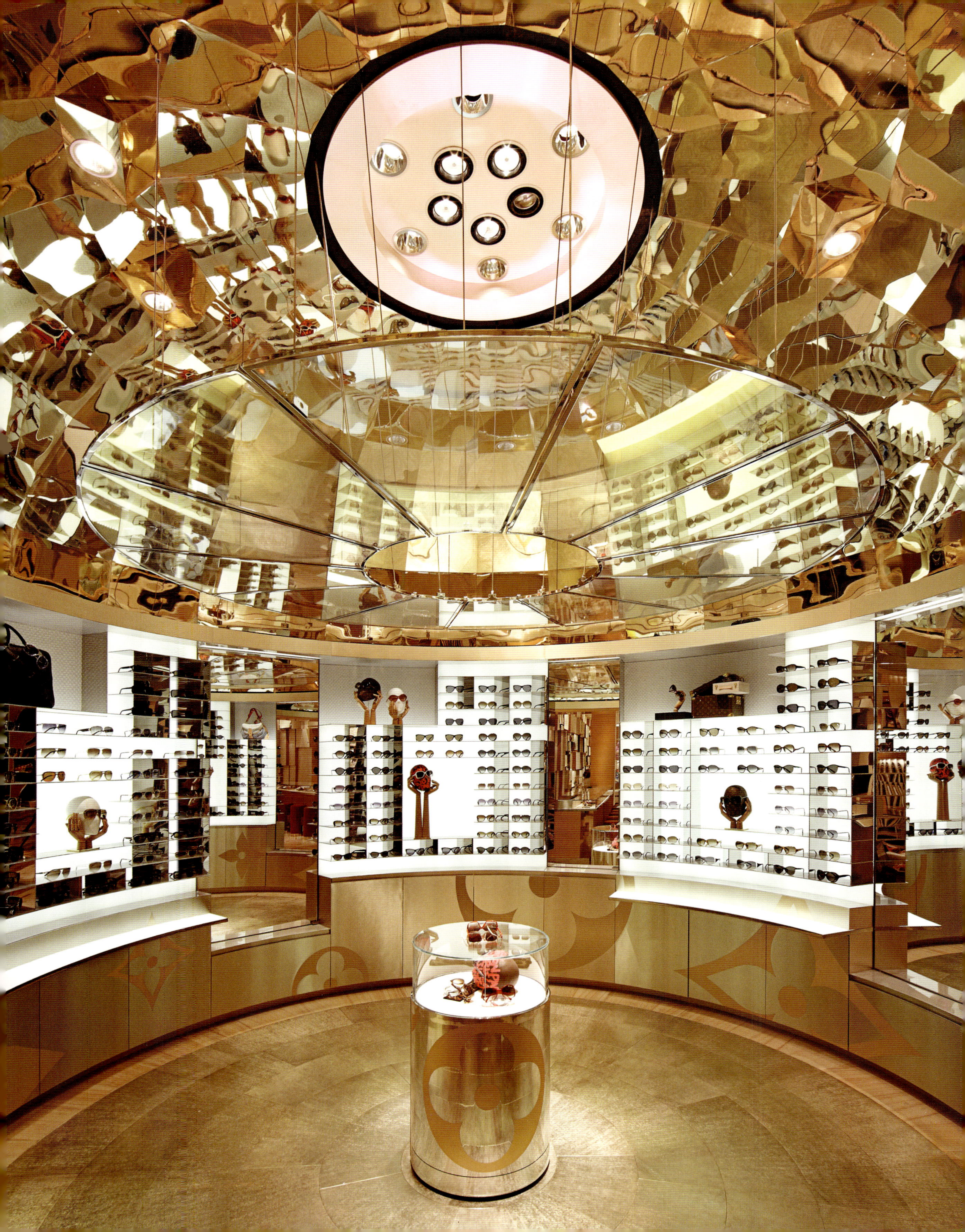

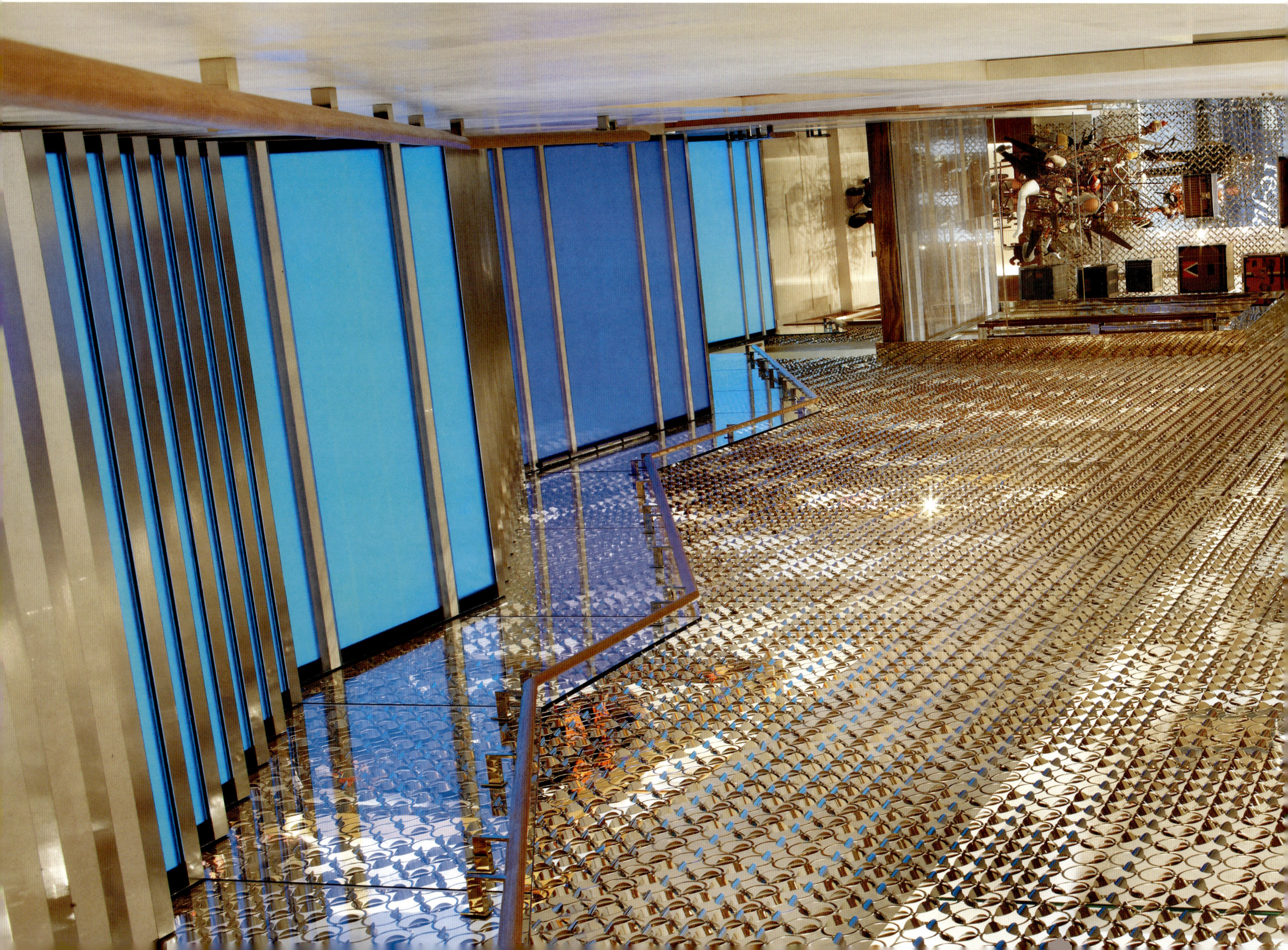

ARCHITECTURE AND INTERIORS 151

LONDON NEW BOND STREET

EUROPE

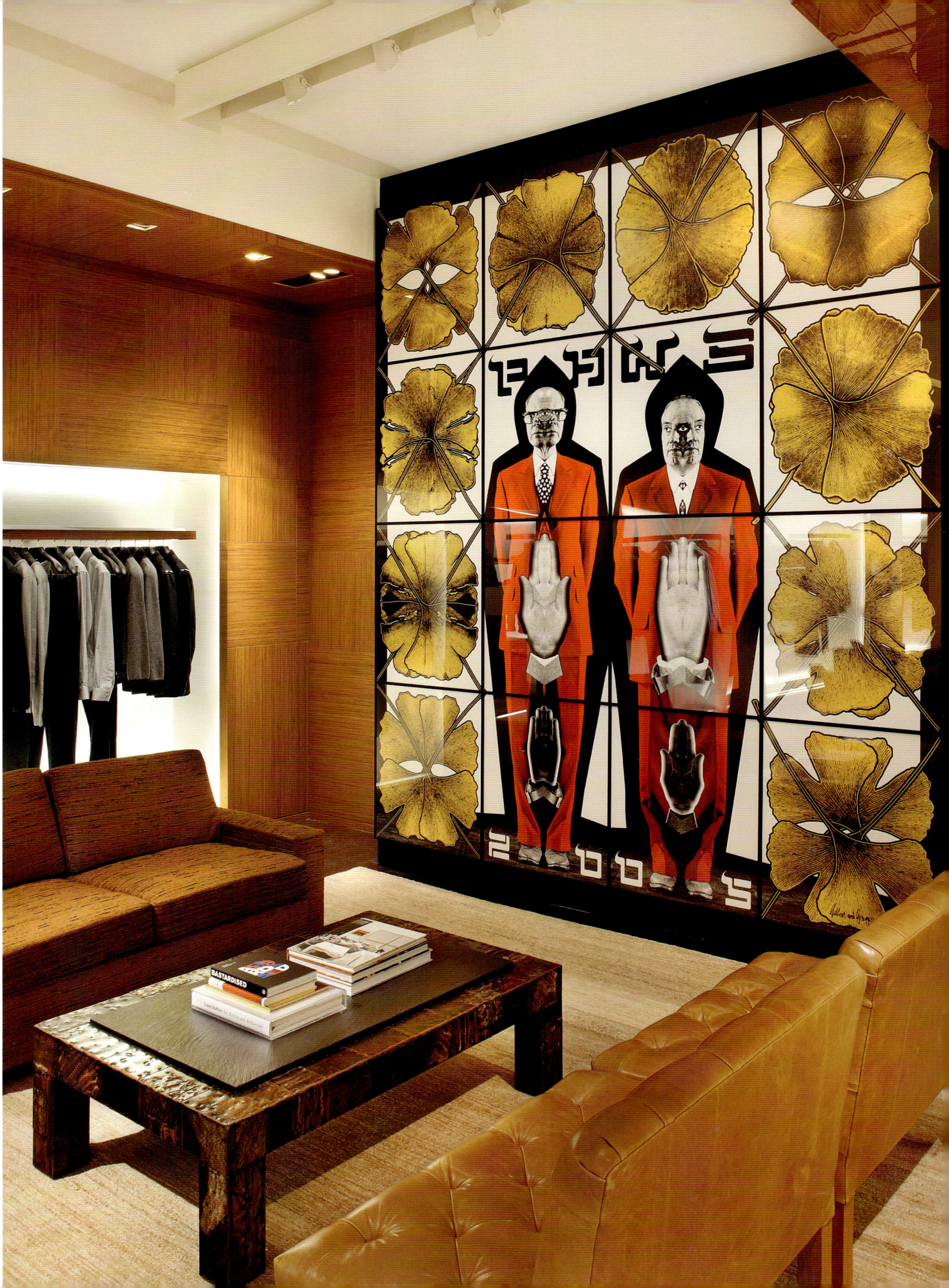
BASTARDISED

ARCHITECTURE AND INTERIORS 153

LONDON NEW BOND STREET

EUROPE

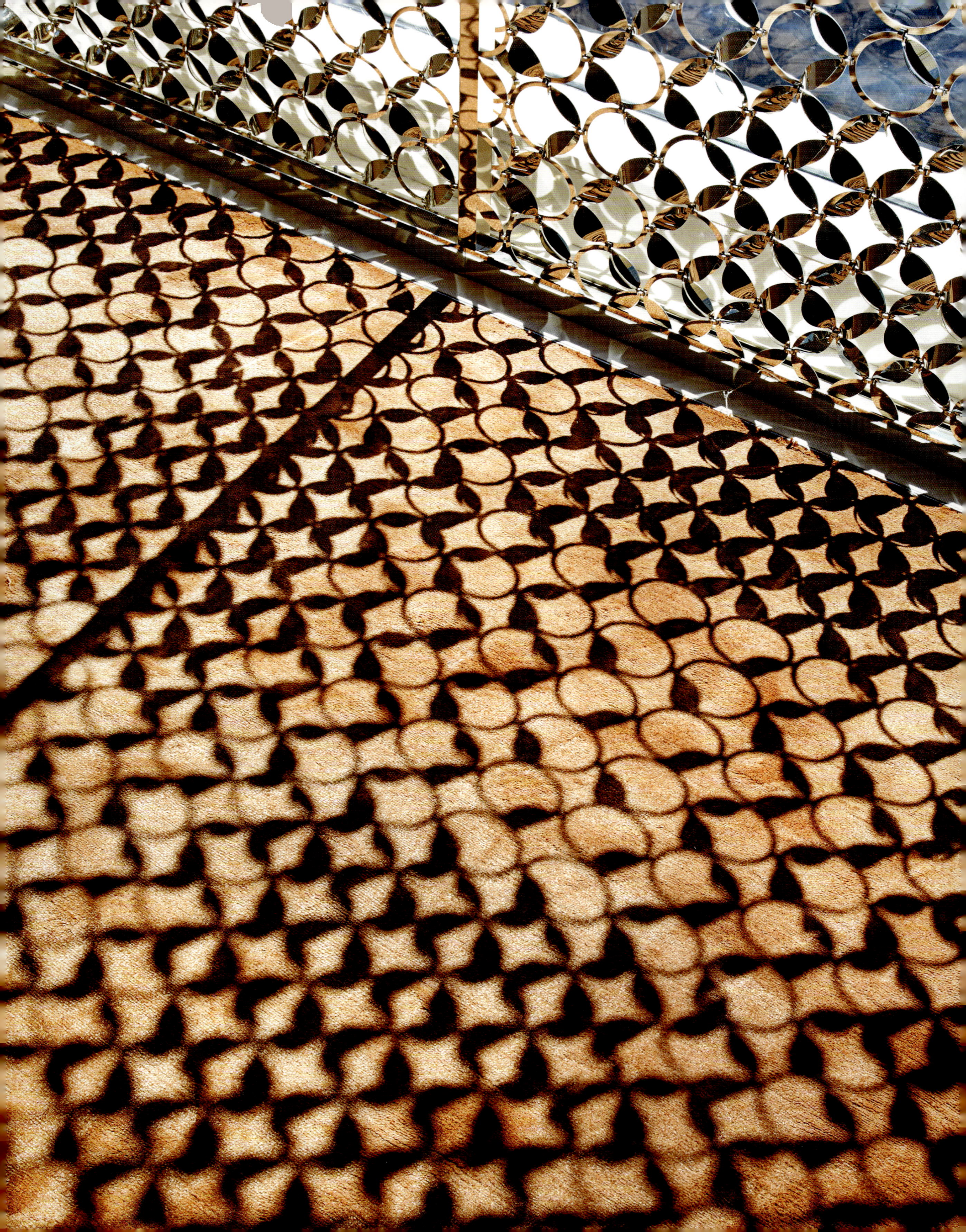

ARCHITECTURE AND INTERIORS

LONDON NEW BOND STREET

PARIS CHAMPS-ÉLYSÉES

architects
PETER MARINO ARCHITECT;
CARBONDALE
2005

text by
RAFAEL MAGROU

Louis Vuitton has come a long way since 1914, when its first boutique opened at number 70 on the Champs-Élysées in Paris. But it hasn't lost sight of what's important: respecting tradition and not renouncing the city that first fostered its growth as early as 1854, with addresses on 4, Rue Neuve-des-Capucines and later on Rue Scribe. It therefore comes as no surprise that in 2005, on the occasion of its 150th anniversary, Louis Vuitton chose the "most beautiful avenue in the world" for its flagship store, returning home after a stint on Avenue Marceau between 1954 and 1998. In 1998, it was at number 101—a lucky palindrome—that the 1,000 square-meter space was unveiled, welcoming all the brand's creations: trunks, suitcases, travel luggage, office accessories and, exclusively, the studio's first *prêt-a-porter* collection. The interior was already designed by Peter Marino, a genius at capturing the brand's DNA and translating the excellence at the root of its fame. History was repeating itself; designed in 1931 to house the Maison de France, or French tourist office, the building is pure Art Deco-style with its tiers and tower that connects the avenues. It was all symbolic, since Gaston-Louis Vuitton, Louis' grandson, was the vice president of a committee for the 1925 *Exposition Internationale des Arts Décoratifs*, which would lend its name to the eponymous building style.

The façades wrap around the corner of the legendary avenue and the no less celebrated Avenue Georges V, remodeled by the head architect of civilian buildings and national palaces, Jean-Loup Roubert, who had spearheaded the restoration of the Grand Palais and the Opéra Garnier. On the first two levels, the existing girth no longer sufficed to accommodate the company's rapid growth after the arrival of Marc Jacobs. Ideally, the brand would have invested fully in the project and made the building a visible epitome of Louis Vuitton, but it was impossible to touch the outer shell. Eric Carlson, the architect in charge of the spatial reinvention of the premises, therefore decided to create a mesh lining covering all the store's levels. Originally invented for the Roppongi store in Tokyo, this lace composed of Monogram flowers consists of an organic structure that allows light to filter through, like the foliage of neighboring trees. 110,000 units were assembled incorporating no less than 27,000 inlays of porcelain, aubergine leather, wenge wood, titanium and colored glass, weaving together to form the backdrop of thirteen, lofty windows. The large-scale, multicolored customization is not only a simple decorative device. "The mesh defines spatial areas and accompanies movement," Carlson explains. For example, when crossing to reach the room dedicated to jewelry, which is covered in silver leaves, the mesh changes in appearance: "encrusted with precious materials, it evokes Louis Vuitton's tradition of craftsmanship." Carlson did not simply expand the façade with this perforated element; he fully redeveloped the interior structure of the establishment. This gigantic project was meant to restore the famous avenue's status as the, "chicest promenade of the French capital," a reputation that has been somewhat diminished over the years. Carriages and sedans have disappeared in favor of heavy traffic and noise, rendering the Avenue much less romantic than it was during the Second Empire, when it was at the height of its splendor.

In order to revive the grandeur of that era, Carlson envisioned creating a "promenade" inside the boutique's stony 1930's shell. This wasn't his first project with Vuitton; he had been intimately involved in other brand developments, notably in the incredible laboratory of Japan, and from these drew inspiration for Paris. Straight away, he sketched out his vision in which clients could stroll inside into a spiral form inspired by Frank Lloyd Wright's design for the Guggenheim Museum in New York. The reference was ambitious, and the execution proved to be colossal since it had to take into account the existing framework and floors without cracking the surface of the façade. Working at the scale of a building, with help from RFR engineers, Carlson toiled like a luthier at work on his musical instrument. He carved, hollowed and sculpted upstrokes and downstrokes until he reached the structure's true essence. He carved into the stony mass until he found the ideal resonator for the Louis Vuitton spirit, creating a circulation system that promoted fluid movement. After months of strenuous work, the succession of gently sloping tiers, reminiscent of the terraces of rice fields or retaining walls in the Mediterranean, produced a new landscape of overlapping levels, all fitting into a unified whole. Each tier offers a specific experience. Together, they form the complex and sophisticated spirit that is Louis Vuitton. This solution did not make the task simple for Peter Marino, who was again put in charge of renovating the interior. Of course, he worked closely with Carlson on the general concept and design, as well as with David McNulty and his in-house Architecture department. To ensure continuity, the interior paving adopts the motif of the avenue, using shades of brown and beige travertine. A range of noble materials are deployed such as essences of anigre, afromosia and wenge wood, epi leather, and stainless steel, all finished faultlessly—a reflection of the company's savoir-faire, whether in leather goods or architecture. The women's areas are accented with Jean Larivière's hand-colored photographs, which are tastefully installed throughout the store. Black shelves and furniture made of anigre and zebrano wood lead to the VIP dressing rooms. A rotunda is home to the women's prêt-a-porter line and looks out onto the Champs Élysées. Here, diverse worlds are strung together: business, casual and fashion. The mesh helps adorn the space, with strong wood accents embedded within.

A staircase, inlaid with checkerboard and mirror, creates a short cut for anyone in a hurry or, equally, for the adventurous. The library creates a break within this winding volume, the first of its kind and one which would serve as a model for other stores following the Champs-Élysées. Above the Bag Bar, on the mezzanine, lies the Book Bar, with its spinning lectern that presents, in addition to an extensive library, the latest releases in art, design, fashion and, of course, architecture.

One can gradually ascend into the store via the "promenade," but most prefer, as was expected, is to instead take the escalator to the fifth floor. This device, at 20 meters long, is framed by fiber optic panels that invite you to immerse yourself in contemporary video art (*Alpha*, by the video artist Tim White-Sobieski, and *Moving Through the Looking Glass* by the artist Haluk Akakce). It is a technological feat, incorporating 720,000 optic points that, in forty seconds (the time it takes to reach the top), immerse visitors in a visual satori. Another route, sought by the discerning client, involves taking an elevator directly from the ground floor to the seventh floor, which is dedicated to temporary installations of contemporary art, thus promoting an emerging generation of young artists. This apparatus, while usually a dull ride, was re-imagined by the Danish artist Olafur Eliasson who created a vectored space where the senses become weightless. There's no use describing it further, one has to experience it for oneself. James Turrell also contributed to the space, installing a luminous sculpture on the ground floor that radiates amid old trunks and other luggage with their unique five-combination locks capable of puzzling the most experienced detective. These pieces represented the first time that contemporary art was presented in a Vuitton store, an experiment that was followed with gusto—notably in London on New Bond Street, where Donald Judd is referenced in a geometric tower of trunks.

At the heart of the design, one cannot miss the atrium, a genuine cathedral at twenty meters above our heads, the equivalent of six stories! Hypnotic does not adequately convey the impression; in this vertical space hang nineteen hundred rods in polished stainless steel, which is, in its totality, the equivalent of almost nine miles of stalactites solidly secured to the ceiling. Their lengths vary and compose a semi-rotunda that is reflected in a vast mirror measuring almost two hundred sixty square meters. The experience is overwhelming. "No trip to Paris can overlook a visit to the Champs-Élysées. In the future, no visit to the Champs-Élysées can overlook a trip to Louis Vuitton," stated Yves Carcelle, chairman and CEO of Louis Vuitton Malletier at the flagship's inauguration. The 6,000 visitors that come on average per day would have to agree.

LOUIS VUITTON
LOUIS VUITTON
VUITTON
LOUIS VUITTON
LOUIS VUITTON

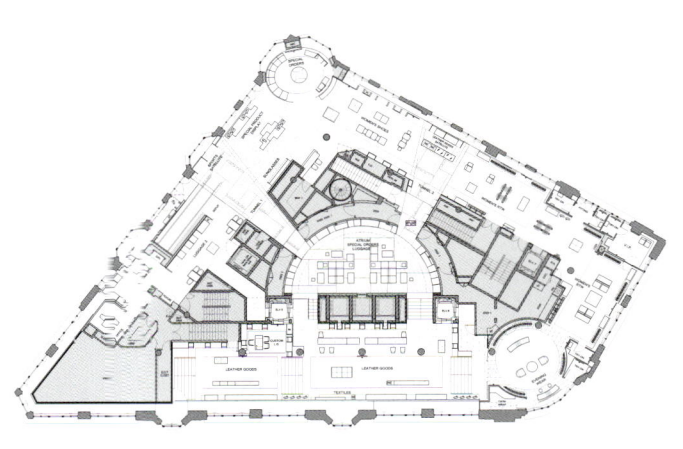

p. 157 windows at night with artwork
by Olafur Eliasson, *Eye See You* (2006)
p. 158 entrance on the corner of
Champs-Élysées and Avenue Georges V
p. 159 right column: entry sequence views

3RD FLOOR

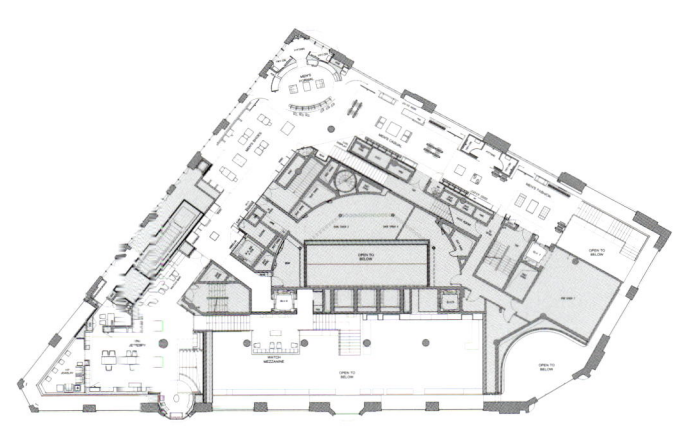

2ND FLOOR

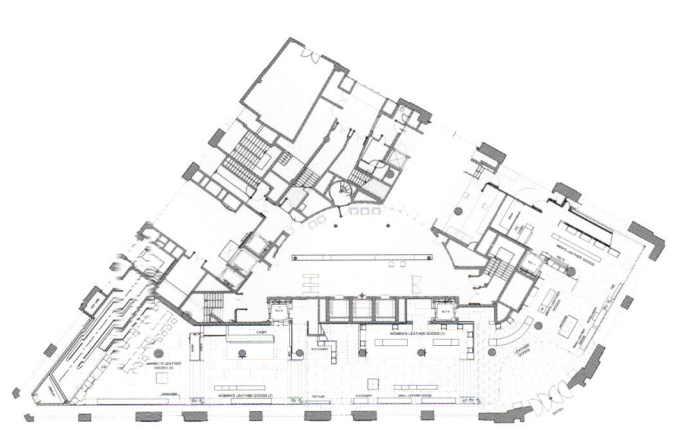

GROUND FLOOR

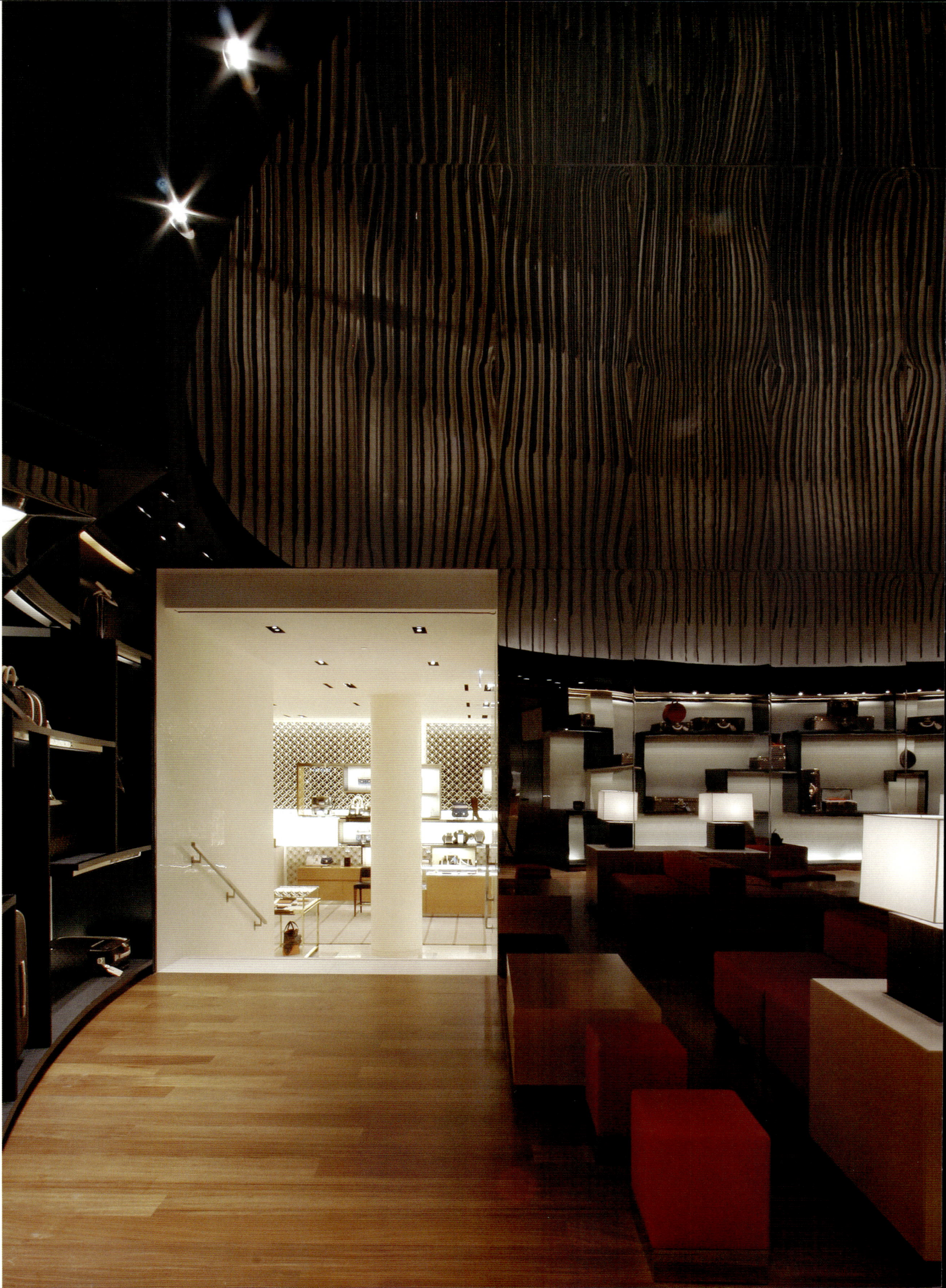

p. 160–161 top: view of atrium luggage area
p. 161 bottom: elevator by Olafur Eliasson,
Your Loss of Senses (2005) leading to the
Espace Culturel on the 7th floor
p. 162–163 ceiling of atrium at night
p. 164 top: view of interiors showing the
manipulation of trademark patterns in a variety
of materials; bottom: VIP jewelry atelier
p. 165 top: bookstore, bottom: VIP jewelry atelier
p. 166–167 Espace Culturel Louis Vuitton on
the top floor with photo-installation by Vanessa
Beecroft *VB 56* (2006)
p. 168 view into VIP room
p. 169 metal screen along ground floor retail area

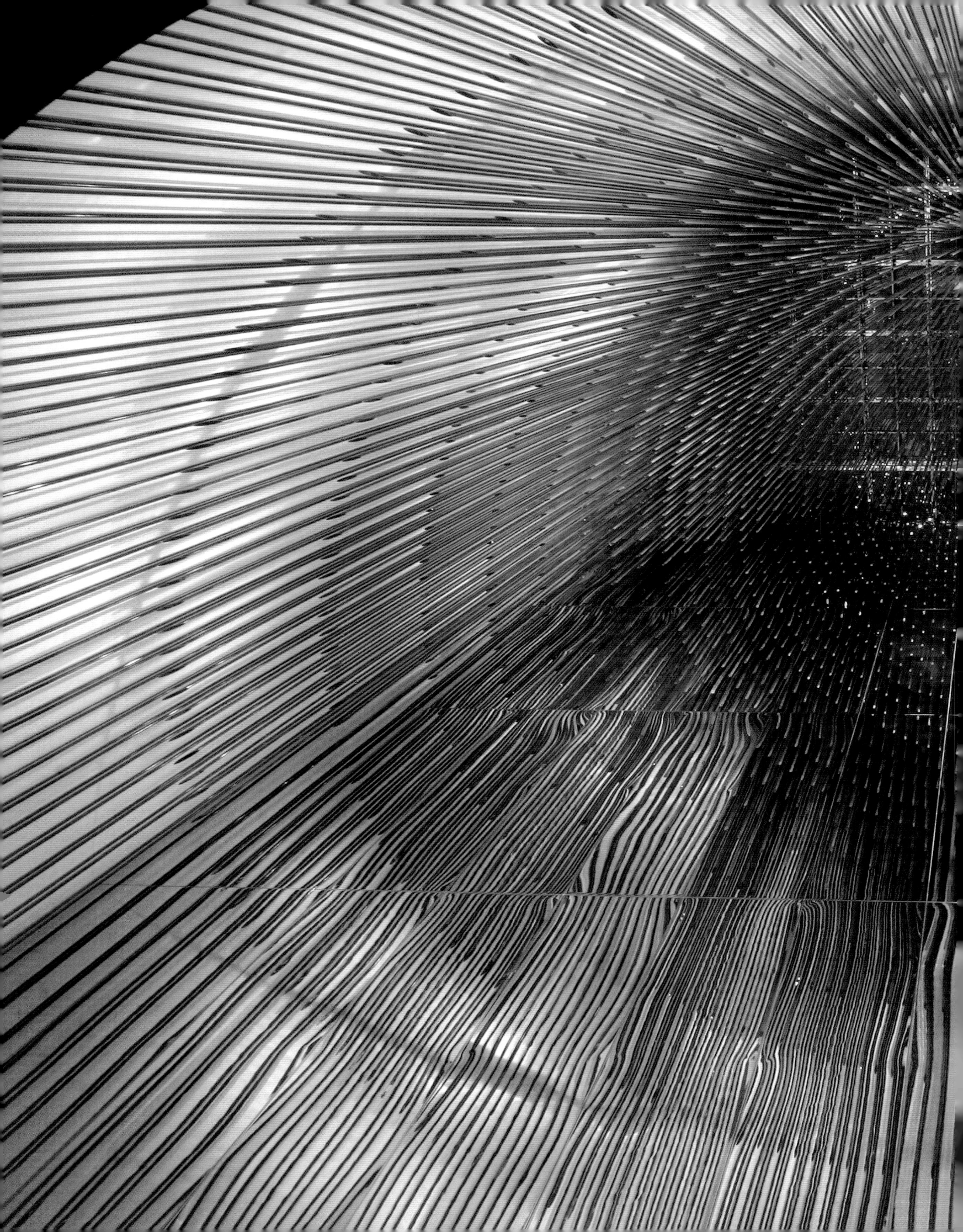

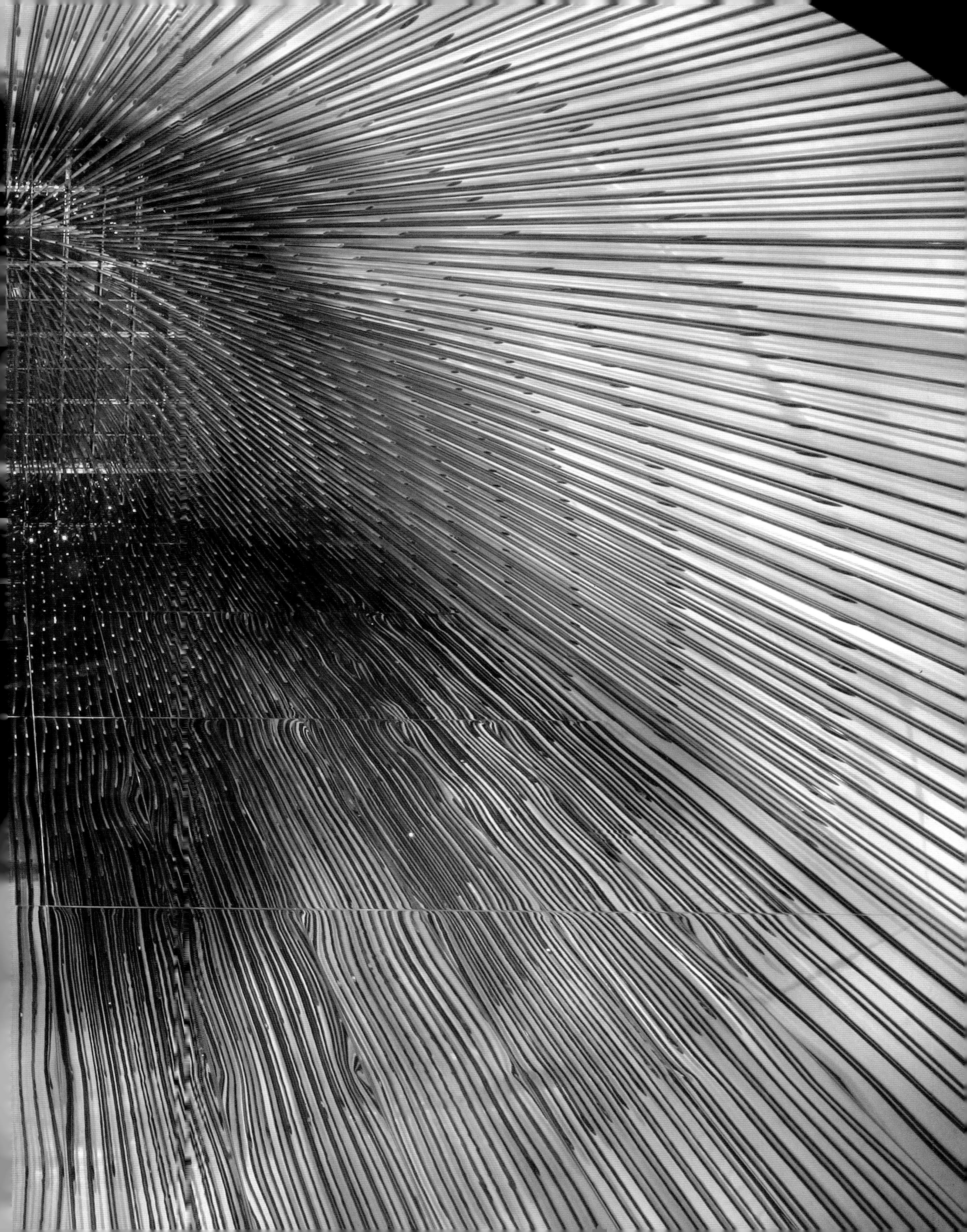

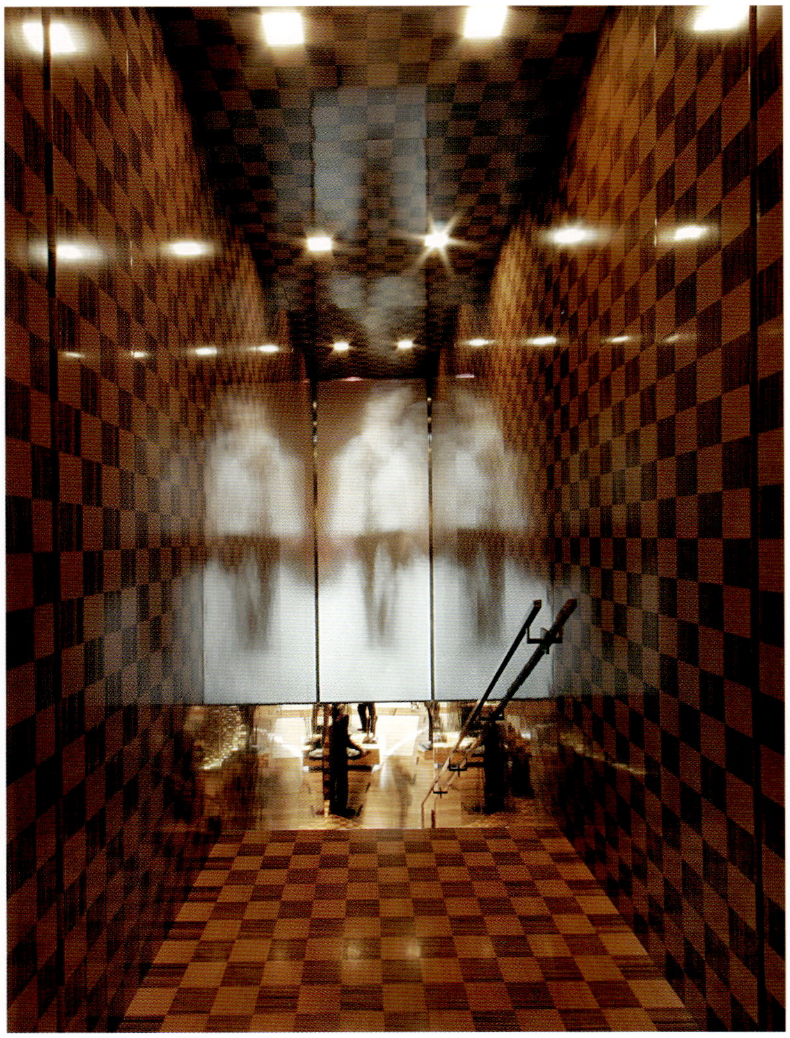

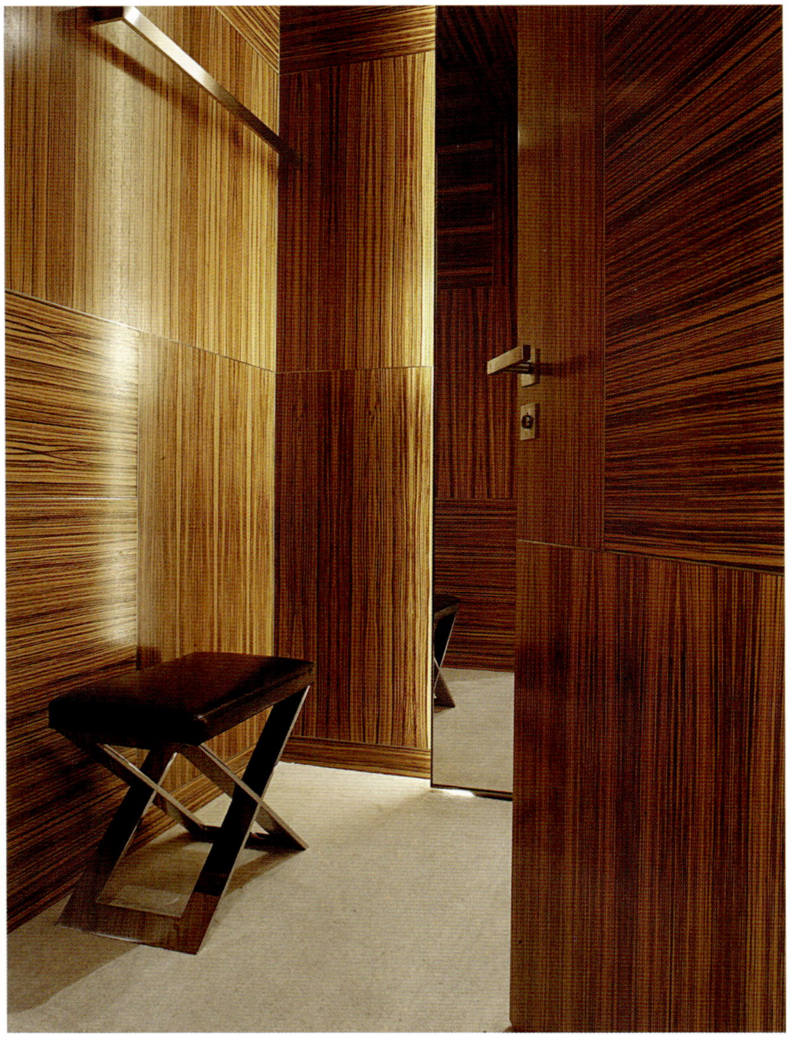

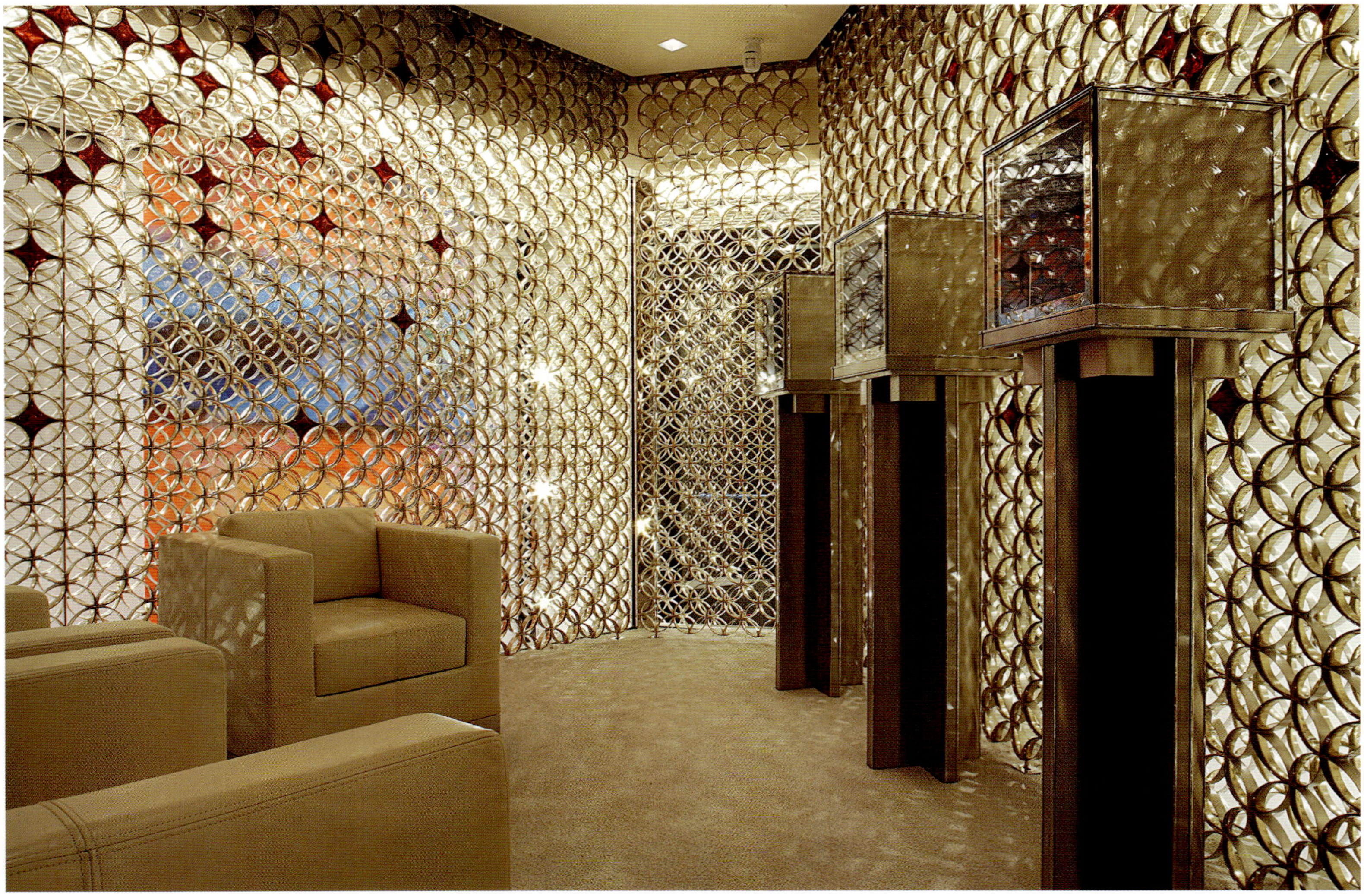

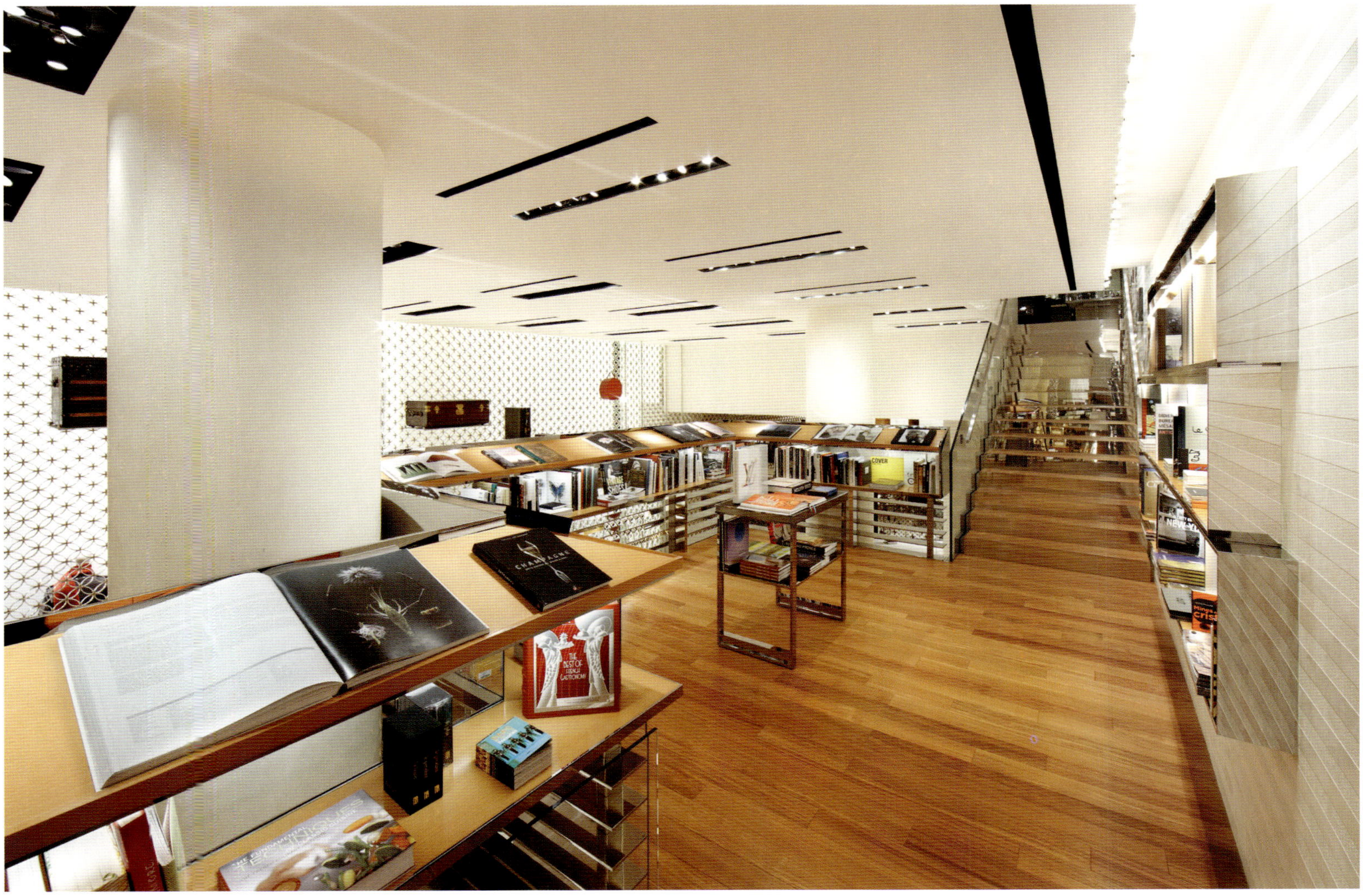

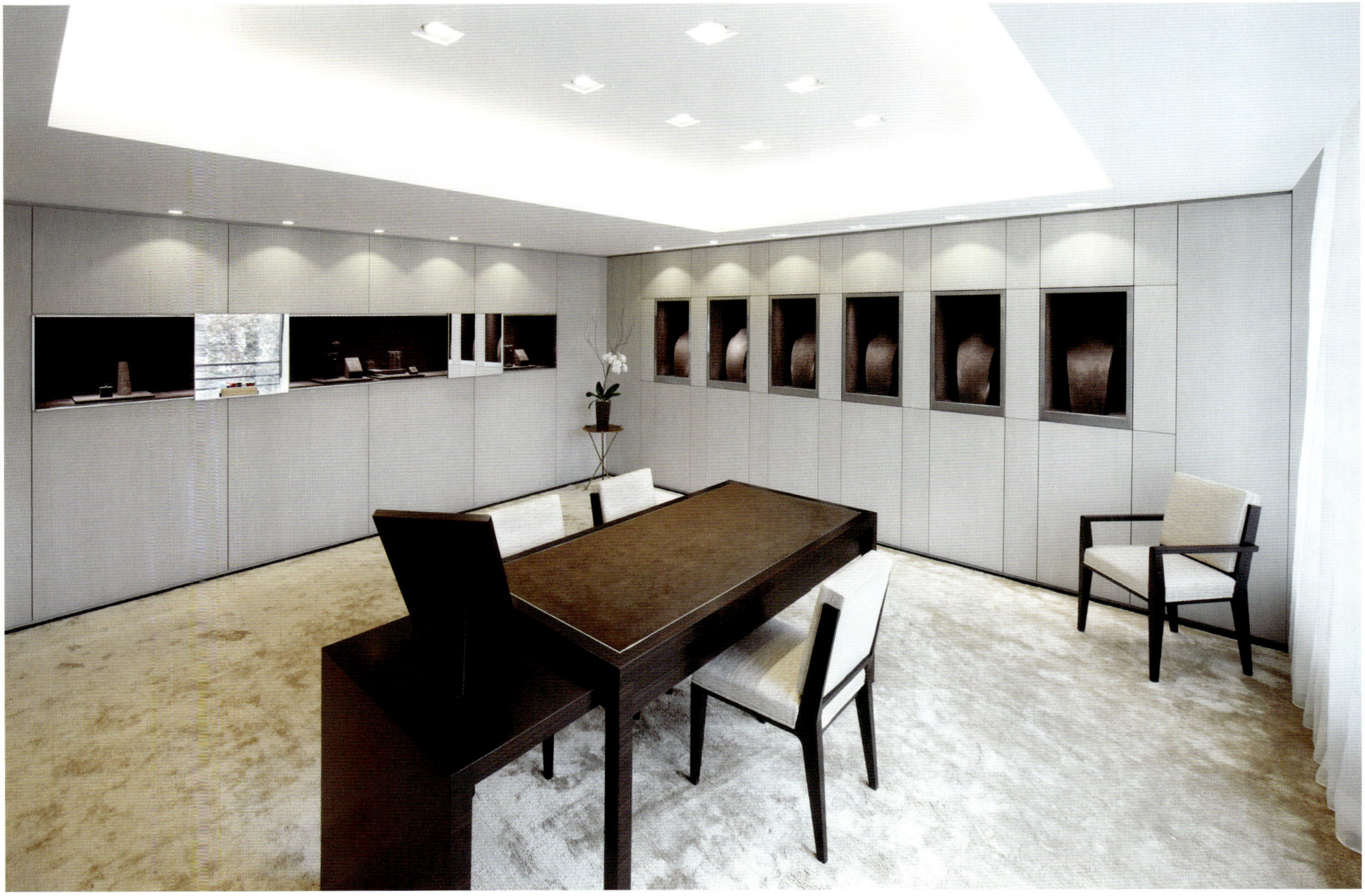

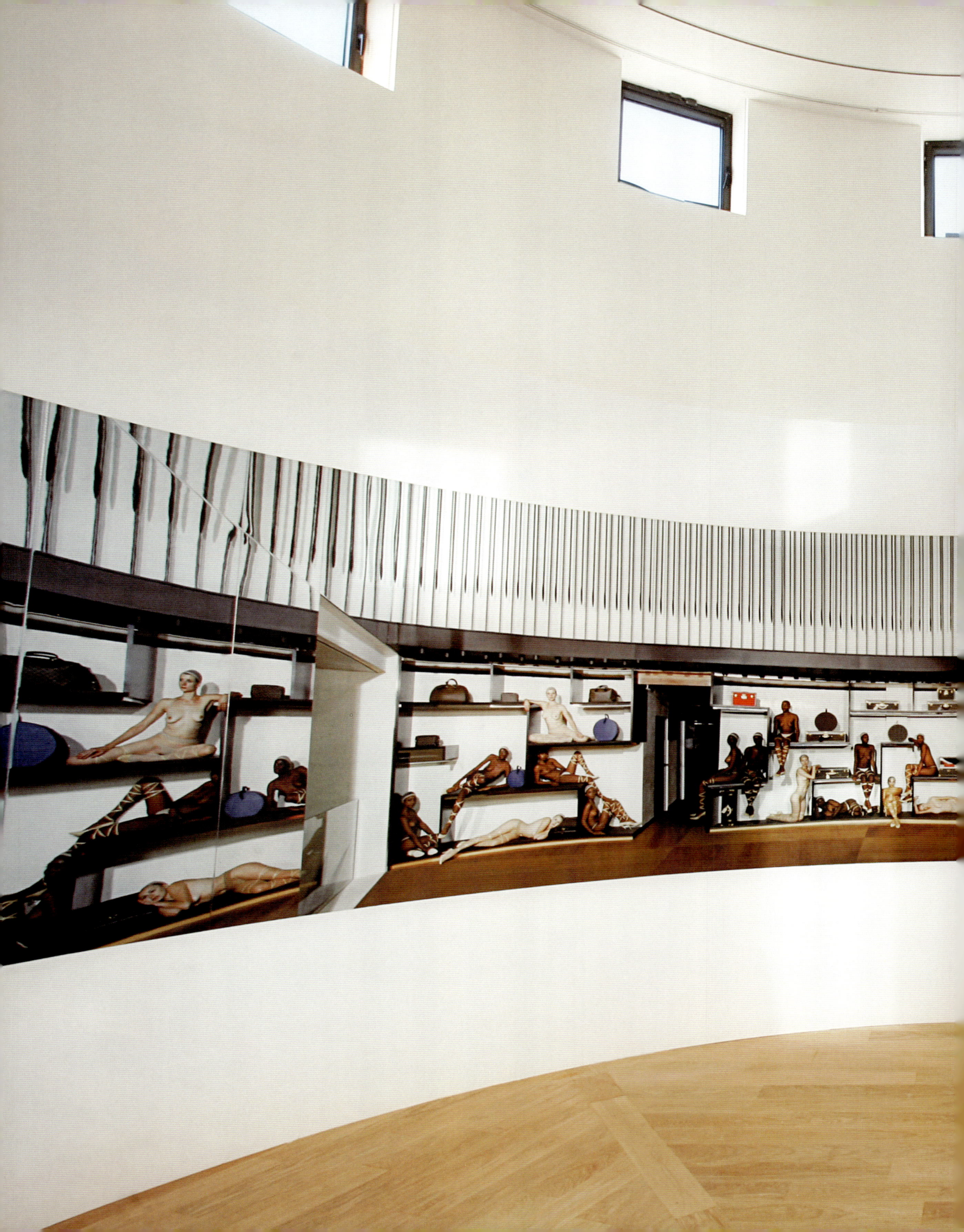

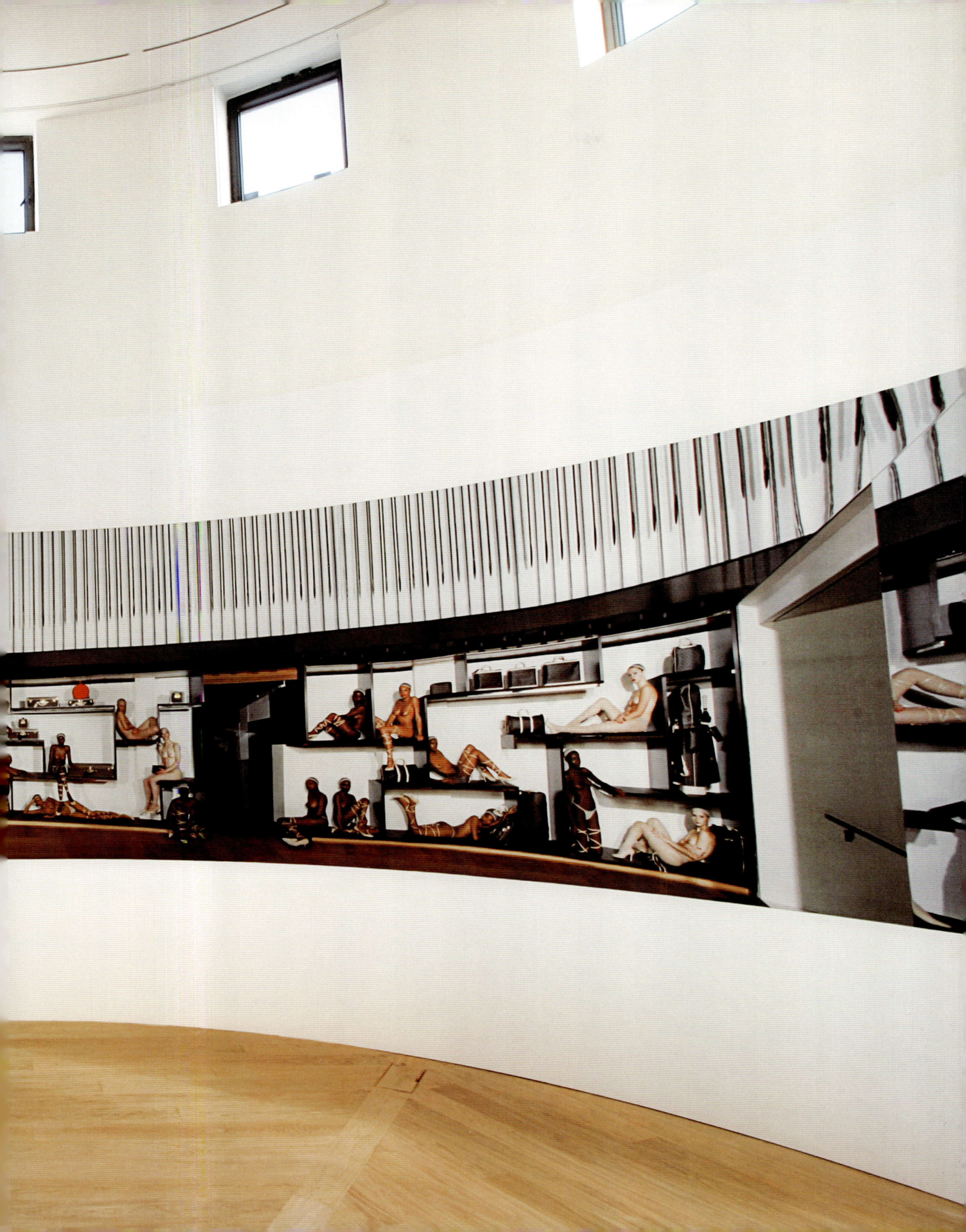

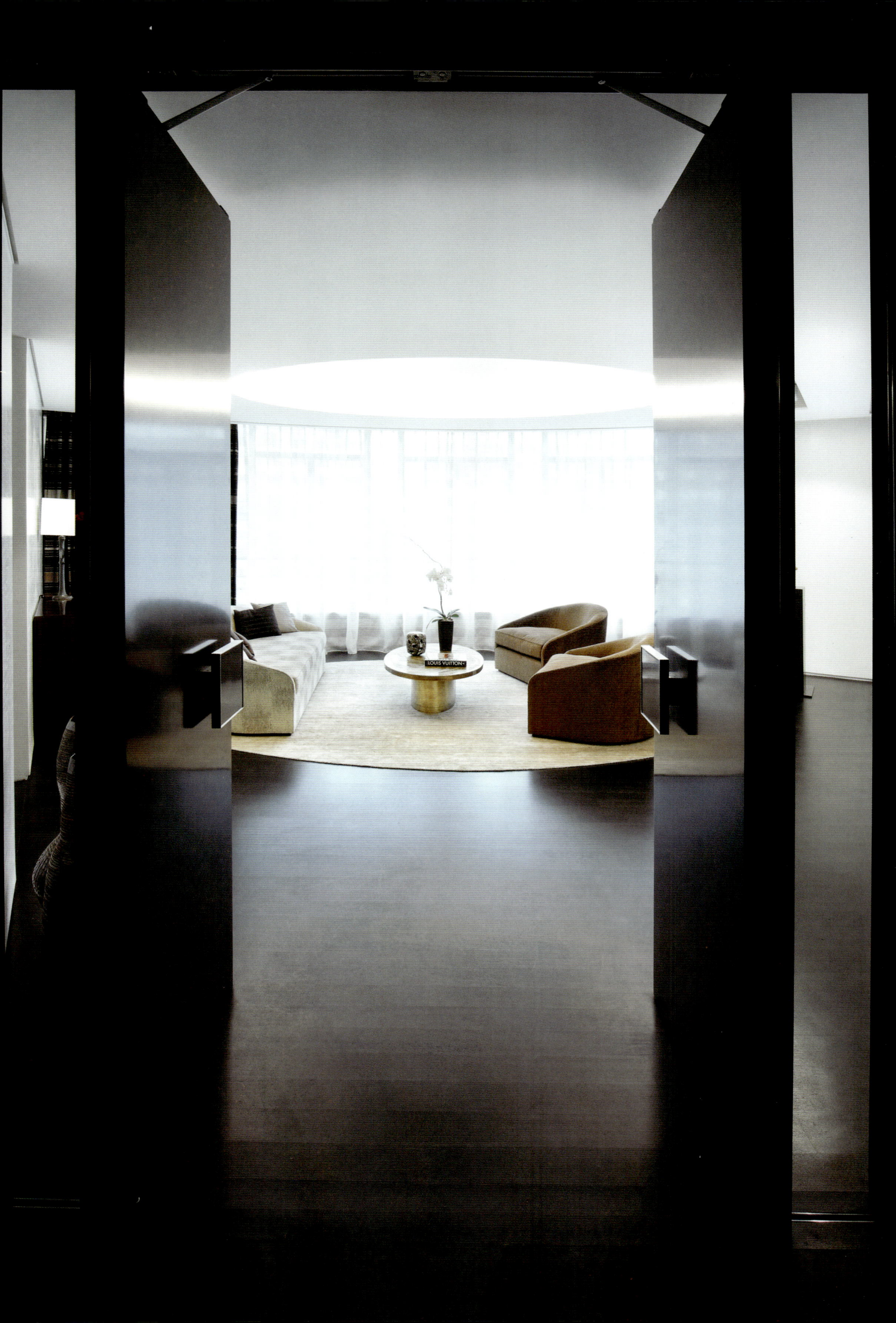
LOUIS VUITTON

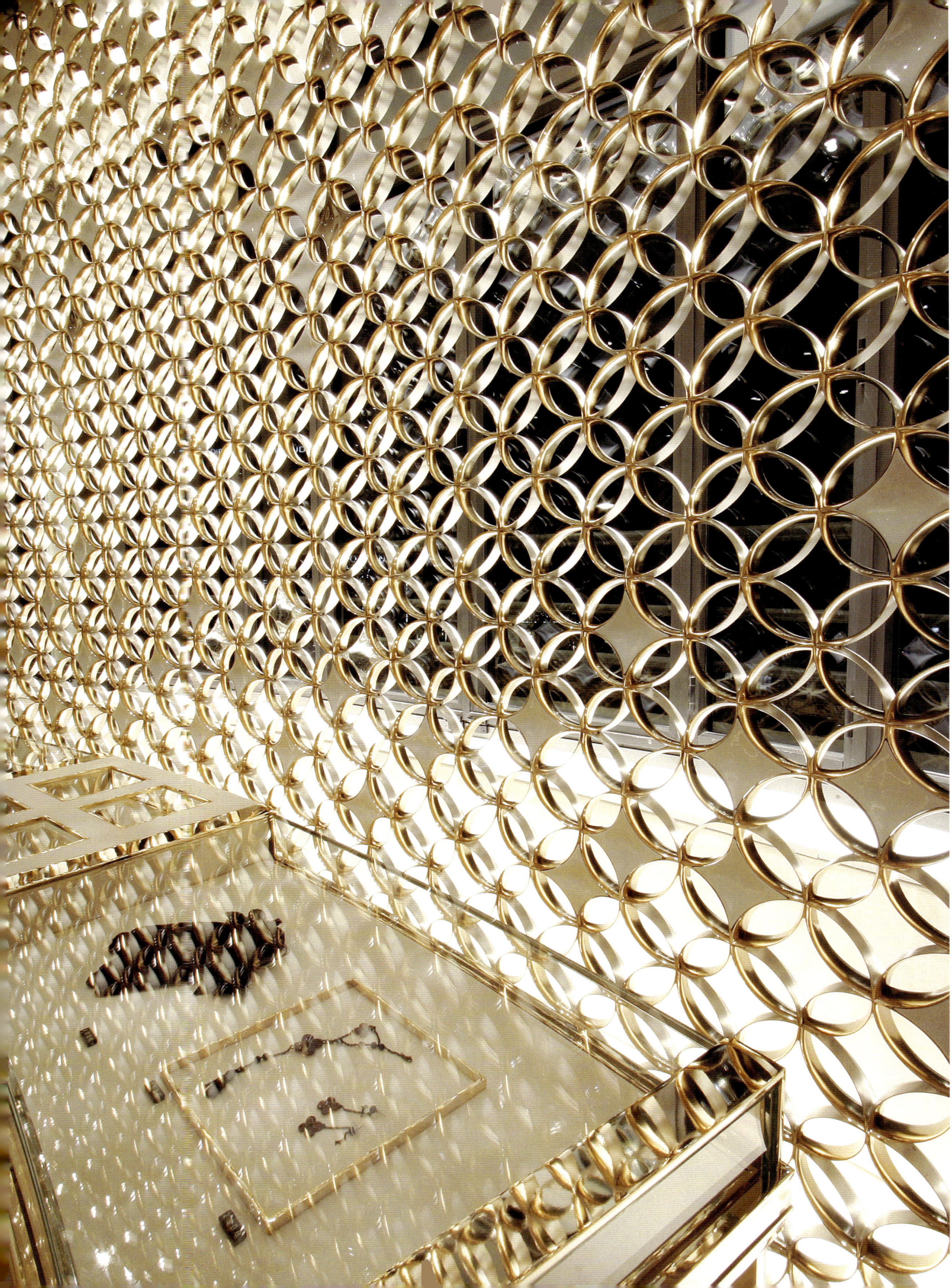

SAINT-TROPEZ

architects
THE LOUIS VUITTON
ARCHITECTURE DEPARTMENT
2010

text by
RAFAEL MAGROU

Nothing but the perfume of nostalgia remains of the fishing village that was Saint Tropez, where, in the 1950s Brigitte Bardot, at the peak of her beauty, was discovered in *And God Created Woman*. The French New Wave passed, Bardot hid herself away at *La Madrague* and fishermen were replaced by tourists who come to this seaside resort, now a symbol of glamour, to gawk at celebrities and other icons passing through. The city's 15th-century citadel and its Mediterranean vegetation are now surrounded by tree-lined private villas, where today's stars in search of rest shield themselves from the public eye. Dominated by the 18-century bell tower in traditional Italian baroque style, with its ochre tones that make the port easily recognizable from the sea, the city's terraces express the soothing nature of the Côte d'Azur year-round.

This is precisely the atmosphere imparted by Louis Vuitton at its new villa located in the heart of town. What's offered is more than a store, it's a way of life, with a lush, adjoining garden—a showpiece that stimulates the senses as much as the leather goods and fashion. From the original boutique, facing the Place de la Garonne, the acquisition of a former pottery workshop nearly doubled the size of the space. One side of this country house borders the street Georges Clémenceau, a destination for any tourist walking from the port to the Place des Lices. Louis Vuitton expresses its presence on this side only at eye-level, with the use of window displays that change with every season and collection. Where the garden emerges, however, if you tilt your head up slightly, you'll see above the wisteria the brand's full name inscribed into the plaster surface of the façade. It's as if the letters have always been there. Respecting and enhancing what was there before, the façade's ochre tint has been restored and the soft peaks of its surface celebrate the architecture of Provence without any pretension. The store's original entrance has not changed, although it opens up onto a wider street that is, unfortunately, still crowded with parked cars.

The renovation of the façade, in light of recommendations made by the *Architecte des Bâtiments de France*, involved developing maximum transparency by discreetly introducing as much daylight as possible through a single, generous glass-paned entrance. Once past the brushed, stainless steel frame, the space is entirely unconstrained. In reality, the depth of the store creates an exhibition space in itself, without any interruptions. The view can be admired from the street both day and night because the designers installed a fine security gate, cast from the best metal in order to prevent any intrusion. When raised, the gate disappears completely and seamlessly into its case. The interior design displays a certain freshness generated by the Mediterranean climate, with exhibited collector trunks revealing endless secrets to relaxation. Metal lines echo the shrouds of nearby sailboats. The floor is a continuous surface with a few inserts, but the texture evokes the rocks revealed by low tide that invite you to walk upon them barefoot. The inside walls made of ash wood lend a light-colored touch to the ambience that is enhanced by anigre wood on the sides of the display cases.

The style is more casual than it is in large cities—the resort atmosphere calls for it—however, the interior design is no less rigorous. Quite the contrary, the attention paid to concept and execution emphasizes transparency and reflection, themes that are presented here without a single blemish. Monolithic furniture, with metal edging and sliding racks with glass partitions, form the reception counter and displays of leather goods. To the left, a tall teak library displays the luggage, which benefits from a narrow patio that allows the leather to bask in the sun without the risk of damage. Above this lofty space, which didn't exist in the store's previous configuration, there is platform made from the same wood, crossing from side to side and announcing the masculine tones that reign on the second floor. A deliciously skewed stairwell takes you upstairs. Although discreet, it relies on artful technique to create its slender frame and to balance its wooden stairs, allowing each to seemingly float in space. An Art Deco chandelier articulates this structural piece, its alabaster globes suspended at different heights by stainless steel rods, forming a light-filled constellation. The magnetism that results is planetary—attracting the eye without being blinding, and diffusing an energy that seems to gently warm the body.

On the second floor, visitors become skippers. The yachting atmosphere of the men's department is carefully created through a combination of rigging and nautical equipment. There's stainless steel for the frames of the display cases, polished teak for the railing, and leather, of course. Even the carpets have nautical accents. Complex furniture arrangements serve diverse functions—to sit, to exhibit, to converse—and optimize the space, just like in the best sailing boats. The maritime air continues until the upper deck that overlooks the area. This passage leads to a uniform, glass wall that reinforces the effect of being in the cockpit of a ship. In the horizon are large yachting images from the Louis Vuitton Cup, a competition associated with the America's Cup.

The building's junction with the newly designed Louis Vuitton villa is through a large bay window, with exceptional dimensions (4.5 meters high). This overlooks a vertical garden, composed of jasmine flowers and a floor paved with a pattern created by multiple fractured sticks. This fragrant interlude is embellished by a spring that runs over rocks along the entrance to the old pottery workshop. Nothing remains of the dusty craft studio, except the main façade. However, the two original wood doors were restored and the windowsills were removed so as to create greater continuity between the villa and the garden. The result is a visual and olfactory dialogue: a unique atmosphere that lies somewhere between interior and exterior. The villa is fully devoted to the world of women, with leather goods on the ground floor and ready to wear on the second floor. An iridescent, spiral stairwell is carved into the mass and leads to the boudoir above. At the top, a cone of light draws the visitor in and creates, by way of a skylight overhead, a celestial eye whose blue ether changes as the clouds roll by. This is certainly a reference to the canons of light in Le Corbusier's *Couvent de la Tourette*. Finding the spiritual in architecture.

Drawn from the patrimony of the brand, framed posters arranged on the wall express the evocative richness of travel at Louis Vuitton and transform the store into a personalized, domestic space. In addition, a portfolio of drawings commissioned from the artist André complete this artistic installation. Between the two overlapping spaces, a Mondrian-like arrangement of light, wooden essences reflects a subliminal theme, with accents of lacquer, mirrors and brass on the garden side. Double curtains dim the sun's rays, their discreet veils floating above silk rugs inspired by those at the *La Madrague* residence. A rectangular light descends from the ceiling to accentuate the display of exotic leathers and special items. In the VIP lounge towards the rear, a mirror triptych hangs against Havana brown lacquered panels, a graphic code expressing the rarity of the products one can try on here. Because the St. Tropez clientele has a diverse taste, nuances of fashion and style have to be attended to.

In front of the façade facing the garden, a long trellis of purple wisteria creates a spatial transition and a protective filter between the sunlight and the sales area. A winding passage connects the private outdoor lounges embellished with furniture inspired by antique wickerwork mixed in with a few glamorous pieces and arranged in the shade of a giant magnolia tree. Figs, exceptionally large datura flowers, oranges, clementines, pomegranates, jasmine, oleander and aromatic plants: it's an ode to all the senses. At dusk, the shadows cast by the plants onto neighboring walls create a theatrical atmosphere. This olfactory garden offers a unique fragrance, its ambient air seeping through the door and gate leading to Rue Clémenceau, traveling like an invitation into ecstasy. It is an exceptional companion to the Vuitton shopping experience, one that calls you to elegance, even at the beach.

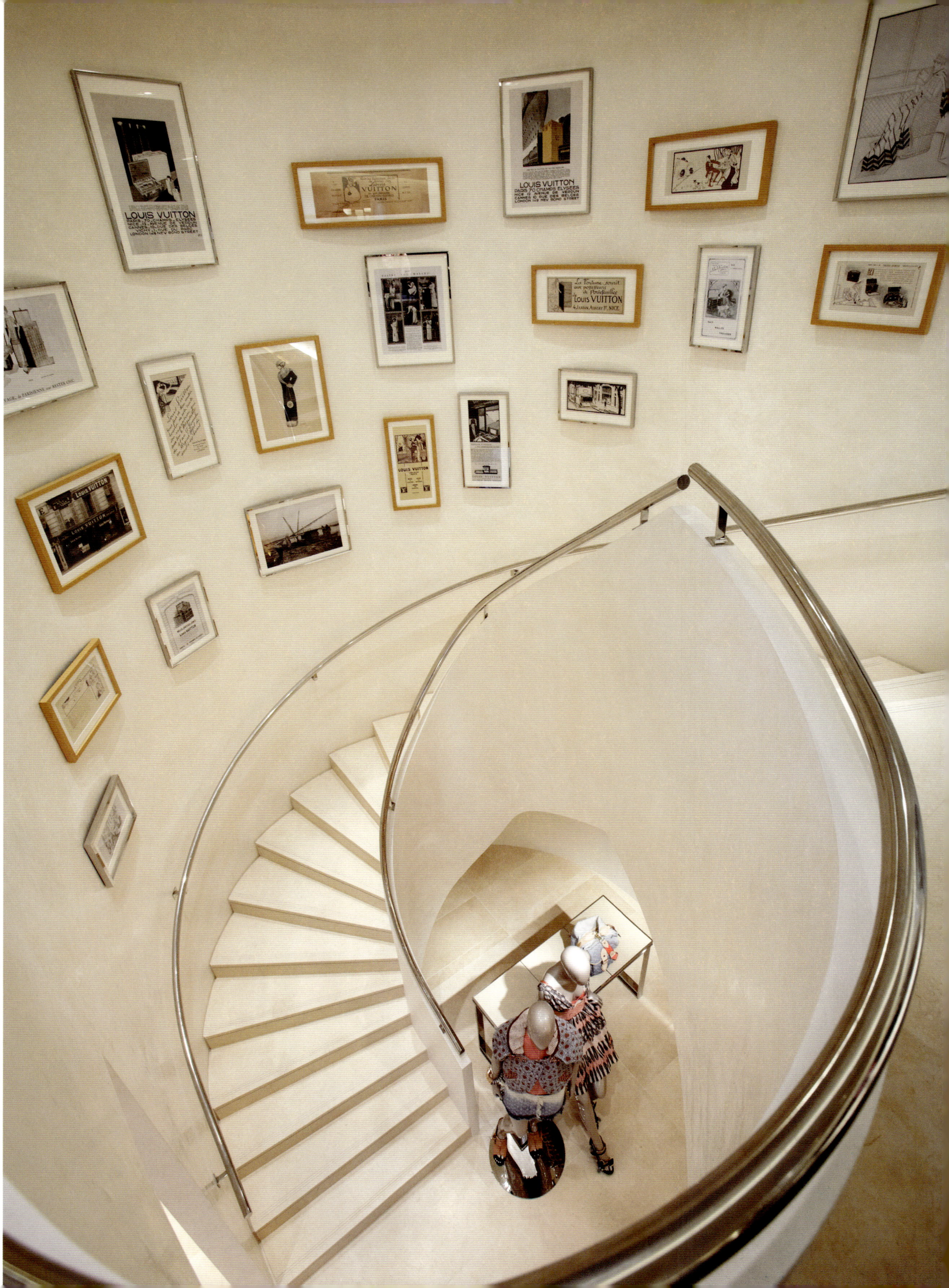
LOUIS VUITTON
LOUIS VUITTON
LOUIS VUITTON

GROUND FLOOR

2ND FLOOR

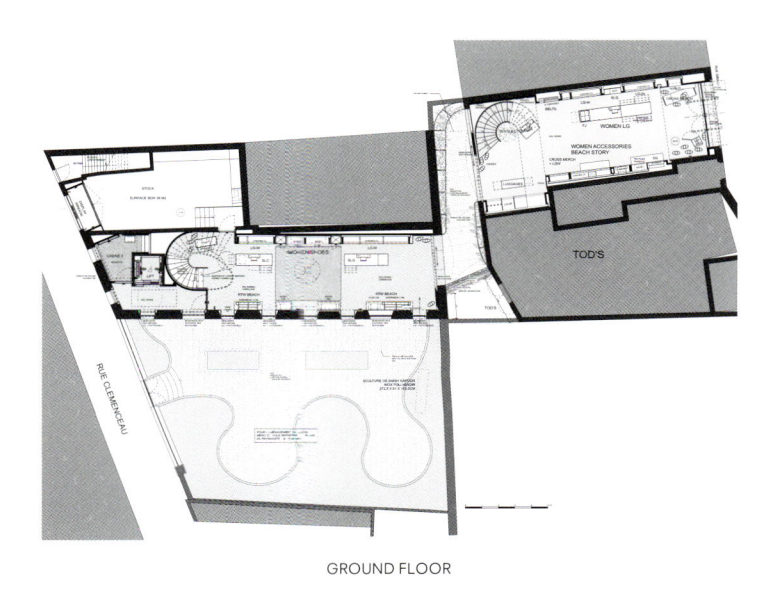

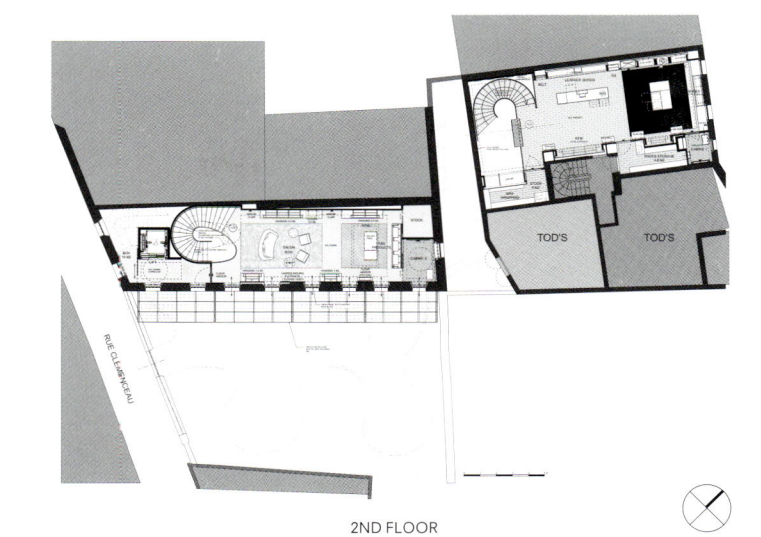

p. 171 garden façade
p. 172 view of staircase
p. 173 bottom: view of Sibili street façade
p. 174–175 garden at dusk
p. 176–177 view of path separating the luggage area and women's universe

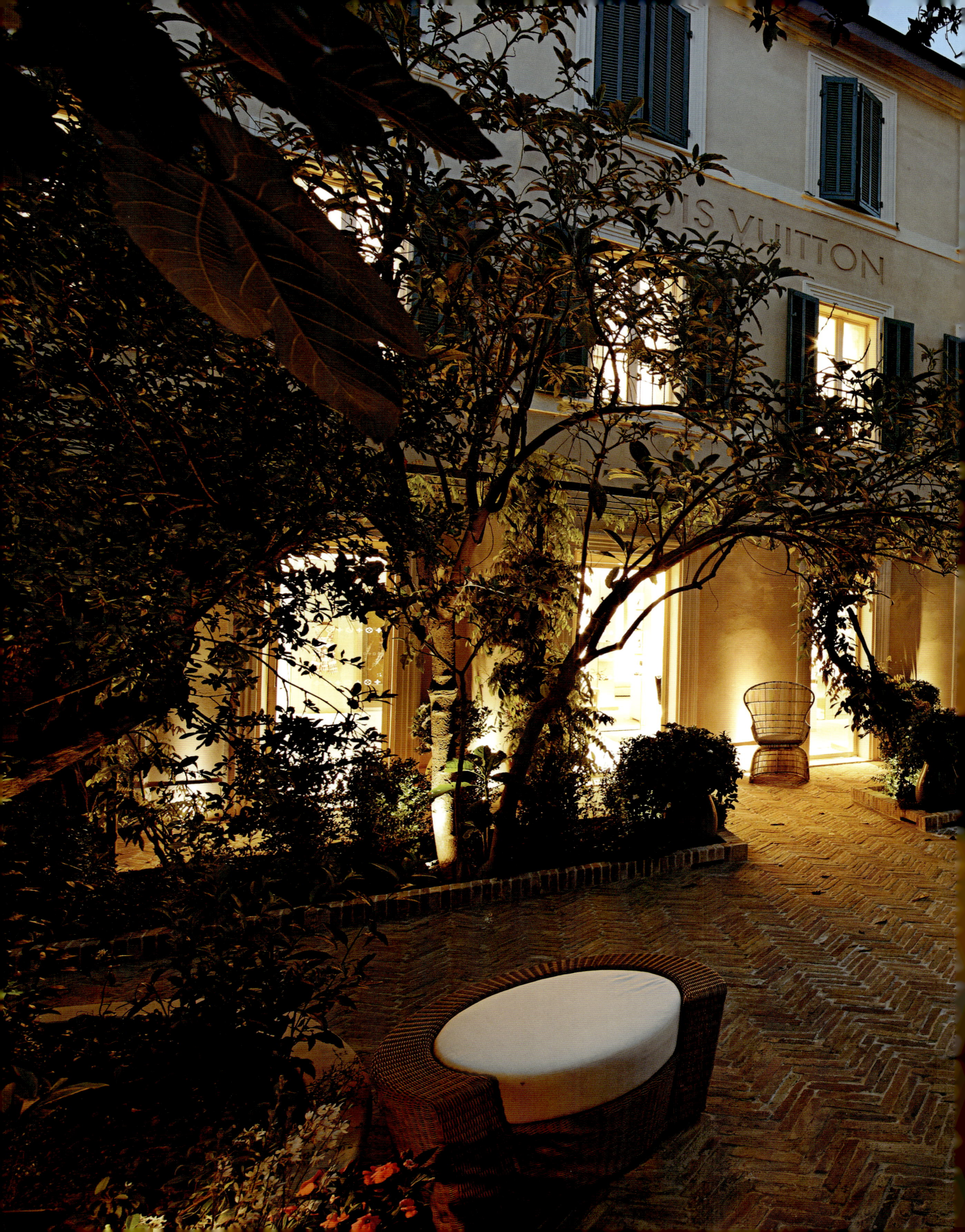
VUITTON

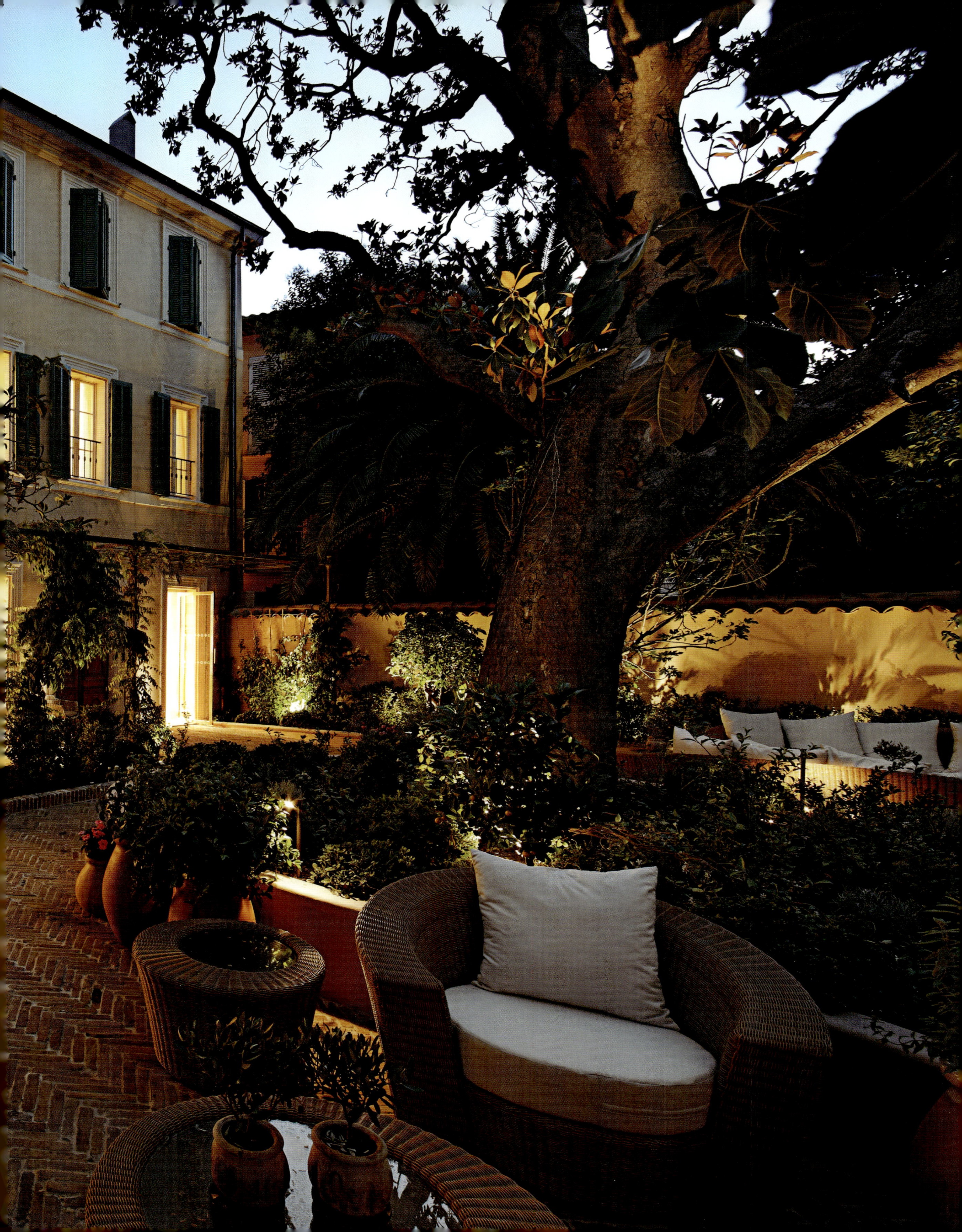

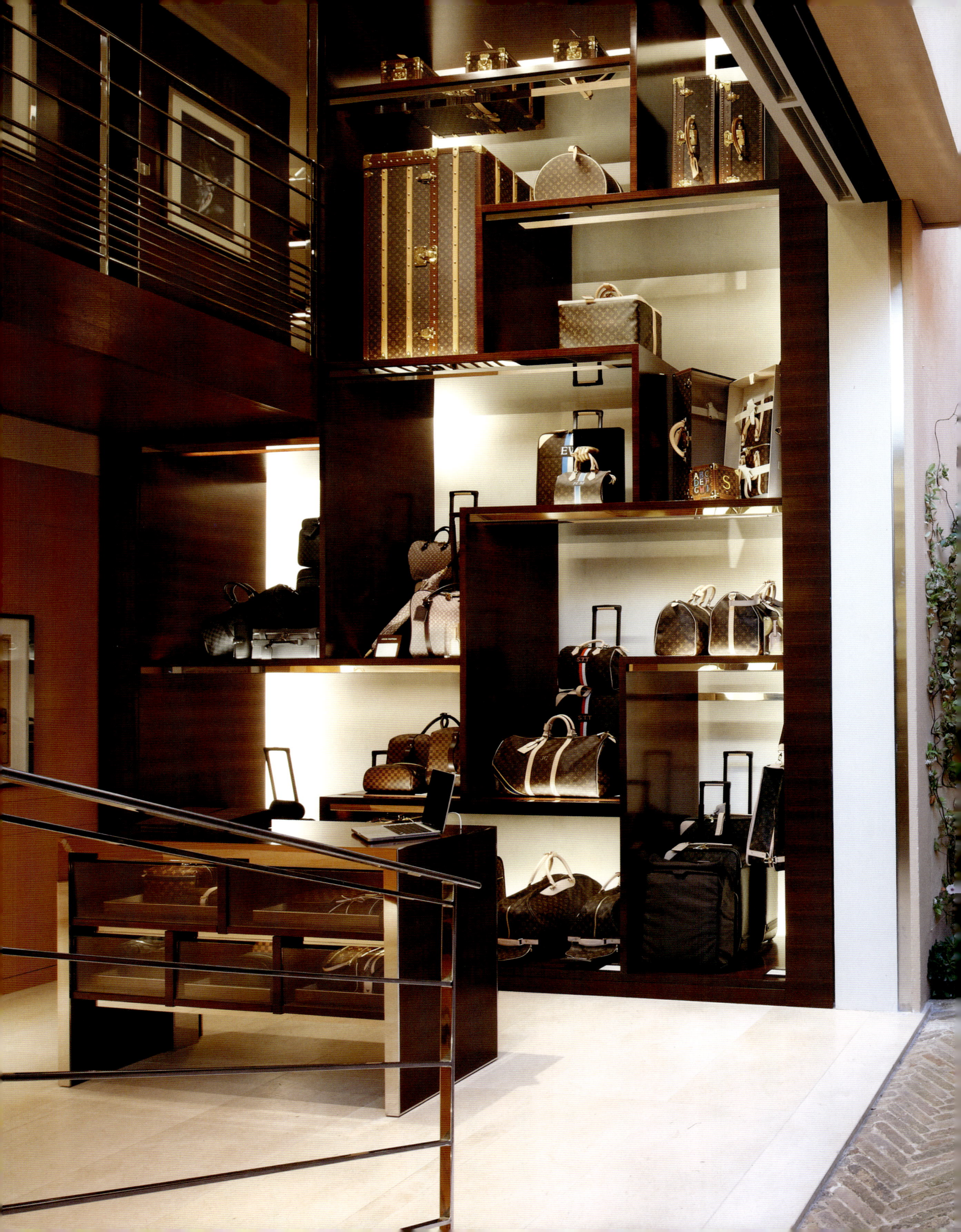

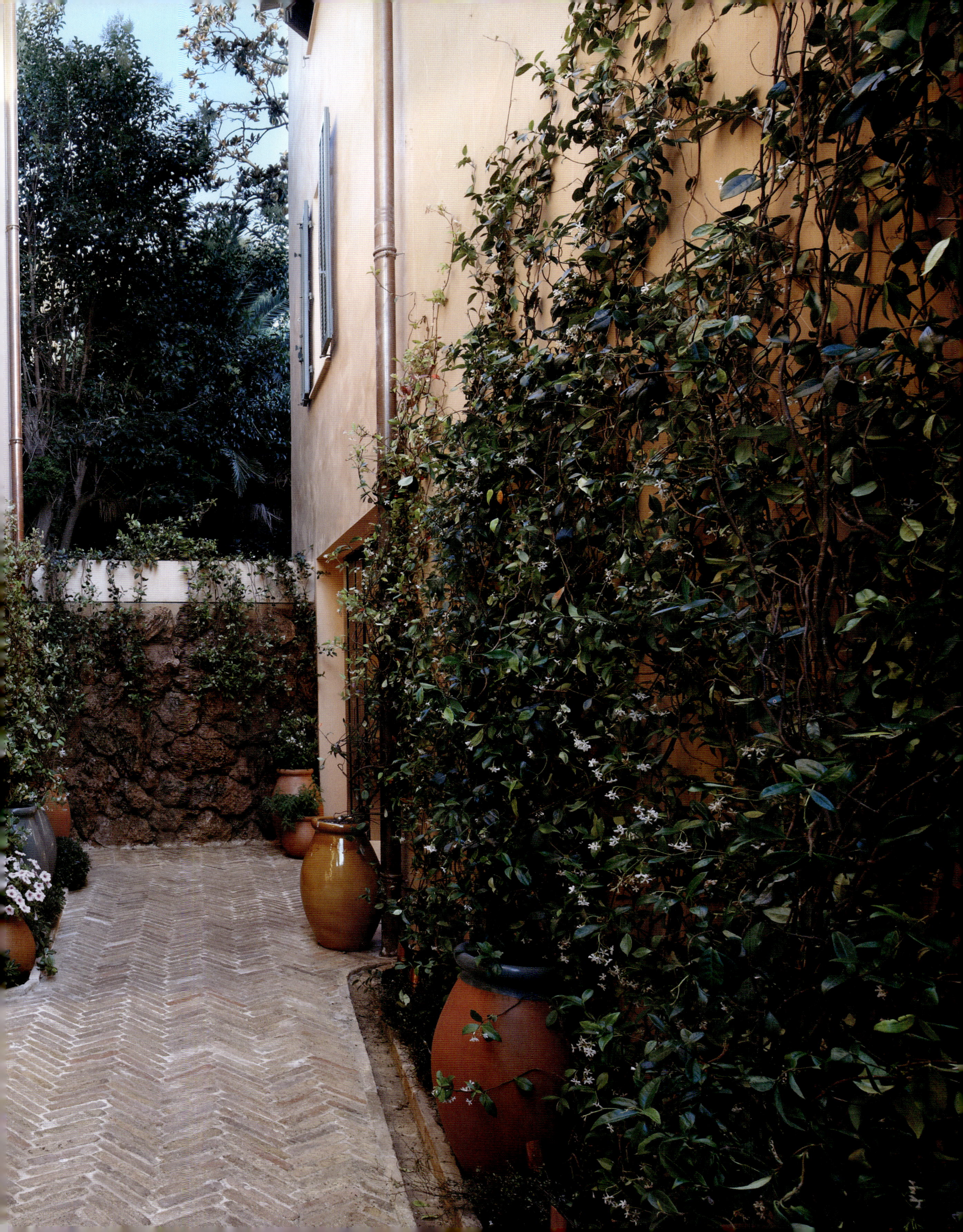

ROME ETOILE

architects
PETER MARINO ARCHITECT
2011

text by
RAFAEL MAGROU

All roads lead to Rome! Everyone knows that the Eternal City is home to architectural treasures and embodies a slightly dulled splendor. Of course, Rome is not Milan, the capital of fashion and design, but it is the cradle of Western civilization, after Athens, and represents historic values held dear by luxury brands, with Louis Vuitton at the top of the list. The Piazza di Spagna, with its cascade of steps falling from the Trinità dei Monti to the Pietro Bernini's Barcaccia fountain, is a cinematic setting that has been many times exploited. A never-ending flow of tourists come here to get lost in the city's elegant streets, among which is the Via dei Condotti, the chicest in the city of Seven Hills. All the renowned labels of Italy and the world beyond are here. Louis Vuitton established residency first at number 13 and then at number 15. Two streets away is the triangular piazza San Lorenzo in Lucina, named after the church there; it's where the famous *malletier* first set down its bags in the 1980s to found its first Roman boutique. Needing to expand, but remaining true to its ways, the brand—a leader in luxury—wanted to stay in the same historic district.

Two adjoining buildings away from the original store, almost directly facing the twelfth century portico of the church, there was a multi-purpose hall called the *Spazio Etoile* that provided the sought after setting for the Monogram collection and offered the possibility of going from 300 square meters to 1,242 square meters. The Italian *maison* could finally be founded. In fact, it was an old movie house from the glory days of Cinecittà that was entirely renovated. Little remains of the theater that once was, with its arabesque balconies, its skylight and its thousand wood and metal seats where the laughter and tears of Roman families once resonated in front of visions of the *città aperta* they lived in. Nothing but the galleries, diminished by an intermediary floor built in the 1970s; the splendor of the initial volume no longer exists. The typical façade elements don't have any real charm, but the city has decided to preserve the geometric features and classify the building as a landmark. *De gustibus et coloribus non disputandum*—it's no use debating taste and colors. Its surface was therefore redone with respect to the existing one, the oculi embellished with light and color, the lintel topped by the name of the company in gilded letters lit from behind. The bays are involved on several levels: as vitrines, visualization through the presentation of the boutique, commercial and cultural displays.

In order to respect the original site, the Louis Vuitton company decided to recreate a movie theater. The question then became how to combine sales and film projections in a shared space without penalizing either one. Calling upon Peter Marino, a permanent member of the brand's architecture department, the answer was found in a two-fold effect. First, an artistic visual mechanism was created in the double-door entrance and turned into an immersive area, perceptible from the piazza. It produces a draw without disturbing the clarity of the urban space, an *ad astra* magnetism—toward the stars—that nods to Eadward Muybridge and Jules-Étienne Marey, who pioneered the moving image through their sequences. Then, beyond this unique area, your eyes take in the new store as a whole, every last inch. This includes a small-scale recreation of the movie theater, whose program promises to be exceptional.

Several stair cavities have been shaped like spirals, loosely echoing the undulations of a film reel, but without the notches. Single, double and multiple loops fill the space, with the railing and curved stringboard of intersecting flights—their steps sealed—composing a round-edged prism around this inspiring open space. The whole is an airborne sculpture, with steps suspended in empty space—an experience of levitation that's bound to make your head spin. For a split second, you'll think you're in the Venice Film Festival or at the Cannes Film Festival, except that there's no red carpet. So that you can see the movie screen from the second floor, the glass-paned railings are fully transparent.

The ground floor is devoted to leather goods and accessories, with the classic Bag Bar in the rear; the second floor is dedicated to women and includes the small theater that is part of the Louis Vuitton sales experience. Visible from below, a screen that can be adjusted to fit the film being projected lines the back wall and offers its nineteen-person audience a cinematic program that combines cult films and exclusive releases, in cinemascope and in 3D, depending on the need. Side panels can be altered to accommodate these formats; sound is frontal, but each high-comfort seat is equipped with individual speakers. The alcove that's formed by this *camera obscura*, although it fits in visually to the store as a whole, is able to reign in attention towards the projected subject. Creating privacy, the bookstore begins at the second row, forming an acoustic barrier and also a functional display for books. Mission accomplished, *libro aperto*, for Louis Vuitton; it has reinstated a silent space for a happy few, once again serving as pioneer by combining luxury and film. It's a kind of homage to the Lumière brothers who invented the principle of moving images some forty-one years after the Louis Vuitton *malletier* was founded in Paris.

The volumes in this Roman House come one after the other, but no two are alike... Under 4.8-meter raised ceilings, stretching along the façade, the prêt-a-porter department enjoys natural light as do the fitting rooms. Perched up there, *belle donne* have a wide-angle view of the urban action below, looking through the oculi on the Piazza San Lorenzo di Lucina façade. They can also examine the tones of the fabric against their skin and the vibrations of the material by the light of sun, which streams in from the main façade that faces south. The depth of the configuration—the former movie theater fills a hollow indentation—usually would have required an artificial adjustment to add light to the building's inner recesses. It exists of course, as it does in every store here and elsewhere, but the old shaft of light remains, filtering through a square glass roof. It is an exceptional device that accents materials *a capite ad calcem*, as well as the lines of architecture, leather goods and textiles, and also the human lines, in the space as a whole. Nothing obstructs this feature; the roof has been converted into a private garden for the home that is located up there. Unfortunately, you can't access it from Louis Vuitton.

The lower level is once again reserved for men. A large unit against the wall is used for luggage and is visible as soon as you walk in. The atmosphere is similar to the one at the store in Britain on New Bond Street, which represents a new model for future developments. The women's department is warmer, exhibiting the brown and red tones that teak and striated leather lend; there's stalactite brown on the floor. This new brand emblem should attract all of Rome, the Hollywood-on-the-Tiber of the 1950s, today re-gilded by this new setting for a modern-day *Dolce Vita*. Instead of Anita Ekberg and Marcello Mastrioianni intertwined in the Trevi Fountain, it is the former movie house turned house of luxury that is announcing a renaissance: *L'amore rinasce à Roma!*

p. 179 rendering of exterior along Piazza San Lorenzo in Lucina
p. 180–181 interior views of main retailing areas: cinema, Bag Bar, main atrium, basement and men's universe

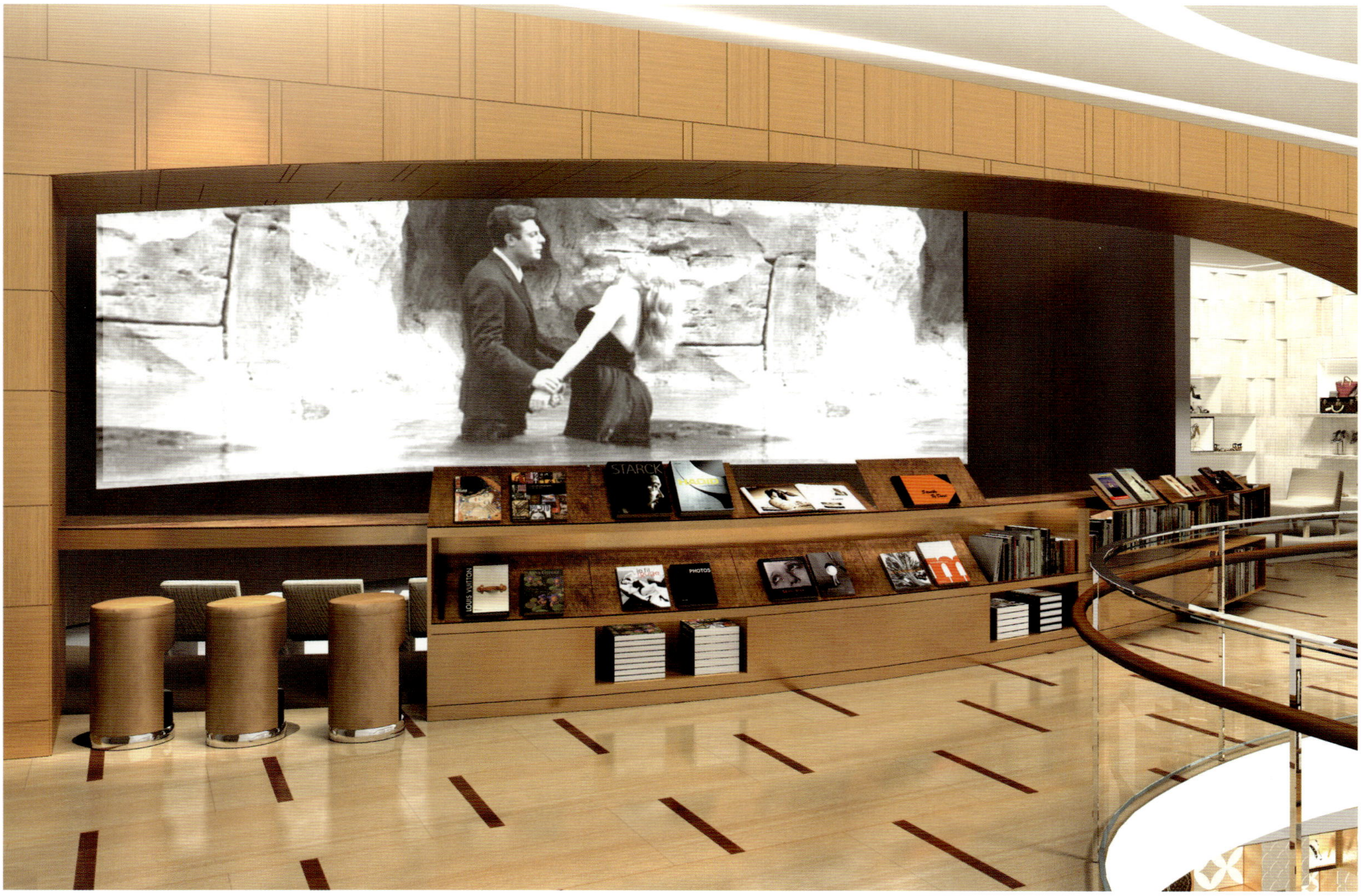
STARCK
PHOTOS

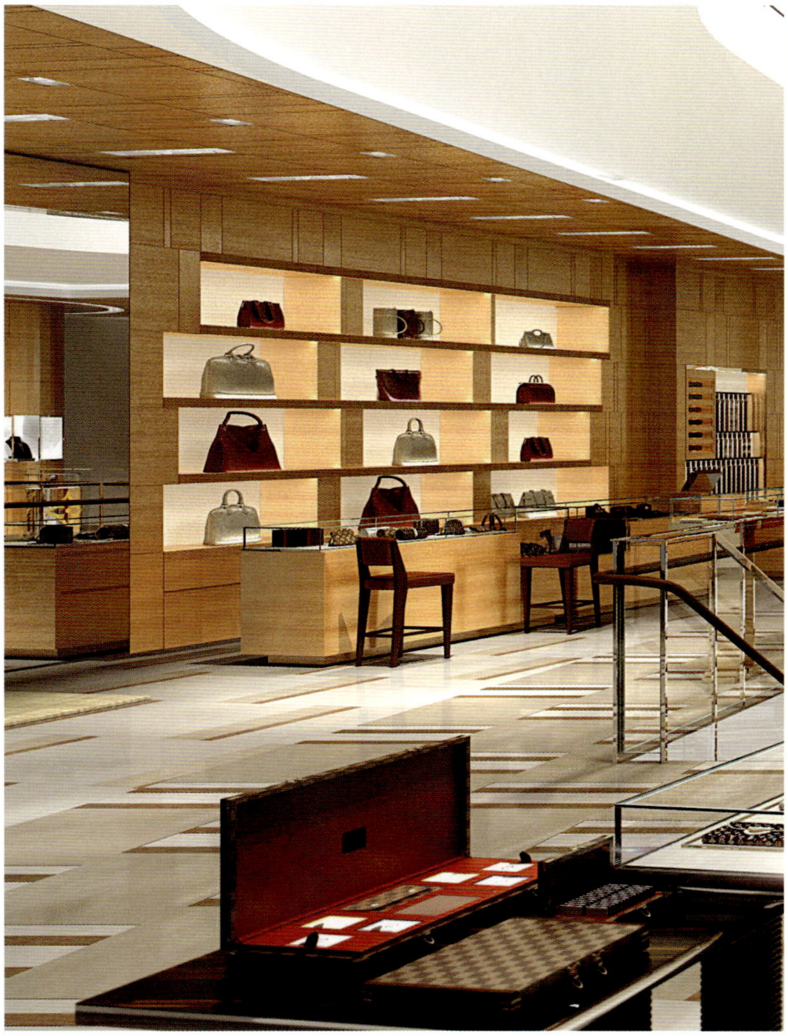

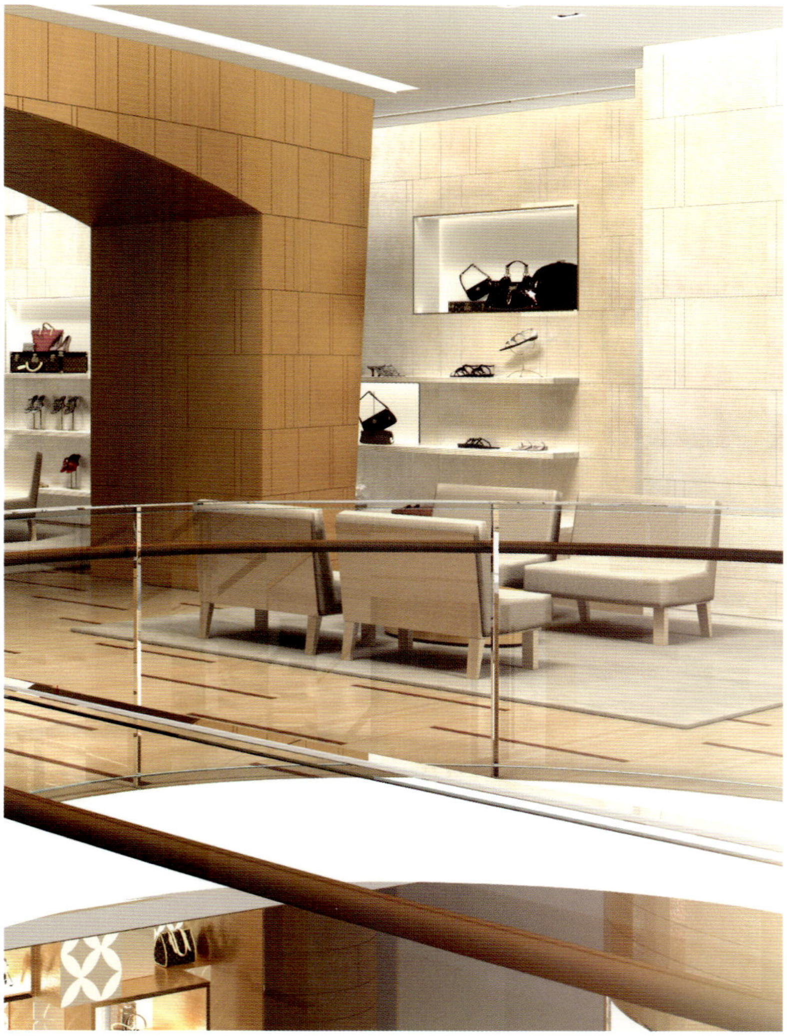

ARCHITECTURE AND INTERIORS 181

MOSCOW GUM

architects
THE LOUIS VUITTON
ARCHITECTURE DEPARTMENT
2004

text by
RAFAEL MAGROU

Who would have imagined twenty-five years ago that Louis Vuitton's famous checkered pattern and monogram from the 19th century would be on display in Red Square, across from the Kremlin? In the heart of Moscow, the capital of the Russian Federation, the location was once named "Fire Square," because of the flames that repeatedly destroyed the original buildings there. When Ivan III embarked on its renovation, the square began to take on its present form, eventually becoming as famous as Times Square in New York, the more animated American version. *Glasnost*, the policy of transparency introduced by Gorbachev that thawed relationships with eastern block countries, unleashed unprecedented growth in the late 1980s in the country that founded Communism and that's now devoted to the Saints of Liberalism. All that remains from the revolutionary period is Lenin's Mausoleum, a remnant of 20th-century revolution. Today, another revolution is raging in Red Square, but without all that bloodshed.

The event is taking place at the GUM department store, which replaced the old hall of the Upper Trading Rows that existed before the Revolution of 1917. In the early 2000's, Vuitton found a choice spot at the northwest corner with a view that stretches from the State Historical Museum to the colorful domes of Saint Basil's Cathedral. While vendors used to sell old icons, *laptis* (traditional woven sandals), saddles, ham and hot soups, the GUM department store is home today to the most sought-after international brands. When it opened in 1893, it was the largest shopping center in the world and also represented a radical turning point in the history of Russian architecture, not only because of its rational and economical dimensions—arguments that allowed Alexander Pomerantsev to win the 1886 competition—but also because of the resurgent, Russian style developed by the architect. The scale, volume and architecture of the building as a whole have all the characteristics of a palace, reminding us that Red Square plays not only a political role but also a leading commercial one. Today, the architecture of GUM, with its incredible vistas of surrounding galleries topped by arched windows is a must-see when visiting Europe's largest city. Since the Revolution and the decades that followed with the occupation of the Council of People's Commissars, the popular vendors at the *Glavnyi Universalnyi* (the State's main department store) who sold everything from fur coats to candles, were replaced by prestigious labels that now stand alongside the many cafés and restaurants.

But, to be incorporated into the GUM is no trivial affair. Made of marble, limestone and granite, the outside and interior façades are classified as landmarks, which inherently limits the signage that can be displayed. From a preservationist point of view, one that aims to conserve the image of the State and its heritage, Red Square must remain intact, as must the GUM. Adding inscriptions and overlays to the windows is also strictly forbidden. The municipality has expressly asked that all windows remain entirely transparent, and has posed a ban on blocking the windows with any kind of article. Despite these regulations, Louis Vuitton has dared to place its initials—although discreetly—on the canopy above its arcades. The celebrated French leather goods manufacturer was already occupying a portion of the ground floor in 2004, when the opportunity arose to expand to the second floor. Already on a single level, the structure of thick pillars at short range from one another necessitated a renovation unlike any other the brand had ever undertaken. Despite its original Russian address on Stoleshnikov Lane, a neighborhood devoted to luxury, Louis Vuitton owed it to itself to have a presence amid the GUM arcades. The design had to be based on a hypostyle structure, but the walls and ceiling vaults could not be touched. Respecting local regulations was an exercise in contortionist dexterity, but it also guaranteed that the architectural unit, with its deep sun-drenched naves, would be maintained. The building is a beautiful testimony of the best in the history of tsarist architecture, and has thankfully been preserved by the regimes that followed.

Divided over two levels, with three vaults from the interior gallery forming the façade overlooking Red Square, the Louis Vuitton store is physically unable to present a singular, panoramic view of the entire collection, unlike its other international stores in London, Tokyo, Hong Kong and Las Vegas. Because these subdivisions were unavoidable—creating new openings is prohibited—an entirely different approach had to be invented and adapted to the geography of the space. The reduced possibilities created a division of sales areas and changed the layout of display cases, all of which had to be carefully considered as well as approved by the board of control at GUM. Luckily, each floor has a separate entrance, with two entrances on the ground floor, one of which opens directly onto Red Square. This layout facilitates the flow of traffic, with leather goods—the core of the brand's identity—on the ground floor and men and women's ready-to-wear on the second.

The staircase connecting the two floors is precisely placed in a hollow recess. In order to reserve maximum comfort for its clientele, the Architecture department endeavored to open up the space as much as possible, using vertical, quarter-inch metal rods to hold up cases displaying leather luggage. This stainless steel diffraction dilates the lofty space, as it is integrated into the risers, banister and beneath the steps, as well as into the open areas that wrap around this unique, ascending structure. Thus, the passage from the lower to the upper level is a jewel of a thousand transient faces and movements milling about the store. It shines all the brighter in contrast to the relatively sober materials used throughout the store, with its travertine floor and plaster of varying textures with checkered and flower motifs on the walls. The archways are left undisturbed, their thick pilasters dividing the space into different areas devoted to timeless or temporary collections. On the ground floor, the furniture is delicately placed against the age-old walls, forming a simple display area accented with anigre wood, in front of which glass counters exhibit top-quality items.

The upper level boasts a ceiling that's almost six meters high, giving breathing room to the men and women's ready-to-wear collections. Here, one can truly appreciate the magnitude of the building, with its deep, wide view of Red Square and its monuments. Here, an opening has been left intact out of obligation, but also by choice, accentuated by hanging chandeliers made from Murano glass created by Barovier & Toso that incorporate blown glass techniques in the form of flowers and butterflies. These chandeliers were specially designed for the GUM, then followed by other versions made for Louis Vuitton's other boutiques such as Nagoya Sakae and Las Vegas. Both airy and aerial, they produce a fixed choreography— a Nijinskian leap frozen in glass and bursting out into three dimensions. Almost two meters high, they hover overhead, upholding the palatial impression that the GUM exudes. The men's space is more confined and suspended in tones of champagne with an ambiance like that of a club, complete with zebrano wood furniture, leather seats and brown rugs. Arching above the suspended ceiling elements, the vaults remain preserved.

For the women, who, according to the great Leo Tolstoy, "hold in their hands the salvation of the world," there's a row of three crystal clusters in the main hall devoted to textiles. The collection rests on metal stands, accented by thin lines of light. Lightness is feminine, and so are the floating, gilded flowers that hang from metal wire and hover around the façades, a second, inner skin that represents the label's ability to adapt to the most delicate settings. The large arched windows of the GUM remain intact, although they're transformed by the constant blossoming of Louis Vuitton that enhances Red Square, also known as *Krásnaya plóshchad* or "beautiful square."

p. 183 and top of 184 exterior views along Red Square
p. 184 bottom left: main shopping gallery of GUM
p. 185 views of women's collections area
p. 186–187 exterior view at night
p. 188–189 views of staircase, screens and Murano glass chandelier

2ND FLOOR

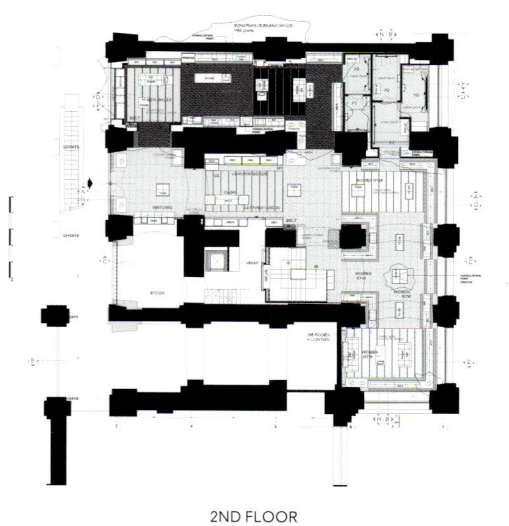

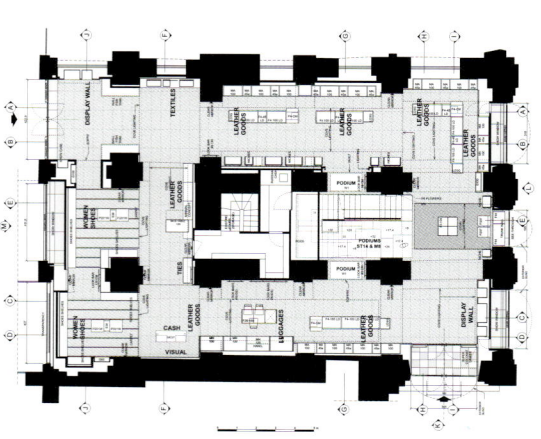

GROUND FLOOR

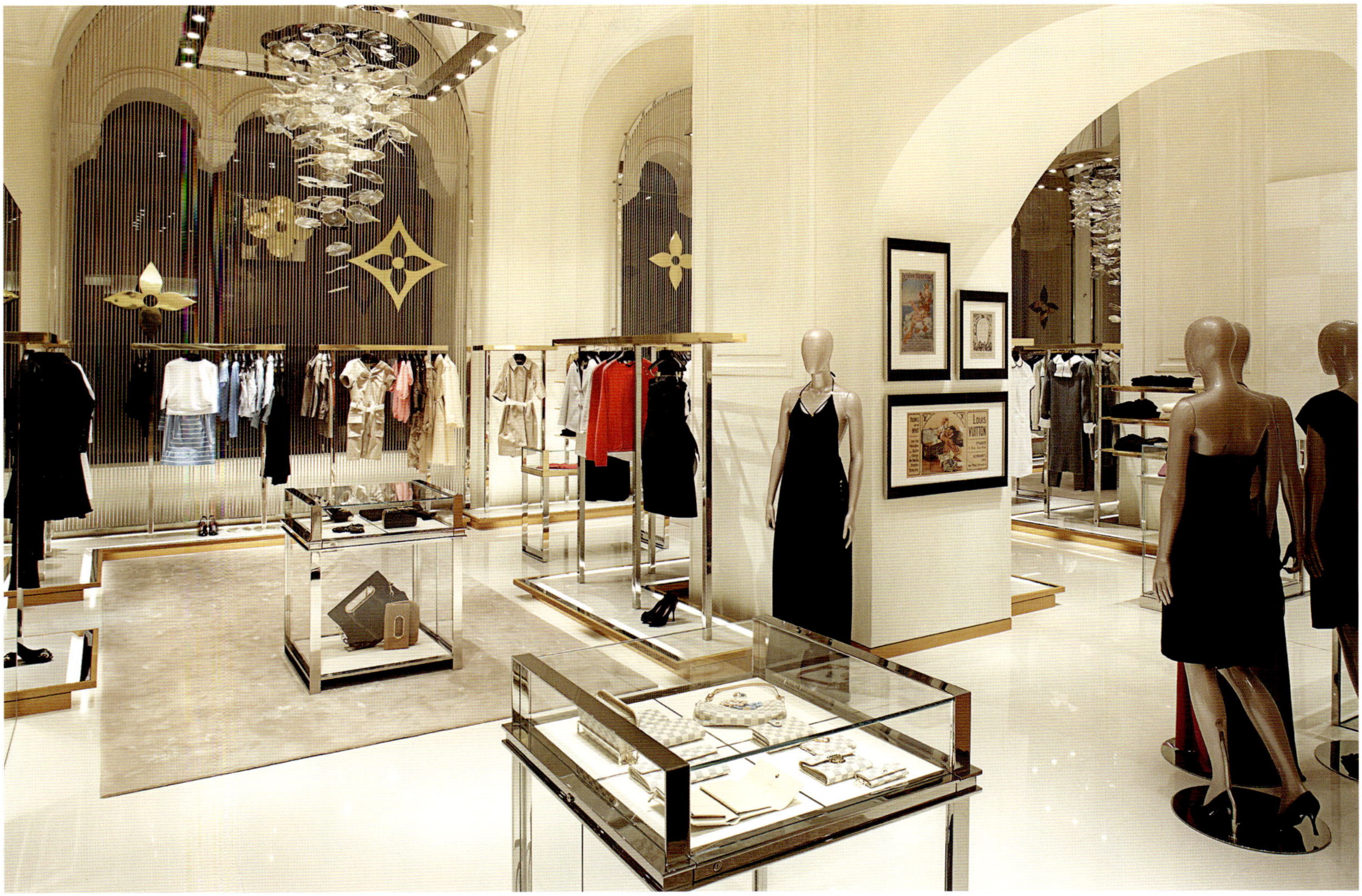

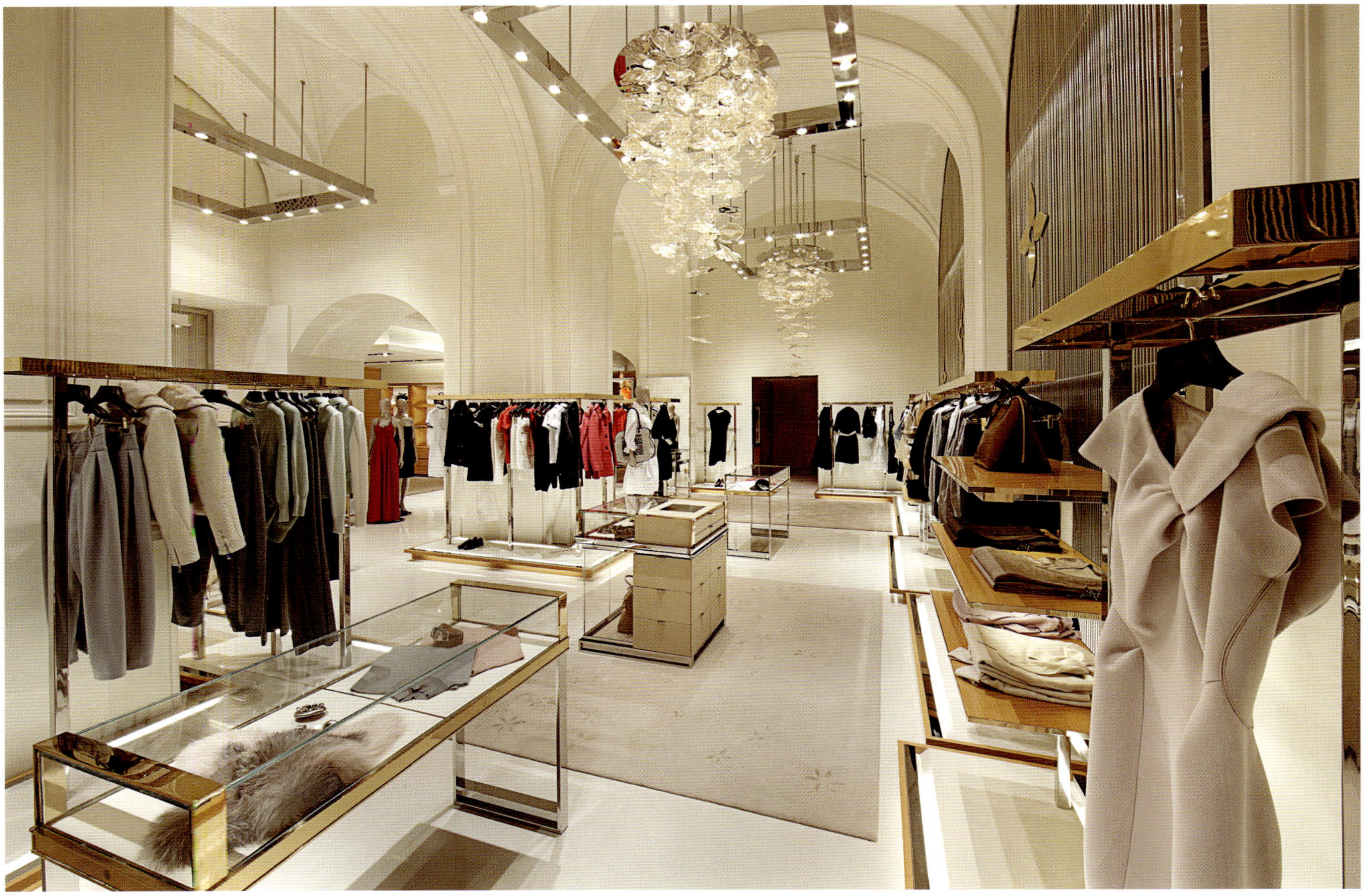

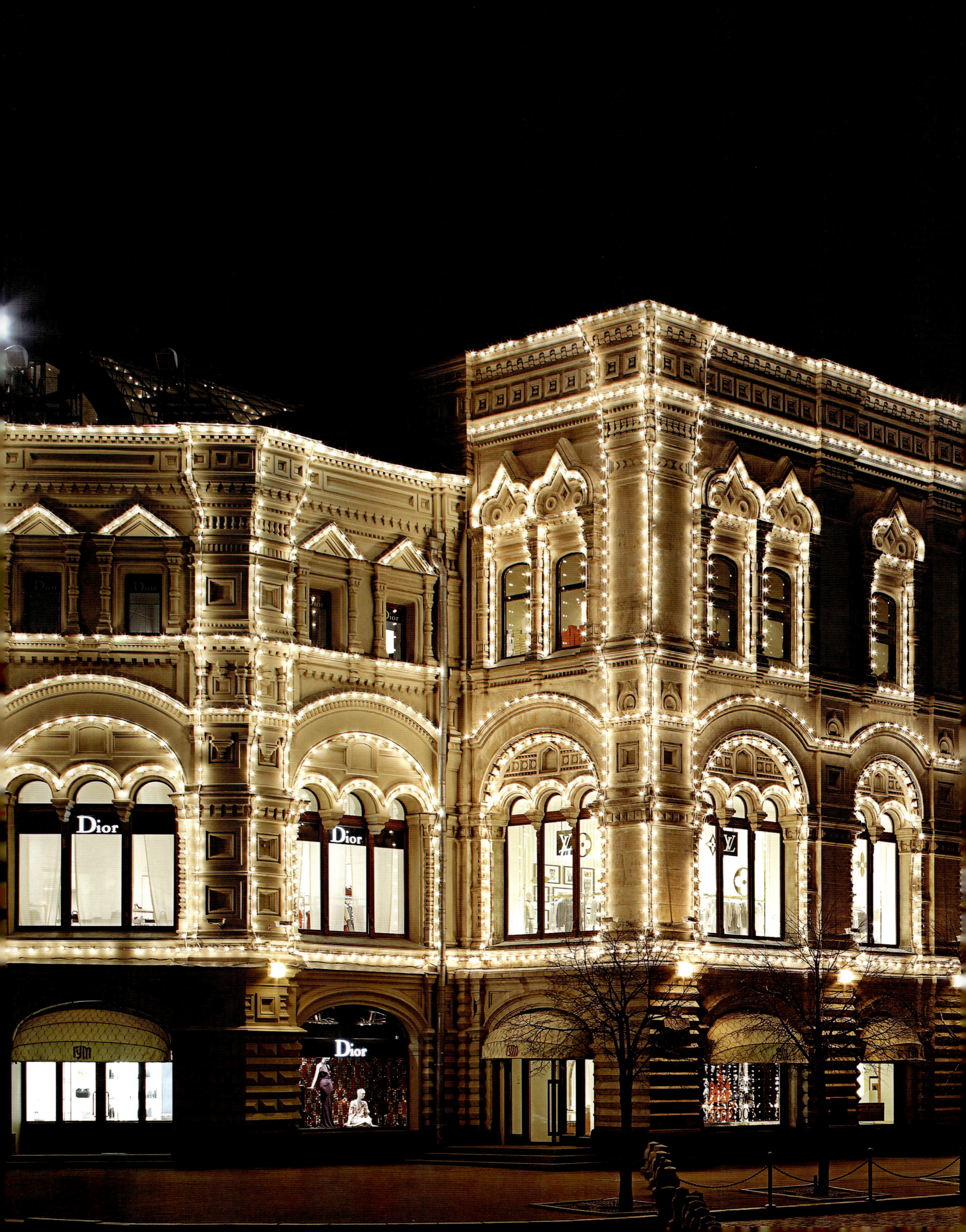
Dior
Dior
Dior

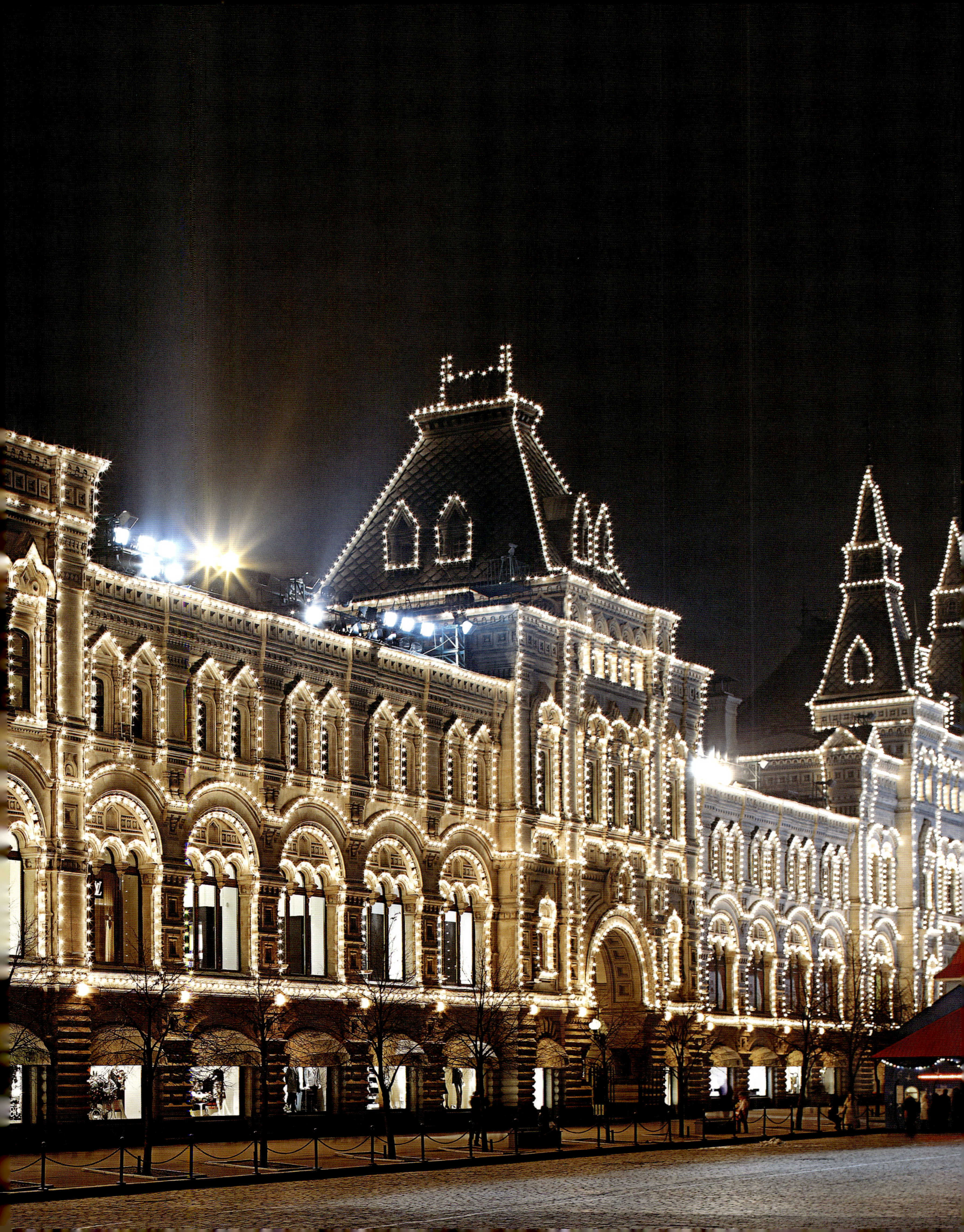

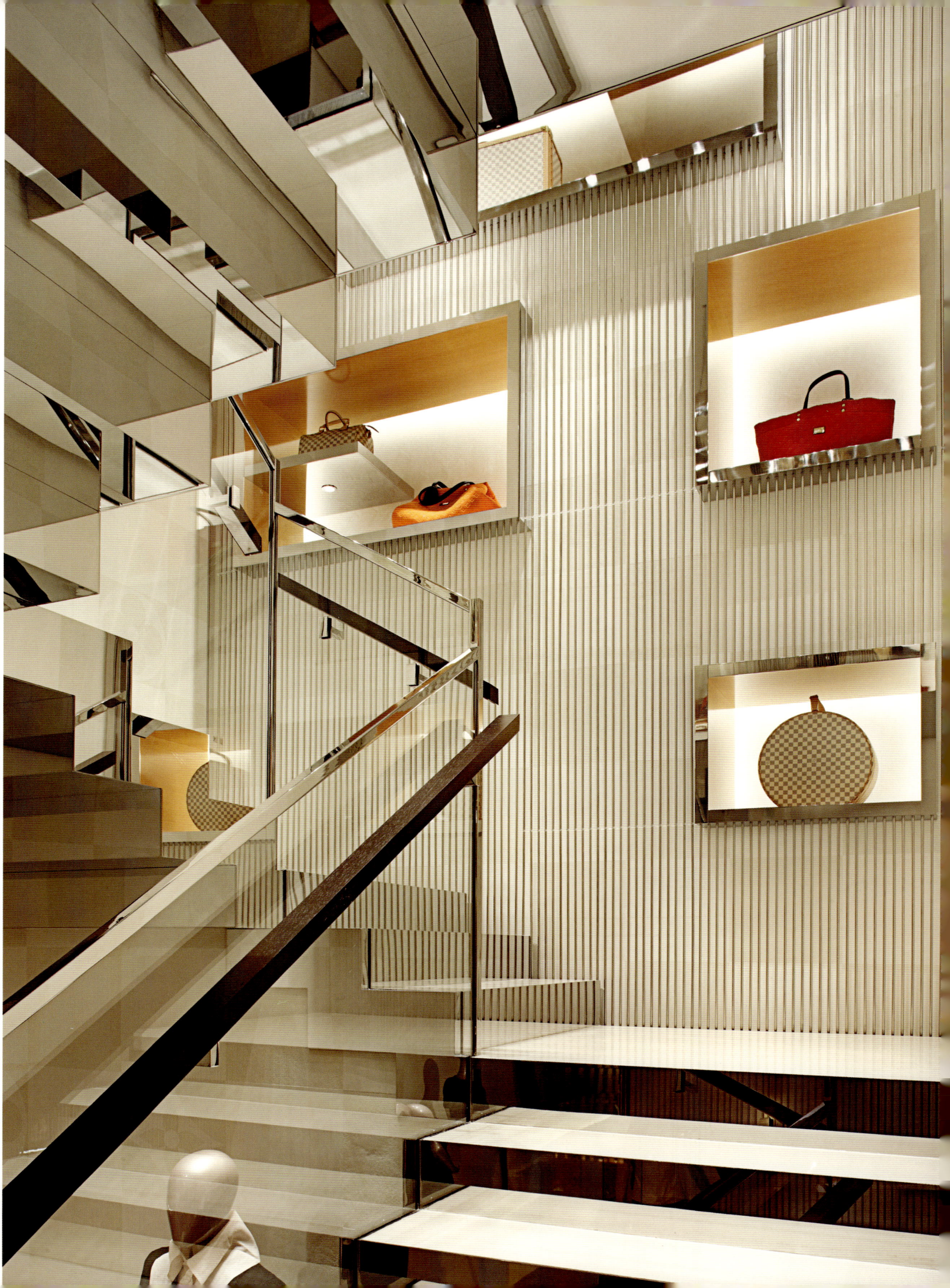

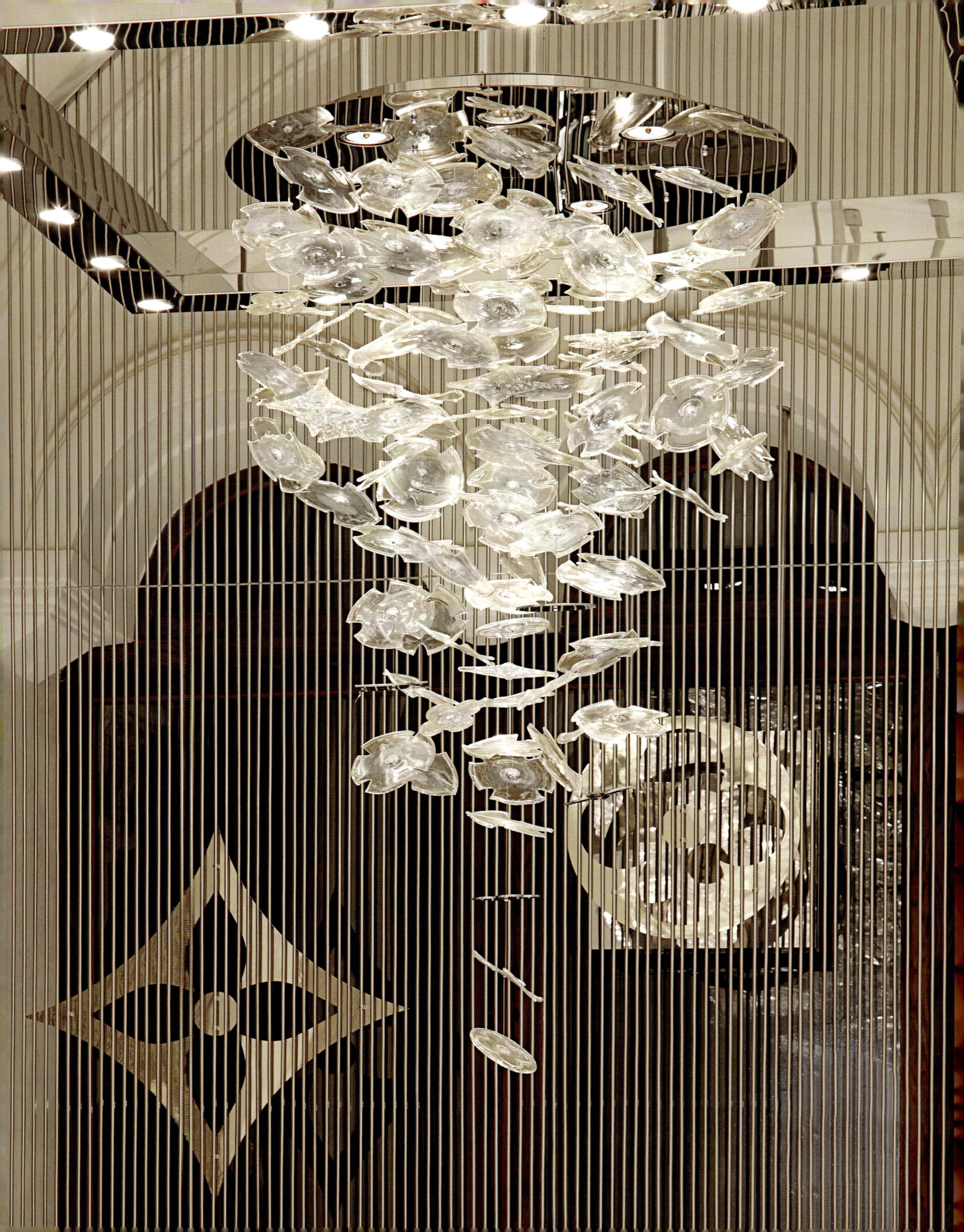

A CONVERSATION WITH CHRISTIAN DE PORTZAMPARC AND FRÉDÉRIC EDELMANN

CHRISTIAN DE PORTZAMPARC: I was just finishing the Crédit Lyonnais tower in Lille. It was then that Yves Carcelle, Chairman and CEO of Louis Vuitton, called me about a "flagship building," as he called it, in New York. And so I went over to see the site with the team Bernard Arnault had been working with for a long time.

FRÉDÉRIC EDELMANN: The Louis Vuitton site had already been purchased?
Yes. It was 1994, and I had just learned that I had been awarded the Pritzker. At a dinner, Bernard Arnault spoke to me about all the problems he was having with fakes and label copies.

Then he said to me, "I bet someday we'll work together." He didn't know about the Pritzker Prize yet. And I had already gone to see the site.

Who were you talking about the project with?
At first, Louis Vuitton was the motor, and obviously I showed my first sketches to Yves Carcelle. When he thought it was beginning to take shape, he said, "OK, go see Bernard Arnault." The first project—maybe you saw it at the '96 expo—consisted of boxes, one on top of the other. The site was very narrow. I had proposed an idea involving stacking boxes, Louis Vuitton boxes, maybe it somehow came from there…

We moved ahead with this project, which he liked. After a few months, Arnault called and said to me, "I purchased the Wally Findlay Galleries, which means the site is bigger. So, your project is very good, you just have to expand it…I really want a flagship building."

I looked at the boxes—the stack, the succession of strata, it worked very well in New York. But I said, "If we expand the building, the boxes are going to be heavy." And that's when I started on the second project. Slowly! It needed to have a strong presence, but buildings with a strong presence also have to stand the test of time. They can't just make a splash or be a UFO on the block. I remember it was on the plane that I drew out the decisive sketches for the tower, based on photographs of the models we were making. I faxed them from the hotel to the firm so that they could make a new model. And when I returned, it was clear.

Ideas sometimes come like that. The same thing happened on a plane between Luxemburg and Berlin regarding the Cidade da Musica in Rio. The plane helps sometimes.

When you sent the fax for Louis Vuitton, was it so that they could translate your idea?
It was so that they could translate the idea into a model, but it was pretty precise: I was doing it on photographs of preliminary models and plans that showed all the angles… It was better than it was as a sketch, and we had already worked enough together; they clearly understood my intentions…

It was a very curvilinear design at first.
Yes and that's when Arnault said, "The previous project was fun. This one could be beautiful." There was a vertical and slender thrust in the idea that was to be largely accomplished through white silk-screened and sandblasted glass. The white sandblasting would reign in the light from everywhere for the inside. And, most of all, it would be a much less reflective wall, so the building wouldn't just mirror the tower across the street. That's what also led me to break the form and create oblique angles. What's more, we didn't do the sandblasting on normal glass, because that would have yielded a green color—I used an extra-white glass, like the kind Pei used at the Louvre. It's a glass in which the iron oxide has been removed. That's what causes that green color. It's more transparent, whiter—even if it's very thick—and when it's sandblasted, you get a white-gray color.

Iron oxide is a normal compound in glass. It therefore has to be extracted through a chemical process, which increases costs by forty to fifty percent. It's a huge financial undertaking. I would use it in every project if I could. We imported glass produced by Saint-Gobain, sandblasted in Canada, sent it to Miami to make what they call cassettes, mounted them in the frames and then delivered and installed it into the framework in New York. All this while respecting codes that aren't the same as they are in Europe—with regard to solidity for example—and while dealing with a company that was telling me, "There's no way a Miami company is going to set foot into New York." You know how American unions are.

You spoke to me quite a bit about unions. There are trades that can't work together on the same site.
Yes and the bricklaying union even demands that there always has be some brick in buildings. But there was also the rest, all those traditions of American construction, like the amazing Indian [Native American] carpenters—the ones in Cartier Bresson's photographs who are putting up the last beams. There were two important elements. First, I was making very thin floors so that their profiles would be imperceptible at night. Then I proposed curved glass, so that the surfaces would be perfect. It came time to find some savings, and in a conversation with Bernard Arnault, we "arbitrated." I had to keep the slenderness of the floors; that was crucial, he knew it. And so I went back to the principle of a prism and flat glass. Ten minutes of consideration, two days of study (we were somewhat prepared for it at the firm) and in the end, it was really lucky: I think it's really better than before, because it's really New York. And there's something there that confirms that, yes, you are on the

block. Even if it's very strange, it's still New York, and in the end, the story about the curves was too sophisticated—"over-designed." It was really lucky that I was forced to cut down on costs.

And during this time, Philip Johnson was doing the Lipstick Building, which doesn't skimp on the curves.
Yes, you can do anything in New York. But I'm sure that the Louis Vuitton headquarters needed to be sharper, more trenchant. In New York, I also learned that if you make a void, you're allowed to make up for the space in height. It allowed me to imagine a huge empty space with a large area on top. I proposed to Arnault that we create a wonderful, very lofty space, one that broke away from the profile of the Chanel building next door.

Of course Arnault was happy. He's deeply interested in design. He analyzed the models and drawings in detail. I can tell you that there aren't many politicians and company heads that take the time to really examine a project. In juried competitions, if you ask them to bend down, they feel stupid. I've even heard some say, "I don't need to see it, I listen to my advisors…" At the time, he was saying, "Frankly, I'm not an expert but I really want to be involved in the project." He immersed himself in it. He asked the right questions. The first time, I said, "I can't go to him, he has to come here because this is where the models are." He was someone who never went anywhere. But he came anyway to look at all our studies. At the end of a meeting about the façade, I heard him say again, "If the point of the meeting was to gain my approval, you could say it was a failure. However, I'm very interested and curious to see this option and others again, as soon as possible." Those were his words. "I want to better understand. You failed this time because I didn't understand." Which makes me think there's also a genius behind the man of finance. In terms of the design, I understood that he was entering a world that he liked and that he felt connected to, personally and directly.

The LVMH tower was well received by critics. What form did that take in the United States?
Recently for example I went to a luncheon in the upper space, LVMH's "magic room." I was invited by a landmark association in New York. Every year, they have a luncheon to raise money, and every year it's held in an old building. This time, they did it in that room and they said to me, "This is the first time we're meeting in a contemporary building. It may become a landmark." That's great to hear.

And at that luncheon at the LVMH building, a guy introduced himself, "I'm the architect of Bank of America. I wanted to thank you because all my work on that bank building—a project that involves oblique angles and prisms too," he said, "comes from you and LVMH. I wanted to say thank you, one for your ideas, but also because I was able to convince the companies that it was feasible…" There you have it: so there are projects inspired by LVMH being developed in New York.

The film in the "Empreintes" series presents how it was received. It's a portrait made for [Channel] 5 by Daniel Alblin and written by Jean-Louis Cohen. The latter thought that I should be interviewed in Rio, New York, Paris, etc; that all these places would overlap. At the beginning of the film, lights go up and down the façade… But really you see how New Yorkers react; you see that they like their city and its architecture. LVMH seems to have made an impression on them. That's a first for the city. They actually say that there hasn't been a building since the Ford Foundation that has so revived the presence of architecture in the city.

When Amanda Burden became the director of City Planning, which heads urban development, she launched an incentive-based policy: she suggested that if developers come with good professionals and if they present architectural and urban planning projects to her—good, sophisticated projects for the people of the city—she'd be ready to change the zoning and to propose new air rights. That's when I was called by several developers, for example for 400 Park on Park Avenue—which seems to be put on hold or stopped by the recession. And the four blocks I proposed for the Riverside neighborhood were just approved by Amanda Burden's City Planning. A tower of mine on 57th Street is also being built. It consists of several volumes that gradually rise up almost a thousand feet, with apartments overlooking Central Park.

These are the happy and sometimes difficult situations that come in LVMH's wake.
In the wake of LVMH and the Pritzker. Because in the end, I have a good reputation in the United States. In France, they know my name at *Le Figaro* and *Le Monde*. The architecture community knows me. But what the firm is doing isn't well presented.

And for you, for your own conception of architecture?
In working on this project, I came to that notion of the slightly prismatic ascension. Maybe I drew on the oblique angles that I developed in the Lille tower. It also influenced other projects in which slender forms and prisms come into play again. It all started in '95-'96 with LVMH. There are projects that are seminal in that they clear a way. And then in time you inevitably reach another stage. I'm now designing skyscrapers in China that have nothing to do with that. It's also that you don't want to repeat yourself. You want to preserve a fresh spirit, but then sometimes the old stuff comes back.

You were also asked to go to China. What's happening there?
It's a kind of large landscape. Unintentionally, I was inspired by Chinese painting. Once I put it down on paper, they said, "Oh yes, but you know the young generations really don't care. They don't look at that kind of painting any more." Except, then an architect who's somewhat Chinese said to me, "On the contrary, yes, young people are finally searching for and finding their roots."

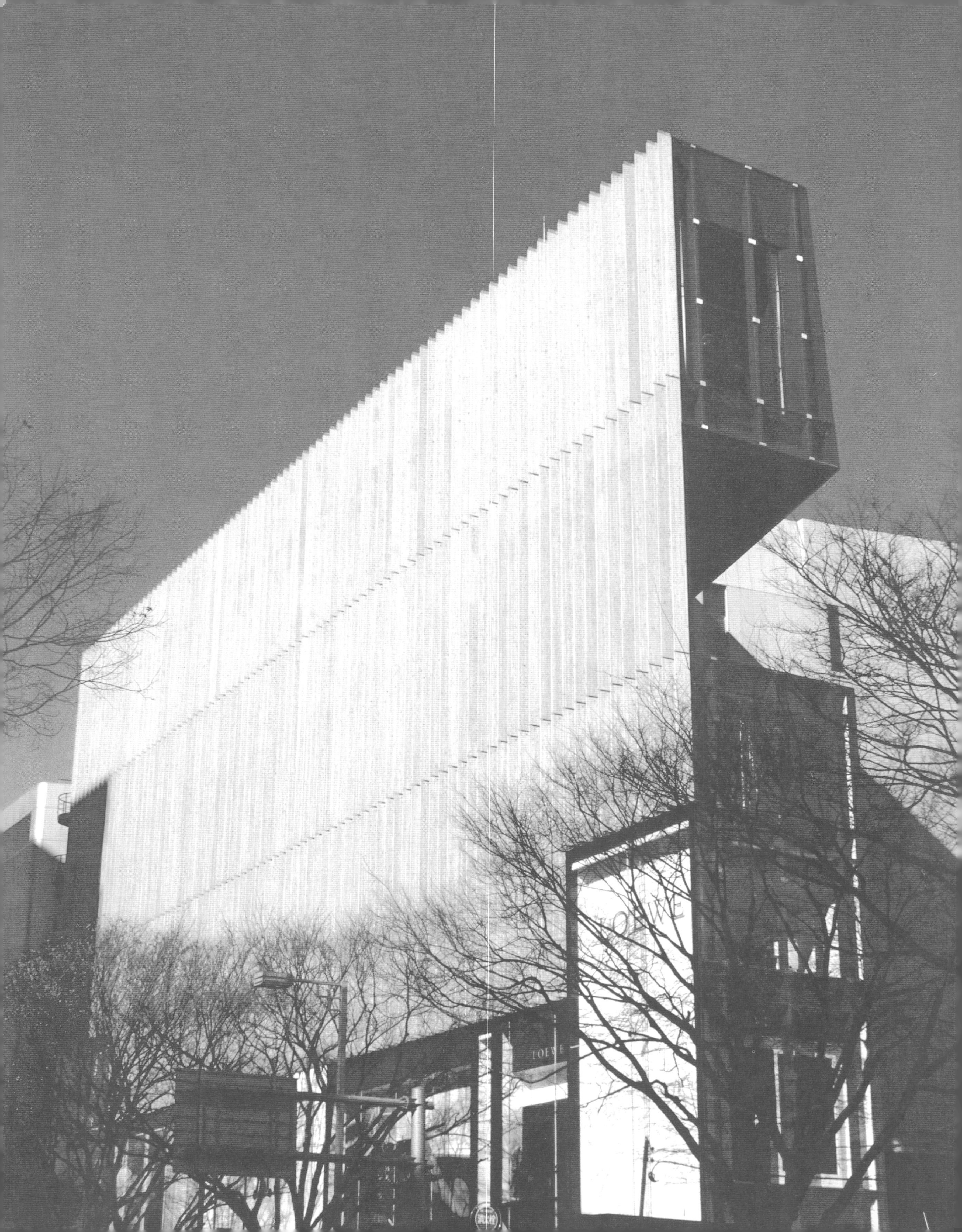

HEADQUARTERS
UNITED STATES, NEW YORK
LVMH TOWER
JAPAN, TOYKO
ONE OMOTESANDO

NEW YORK LVMH TOWER

architects
ATELIER CHRISTIAN DE PORTZAMPARC
1999

text by
FRÉDÉRIC EDELMANN

The inauguration of the LVMH tower (Moët-Hennessy/Louis Vuitton) in New York on Wednesday, December 8, 1999, was marked by an explosion of golden glitter and the presence of Hillary Clinton, back then the first lady of the United States. It was no flash in the pan. The building is located in the heart of Manhattan, like every company of a certain stature, close to the corner of Madison Avenue and 57th Street. Its unveiling has gone down in history as the first New York architectural event since Kevin Roche and John Dinkeloo's Ford Foundation (1967) and Frank Lloyd Wright's Guggenheim Museum (1954), and has even dethroned the postmodern tower of AT&T (today the Sony Building) designed by Philip Johnson in 1994.

For nearly thirty years, until Rudolph Guiliani became mayor in 1994 and began improving the perception of an impoverished and dangerous metropolis, New York was mired in architectural mediocrity because of the timidity of commissioners and the rigidity of construction unions. Although supported by Bernard Arnault and by his very recent Prizker Prize (1994), Christian de Portzamparc's work, from the moment it was initially commissioned to its completion, was no easy task in terms of its structure or concept. New Yorkers had cultivated a certain kind of protectionism that reinforced antagonistic traditions in the field of construction: steel was king in the US, while concrete was exclusively devoured in France.

So how can the success of this modest, 24-story building (resting at 112 meters high, and 580 square meters) be explained? Herbert Muschamp, then the fearsome critic for the New York Times (he died in 2004) was one of the first supporters of the building. Portzamparc restored his joy of discovery by reinterpreting the principle of the "skyscraper," however small, at a time when building regulations and the standards of constructors were fixed. The building created a spark in the nearly endangered architectural world of the East coast, which was only spared by a few villas and a bouquet of superbly designed stores. A French observer, accustomed to the theatrics of European architects, might have passed by without noticing the narrow façade, its sensible ground floor already occupied by Dior, one of the group's pearls. But for him too the "Portzy" design would have represented a rupture reminiscent of the spontaneous expressionism of French architects like Henri Gaudin or Frédéric Borel, or that of an exuberant Gehry, who was already at the peak of his fame in Europe, whose Guggenheim opened in 1997.

An American enthusiast could immediately comprehend the novelty and freshness that characterized the tower. The building clearly departs from the old three-part principle (broken masterfully by Mies Van der Rohe) that calls for a foot, a body and a head—which cleverly crowned skyscrapers built between the wars and after. But, above all, the structure stays clear of the arrogant gravity of recent towers, simplistic geometric volumes: a cube topped by a cylinder, and capped with a cone (Helmuth Jahn, 750 Lexington Avenue), or the Lipstick Building, so named for its tubular shape (Philip Johnson, Third Avenue). With Portzamparc's design, the four, large receding glass panels of the LVMH tower, white or dark, form a kind of photon trap, allowing the internal structure to escape analysis. Day and night, one cannot ignore the discreet elegance of this large, glass gentleman who seems to wrap around himself a building-gown whose materials capture every nuance of light, without reflecting the image of his neighbors.

The approach is a conventional method for a French architect, one that had been often used before by Le Corbusier. "The building is a body, not a façade," Christian de Portzamparc explains. "Folds are not random. It is a visual device. A machine guiding what you see. It's a building that I developed as a visual expression while at the same time getting around New York regulations." He expounds on his device with the same constant poetry that enlivens his design: "From the inside of the building, the view of Manhattan becomes strange and mysterious as a result of a network of lines sandblasted on very rare, extra-white glass, produced by Saint-Gobain, sandblasted in Canada, and assembled in Miami."

"It involved," he adds, "imagining a system capable of filtering light in order to convert it into bluish white tones. With the windows being very high, the transparency allowing for visibility is retained in their lower part. Towards the top, this visibility is degraded and changed with light. Hence, we arrive at the paradox that the least transparent part is the most luminous." This was certainly needed to light the twenty-four little stories, variously discernable, behind the façade overlooking the street, and delimited on the inside by mostly opaque, brick partitions. This disrupted design creates on every level a range of spaces that reflect the diversity of the brands that belong to the group: Dior, Lacroix, Guerlain, Louis Vuitton, Céline, and Givenchy, to name only a few of the first occupants.

An elevator shaft, a slanting partition and the projection of the façade's lines on the interior spaces allow the invention of variable geometric volumes, all of which share three constants: an almost spiral arrangement, like a crustacean; a compactness only rivaled by the common areas at the Pierre Hotel (real New York chic is not always about space); and finally an amazing capacity to support changing amounts of "style" from each brand in the group—from Louis XV, numbed by the use of white, a bit of raspberry red for the sexier among them, a touch of tomato green, harvested early for aesthetic versions of luxury. In this manner Portzamparc and his team (Bruno Durbecq and Wilfrid Bellecourt, assistant architects) offered the interior designers a versatile support system capable of accommodating a range of vocabularies. There's one more space that bears the signature of the French architect; the lofty hall that crowns the building with an open, panoramic southern view of New York. This is a place called the Magic Room, for parties or formal occasions. As the architect explains, this space resulted from negotiations regarding air rights but also the complex regulations of the surrounding area. The tower's hollow belly greatly contributed to the volume at the top.

Portzamparc didn't immediately settle on this white, glass tulip. Often exhibited, the succession of models illustrates the evolution of the design; it's practically dizzying. In very small scale, you can see the different possible forms being developed—from a model with receding stories to the idea of piled up boxes that was the point of departure for more detailed considerations of the LVMH tower, and every variation in between. Portzamparc's first, large-scale models resemble a stack of different kinds of luggage. The acquisition of a small plot where the Wally Findlay Gallery was located led the architect toward a more supple direction, and gradually to the large glass panels, which he initially imagined would be curved. The strictness of American construction denied him this freedom however, and led him to the broken lines of the final design.

Bernard Arnauld, the CEO of the LVMH group, got a good deal out of Portzamparc, whose knack perhaps came from his first job when he graduated from the École Polytechnique as head of construction at Ferret-Savinel. From here, he went straight to the top: the ballet of New York muses welcomed Portzamparc both as the savior of a misguided architectural community and as the inspiration for a new movement that was generously hailed by critics and will always be recognized by posterity.

p. 192 One Omotesando Building, Omotesando, Tokyo
p. 194 exterior along 57th street
p. 197 exterior view of South façade
p. 198 view from across 57th street
p. 199 top: "magic" room on top floor; bottom: view of clear and fritted glazing, looking into a typical office
p. 200 view from Madison Avenue and 57th street
p. 201 conference area and elevator lobby

GROUND FLOOR

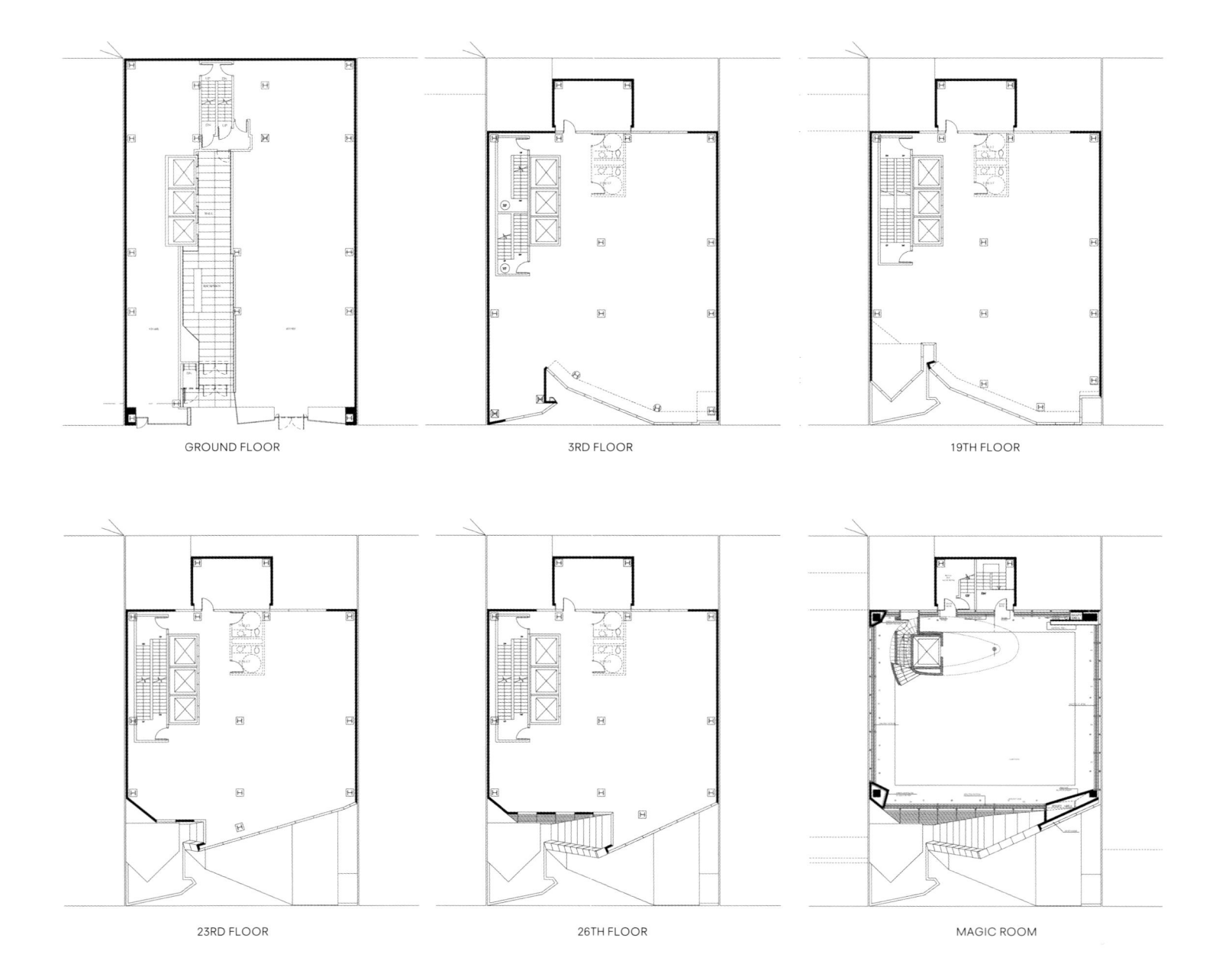

3RD FLOOR

19TH FLOOR

23RD FLOOR

26TH FLOOR

MAGIC ROOM

ARCHITECTURE AND INTERIORS 197

NEW YORK LVMH TOWER

UNITED STATES

Christian Dior

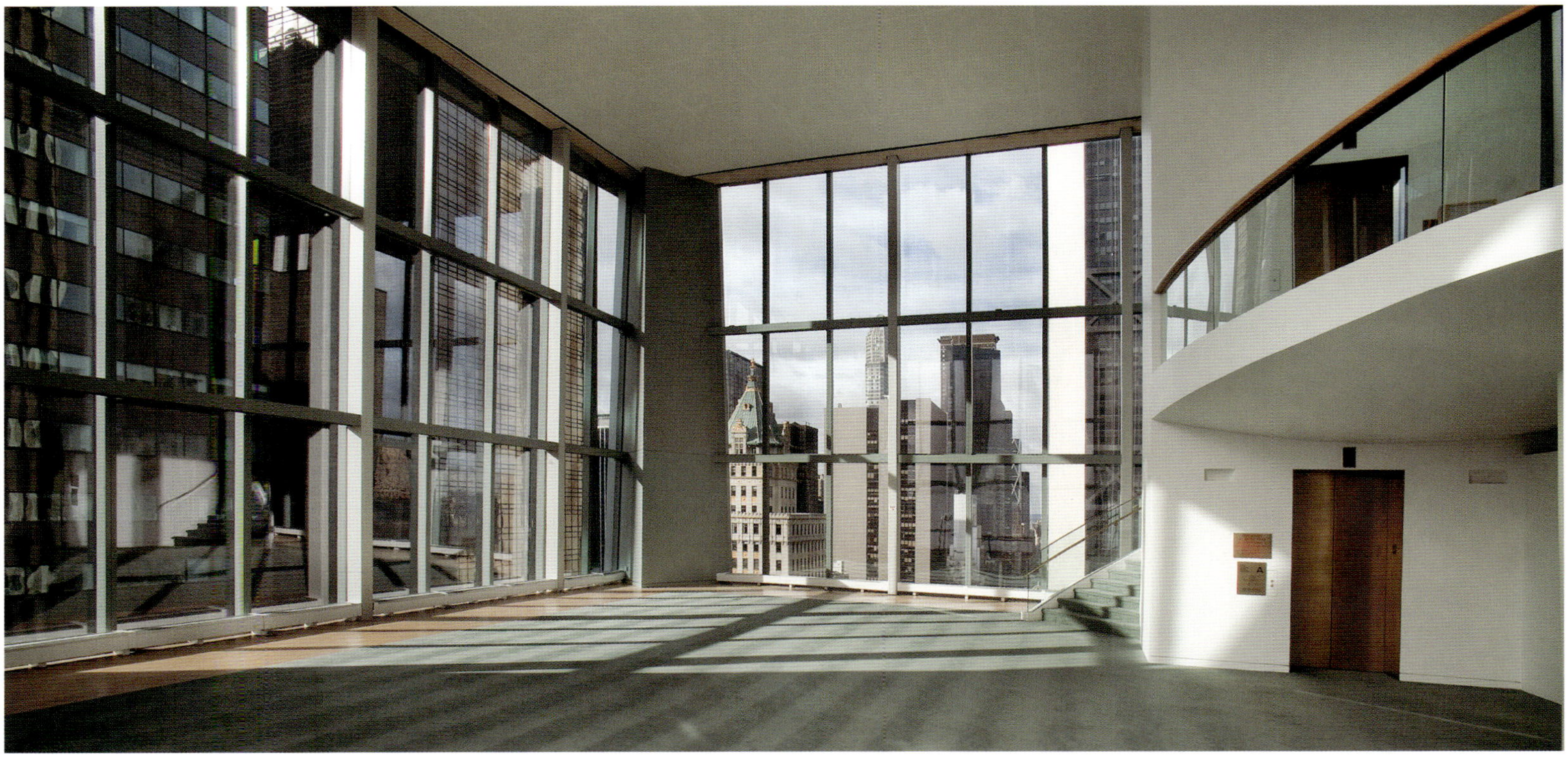

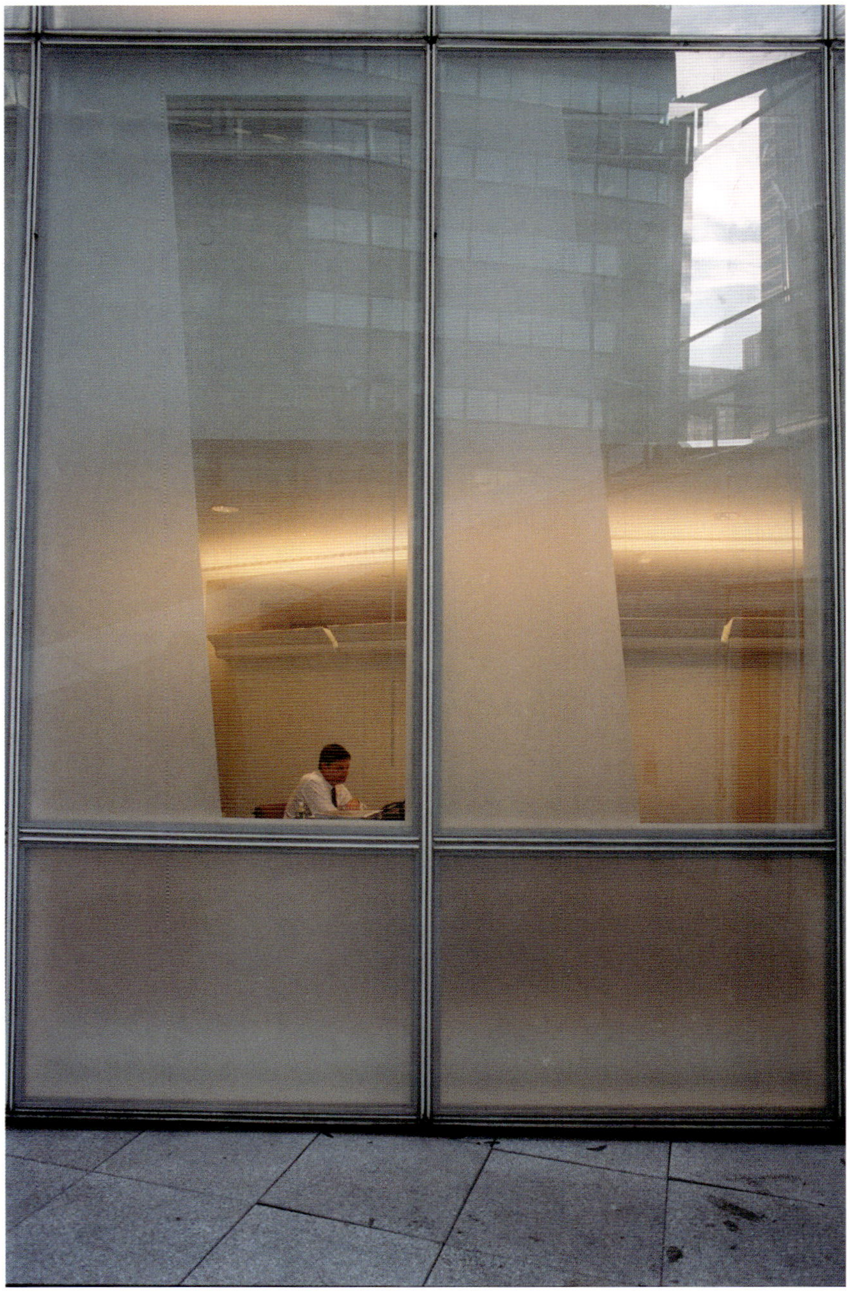

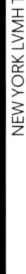

ARCHITECTURE AND INTERIORS 200

NEW YORK LVMH TOWER

UNITED STATES

ARCHITECTURE AND INTERIORS 201

NEW YORK LVMH TOWER

UNITED STATES

TOKYO
ONE OMOTESANDO

architects
KENGO KUMA
2002

text by
FRÉDÉRIC EDELMANN

It took Kengo Kuma nearly twenty years to achieve the international recognition that he enjoys today. One Omotesando, completed in 2002, is an important milestone along the way.

Some had raised doubts that he'd succeed especially since he'd employed such endearing aphorisms like "I want to erase architecture," something he'd initially embodied in composite, mostly unassuming structures. This philosophy combined virtually all styles and fashions; take for instance, the simultaneously postmodern and metabolic building dominated by a colossal Doric column, which he built for the M2 car salesroom in Tokyo's Setagaya neighborhood (1991). On the opposite end of the spectrum, if you can call it that, he created the extremely sophisticated design for the Great (Bamboo) Wall House outside Beijing (2003), One Omotesando, and subsequently, the LVMH building in Osaka on Midosuji street—a sleek, quadrilateral structure covered in stone and glass strips (2004).

No two Kengo Kuma projects are alike. Each one has its own, its own manner of seduction, and at the same time, its own way of confusing the public. When he renovated the empyrean Nezu Museum (2009), on the edge of the Aoyama neighborhood, and extending Omotesando's hip strip south, his bad boy image began to take on that of a Zen master. It's been more than four years now that the architect completed the headquarters for Louis Vuitton at the corner of Omotesando and Aoyama Dori, a building that reminds people that he is of Japanese descent, but that he completed his studies at Columbia University in New York. In a country that generally tends to forego street names for a more complex numbering system, the building's official address is 3-5-28 and 3-5-29 Kita-Aoyama, Minato-ku.

One Omotesando is obviously easier to remember; it's a name as distinguishable as a flag. But, does it stand like a "flagship," as they like to say at Vuitton ever since Christian de Portzamparc finished the New York headquarters? Regardless. With the utmost seriousness, Kengo Kuma here makes use of a large rectangular screen, striated with vertical slats of wood: "a star-spangled banner" without the stars. This device was meant to recall traditional Japanese architecture, while serving as a filter and a screen. In fact, he drew inspiration from the curtains of wood of the Shinto temple dedicated to Emperor Meiji and hidden in the Yoyogi Park, so as to protect the building from the "bric-a-brac environment," to use Kuma's own words. Is he referring to Harajuku's extravagances, or to the collection of architectural examples that—like a neoclassic pastiche of Ricardo Bofill—practically face the Louis Vuitton headquarters, including buildings by Toyo Ito (Tod's), SANAA (Dior), Tadao Ando (Omotesando Hills), and even Jun Aoki (Louis Vuitton)?

Administrative approval for the structure's solid wood façade, which stands in front of a classic, glass wall-curtain, was very difficult to obtain due to the stringent fire-safety codes in Tokyo. At 50 meters long, it masks the structure of the building, while also revealing its unusual complexity. The architect explains that it resulted from his desire to incorporate the specificities of Japanese space: the juxtaposition of autonomous volumes and integration of the landscape. This effect in particular is achieved in the strong presence of the avenue's tall trees, zelkovas (or *keyaki* in Japanese, a species similar to the elm), which conceal the lower part of the building, its row of four windows and the emblematic name of the building: One Omotesando. At this level, neither Louis Vuitton, nor LVMH are apparent.

To a great extent, the overall form of the structure appears to be influenced by Tokyo's codes, which, as in New York—and to a lesser extent, in Paris—obey building and neighborhood conventions that, when combined with fire-safety and earthquake regulations, can become debilitating or valuable depending on the skill and imagination of the architect. Many of the neighborhood's constructions wriggle into their space, giving up a few meters in one direction to gain a few elsewhere by increasing the height or depth of the building. At the much larger scale of an eight-story building, the ground plan of One Omotesando winds up recalling an exceedingly comfortable airplane seat (think business class). In other words, it benefits from a comfortable and unusual width, on the ground floor at least, with a total surface area of more than 1,600 square meters for the in-house brands that have made One Omotesando their home (Fendi, Celine, Loewe, DKNY).

The cross-sections, which vary from one part of the building to the other, reveal mysterious gaps, empty and solid, which find meaning only through Kuma's skillfull distribution of the interior spaces. For Louis Vuitton (and LVMH), life begins on the second level in a spacious lobby, where white and metal dominate over a wooden floor that glistens beneath the artificial light. A large "L" and a large "V," both in relief, intersect to form an abstract sculpture—the only reference to the company, unlike in their stores. A bank in the shape of a half moon allows a hostess to welcome and direct visitors either to the various offices of other brands, or to the Louis Vuitton spaces.

Metallic stairwell or elevator? Both routes lead to the offices that, in essence, preserve their secret. They also lead towards two large volumes—a hollow area between the fourth and sixth levels which serves as a festive terrace, explaining the building's strange profile, and another area that is surrounded by glass and isolated from the world by tall, adjustable blinds: the boardroom of the Japanese branch of Louis Vuitton. Here, luxury is tempered and functional: when the blinds are raised, a large part of the city appears—a striking model where one can imagine the presence of already existing stores and conceive of future projects.

p. 203 aerial view from across Route 246
p. 205 façade on Omotesando
p. 206–207 interior views of lobby and staircase
p. 208 top: detail of wood louvers as seen from the interior; bottom: roof terrace
p. 210–211: view looking up South façade

ARCHITECTURE AND INTERIORS 204

TOKYO ONE OMOTESANDO

JAPAN

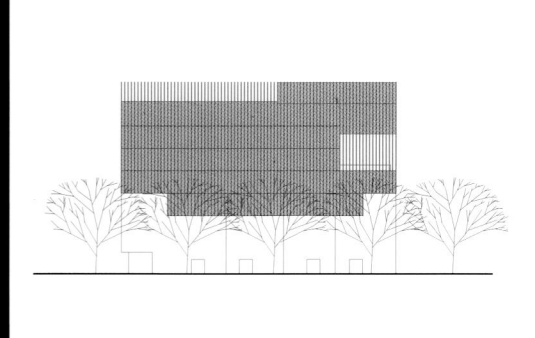

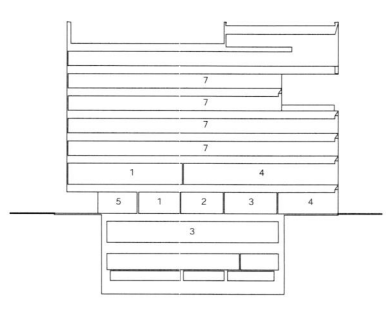

GROUND FLOOR

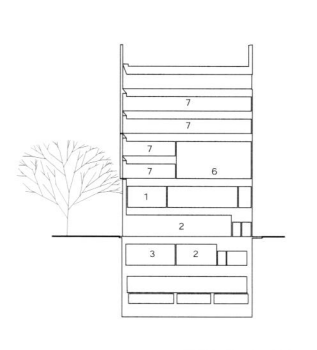

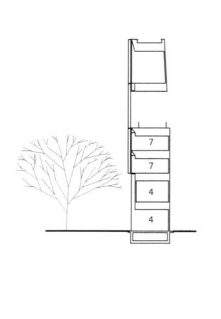

SOUTH ELEVATION

SECTION LOOKING NORTH

SECTIONS LOOKING WEST

ARCHITECTURE AND INTERIORS

TOKYO ONE OMOTESANDO

JAPAN

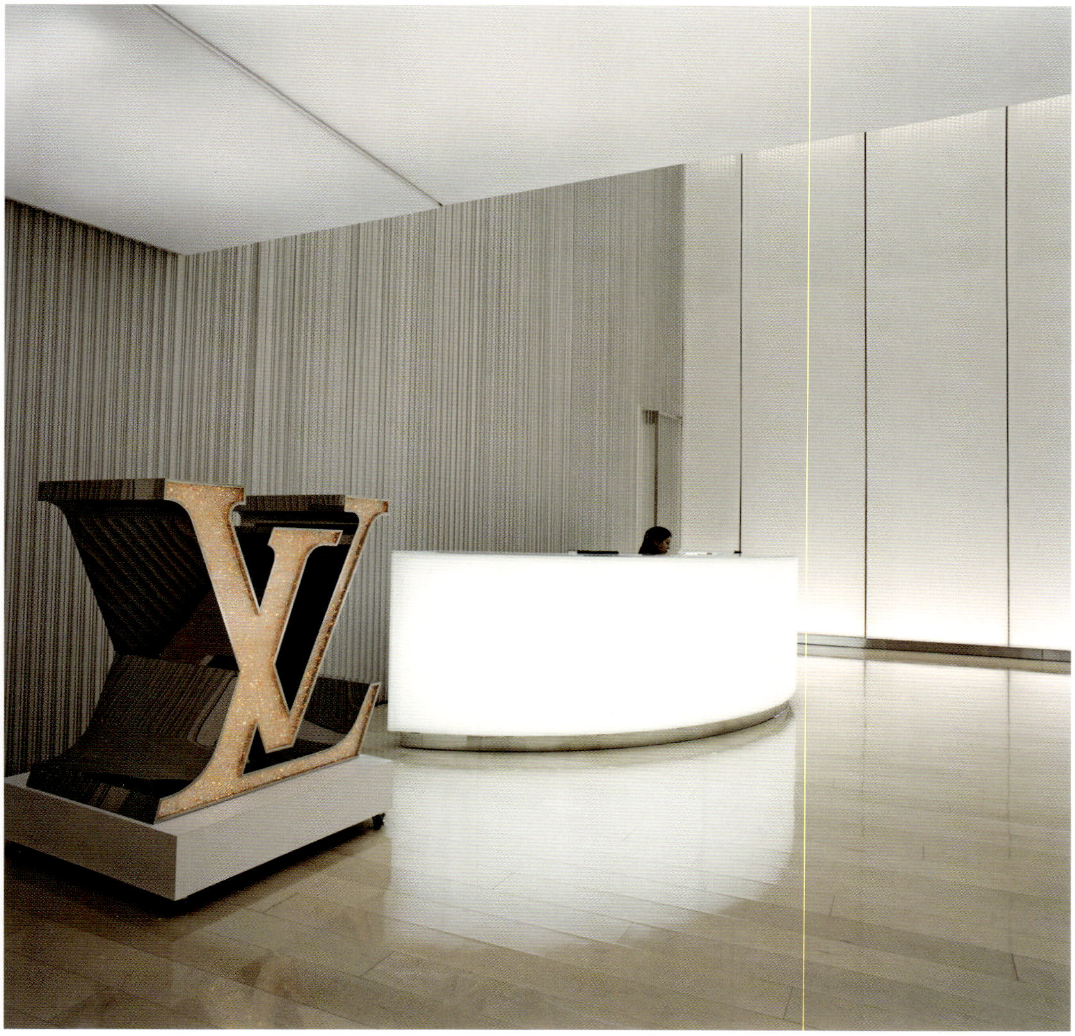

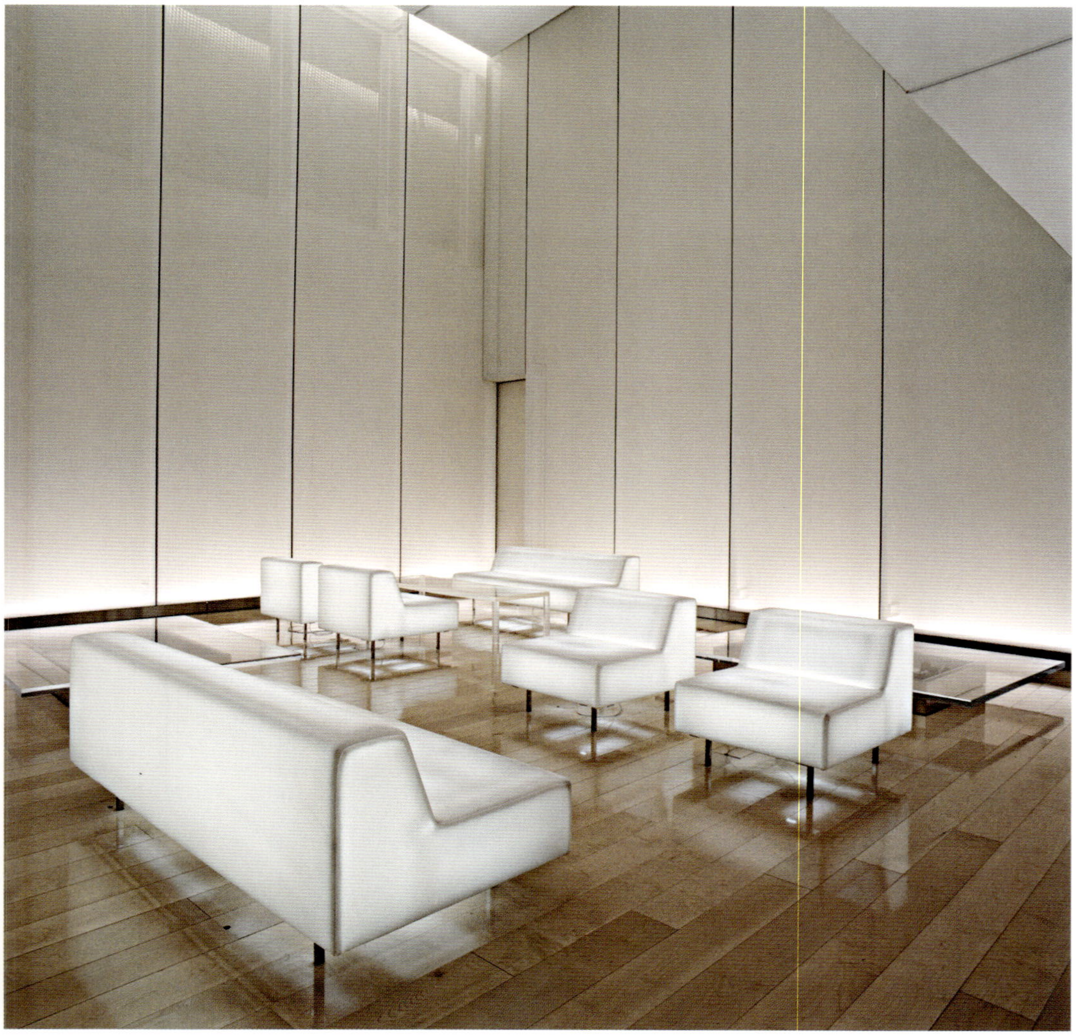

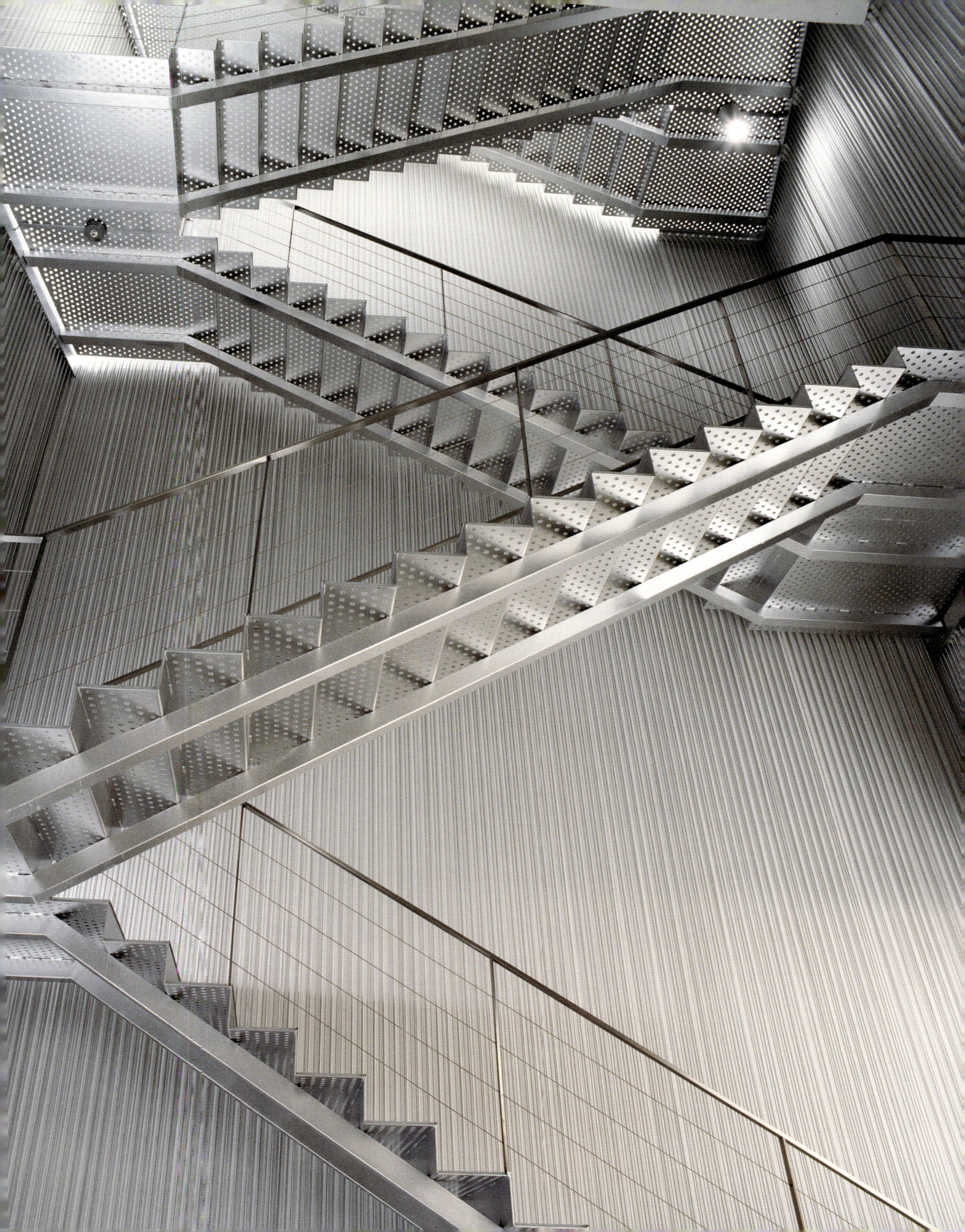

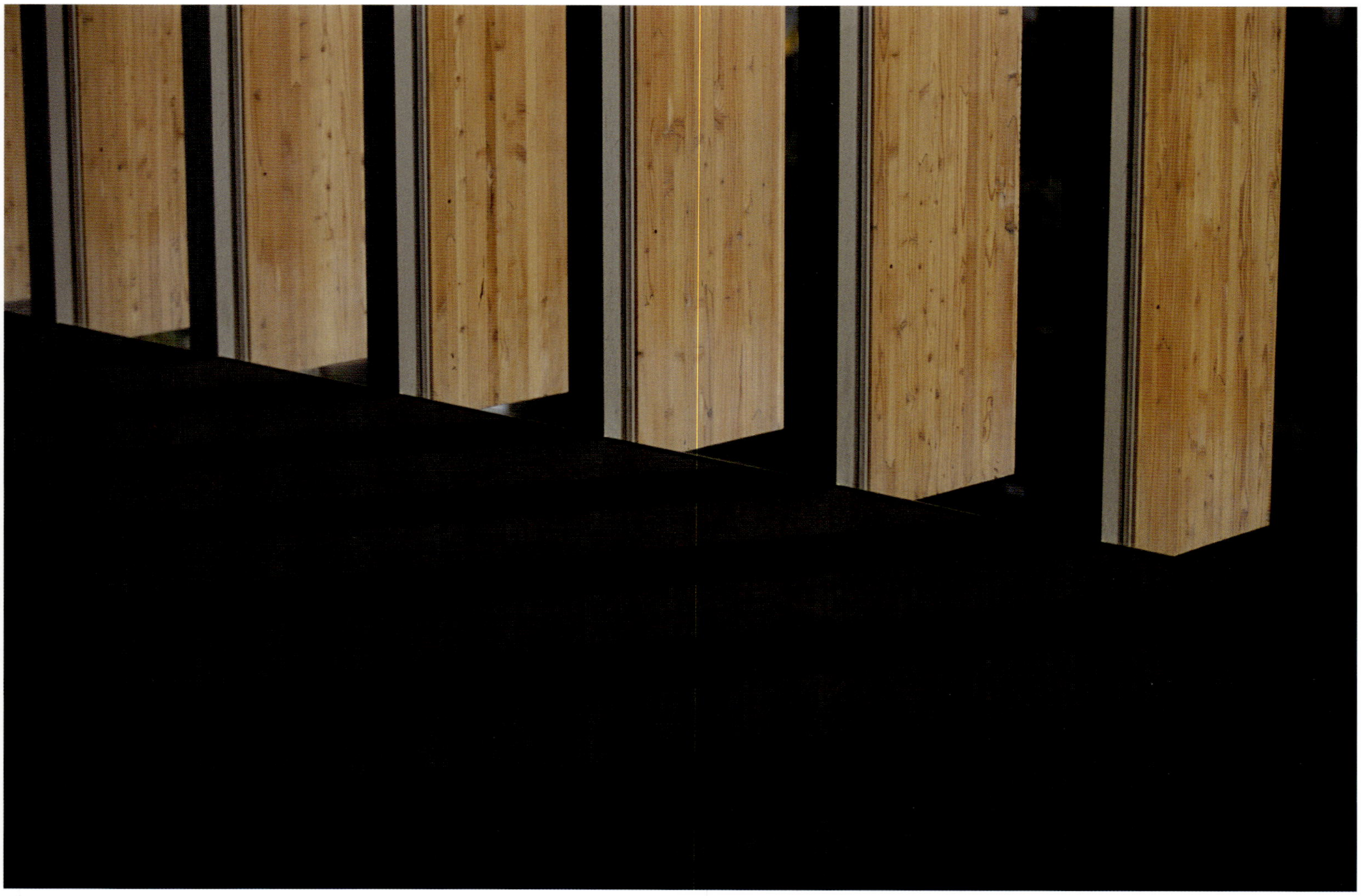

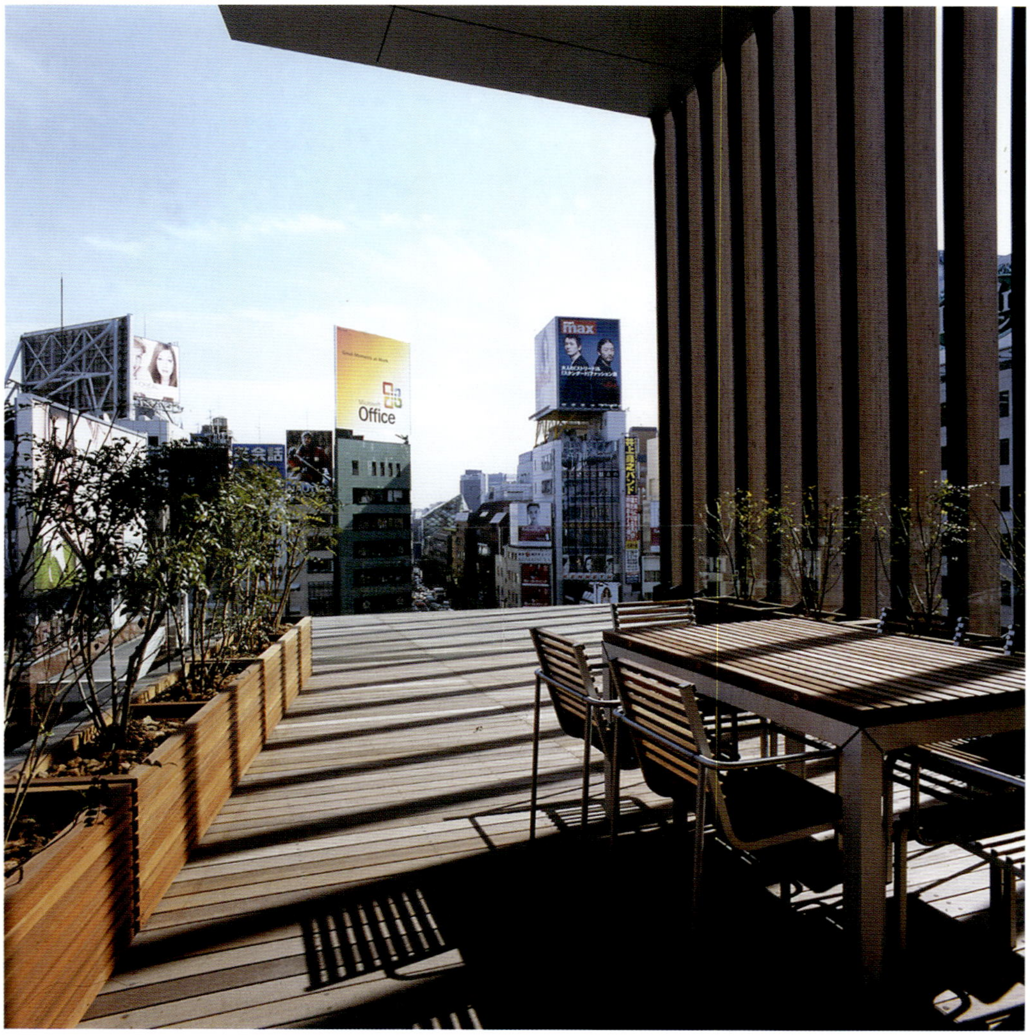
Office
max

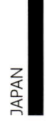

WALL SECTION

LOUVER DIAGRAM

4TH FLOOR

5TH FLOOR

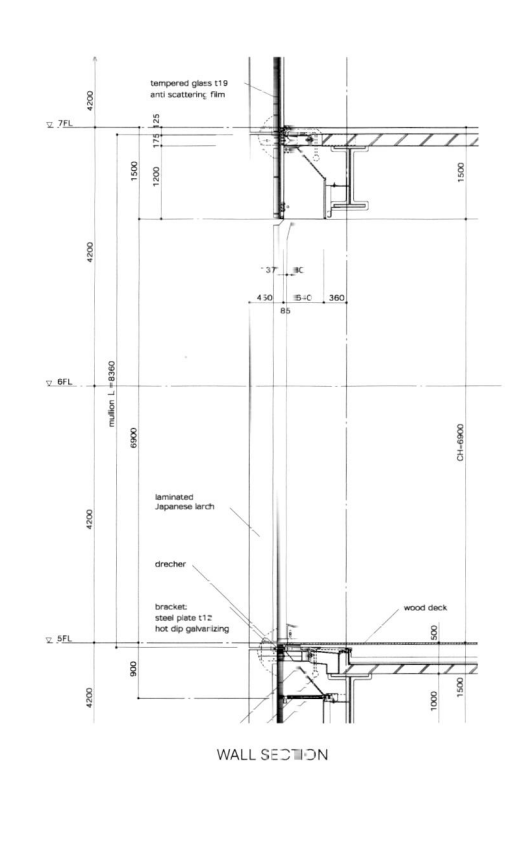

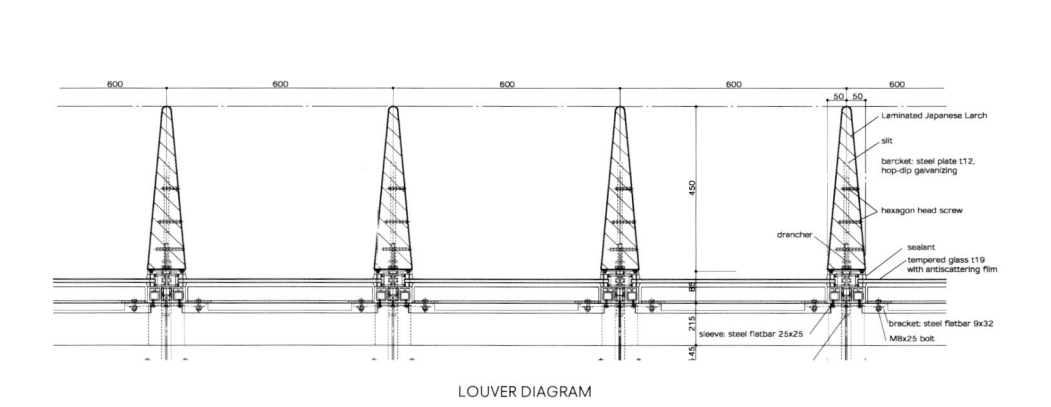

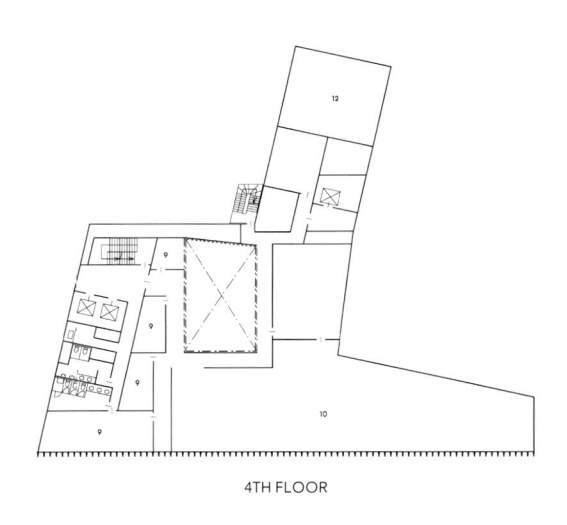

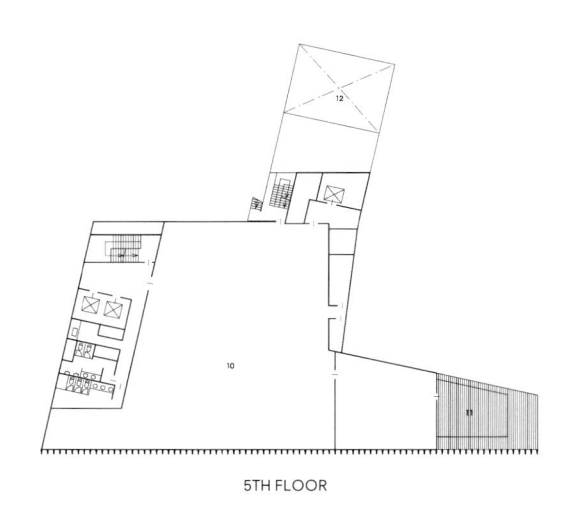

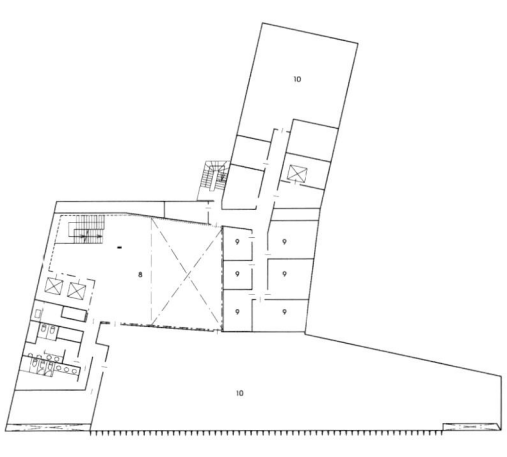

3RD FLOOR

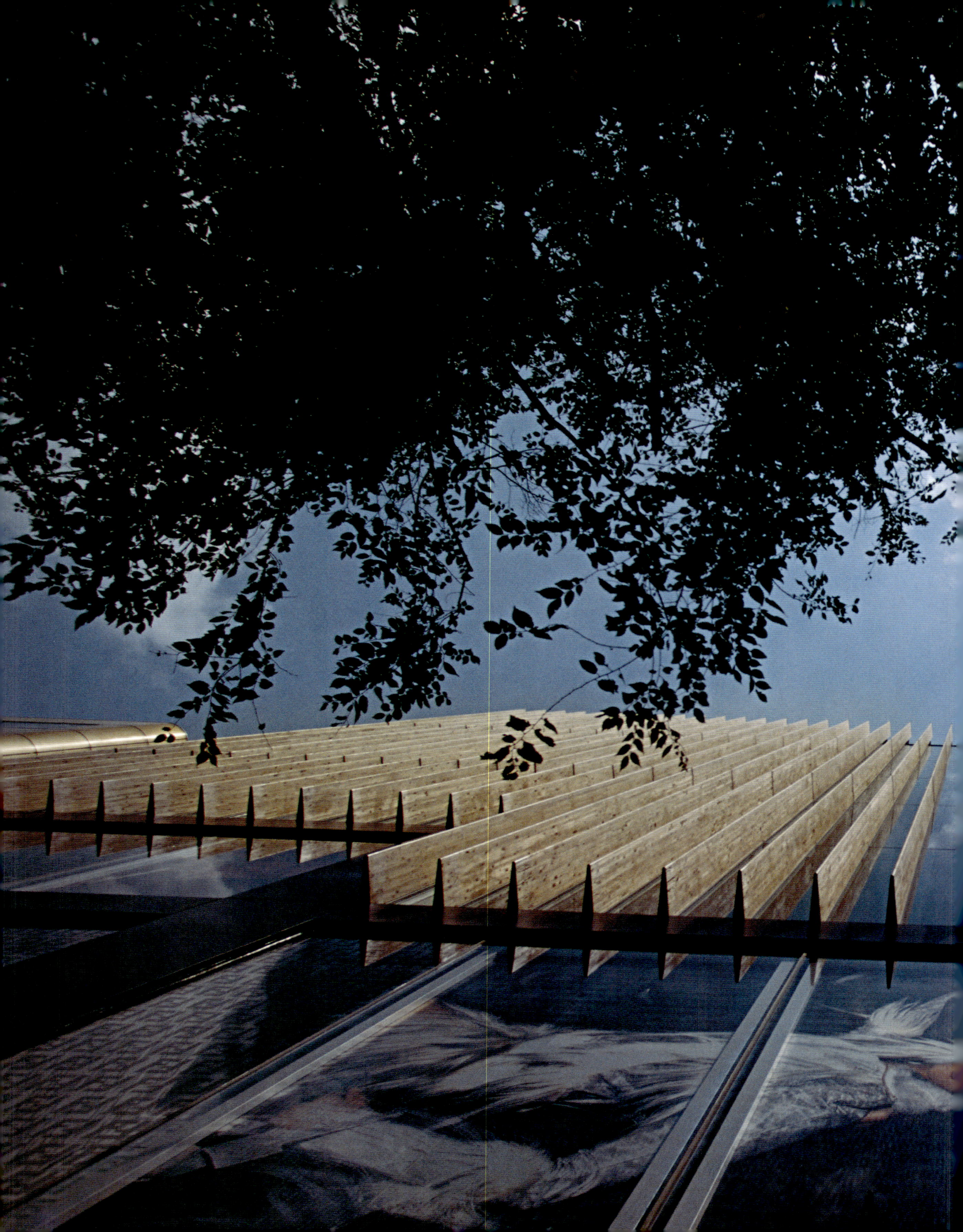

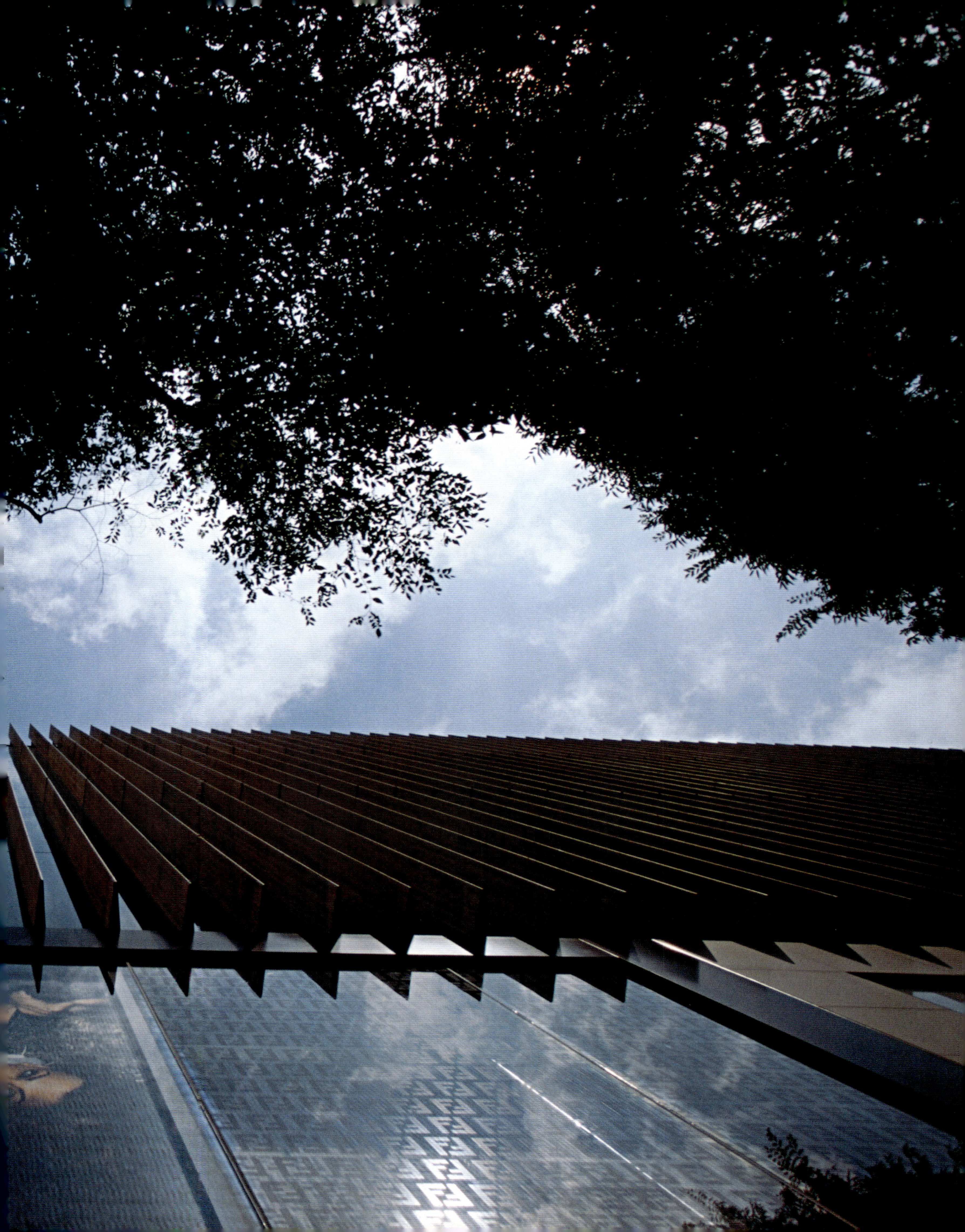

A CONVERSATION WITH CHRISTIAN REYNE AND RAFAEL MAGROU

RAFAEL MAGROU: Louis Vuitton is a brand that has become famous across the world. Once associated exclusively with the world of luxury travel, offering trunks and leather goods, today it offers a full range of products that includes men and women's fashion. This established the company as a world leader in luxury whose merchandise, especially bags, is coveted worldwide. Has this change radically transformed the in-house mindset?
CHRISTIAN REYNE: Since being founded in 1854, the house of Louis Vuitton has gone through several periods of transformation, but has never lost sight of its rising standards for quality. This has maintained and even strengthened its reputation throughout the world. After 1997, when Marc Jacobs came from the heart of the fashion world and expanded the brand's catalogue, it truly sent shockwaves through the company. We had to adapt to new activities and expand our industrial capacity to respond to the exponential creative growth. However, as surprising as it may be, we have retained a very participatory operational mode at Vuitton, one that is developed through dialogue. Our exchanges are particularly iterative. When making decisions, such as making choices for a site, project or technical details—despite the size of the brand and its fifteen thousands employees located in fifteen workshops and over four hundred and seventy stores worldwide—we operate according to the same spirit of the original brand, with a side to it that's rather familial.

The architectural visibility of the brand is developed primarily for stores and spatial and material inventions there. What is required of the workshops—which are the mainsprings of production—in order for the massive demands to be met? Do they have the same operational mode that they always have had?
No, quite the opposite. The concept of the workshops has greatly evolved, principally through architectural choices but also for production reasons; we went from a very artisanal approach to production, without that being pejorative—you are well aware of the effort Louis Vuitton has made to reconcile tradition and modernity—to 3D designs that involve the latest advancements in this domain.

If you take a look at the Louis Vuitton workshops, you'll see several "generations." First, be aware that, traditionally, our workforce is concentrated in metropolitan France where we have eleven leather goods workshops; we only have two workshops in Catalonia and one in California. For other areas of competence, we have a workshop devoted to shoemaking in Veneto, Italy—a traditional region for this skill sector—and another devoted to watch making in Chaux-de-Fonds in Switzerland. Apart from the workshop in Asnières—which is the cradle of the company and produced the first trunks, thereby establishing the name of Louis Vuitton as being synonymous with luxury and world travel—the first generation workshops date from the end of the 1970s, with the acquisition of buildings in Saint-Donat in the Drôme region, Issoudun in the Indre region, and Sarras in the Ardèche region. Three functional structures.

The second generation emerged during the 1990s, with the construction of workshops such as Saint Pourçain, in the Allier region—the first in a long series built by Gilles Carnoy. It was there in fact that he first sketched his unique skylights, inspired by the nautical world. These became a distinguishing feature at Louis Vuitton workshops, serving as a fifth allegorical façade. It was also here that the square building plan, with adjoining patio, came into being. The Sainte Florence workshop in the Vendée marked a new stage, bringing about the third generation. Built at the dawn of the 2000s, it expressed an architectural identity all its own, with its canoe-shaped skylights. The idea of constructing workshops in the countryside was reinforced, providing the most serene possible setting for the leather craftsmen. We're in constant search for a horizon that provides them with a place to rest their eyes during breaks, given the extreme concentration required by their professions. This is the case in Ducey, with its view of Mont Saint-Michel in the distance, and also in Condé, designed by Jean Marc Sandrolini, with its views onto the crop fields of the Indre. Marsaz, which opened in 2011, represents the most recent generation with its vast shell opening onto the landscape, and the Vercors Mountains skirting the sky. This facility expresses the desired balance of treatment that exists in our factories now, with an optimal working comfort. What's more, the decision to settle in areas far from cities generates employment in what are sometimes depressed areas. Accessibility requires LV employees to adapt their operating procedures, but carpooling is no longer an issue and it strengthens bonds inside and outside company walls.

Finally, whenever possible, we avoid distinguishing between workshops and stores in terms of space and organization; if our craftsmen feel good, our clients will sense the pleasure in the products they're purchasing.

How does this translate into the way the workshops function? Have you replaced hand-made processes with machines?
In Fiesso D'Artico, which was built by Jean Marc Sandrolini near Venice, we installed an automated section for the first time, replacing the hand of man. But this was put in place at a specific part of the production process and only serves to lighten the workload

and to execute the most daunting portions of the shoemaking process. Under no circumstances do we want to turn our workshops, where human expertise reigns over machines, into factories that spit out products. Even if there's great pressure to meet the demands of our ever-growing clientele, we don't want to run the risk of sacrificing the quality of our products just to fill orders. On the one hand, this means we have to anticipate needs by creating new production sites and, on the other—and this is unfortunate—we sometimes have to ask our clients to be patient, for the sake of quality. The rule is that we must automatically be one workshop ahead!

Our workshops are therefore never larger than 8000 square meters, half of which is devoted to production, strictly speaking. This scale allows us to retain acceptable production units, in which the foreman knows each leather worker by name. It's very much like a family, like I was saying, since conviviality is our way of guaranteeing the quality of our products. Comfortable working conditions are a priority for us all, and our architecture meets these objectives and evolves along with our aspiration to always do better, to satisfy our clients.

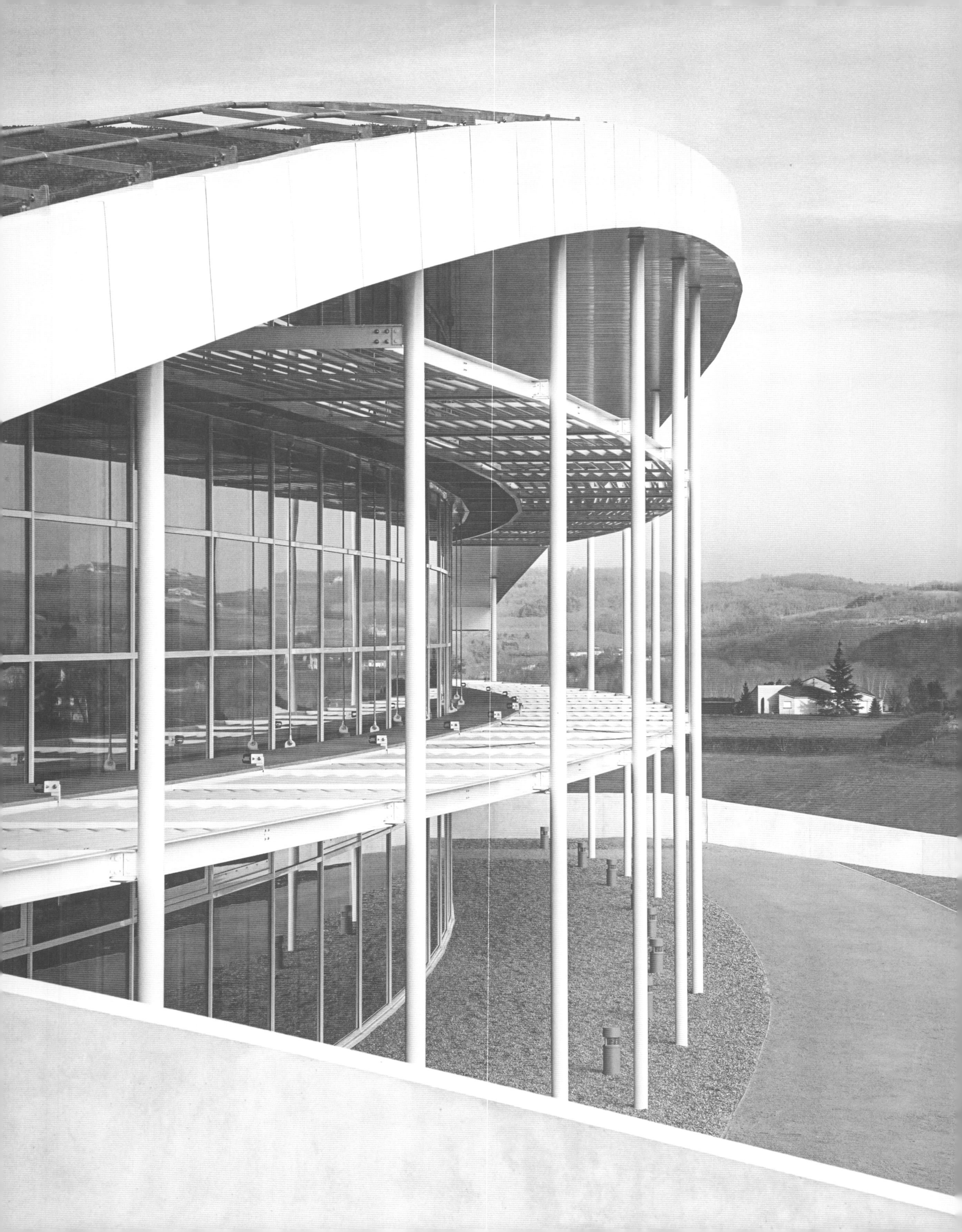

INDUSTRIAL
FRANCE, DUCEY
FRANCE, CERGY EOLE
ITALY, FIESSO D'ARTICO
FRANCE, MARSAZ

DUCEY

architect
GILLES CARNOY
2002 AND 2006

text by
RAFAEL MAGROU

"The good building is not one that hurts the landscape, but one which makes the landscape more beautiful than it was before the building was built," stated Frank Lloyd Wright, the architect behind the Guggenheim Museum in New York, during a 1931 lecture. It became a universal reference for architects, specifically for Gilles Carnoy when he began his formal architectural research for the factory that would manufacture Louis Vuitton's leather goods. This attention to context is perfectly consistent with the monogrammed brand's philosophy: to blend seamlessly into the environment, in both the literal and figurative (or ecological) sense of the term. The approach was first taken as early as 1998 for the Sainte-Florence site, in the Vendée region of France, where the luxury company established two production facilities for leather goods as the basis of a new industrial strategy: implementation outside of urban centers, square surfaces to install production lines, natural light captured by large bay windows and skylights. The forms of these immense skylights, inspired by the maritime world of the architect-navigator, immediately transmit the unique identity of the Louis Vuitton workplace. The question of work conditions, which became key in attaining the highest possible quality, was raised in comparison to previous factories that existed in Issoudun in the Indre department, in Saint-Donat in the Drôme department, and in Sarras in the Ardèche. In the 1990s, Gilles Carnoy had already begun work on the historic ateliers of Asnières-sur-Seine. In a building where Louis Vuitton had centralized production since 1859, which included on its site the family home that is now a museum, the architect undertook the delicate task of volumetric couture. In several stages, he modified the original character of the building, introducing in particular the two adjacent skylights, made in the purest industrial tradition.

In 2000, the Ducey project hit a new stage. Louis Vuitton launched the idea of establishing leather production facilities in Normandy, near Mont Saint-Michel. Generating new jobs, this opportunity mobilized local communities to propose several sites for construction. After a visit to the area, and wishing to maintain a distance in relation to the monument, the choice fell on a site between the border towns of Juillet and Ducey, a rural area in the south of the Manche region. Seven and a half miles away from the Benedictine Abbey, Carnoy developed a new 4,000 square-meter factory. The structure is nestled into the groves of Normandy, thereby adhering to the idea of fitting into its context. Workshops, offices, social spaces: all its facilities are on the same level, save for the restaurant which is up on the second floor. Here, the architect created a lone gazebo that offers a panoramic view of Mont Saint-Michel when it's clear enough, keeping in mind that, "in Normandy, the weather is always great, at least ten minutes a day." Contrary to Sainte-Florence, where the patio is central to its design, in Ducey, the skylights are distributed in order to offer both the utmost flexibility to production lines and to benefit the CAO DAO (computer-assisted concept and design) offices and method development. It should also be noted that the extended North and South façades procure optimal light that is controlled by overhanging roofs, sun-shades and other adjustable shutters, and echoed by two huge, scallop-shaped skylights. These maritime allegories are bolstered by four, tree-like beams—another nod to the master Frank Lloyd Wright, whose flared lily-pad columns at the Johnson Wax Headquarters (1936) in Racine, Wisconsin, were a revolutionary system devised to support the floor. Carnoy instead references palm trees, which take on an airy form so as to preserve the softness of the northern light captured by their openings.

Lighting is key for the lines of production. Firstly, it allows an employee to "listen to the leather," that is, to verify the quality of new leather shipments and organize materials in one of four categories, each corresponding to the different parts of a bag, or to discard bits as waste. Here, only calfskin and goatskin from La Comète tannery in Belgium are dealt with; exotic leathers are assembled in Asnières. 1,500 square meters of material arrive every week, with an average of 500 square meters per day. Secondly, lighting levels need to be as close to natural light as possible in order to test the leather's "stretching" and "rolling" directions, and to ensure that the thread sewn on the leather matches it tone for tone. LEDs complete these verifications. In addition to the natural light that floods the workshops, sheets of fluorescent tubes maintain consistent lighting levels throughout the day. It is vital that leather workers—76% are women—can guarantee an optimal level of concentration. Especially considering that there are close to 8,000 Louis Vuitton products, 700 of which are new every year, and that every *Speedy* bag undergoes 136 operations, the comfort of every employee has to be ensured in order to allow each worker to remain focused to the utmost extent—producing the quantity of articles in question without compromising on quality. Everything here is set up so as to promote and embellish the "*beau geste*."

The ergonomics of the workplace are constantly being studied. At Louis Vuitton, it's a verifiable culture. Every day, the tiniest improvements are considered, and the results are evident in the articles presented in-store. The brand's philosophy is as such: if the worker enjoyed making the bag, the client will sense this during its purchase; especially since acquiring a Louis Vuitton bag means procuring an object that will accompany you for a lifetime. The leather workers feel a certain pride in the fact that they are producing collection pieces that travel across ages and oceans. Architecture should be, and is, at the service of this vision. The spatial organization promotes the establishment of U-shaped work environments, in order to manage teams of at least 25 people, and guarantee a certain proximity to the manager. These arrangements have to be extremely mobile in order to be able to adapt both to specific orders and to developments in the field. The incorporation of the latest technologies like giant scanners and digitalization to map out the hides, and digital cutting tables capable of generating as little waste as possible—which in the end leave only a five to ten percent differential in comparison to man—attest to the level of specialization of the House. Moreover, multi-product lines are put in place in order to be able to accommodate six or seven models in one geographic area. The square shape of the workshop facilitates this arrangement and includes three main parts: to the North, cutting, which benefits from constant light; in the South, assembly; and in the middle, preparation, the intermediary stage. The core production practices come from a legacy of ancestral tradition, transmitted to apprentices who must take a particularly challenging exam, of which only 10% pass successfully and are integrated into the factory. What's more, every leather worker has expertise in multiple areas, and is able to work with leather, canvas, textiles. A single outlet joins the docks that distribute raw materials to those that ship materials to the international logistics center in Cergy Eole. No one worries about ventilation here since the adhesives used do not contain solvents; they're entirely aqueous. The strength is in the stitching.

Health is at the heart of all work. To start the day off well, five minutes of *taichi* are offered in the morning. A complete health routine is equally envisioned. While an employee spends most of her time in fabrication, several measures have been developed to prevent any stress related to fluxes in volume—some products surpass even the most audacious sales forecasts! Because orders are always varied and because new products are tackled every day, the "Marelle," a synthetic table of problems and solutions, brings each team together and strengthens team spirit. Team leaders set a tone for excellence that is the goal. Everything is established to optimize quality and to improve day-to-day operations. Many solutions are proposed by workers themselves and are passed from one area to the next, from one production line to the next, so that all can benefit. Solidarity reigns. Carpooling, for example, is a daily service for all employees. Parking, moreover, is hidden behind hills in the landscape, allowing one's eye to gaze uninterrupted into the distance. On the southern hillside, perched some twelve feet above, one sees an almost exact copy of the workshops, with a single shell. This second site, built later, includes production facilities, but also houses personalization services (for initials and colored stripes) and the parts department in case repairs are called for. There is an inevitable dialogue between the buildings, which are connected by a system of "company bikes," and both are immersed in a lush environment that can be admired through wide, cinemascope windows. The only twist to the initial vision is the fact that the restaurants are up on the second floor, where the panorama of Normandy can be embraced. In the distance, the spire atop the rocky island of Mont Saint-Michel reaches towards the ever-changing sky of Normandy. An invitation to go beyond.

p. 214 exterior view of Marsaz atelier
p. 217 model views
p. 218–219 views of the building set against the landscape of the Manche
p. 220 view into the production atelier from a staircase, with an installation from Stephen Sprouse's *Roses*
p. 221 the atelier at dusk
p. 222–223 view into the main hall supported by pillars resembling giant palms

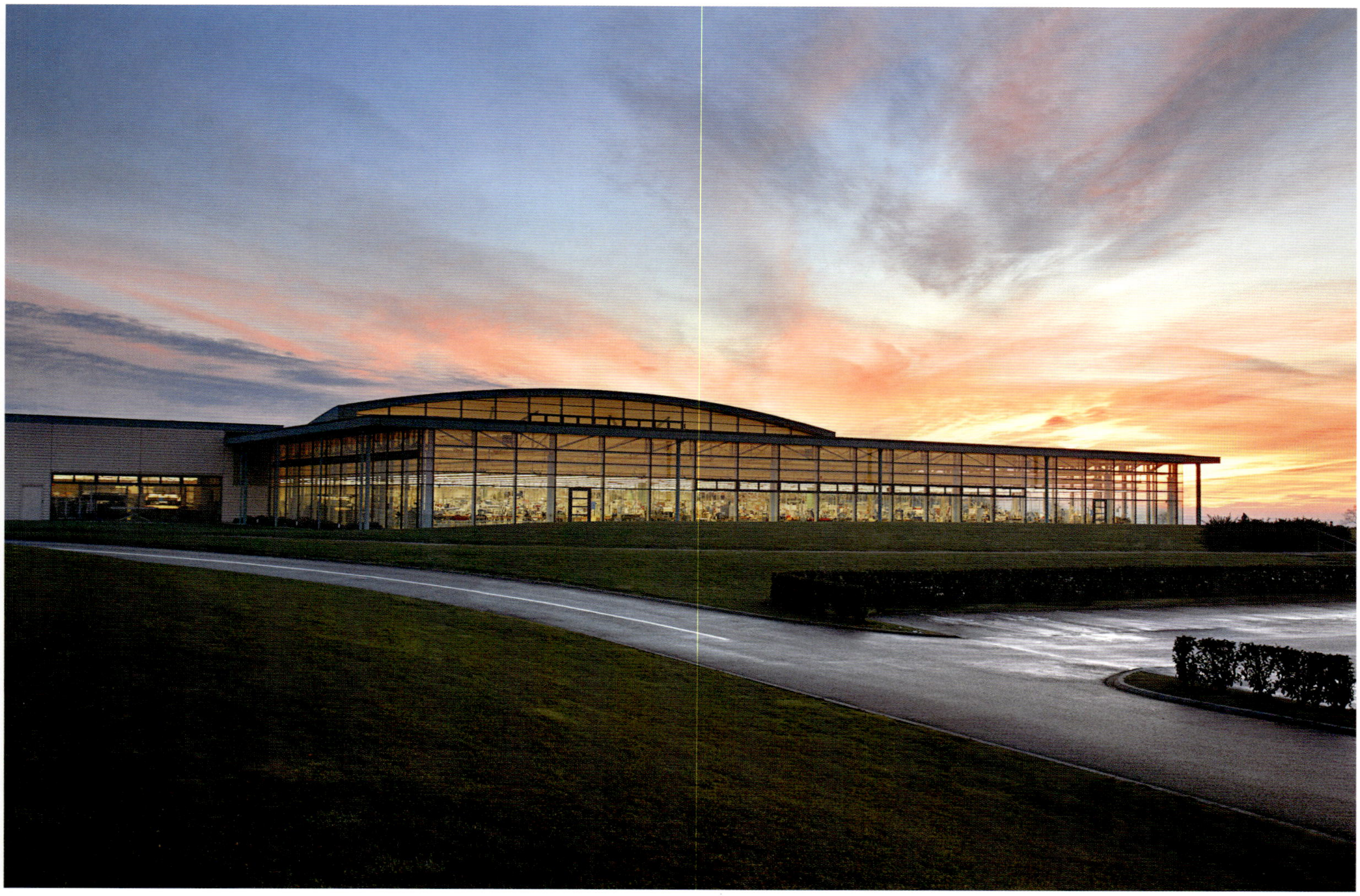

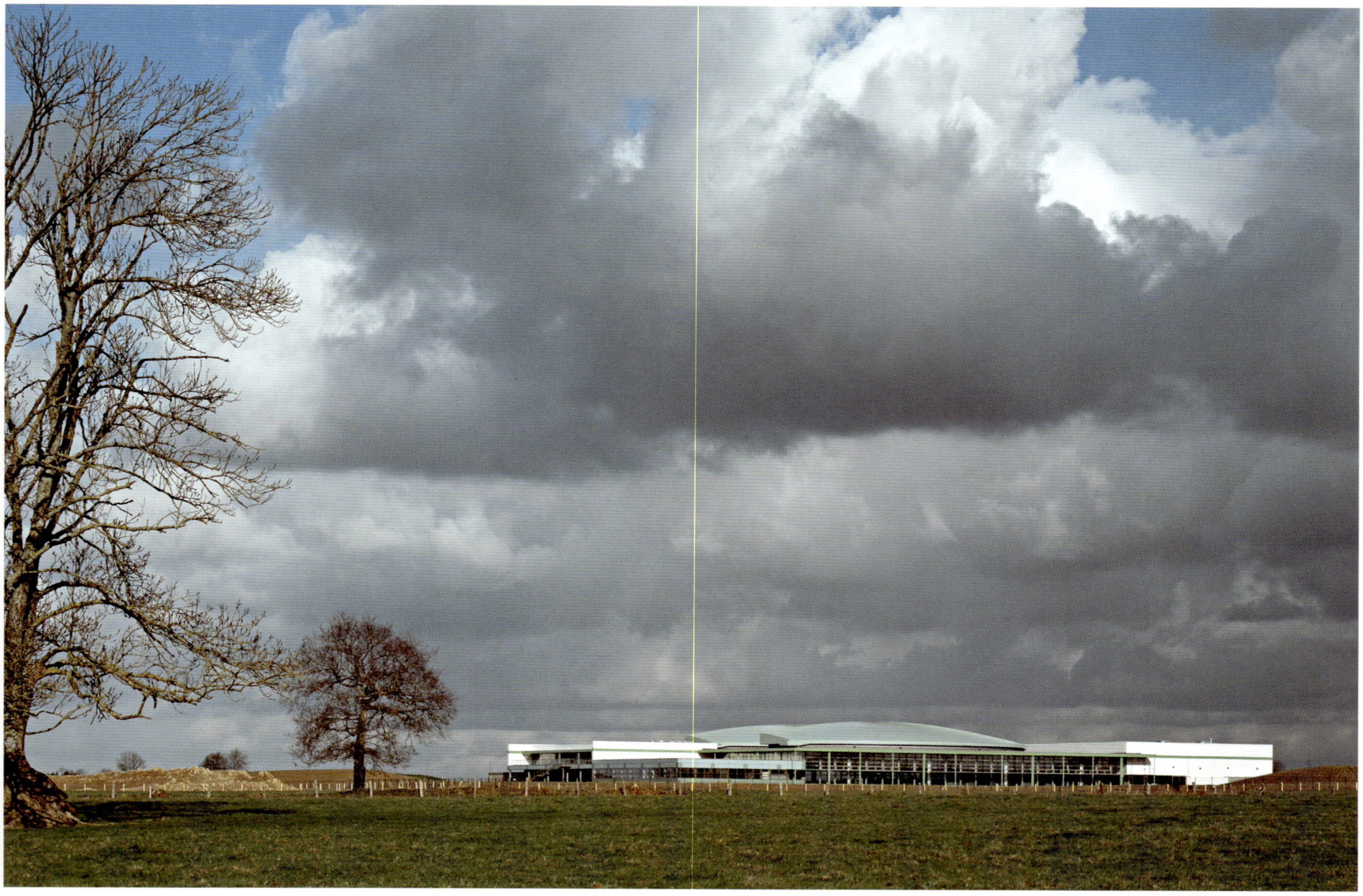

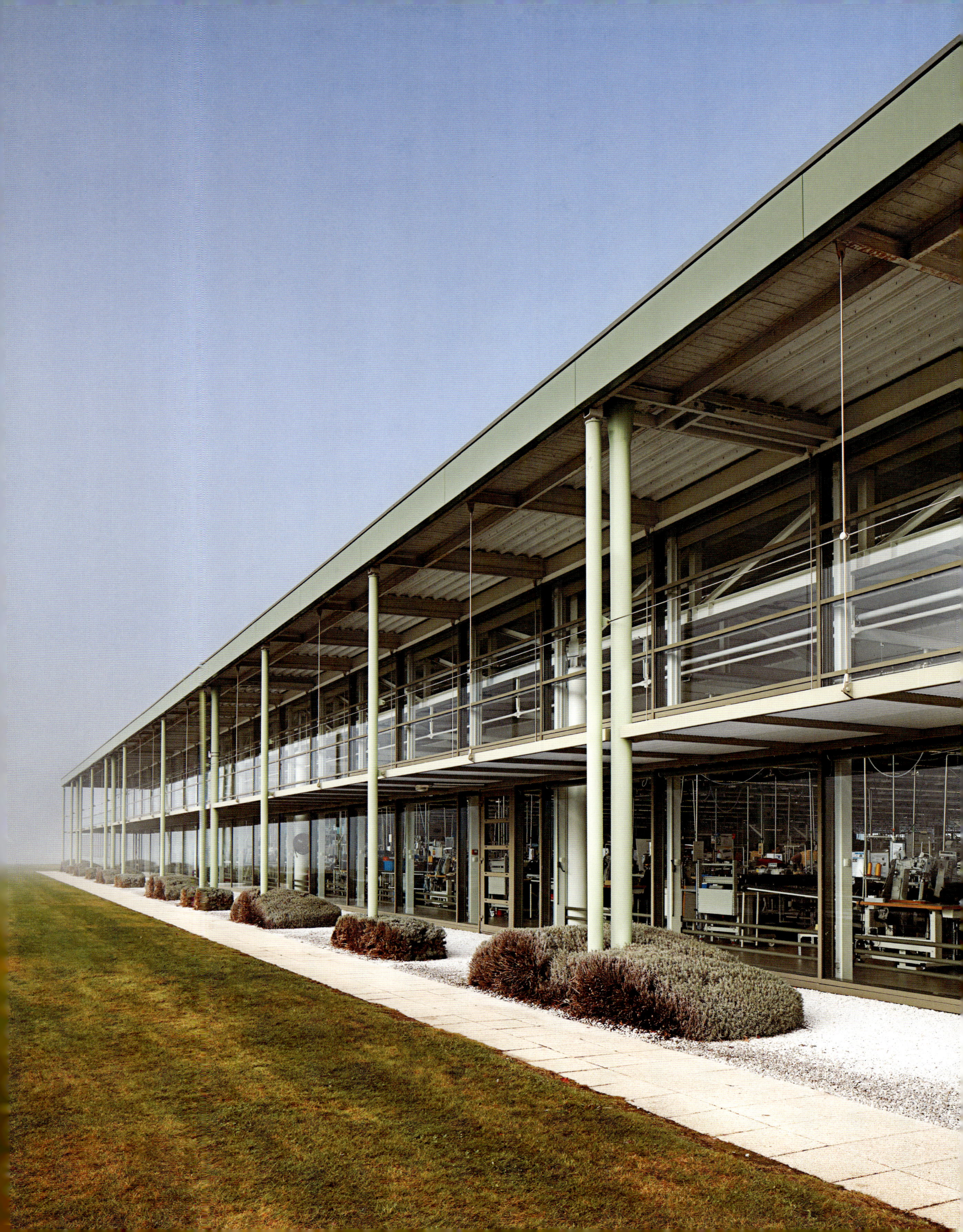

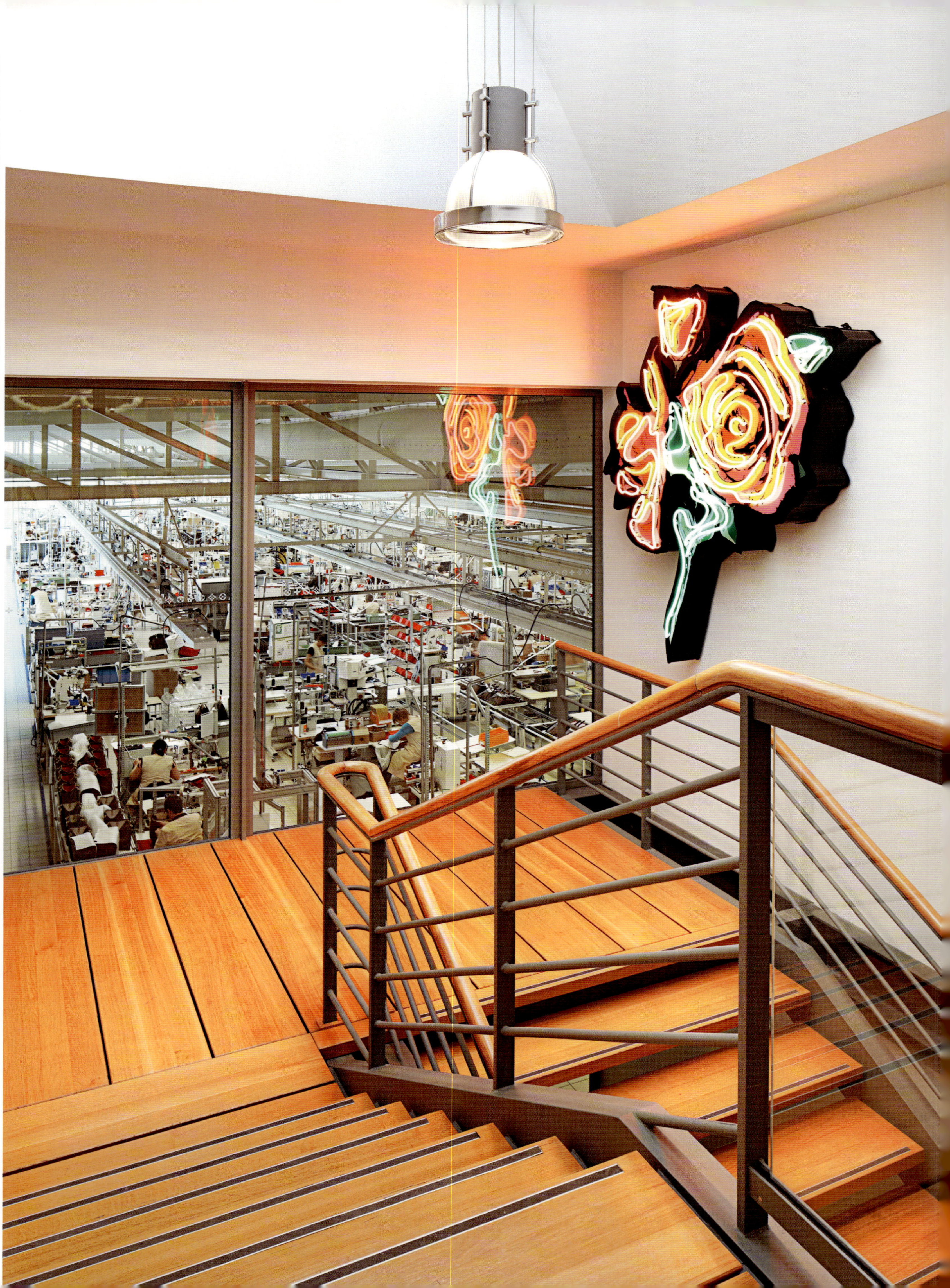

ARCHITECTURE AND INTERIORS

DUCEY

FRANCE

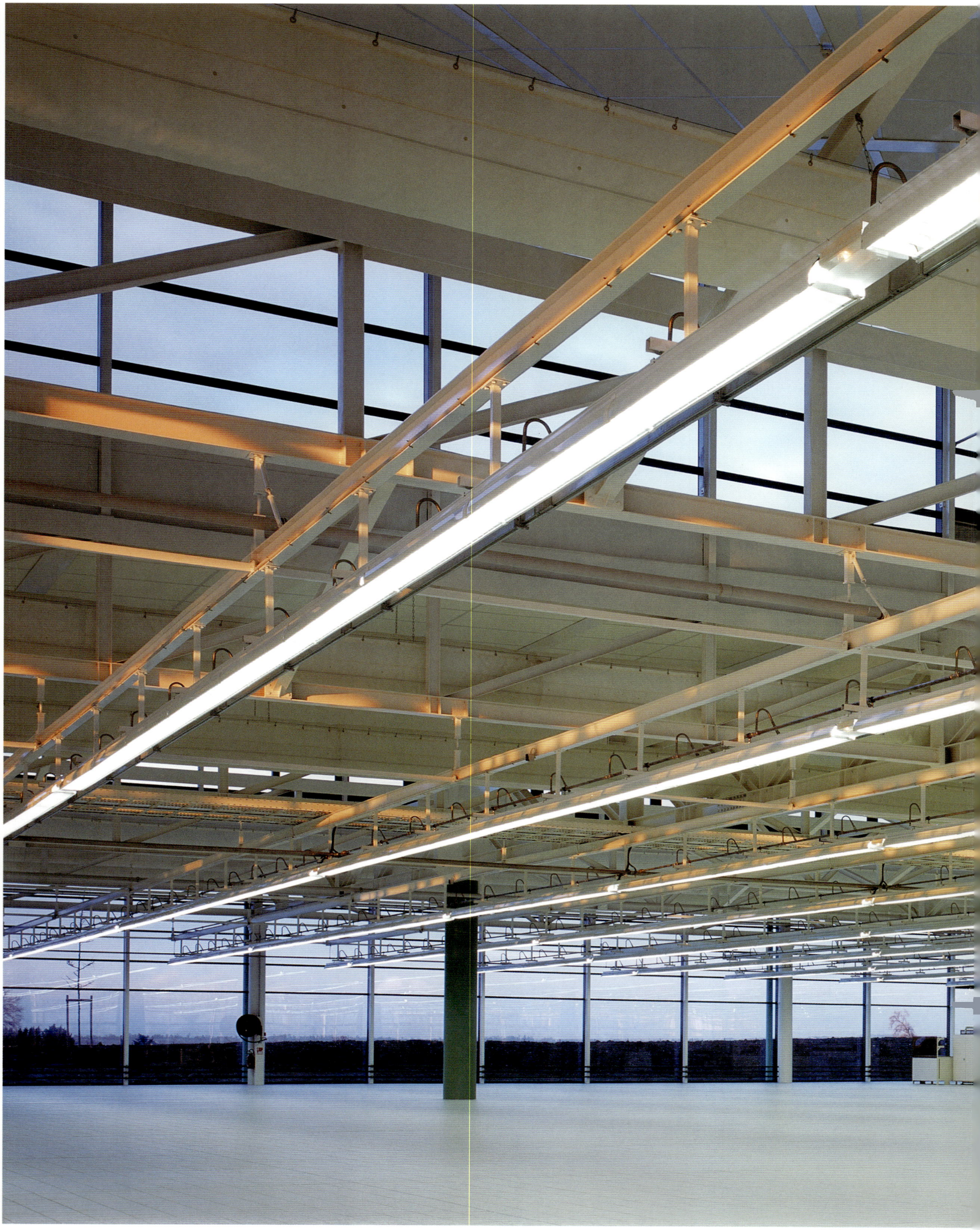

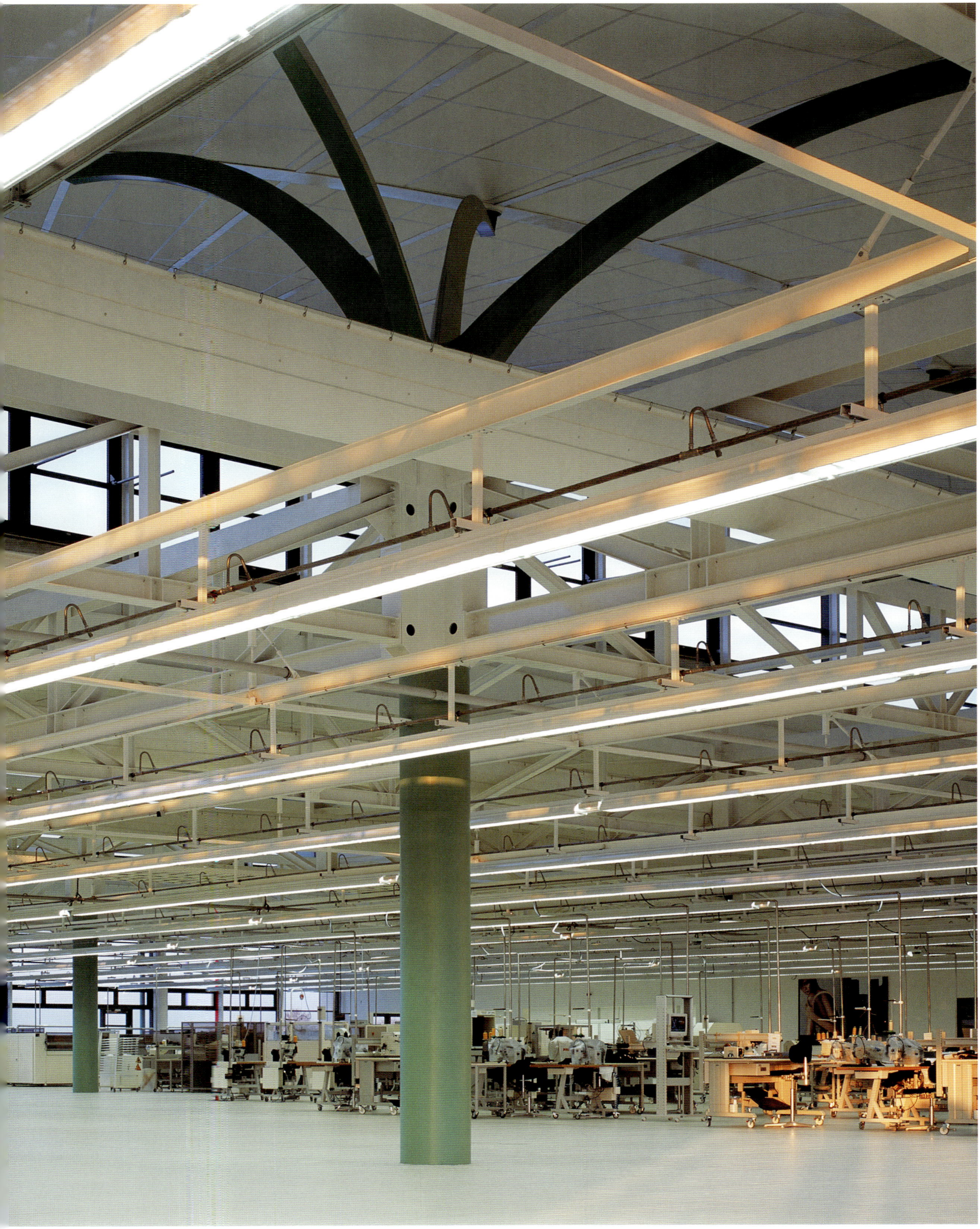

CERGY EOLE

architect
GILLES CARNOY
2007

text by
RAFAEL MAGROU

Louis Vuitton trunks have traveled the world, as evidenced by the labels of great hotels that tattoo their hides. Their graphics are evocative of an era in which exoticism was associated with expeditions by adventurers. The tradition, at once aesthetic and nostalgic, has now been lost since anyone can travel the world. Nevertheless, the one hundred and fifty year-old brand hasn't left its globetrotting mindset behind; its products can be purchased in every corner of the globe. To respond to a demand that is constantly growing at a dizzying rate, it established a logistics center near Paris. True to form, this industrial building is distinguished from similar structures by a certain elegance. Generally speaking, warehouses are metal boxes that have little affinity with the surrounding area; they're simple envelopes for large spaces that can be used for their storage potential. The specifications of these buildings do not create the most exciting work for architects. For this third-generation, leather goods warehouse, situated on the windy flats of Cergy, outside of Paris, the architect Gilles Carnoy aimed to go beyond the basic model by splitting and shifting the volumes and arranging them so that employees could benefit from natural light entering laterally. Thus, from the monumental monolith, he extracted fragmented parts and introduced more human profiles and scales.

The façade imparts Vuitton's identity, but in an almost subliminal manner; the eponymous checker motif is visible in alternating strips of smooth and grooved metal, which softens the immensity of this kind of building. The architect, moreover, played with a quasi-musical rhythm by introducing three large panels of colored glass, inspired by leather tones—burgundy, orange, brown—and their complements, like the color blue. The cubic mass is interrupted at the southern end by reservoirs put in place for fire safety that form a series of undulations which are intentionally left visible and ribbed at the top. Here, technology and aesthetics have become one.

Around the entrance and its security control, the waltz of trucks coming and going is endless. This mechanical ballet is conveyed through the maneuvers of these giants on wheels who attach themselves to the open mouths of the western façade. There are sixteen docks for loading and unloading that govern these merchandise exchanges—inbound or outbound—to France or abroad. One dock is specially dedicated to shipments by air, due to special packaging. Everything is done in a way that every corner of the world receives its merchandise in the shortest possible time. These virtual windows onto the world are alternated with glass sequences, which are particularly exceptional since these areas are usually blocked. This decision was made, on the one hand, to bring natural light into the large, lateral corridor where outgoing boxes are received. On the other hand, in addition to offering a framed view of the outside world, they ensure another level of security for all.

"Emphasis is placed as much on the comfort of working conditions as it is on the aesthetic quality of the work," states Grégoire Gilliot, a former colleague of Carnoy, who took over as head of the firm after the latter's death. "It's even possible to indulge in the luxury of space in order to significantly improve working conditions," he adds. As a result, the 21,000 square-meter warehouse benefits from light transmitted through skylights shaped like airplane wings—a formal variation that's signature to Carnoy—complemented by strips of fluorescent lights that adjust to provide necessary and sufficient levels of light in the hall. In this space, rows of floor-to-ceiling stock racks seem to stretch out into infinity, leaving a vivid impression of the remarkable size of this monogrammed brand.

In this graphic labyrinth echo the melodies of the horns of forklift trucks, swarming as though they're in a real metropolis of predestined boxes. Like insects buzzing, they create a choreography directed by the order book and structured by stores throughout the world. The tempo is mesmerizing, but the human dimension isn't lost. This dynamic seems to be a breeze for employees. It goes without saying that the control center includes a restful retreat for these cadenced workers. Because the warehouse is closed to outsiders—confidentiality and protection require it—the lack of a view onto the Val d'Oise countryside is replaced by other windows that, through photographs and other personalized images, create a visual respite. From the offices, the field of view is expanded, with glimpses of the ever-changing sky of Île-de-France. This administrative section complements the stocking area and, moreover, is in direct communication with it. From the entrance, visitors are immediately taken in by the view of the large corridor, with its laminated wood framework. A slight feeling of vertigo overcomes them. Total transparency, which immediately puts the quality of the work in the foreground, is achieved without sacrificing usability, since leather couches next to product displays welcome visitors as they would guests. The adjoining meeting room, which is entirely glass-paned, hides nothing of its objectives and devices, and constantly improves the space-time relationship Cergy has with its shipping destinations. Finally, a quality control office, under the eagle eye of its team, is in charge of separating defective products; the slightest imperfection at Louis Vuitton relegates a product to leatherwork limbo. To comply with the company's environmental standards, several high-quality environmental goals are attained, even in these warehouses. With assistance from Michel le Sommer, phytorestoration basins composed of plants—reeds for the most part—feed on organic compounds emitted by rainwater and wastewater, naturally purifying them so that they can be recycled. This system is utilized to water lawns and to allow water to be re-infiltrated without the risk of pollution. This component creates a landscape that surrounds the storage area—a kind of wetlands where ducks have settled, with bees at work in the chambers of hives towards the rear of the building. The role of landscaping is essential to the site; the transparency of the gates are lined with thorny shrubs known as Pyracanthas that deter uninvited guests, while also providing berries for the birds. The horizon, a major element of all Louis Vuitton sites, is here organized around planted knolls that mask the parking garage and some of the surrounding area, offering to one's gaze—despite the unappealing environment—a palette that changes with the fluctuating seasons and light.

p. 225 exterior view of the building, located in the Val d'Oise
p. 226–227 views of the exterior with details of the stained glass façade inspired by the trademark damier
p. 228–229 view of the industrial conveyors in the depot

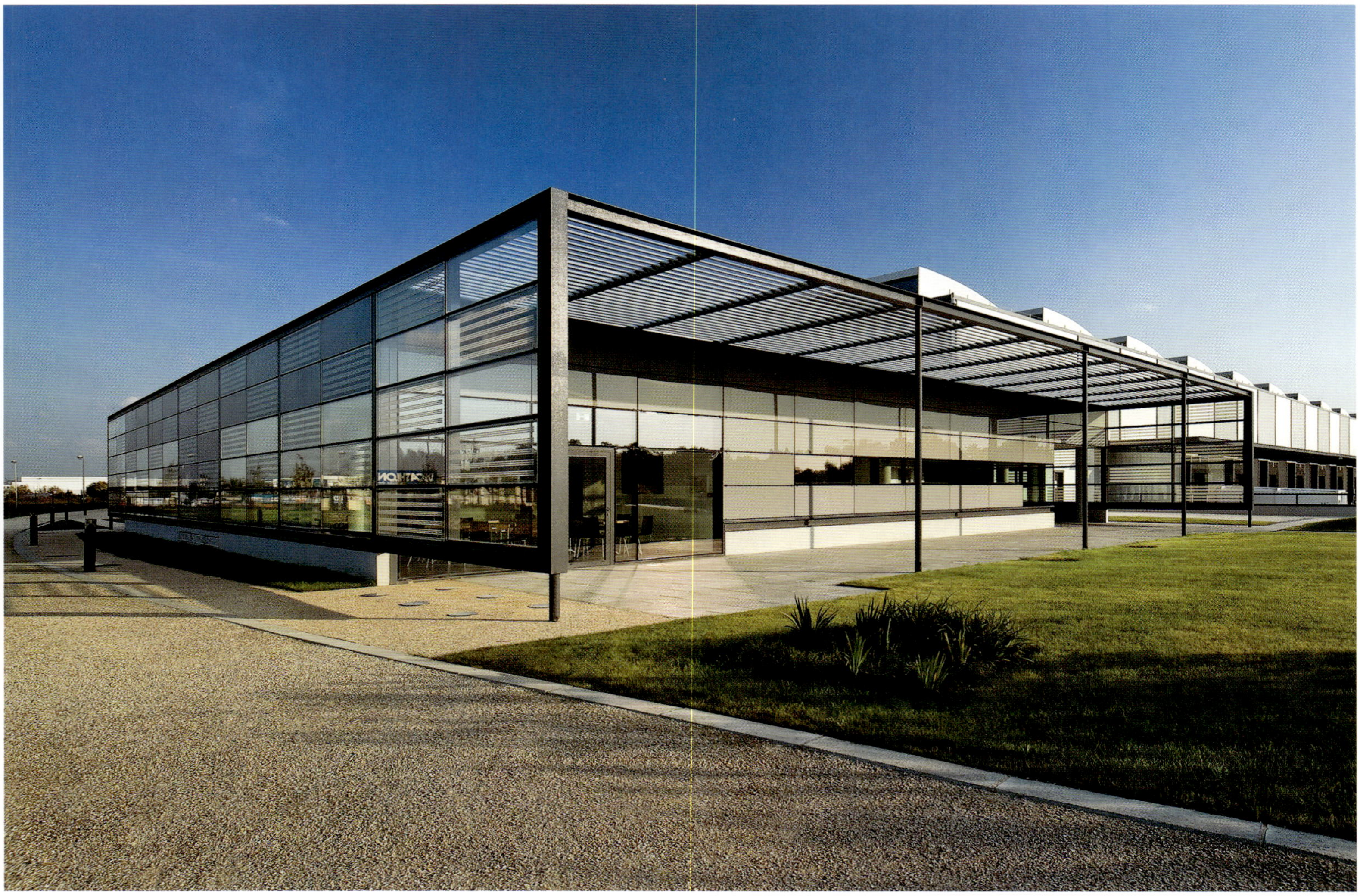

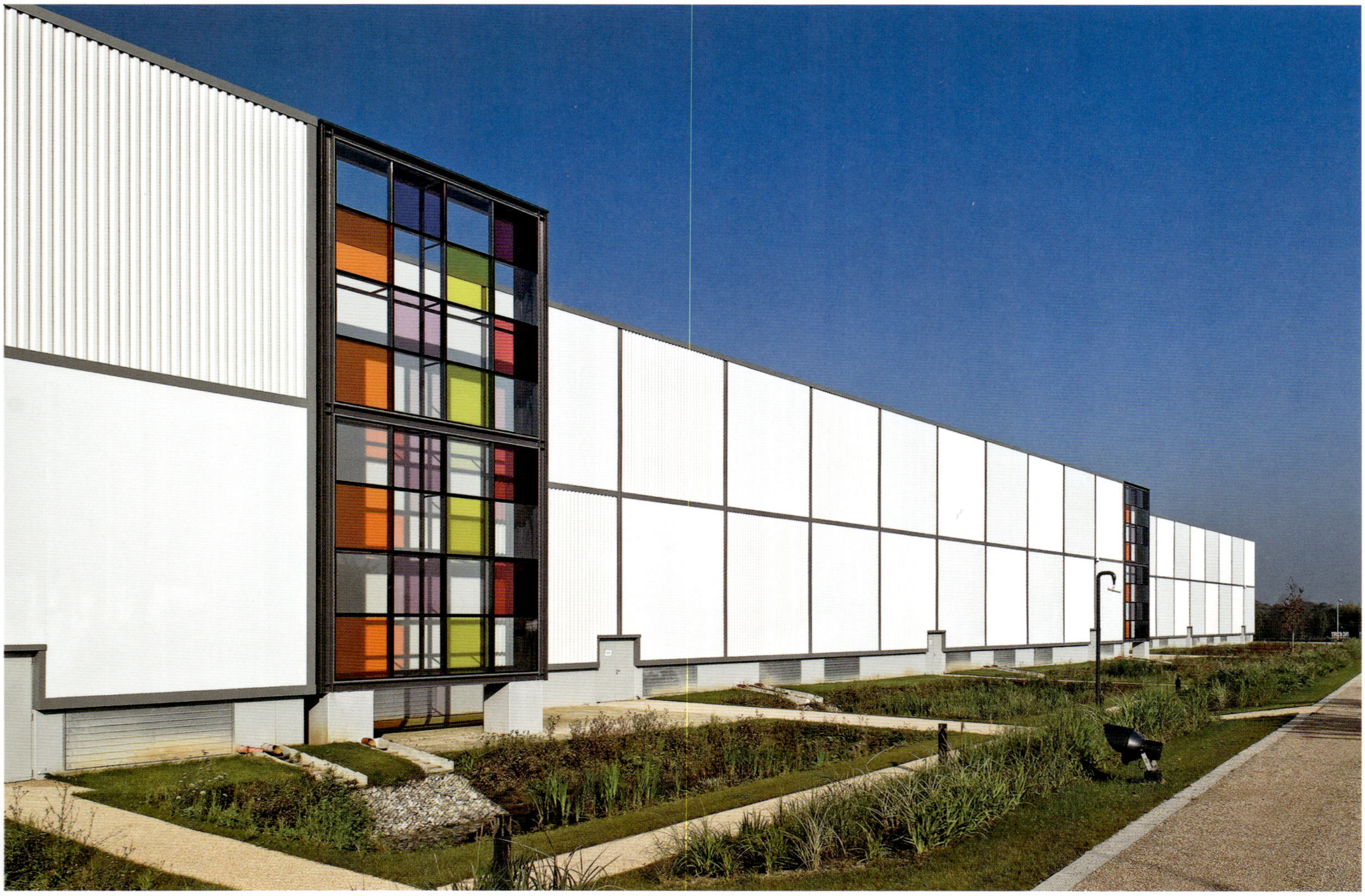

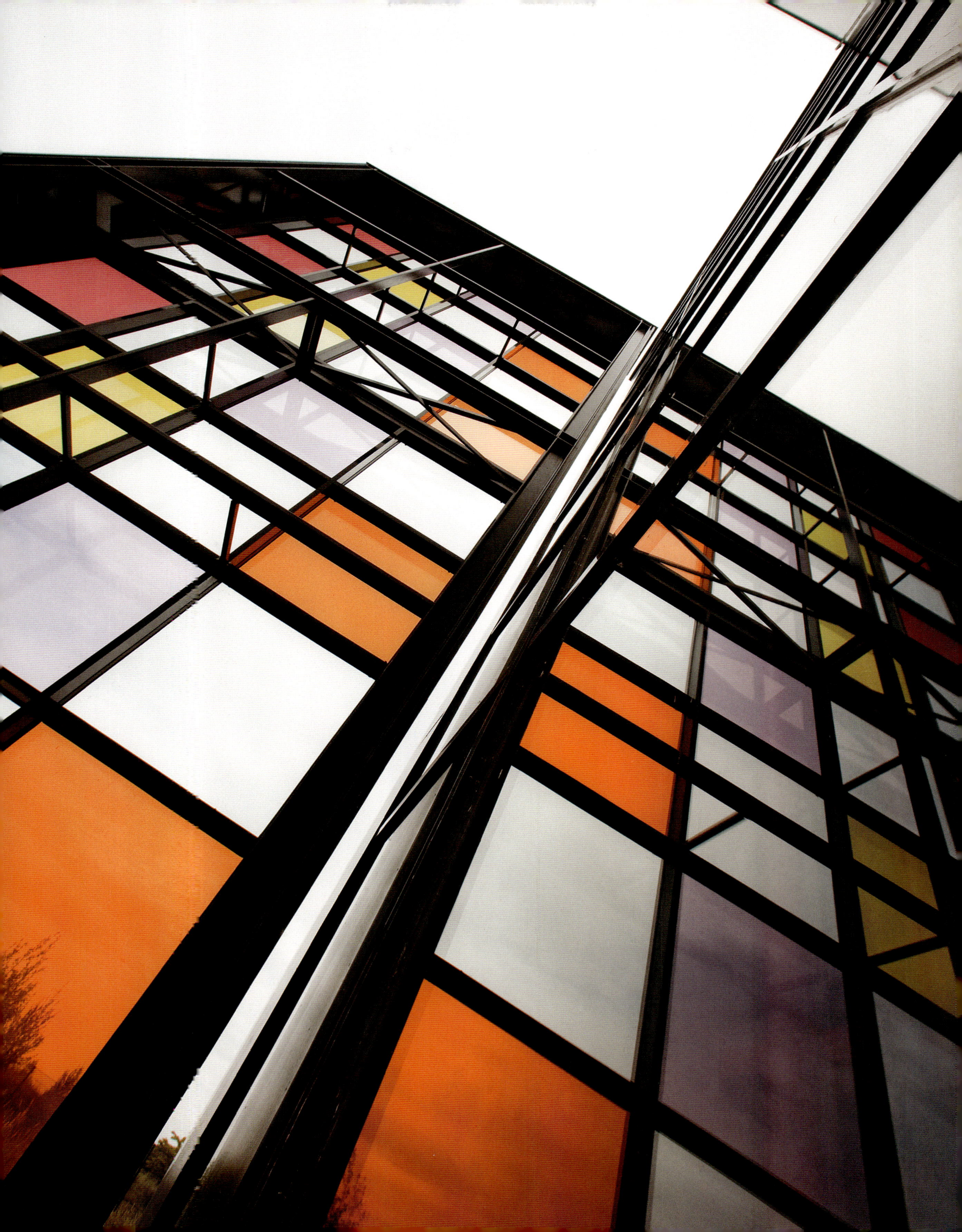

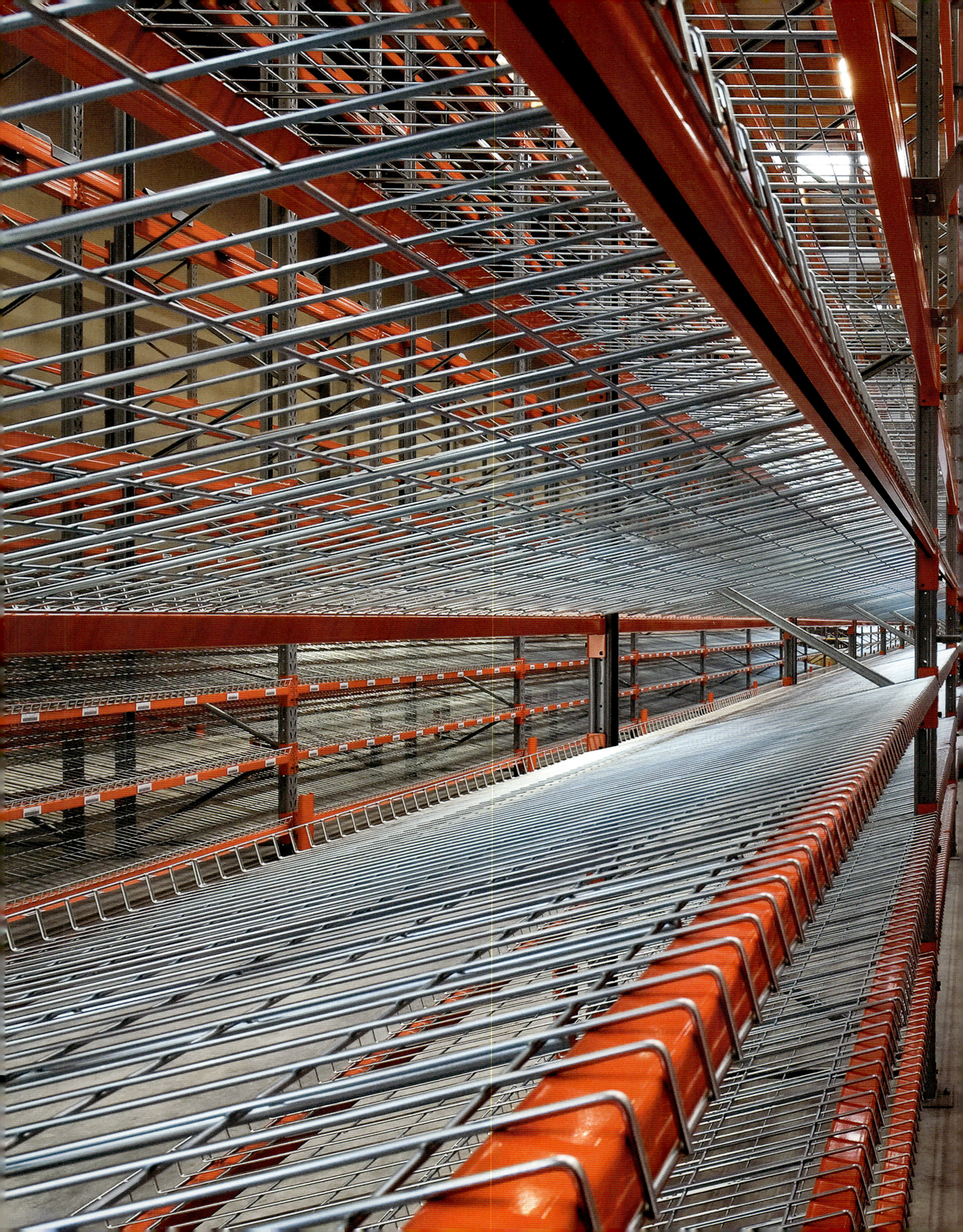

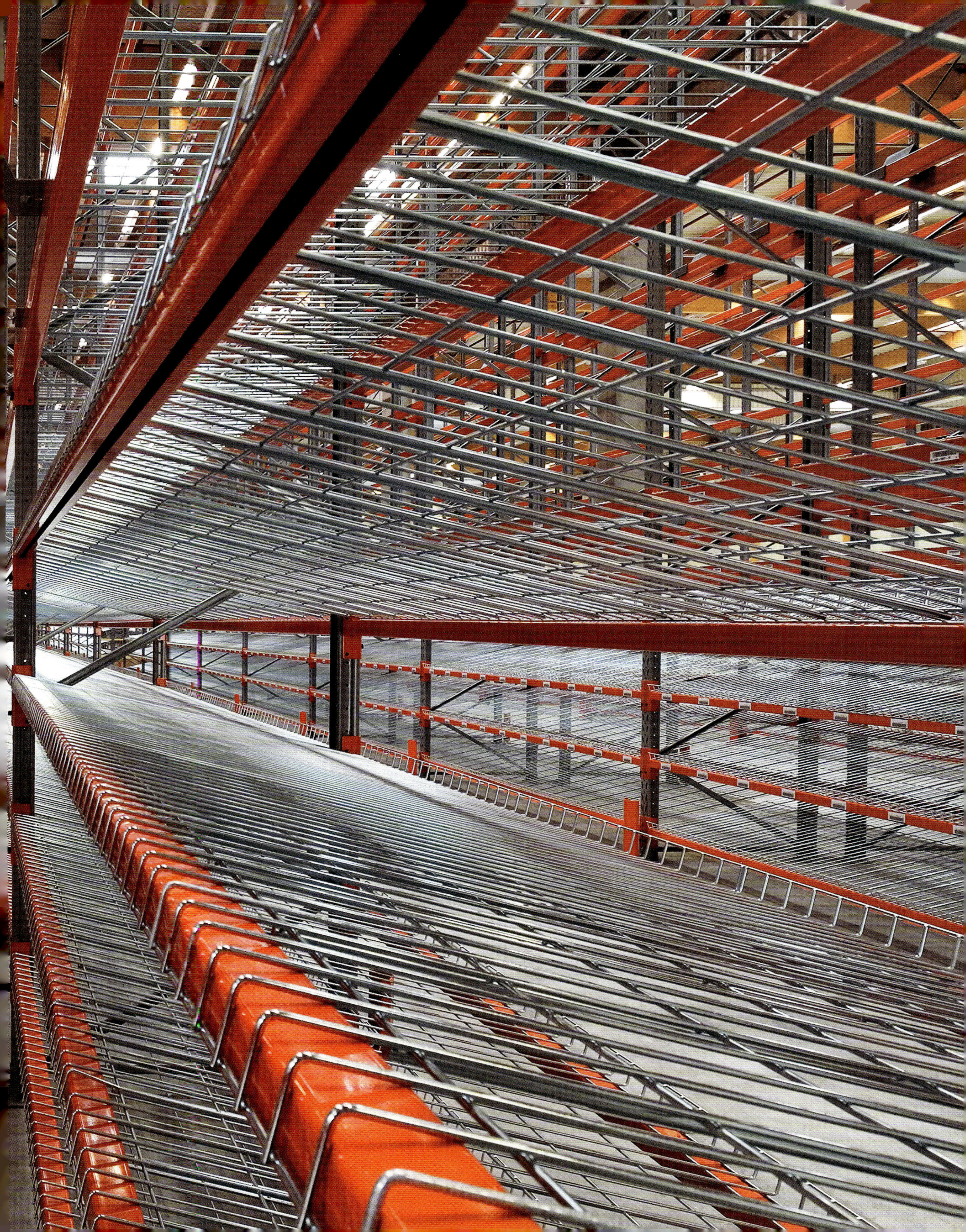

MARSAZ

architects
GILLES CARNOY
AND GRÉGOIRE GILLIOT
2011

text by
RAFAEL MAGROU

In the tradition of their leather goods ateliers in Sainte-Florence and Ducey, Louis Vuitton is undertaking a new generation of buildings that will boast improved comfort in the working conditions for its employees, as well as create a clearer dialogue within the context in which they are situated. Such is the case in Marsaz, the youngest of its manufacturing sites. This project was enthusiastically led by Grégoire Gilliot, a former colleague of Gilles Carnoy, whose designs for Louis Vuitton's industrial architecture are famous for their elegant silhouettes and distinctive lighting, with maritime undertones. After Carnoy's sudden death in 2006, the young designer took over the project, making the Marsaz site a collaborative work conceived by two minds. Indeed, Gilles Carnoy and Grégoire Gilliot were engaged in a sort of in-house, fraternal competition as they confronted the ideas of two generations of architects, two sensibilities and two visions in response to Louis Vuitton's extremely demanding needs. Out of their respective arguments, the sketches for the final project were produced, drawing on the positive points of each exploration without choosing exclusively between one or the other's designs.

This proved to be an enriching approach for the project, allowing them to improve upon any possible flaws.

Thus emerged the new leather goods factory, located four kilometers from Saint Donat, where Louis Vuitton already had workshops of a more standard, industrial silhouette. It is a sensitive site for such a building, as it is extremely rural and radically natural. On the outskirts of the northern Drôme region, only a few strides from the famous "Ideal Palace" of the postman Ferdinand Cheval, Marsaz wraps around a landscape of undulating hills punctuated by groves of conifers and striped with alternating vineyards and orchards. From Tain to the plain of Montélimar, both the lifestyle and the countryside are deeply rooted in viticulture, and the region has become a destination for wine tourism, boasting a route rich with vineyards that wind around the meandering Rhône River. This favorable location allows Louis Vuitton to invent a new concept in a space capable of absorbing the production capacity of Saint-Donat, and offering a large enough scale to accommodate current order volumes. The size is also the challenge, however, since the workshop's architectural forms must be as discreet and respectful as possible in relationship to the agricultural environment around them—all the more so since the land proposed by the town overlooks the tiny village's slate bell tower. The architects have taken care to integrate their work with an immense, curved roof, which not only echoes the polished reliefs surrounding it, but also disappears in its rustic environment under a green cloak of plants. Thus, Grégoire Gilliot and Gilles Carnoy compose a gentle architectural prominence, marvelously married with the geography of the landscape—a choice that nevertheless required them to sacrifice the emerging skylights that distinguished the last Louis Vuitton workshops at Sainte-Florence and Ducey, and the obligation to fit smoke control devices on the façade. They find an alternative by installing a giant bay window oriented to the south, with a view of the crenelated Vercors mountains—the "French Dolomites"—which trace a limestone line to the east; it was worth the trouble as the edifice overlooks not only the town of Marsaz, but also the surrounding hills, in a 180-degree view.

The natural 10% gradient requires a staggering of levels, allowing for physical and visual communication, combined with architectural and environmental screens. In particular, it helps to absorb the volume of the offices, flanking the eastern side and integrated with the ground-level restaurant overlooking the natural terrain and the Vercusien peaks in all their majesty. Past the row of tall-stemmed poplars—emblematic of the region's grand properties—and starting from the ground parking lot punctuated with shrubbery, the visitor is guided by the slightly modified geography of the site, sliding along the platform that runs along the studios from below to access the main entrance and its window display of legendary bags. Discretely placed, it invites the visitor into a double-height space, accented by two crossing flights of stairs, which, along with a peripheral gallery, create a direct visual dialogue between the offices and the workshops via a window.

Following the custom at Louis Vuitton, it was necessary to ensure the building's discretion within its surroundings in order to minimize its visual impact and environmental footprint, but also to find the desired—and desirable—horizon, capable of offering a calming panorama for the tired eyes of the craftsmen, concentrated as they are on their rigorous work. This audacious design is balanced by the cleverly weighted proportions of the great hall housing the workshops. Its inverted, umbrella-like structure is expressive. Outside the lateral walls that seem swallowed up by the terrain, the four main pillars (instead," of the webbed curves at Ducey) extend phalanxes bearing the load of the curved roof, aided by slender repeats on the façade. These metallic fingers stretch up to the top of a cylindrical base of poured concrete, whose texture resembles skin, thrusting upwards 9.4 meters to the maximum height of the ceiling. It's a luxury for industrial architecture to be able to provide such a space for these leather craftsmen. Laminated timber beams shoot off from this primary structure; this is a first in the tradition of the company's edifices, which are often pioneering in their architecture, as well as in their boutiques' spatial and material experiments. With a total range of 11.4 meters, the weight is taken up on the north façade by an extra large, 44-meter metallic trellis beam—an impressive work indeed. Finally, an aerated technical mesh creates a floating ceiling that weaves together the complementary artificial lighting (fitted with exterior light readers), compressed air for the machines, and electrical connections. In so doing, the architects have developed a constructive solution that leaves the better part of the space to the fabrication lines; organized over 4,000 square meters for maximum flexibility, the loop and U-shaped set-up keeps the teams in close proximity and optimizes the work flow. As Emmanuel Mathieu, the Industrial Director has explained, the project's target is to have the atelier working at full capacity directly after it opens. Contrary to mechanical production means, the system here makes it possible to humanely manage the pace of production. The square is therefore the basis of the matrix, as it limits the distances from the workshops to the related services, allowing for wider points of contact and favoring the exchange of information. Louder than the other parts of the complex, the so-called "cutting zone," where the leather is detailed before assembly, forms a buffering space between the logistic area and the stock area situated at the back, partially underground. Along with the grand hall, the lower volume of this section is fitted with a high window stretching across its length, illuminating the space with soft northern light, particularly appreciated by artists and craftsmen for its constancy. The front ateliers benefit from southern light, which is filtered and controlled by an ad hoc solar protection device: a metallic grate is fitted with blades and twinned with an interior shade for especially bright days.

This project rates even higher than Louis Vuitton's other buildings with respect to French sustainable building standards (*Haute Qualité Environnementale*), responding to the 2005 regulations for thermal requirements and centralizing the building's technical management for optimal energy efficiency. This economy of resources is achieved, in part, through the use of natural pozzuolana rock as a substrate for the green roof, and a rain-water catchment system for irrigating the roof's vegetation. Additionally, an arsenal of energy-saving devices is deployed, including a heat pump for central heating and solar panels for hot water generation. Even the morphology of the structure limits energy loss, and its integration into the landscape is remarkable. Its architecture celebrates the aesthetic of disappearance, and combines with a minimal carbon footprint. Despite its dominant position, this ensemble enhances the landscape, rather than overwhelming it. Visible from the high-speed rail line between Paris and Valence, it creates, along with the Vercors Mountains, a geographical, karstic work of art against the azure sky that is similar to the evocations of the Shinkansen passing Mount Fuji in Japan—an allegory that the architect and his employers rightly defend.

p. 231 view from the parish of Marsaz, Drôme
p. 232 top: interior views; bottom: view of the atelier façade at dawn
p. 233 exterior view with detail of sunshade louvers

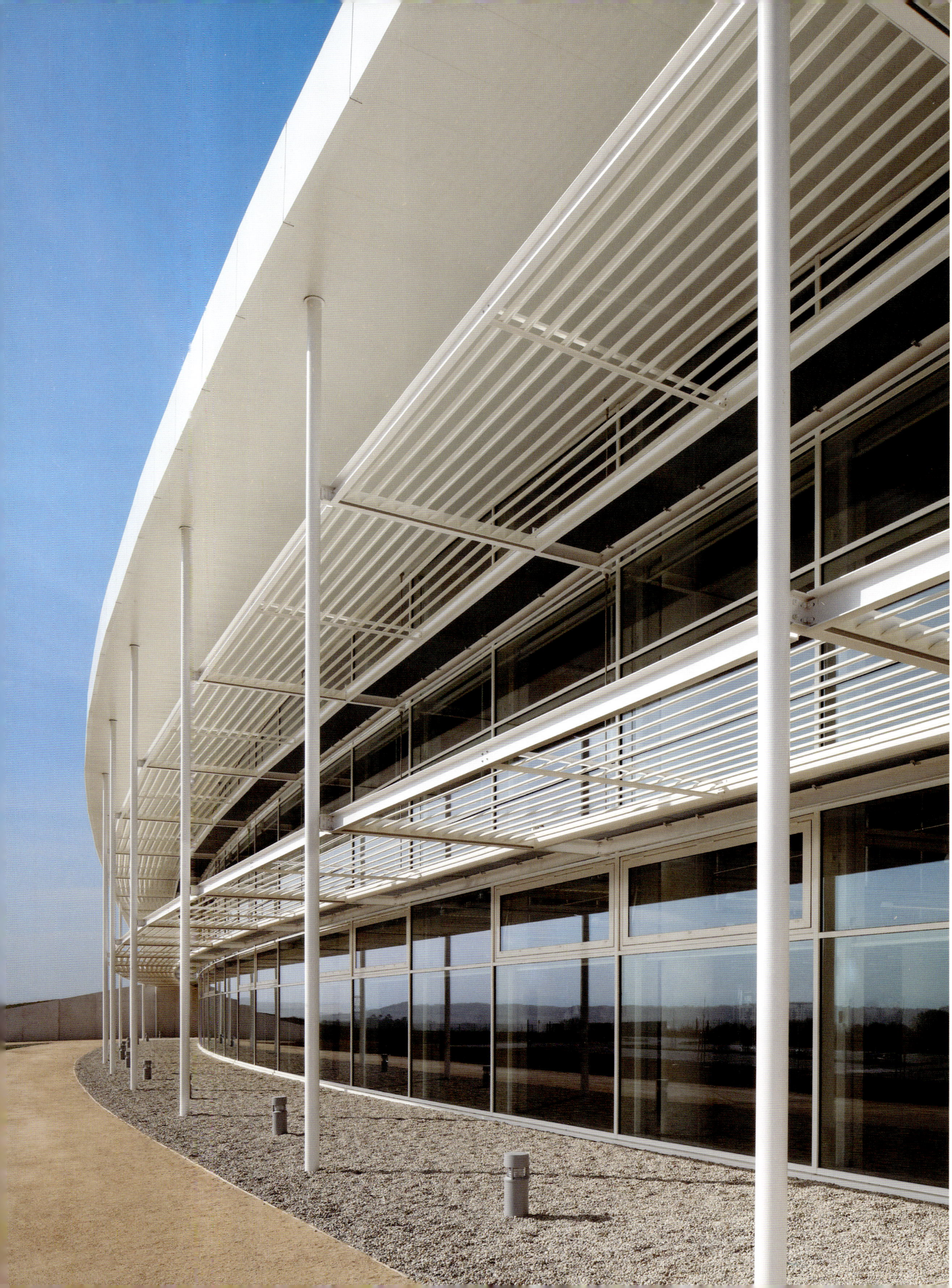

FIESSO D'ARTICO

architect
JEAN-MARC SANDROLINI
2009

text by
RAFAEL MAGROU

Initiated by the historical workshop of Asnières, established in 1859, the manufacture of most of Louis Vuitton's leather has taken place in France, save for the leather factories in Barbera del Valle, Spain and San Dimas, California, and the watch-making factory in La Chaux de Fonds, Switzerland, a French-speaking region reputed for producing complex watch mechanisms. For the production of its fine-crafted "luxury footwear," the brand also sought out the most qualified sites. Research proved it was in Venice, specifically in the Brenta valley that is celebrated for its shoe manufacturing facilities. Workshops devoted to creating curved ornaments fitted to the instep—a few examples of which had already made some film actresses famous for their fashion sense—could be found along the waterway that feeds into the Venetian Lagoon, after having passed through what is today Fiesso d'Artico. It is also in this fertile region that the master of the Italian Renaissance, Andrea Palladio (1508–1580), built various villas, some of which still bear their majestic columns.

It was in the middle of this dispersed region, which consisted of small manufacturing facilities and residential housing, that Louis Vuitton developed a shoe factory. It quickly outgrew its premises (three thousand pairs in 1999, almost one hundred times that amount ten years later), and the decision was made to build a new workshop adjacent to the original one. In light of the quickly growing demands of its clientele and in anticipation of further growth, the surface area grew from 1,200 square meters to 11,000 square meters—in other words, the space was ten time larger than it was originally. In this case, can one truly speak of expansion? Instead, this became an opportunity to create significant architecture, a new window into the brand's craftsmanship and *savoir-faire*.

Noted for his experience in the realm of architecture, his listening skills and his sensibility while building the Condé leather goods workshop (the architect's first collaboration with the company), it was Jean-Marc Sandrolini who was invited to take part in the project. In Fiesso, he had to contend with a particularly unattractive site. "Architecture is a perpetual renewal," he explained. Unless he defied height regulations, there was no evolution towards a potential horizon or an optimal orientation. He quickly opted to create a casing—or should we say, trunk—that would absorb all the organs of the program: three workshops and their social areas, design offices and a gallery for exhibitions, and a two-hundred seat restaurant, located upstairs. What resulted was a singular showcase that expresses simplicity and elegance—as well as a certain discretion—so as not to overwhelm its already busy surroundings.

After developing several schematic sketches—an inherent part of the process of architectural design—Sandrolini was able to balance the volume by drawing a plan that articulated the workshops and offices around shafts of light and a vast rectangular patio; sensibly decentralized, this was conceived of as a court that connects the three workshops and the gallery. From the outside, one sees nothing more than a small fort of concrete poured on site. Too brutal for the designer's taste, this surface required a more luscious covering that would be softer to the eye and light. The idea was to situate the noble trade of shoe craftsmanship in a place at the height of this art. As a sort of artificial skin, the architect implemented a stainless steel wire mesh, echoing the textile that his Japanese colleague Jun Aoki used to wrap the stack of trunks at Omotesando. Consequently, like an art piece by Christo & Jeanne-Claude, the stony monolith was enveloped in architectural tissue paper. Stretched over the stony structural wall, this enormous piece of gauze measuring over 7 meters in height, made of interwoven threads of different kinds, doesn't only serve an aesthetic purpose: it simultaneously creates a visual filter that hides the façade openings and also acts as a translucent screen that blocks the sun, helping to keep the premises cool.

Transmutation. At dusk, the materiality of the structure turns into a screen that vibrates beneath projectors installed above and below. It's as if the energy absorbed during the day were reproduced in the radiant veil of night. To use the term "box" would be offensive to the attention to detail, to the precise elements that develop this architecture. Just as certain shoes manufactured here require almost eighty different processes, the building required an equivalent amount of care so that its many functions could be combined into one single element. This is how it attained its minimalist quintessence, and, thereby, its luxury.

On one side, the outside veil is interrupted in order to make way for a vast chamber, twice as high, that is the entrance. This expansion of space is bordered by a lateral Japanese-style walkway that relies on a framework of bamboo plants to provide shade for benches dedicated to workers who go on break. This perspective ends with a glass-paned umbilical cord that connects the first unit to the waist of its older, larger sister. Once the evanescent glass wall has been penetrated, the lobby reveals an unexpected openness. The sacredness of the place is fully respected by the structure itself: the rectangular court absorbs a natural light that diffuses to the surrounding areas. In a relationship of one by two-and-a-half, at 60 meters deep and 24 meters wide, the dimensions are awe-inspiring. Despite the multitude of people that work here, silence reigns. The building acts as an invitation to worship the beautiful materials celebrated by Louis Vuitton. In this contemplative garden overseen by the three workshops and gallery, the groomed grass is embellished with a thread of water, symbolizing the source, subliminally gathering rainwater in a 200 square-meter basin so as to reduce the amount of drinkable water used for irrigation. Such details contribute to the environmental soundness of the building, which deserves recognition for its efficiency and incorporation of effective insulation, geothermal facilities and solar panels, all of which dramatically reduce energy consumption.

A room under the open sky has been created here, framed by poured concrete walls whose quality and signature—with framework holes left visible on purpose—follow in the tradition of the master of cast aggregate, the Japanese architect Tadao Ando. The austerity suits the nature of the premises. A bolstered tubular structure bears a canopy that is covered by the same texture as the façade, protecting against the sweltering Venetian sun in the summertime. There is no distinction between the features of the workshop and gallery. Everything exists on the same level. The two can watch each other in a never-ending dialogue between trade and art, fabrication and exhibition. The presentation of collectible pieces alongside the latest designs provides a genuine window into the brand that is useful for both for suppliers and employees-in-training. Above, the restaurant overlooks the green depths of the central court where a constellation of patios—whose plants each assume a theme—direct light into the adjacent offices. "Fiesso d'Artico is not architecture, it's a philosophy," states Serge Alfandary, the director of shoemaking, and rightly so. Named after three legendary bags, "Alma," "Nomad," and "Speedy," the three workshops divided by families of workers are respectively dedicated to the elegant woman, moccasins, and sneakers. A fourth area, "Taiga," named after one of the House's leathers, is found in the first building, where classic models for men are created. They revolve around a large, longitudinal street, whose dense colors alternate between red, yellow, blue and green—identifying with and absorbing, with slight flair, the adjoining social areas that include changing rooms and restrooms. Aside from the floor made of cumaru—a very strong wood—the working corridors boast a whiteness worthy of a laboratory. Walls and ceilings are treated to provide maximum reflective light so that working conditions are of optimal comfort, and skylights with a fabric shade prevent any glare. A sound-proof room is supported around the edges by a taut fabric that lets air pass through, completely recycled at the rate of eight times per hour. The least noble tasks are automated and are part of a mechanical choreography that complements human activity. The suction ducts at the cutting tables, buffing tables and other polishing machines form gleaming, winding shapes in the space—a network that is connected to the roof structure and camouflaged by the design as a whole. The right balance is struck between expression and concealment.

Finally, the pathway is studded with artistic footwear. In the court, one can view *Priscilla*, a giant construction of 600 pots made by the Portuguese artist Joana Vasconcelos, and a metal circle with a blood red shoe hanging in the middle, Natalie Decoster's *Objet du Désir*. For the entrance, Jean-Jacques Ory created a giant shoe lined on the inside with Botticelli's venerated Venus. There's also an Andy Warhol silkscreen from 1984; having worked as a shoe designer for Israel Miller before achieving fame, the king of Pop Art drew dozens of them. One bears the inscription, "To shoe or not to shoe?"—a borrowed expression that fits Fiesso d'Artico perfectly.

p. 235 view of main entrance
p. 236–237 view of mesh screen along principal façade
p. 238 views of entry sequence with artwork by Jean-Jacques Ory, *Venus à l'escarpin* (2008)
p. 239 top: detail of the façade mesh screen; bottom: courtyard view with artwork by Joana Vasconcelos, *Priscilla* (2008) and by Nathalie Decoster, *L'objet du désir* (2008)
p. 240 detail of flower monogram from the Champs-Elysées Maison, France

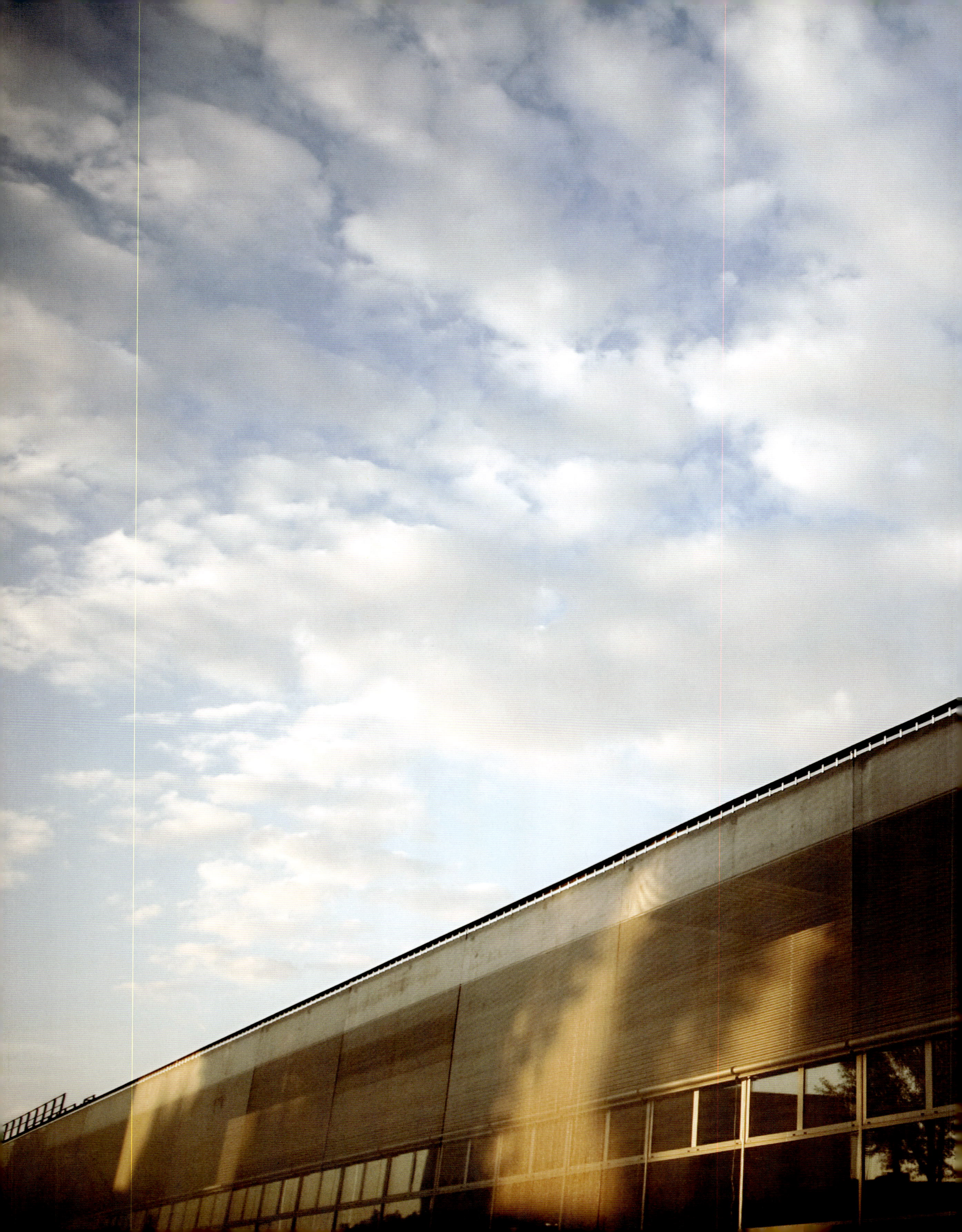

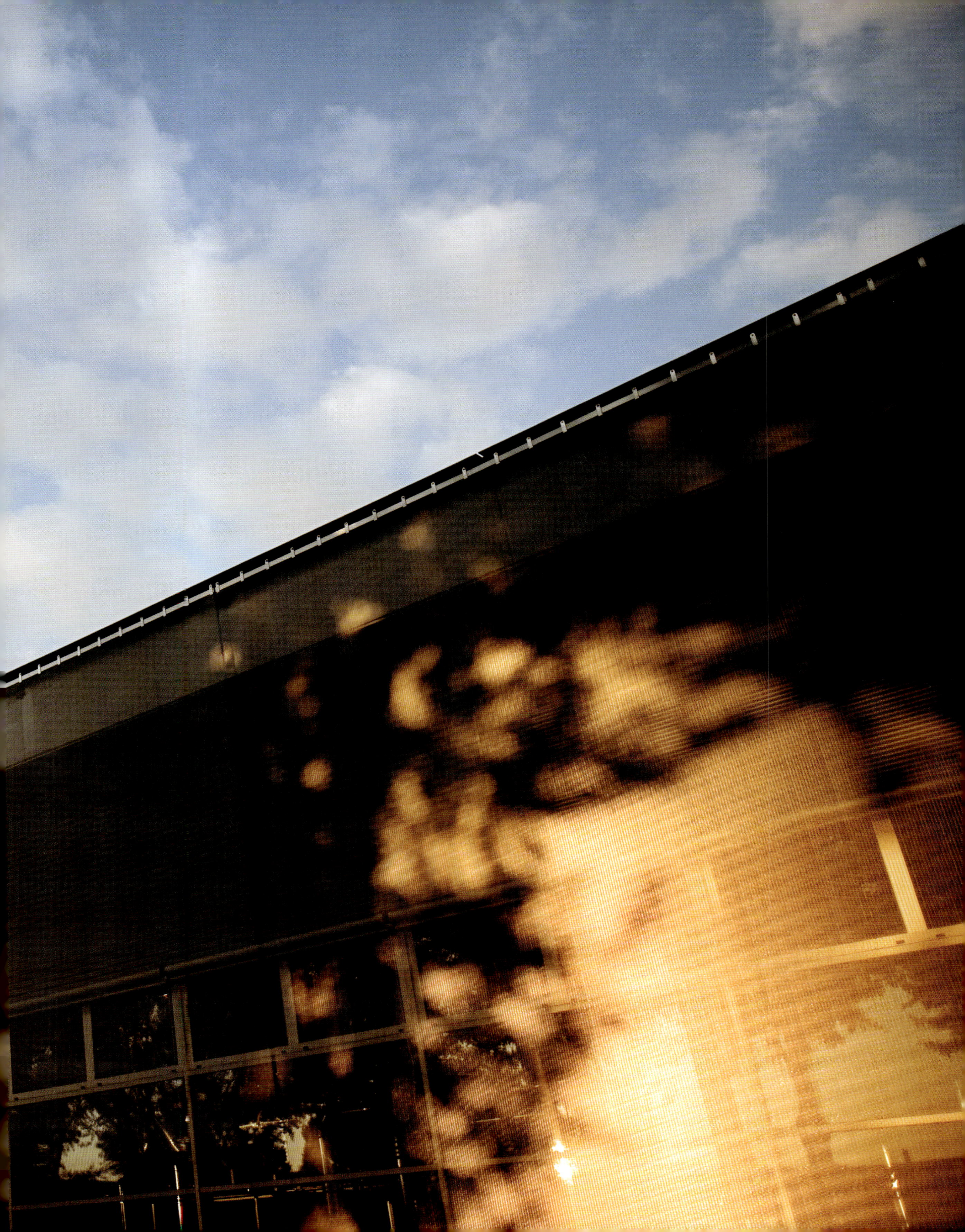

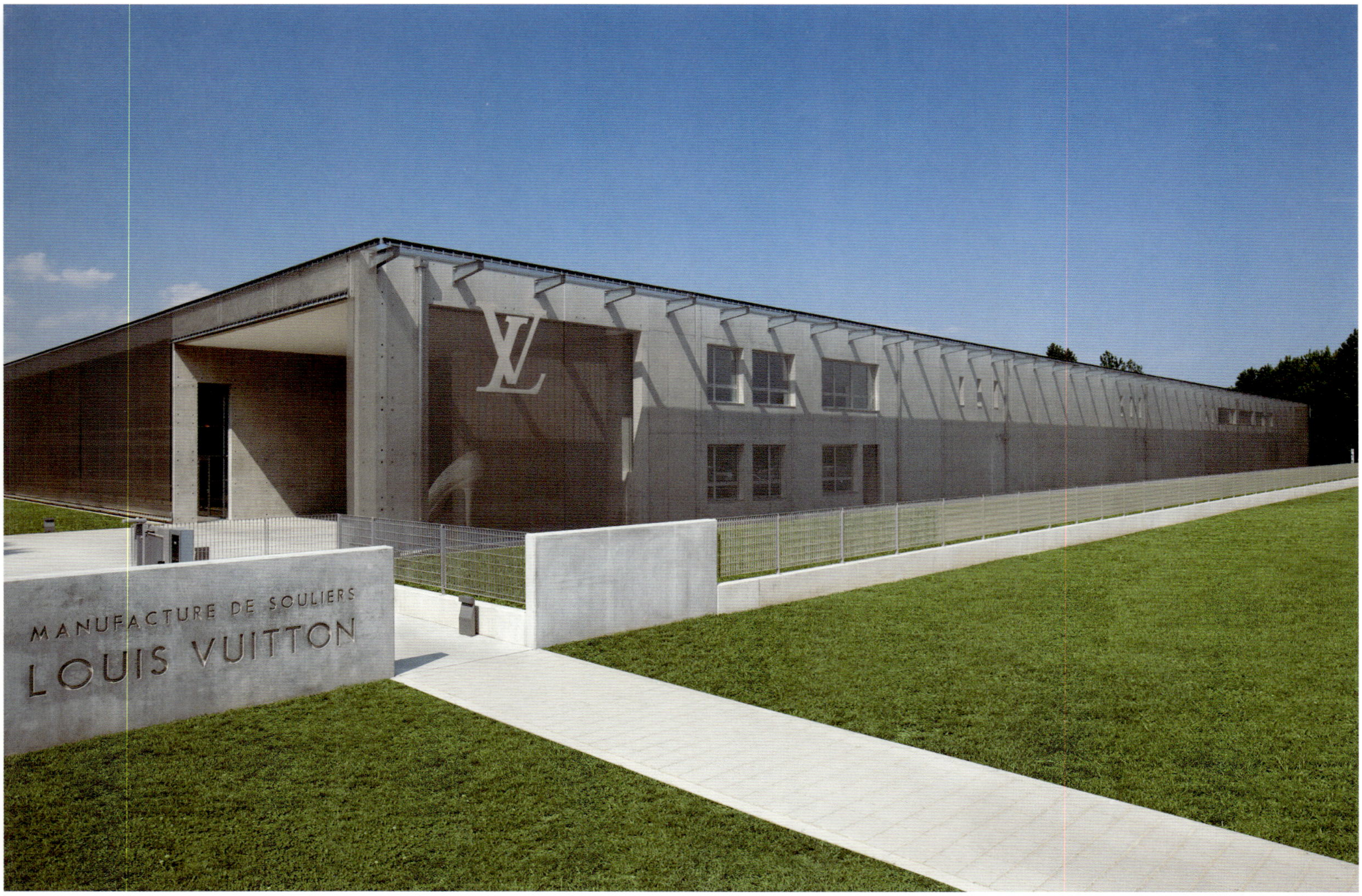
MANUFACTURE DE SOULIERS
LOUIS VUITTON

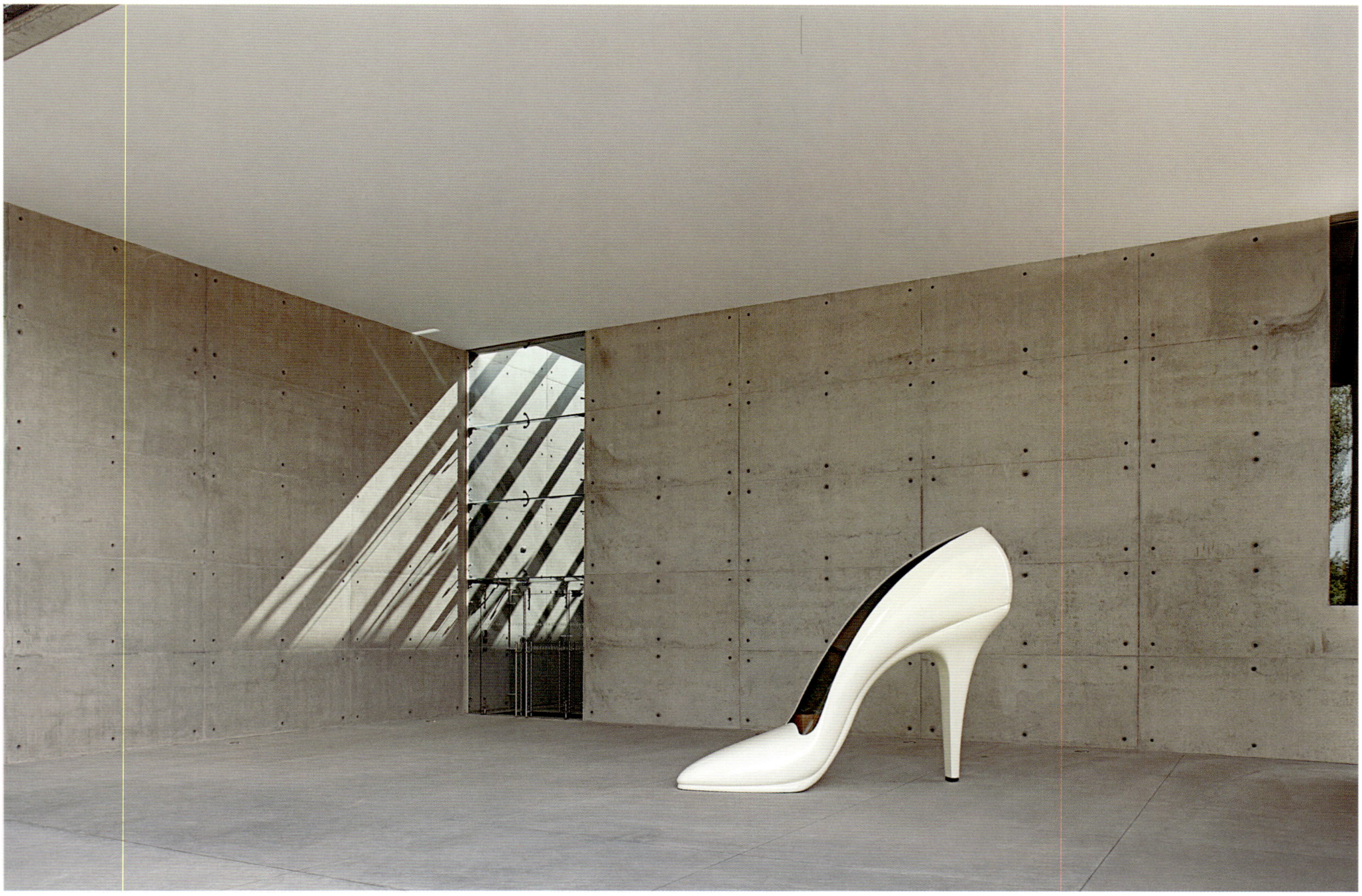

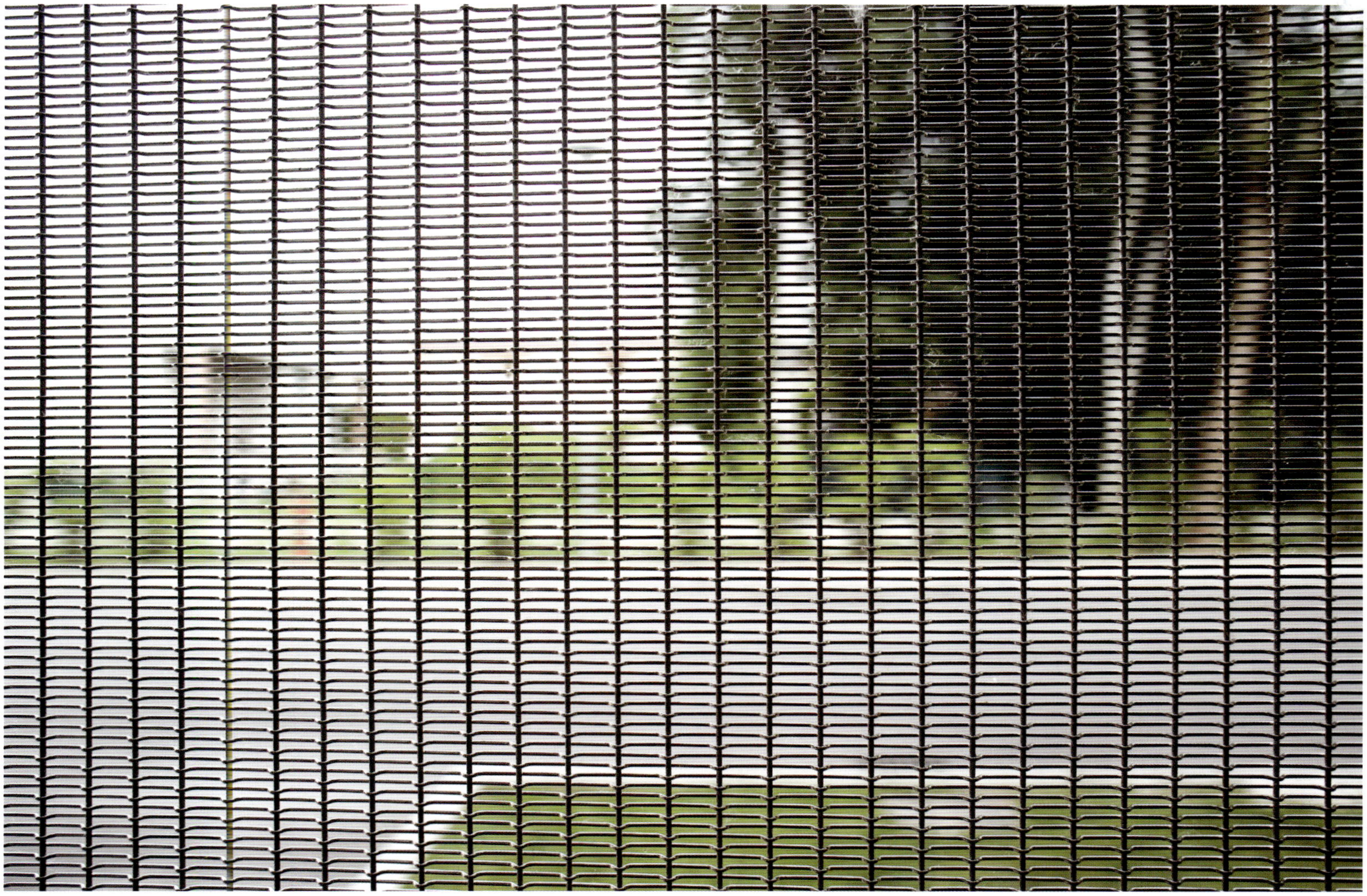

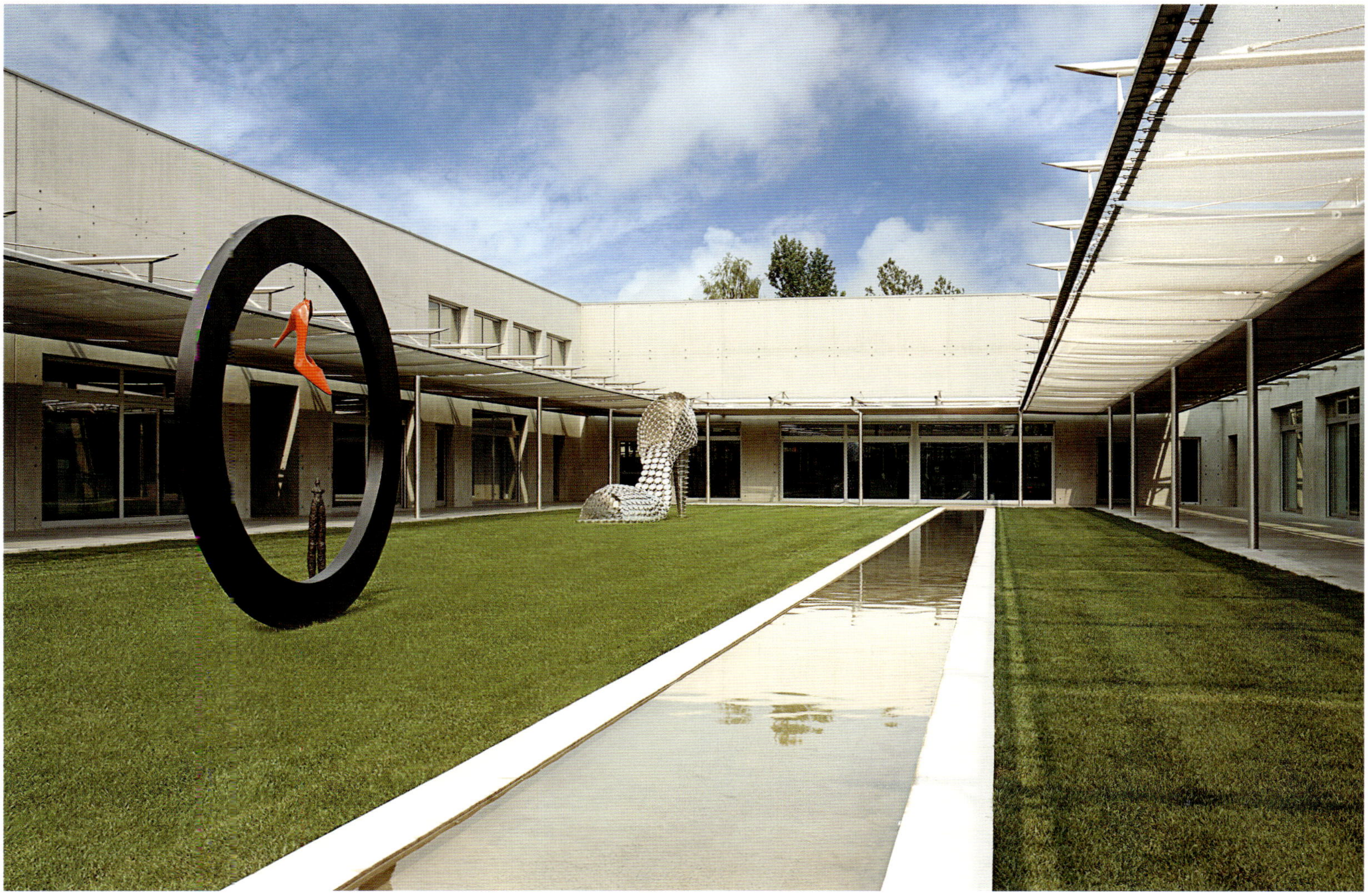

CODES
SKINS
FAÇADES
SIGNAGE

LOUIS VUITTON—ARCHITECTURE, FASHION, AND FABRICATION
MOHSEN MOSTAFAVI

It is true that one of the main tasks of any architecture associated with a brand is to create a visual and experiential identity. The architecture of Louis Vuitton clearly fulfills that task, but it also does more—it transcends brand identity. While using architecture as a tool for achieving its retail ambitions, it delves into the realm of design exploration to an extent that few other companies have matched. Louis Vuitton's commitment to design goes hand in hand with a willingness, clearly for sound business reasons, to pursue unorthodox procedures of implementation and construction. And this experimentation has been good not just for business, but for architecture.

Given the long history of the brand as a maker of premier-quality travel luggage, bags and suitcases, it is interesting to witness the relatively recent and yet spectacular growth and ascendancy of the firm within a more general and diverse category of luxury fashion goods. As part of its strategic global expansion Louis Vuitton has used not just one but a number of stand-alone buildings and larger stores, a fairly uncommon strategy. Until this development, their stores were mainly what are referred to as "bowling alleys"—relatively small, maybe 1,000 sq. ft. stores, consisting essentially of a long internal display wall with a counter in front for interaction with the sales staff. The replacement of this type of store with much larger premises that could accommodate and display a much wider variety of clothing and travel items presented both challenges and opportunities. One of the opportunities has clearly been the mining of the relationship between the design of Louis Vuitton goods and its architecture.

Architects and architectural writers often use analogies with other fields to address the characteristics of a particular stylistic tendency. In the nineteenth century, for example, cooking provided a vivid device for discussing the differences between French and English architecture. The culinary techniques, preferences and traditions of a nation were held to resemble its architectural output; the materials and methods of making things were transferred from one field to another. This phenomenon, which also accounts for the introduction of the concept of taste in architecture, can of course be applied to many locations. Think, for example, of the parallels between the making of Japanese food and traditional Japanese architecture, with its emphasis on simplicity and restraint.

Likewise, the correlation between architecture and fashion go back a long way. The Viennese architect Adolf Loos, who designed the controversial modernist gentlemen's outfitters Goldman and Salatsch on Michaelerplatz in 1909, was fascinated with English tailoring. Loos's modernism and his fascination with English gentleman's clothing were both linked to tradition and a concern with the continuity of crafts. One of Loos's famous quotes exhorts us not to be, "afraid of being called unfashionable." He himself liked to wear English bespoke suits, which had already evolved into more or less their current form by the 1880s. The elegant simplicity of these suits made him appear different—ironically more rather than less fashionable compared to his Viennese contemporaries. But through association, his sartorial habits also linked him with others of similar taste and standing who had a preference for bespoke English tailoring. This duality between individuality and conformity is one of the key features of fashion, a fact well articulated by one of Loos's contemporaries, the German sociologist Georg Simmel, who wrote one of the most insightful essays on the subject.

For Loos the parallels between architecture and clothing reinforced his belief in the value of craft, where a trade was learned through the repetition of proven methods. His building on the Michaelerplatz, including its club-like interiors, is by no means a direct replication of traditional Viennese architecture, but represents an important manifestation of the interplay between tradition and modernity. It was criticized at the time for its reductive and planar simplicity, for it gains its force not from the addition of ornament, but from the affects and qualities of the materials and the methods of construction.

The emphasis on the craft of making things is also something that distinguishes Louis Vuitton from most other companies. The history of the company's products is valuable in this regard. The methods used by Louis Vuitton are those of master craftsmen adopting and practicing tried-and-tested techniques developed over many years in a Paris workshop. Despite the globalization of the brand, the firm's core product—the making of all manner of travel cases—remains deeply tied to the preservation of the company's traditions of manufacturing. At the same time, for the adventurous traveler, Louis Vuitton luggage has always been more than a convenient means of transporting clothes. What the company provided was more akin to an infrastructure—equipment that, when unfolded, made travel to far-off lands possible, maybe even enjoyable. These associations remain part of the mythology of the brand, and are important factors in owning a piece of Louis Vuitton luggage even today.

The current culture of architectural production at Louis Vuitton is sensitive to this history. And the company has based much of its approach to making buildings on the inspiration gained from the visual reappropriation and reframing of traditional Louis Vuitton products and motifs.

From the beginning there were at least four layers of organization that were vital to the success of the firm's architectural ambitions. The founding of the current version of Louis Vuitton's Paris architectural office in the mid-90s has been a cornerstone of both its brand and its building strategy. The company decided early on to make a distinction between the inside and the outside of their stores. And like other companies, they wanted the inside to have a similar palette throughout their stores despite the variations in location. They delegated this task to Peter Marino, whose architectural practice, amongst other things, provides the designs for a number of LVMH-owned fashion brands.

Initially Japan provided the best opportunities for what Louis Vuitton called its "global stores" strategy, and a limited competition was held in the late 1990s for the design of the new store in Nagoya; Louis Vuitton made a deliberate decision not to appoint signature architects for its projects, so the focus would be on developing the firm's own identity rather than propagating an architectural brand. From this, the practice of Jun Aoki was awarded the contract, and the competition concept was developed by Eric Carlson and David McNulty, the team that led the architecture office in Paris at the time. (Carlson has since left to set up his own practice.) According to David McNulty, all the participants in the Nagoya store competition produced classical design schemes, with the exception of Jun Aoki, who presented a simple double-layered façade with a checkerboard pattern on both surfaces, reminiscent of Louis Vuitton patterns.

The final organizing layer in Louis Vuitton's architecture involved the various teams of consultants and contractors who were charged with the speedy construction of all of the projects, beyond the usual emphasis in Japan on fast construction techniques. This is an aspect that Louis Vuitton has always been willing to push to the maximum, since in the boom years for the retail industry it is always more profitable to finish construction sooner, even if it means spending more, as the profits quickly make up the difference. In recent years this organizational model has changed to the point where the Paris office now designs most of the projects worldwide.

The Nagoya store was a fresh idea. Neither the client nor the architect knew what to expect, but the collaboration between the various parties produced a series of design ideas that shaped the firm's signature architecture. The concept developed by the architects in Japan and Paris avoided the use of traditional materials such as stone, with their associations of solidity and opulence. In place of this representational architecture, Aoki developed a more experiential form of architecture that relied on the dynamic participation of the viewer. One of Aoki's ongoing preoccupations has been the use of semi-transparent patterns based on Louis Vuitton products—a graphic device that creates an ever-changing external ambience activated by the movement of the people around it.

At Louis Vuitton's flagship Omotesando store in Tokyo, completed in 2002, the use of various types of see-through wire mesh creates a similar interaction with passers-by. Here, Aoki envisaged the composition of the building as a series of trunks stacked randomly, one on top of the other. The juxtaposition of the volumes helps to break down the building's scale on the famous retail street, while occupying the inside of the building is akin to occupying the empty interior of Louis Vuitton's exotic travel luggage. The shimmering wire mesh drapes the inner glass façade like a dress, becoming more revealing and transparent at night than during the day. The sensual associations between the body and the building are not lost on the viewer. The building's task is to construct desire, to help draw people in.

The dichotomy between the reassuring familiarity of a more traditional luxurious interior and the external envelope as the primary site of Aoki's design has led to greater focus on the material effects of the buildings. In this respect, the use of a double-layered façade as an optical device in many of the stores created a distinctive look that made a Louis Vuitton store immediately recognizable to potential customers. The optical qualities of these façades also generated ever-changing impressions that became the source of their attraction. In many ways, the Nagoya and Omotesando stores provided the seeds for most of what was to follow.

The design of these buildings does not rely on conventional modes of architectural representation, in part because the ornamental qualities and dynamic effects of such façades cannot be fully experienced by drawings or computer renderings. As a consequence, the company has invested heavily in full-scale mockups of the buildings' external skin as a means of testing their impact on the viewer. This aspect of Louis Vuitton's architecture closely parallels the way fashion designers develop ideas by making various samples of their work—a creative method that is beautifully captured in Wim Wenders' documentary about the Japanese designer Yohji Yamamoto, *Notebook on Cities and Clothes*, 1989.

There is something extremely powerful about the directness and immediacy of the methods of fashion design that have been co-opted by Louis Vuitton in its various building projects. With Louis Vuitton, the use of prototypes is an indispensible part of testing the effects of the building, enabling the architects and the client to have a real sense of what the finished product will be like. What these prototypes explore best are the qualities of the external skin as both ornament and function. Unlike Adolf Loos, who saw ornament as a form of 'crime,' these facades do not envisage ornament as appliqué—an addition—but rather as the primary material for the aesthetic logic of the building envelope. As with certain types of clothing, their seductive qualities, patterns and textures are all essential parts of their function.

The evolution of double-layered façades and the use of wire

mesh are the props of the architecture of Louis Vuitton. They provide a kind of apparatus or scaffolding, a spatial envelope that explores potential variations in the depth of the building's skin. This approach undermines the implied solidity of traditional tectonic models. Indeed, some of Louis Vuitton's tactics deploying three-dimensional patterns are closer to Op artists such as Victor Vasarely or Bridget Riley, whose early works have an unsettling impact on the eye. By redeploying Louis Vuitton historical patterns on the surfaces, first Aoki and then the Paris-based team of architects have developed a range of manifestations of the architecture of sensations.

The interiors of Louis Vuitton stores provide a contrast to the noise and pollution of the outside world and to the illusions constructed by their exteriors. These interiors, made of wood, glass, leather, stainless steel and fabrics, have a calming effect on the shopper. They are cleverly designed to slow down the activity of shopping. On one level they seem to lack the experimental qualities of the building envelopes, deliberately appearing more traditional, perhaps even conservative. Yet they have also gone through a variety of design and material transformations and are often modified from place to place. In Japan, for example, the relationship of the client to the clothes is more restrained, with the more expensive items of clothing being handled with great care. This care is not always evident in China—now the fastest-growing market for the firm—so the design team have had to take into consideration this social characteristic within the definition of the interiors.

Another shift in the design of the interior has been the increasing domestication of the environment, making it more akin to a home than a department store. Various techniques for the production of intimacy have been explored to create the sense of a unique experience—like being invited into someone's home. Other initiatives have included club-like spaces reserved for the more regular, high-spending customers. And more recently, the company has been developing the concept of separate zones or stores for different goods and genders. At the heart of most of these variations, however, is the provision of a sense of security—the idea that a Louis Vuitton store has to be a kind of sanctum, a protected environment. This is particularly the case in high-traffic areas like China, where there is a disjuncture between the number of people who visit the stores and the need for a certain level of quiet luxury. This is an additional reason for the partial separation of zones within some of the latest stores.

The design of the exterior has shifted too, over the past five years or so, as the Paris office has become involved in most of the company's architecture. Divided into teams responsible for various global sectors—Asia, Europe, US, etc.—the Paris office has become increasingly engaged with external consultants and construction companies, and plays the role of designers, coordinators and implementers of a complex matrix of design decisions. More recently there has been a shift from the idea of the double-layered skin. Instead they have created an amalgam of the wire mesh and glass façades by texturing glass. Working in Singapore with Front, a New York-based façade engineering firm, they have advanced these techniques to give glass the malleability of a piece of fabric or of wire mesh by molding it like a curtain. Here the glass is used not as a transparent screen but as a building material to define opacity. In these examples, the characteristics of earlier designs act as catalysts for creating new materials with similar effects. This mode of research represents a mixture of tradition and innovation. Ideas that have become the hallmark of the company's architectural brand identity are now being rethought or recalibrated through collaboration with manufacturers and construction companies. And the reality is that many of these companies are now based in Asia rather than Europe or the US.

When Louis Vuitton began its current phase of architectural projects in the late 1990s the visual references for the exterior designs were largely based on the patterns of the company's travel products. Now a reverse process seems to be taking place, with a number of fashion designers drawing their inspiration from the visual effects, patterns and textures produced by the surfaces of recent Louis Vuitton buildings. Such reciprocities may become even more instrumental and intended in the years to come, with the possibility of architects and fashion designers working together on the tailoring, fabrics and coloration of buildings—one thinks here of designers like Issey Miyake, Jil Sander and Rei Kawakubo, who have already made major inroads in this area. But there also remains the question of the next phase in the story of the architecture of Louis Vuitton.

Only a few architects and fashion brands have made a marked impact in the area of retail architecture in the recent past. Among these are the early and "minimal" projects of David Chipperfield and Stanton Williams in London, Future Systems for Marni, Herzog & de Meuron for Prada, Toyo Ito for TOD's and SANAA for Dior in Tokyo and Jun Aoki and others for Louis Vuitton. It took a particular economic climate, a series of enlightened clients and a handful of talented architects to produce some inspiring buildings that also happen to be retail stores as well.

It seems, at least for the time being, that the current global fiscal crisis has put a hold on the type of adventurous building programs exemplified by Louis Vuitton, Prada, Dior and TOD's on Omotesando in Tokyo. In the case of Louis Vuitton, the greater centralization of resources, with the ensuing emphasis on stores attached to malls, has made the separation of the inside and outside of their buildings even more explicit. This separation is neither new nor unique to Louis Vuitton, but is rather a symptom of the realities of contemporary architectural practice, with the result that the outside—whatever the complexity and sophistication of the interior—assumes a greater status as a sign for the brand. On one level this is clearly deliberate: the building envelope and the interior have become two separate domains with distinct areas of expertise. But in many ways, the cited projects of Aoki, Ito, SANAA and Herzog & de Meuron defy this logic and produce architectures still capable of establishing relations between the inside and the outside.

It seems that Louis Vuitton will be continuing their policy of architectural differentiation between the inside and the outside for the foreseeable future. One of the challenges for the firm in the coming years will be to find a way of recalibrating this relationship. It would be interesting to see how the various forms of porosity between the inside and outside articulated at Louis Vuitton's Omotesando store, amongst others, will develop. If the outsides are to lure the clients into the store, then the interiors are to seduce them with their moods and atmospheres. And the interiors have moved towards greater levels of luxury and intimacy, with an increasing number of VIP rooms and differentiated spaces such as travel rooms. The ambience and techniques used to construct desire are becoming increasingly specific and distinct. In Singapore alone, there are stores that are oriented towards tours by Chinese visitors; others focus on younger clientele and recruiting new customers or the more sophisticated female client.

In recent years art has played a significant role in helping create differentiation between the stores. The New Bond Street store in London displays the work of the British artists Gilbert and George. The Champs-Elysées store has its own art gallery. The concept of the store as a mere place for buying goods has been supplanted by a much larger set of environments of affiliation. These environments not only construct desire but they also confer a sense of belonging. These are precisely the qualities that Simmel also identified as belonging to fashion.

Architecture and fashion have become intertwined in the projects of Louis Vuitton and there are now signs of an amalgam between the two. The restricting of architecture to the fabrication of the envelope and the surface—involving a deeper understanding of materials, such as glass—has produced a new taxonomy of visual regimes. Following Pierre Bourdieu, the specificity of Louis Vuitton's visual regime is an example of what he called 'La Distinction'—distinction. It is this distinctive quality of the work that accounts for both its architectural contribution and its recognizability, and identity. The question is, what will come next? How will Louis Vuitton develop the conjunction between its retail and its architectural aspirations, between the inside and the outside, between atmosphere and envelope? It is only upon answering these questions that we will have a sense of the next phase in this evolution.

SKINS

The building exterior is a chief preoccupation for Louis Vuitton's architecture. It is through this skin that the brand announces itself to the city and its clientele. Many of their recent buildings are sheathed in materials meant to evoke fabric. And, like clothing, they project a sensation that is almost soft, either physically or visually. Often they involve malleable materials that are not inherently luxurious but are made to appear so through their handling and placement. It is the experience of these effects that is of paramount importance. The layering of materials such as glass or metal mesh has been a key factor in developing complex, perceptual qualities that are intended, all at once, to evoke feelings of comfort, sensuality and luxury.

  The effects produced by the façades of LV buildings are invariably discreet and more likely to rely on the changing conditions of light, whether between day and night, or the seasons. For example, the metal mesh of the buildings in Seoul and Sapporo change completely in appearance once the winter snow attaches itself to their perforations. Such transformations are metaphorically akin to the seasonal dimensions of Vuitton products. The other quality of these exteriors is their sense of mystery. The veil-like appearance of the façades only hints at the objects of desire offered within. The skin of these buildings, therefore, both reveals and conceals.

p. 246–247 façade detail seen from the exterior of the abstracted damier pattern composing the principal elevations of the Hong Kong Landmark store
p. 248–249 view at night of Nagoya Sakae, Japan
p. 250 detail of Louis Vuitton Store in Kochi, Japan, by Kumiko Inui (2003). Screening the façade are 14,000 blocks of limestone
p. 251 marquetry done in an abstracted damier pattern at the Tokyo Omotesando Maison, Japan
p. 252 transformation of the exterior façade at night of the Hong Kong Lee Gardens store, by the Louis Vuitton architecture department (2005)
p. 253 view of interior detail from Macao One Central store
p. 254–255 interior views of the flower monogram mesh from the New Bond Street Maison, United Kingdom and the Kobe Kyoryuchi store, Japan
p. 256–257 exterior details using patterns derived from Louis Vuitton's L & V initials, from the Las Vegas City Center store and Guam store, United States

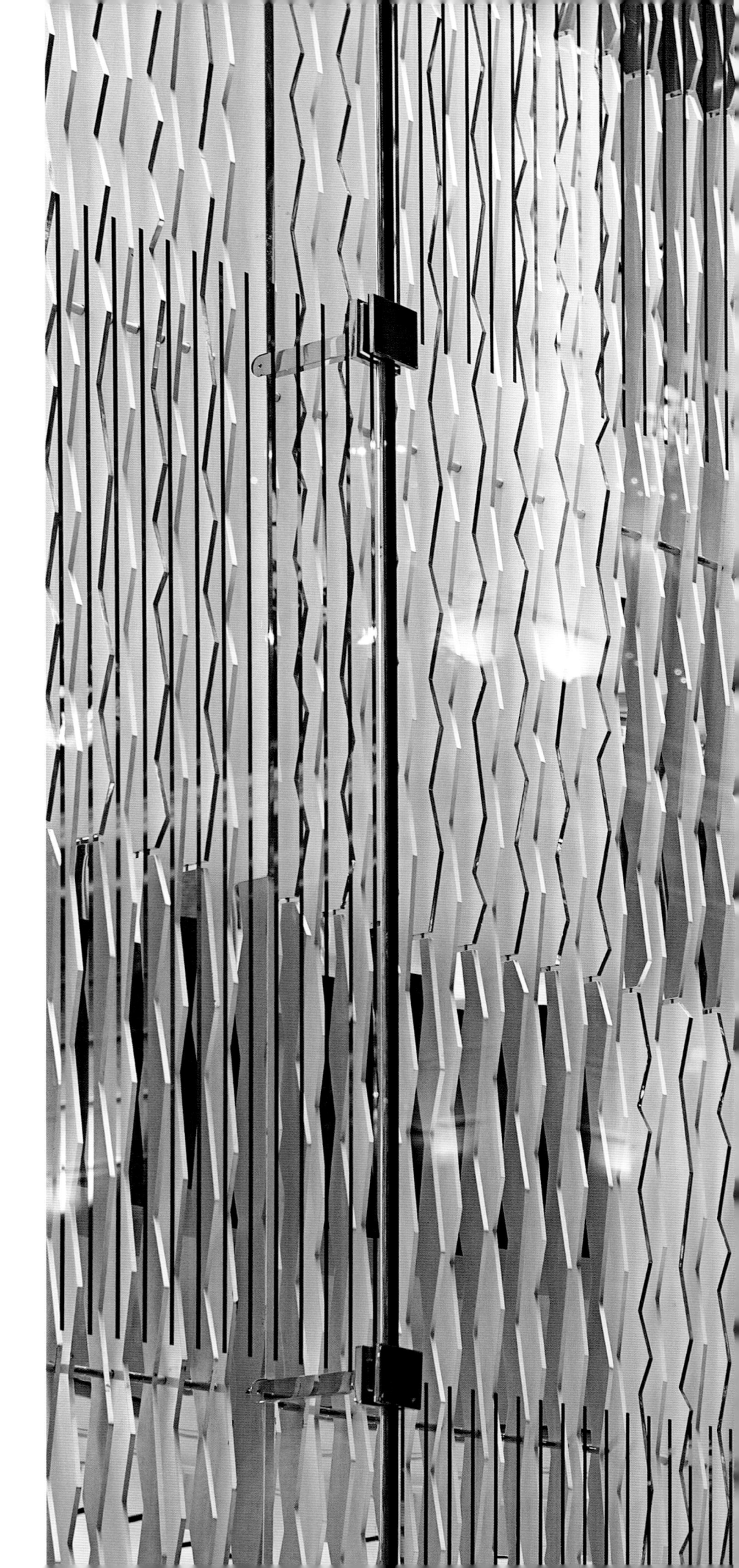

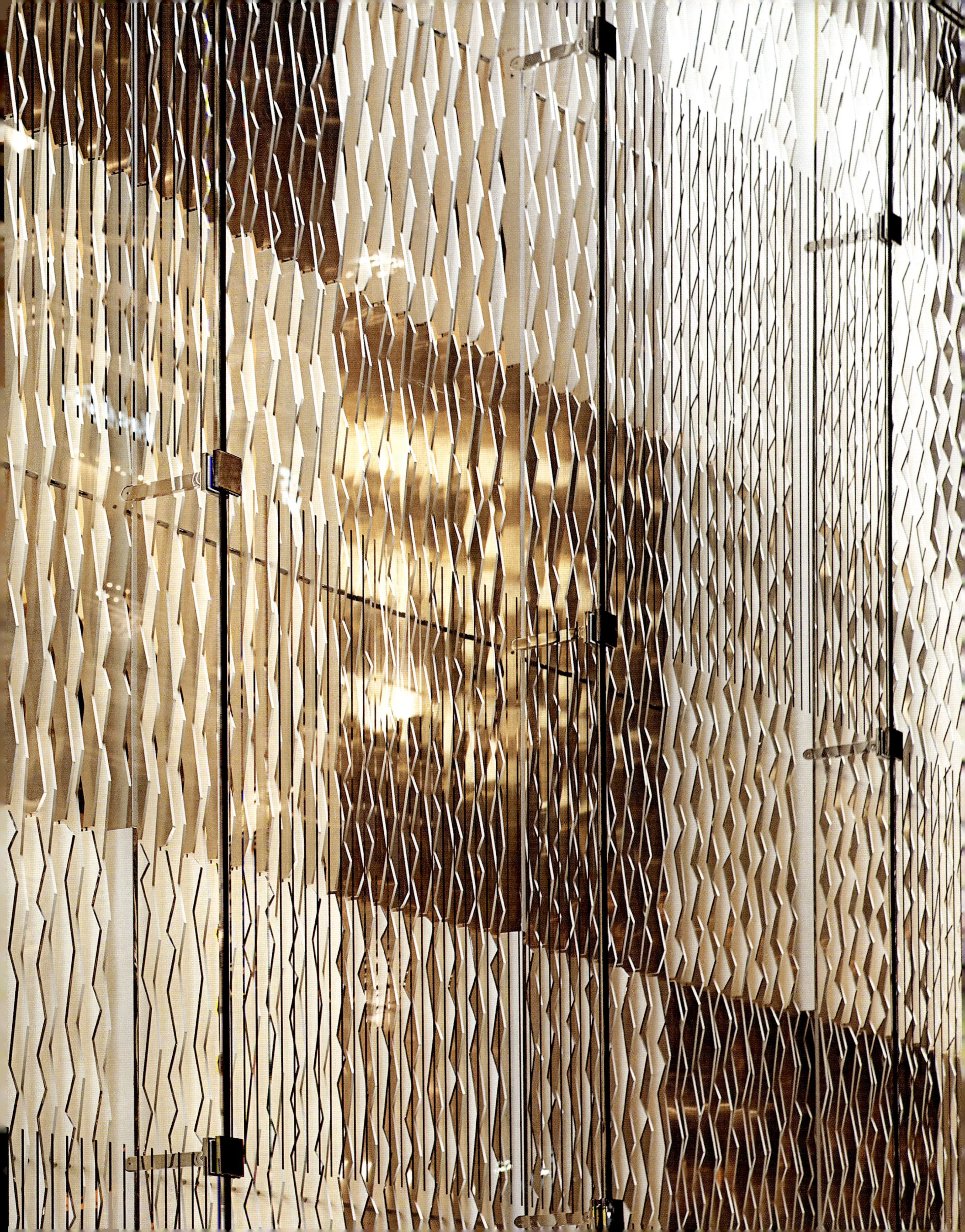

LOUIS VUITTON

LOUIS VUITTON

LOUIS VUITTON
MEN'S

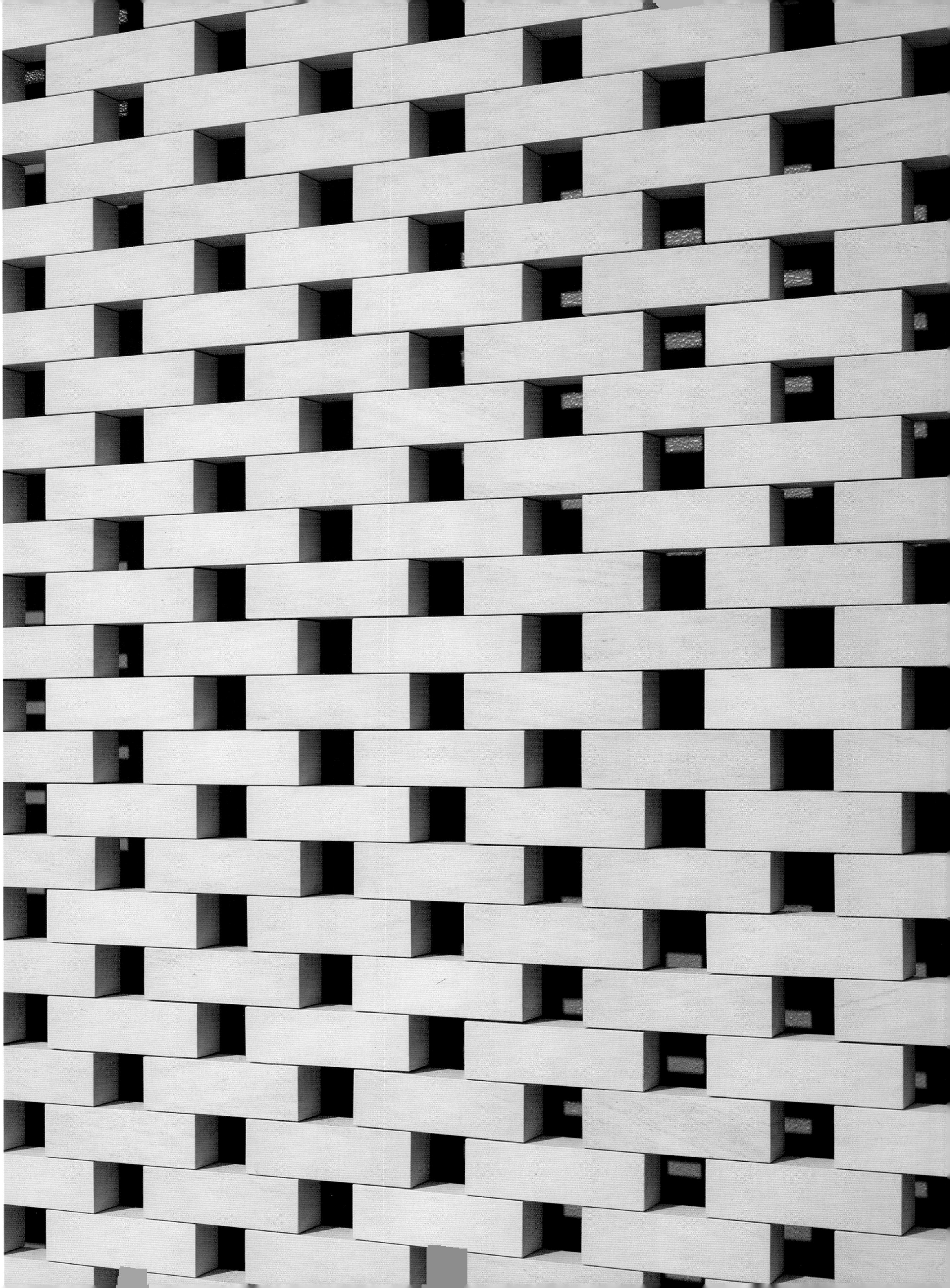

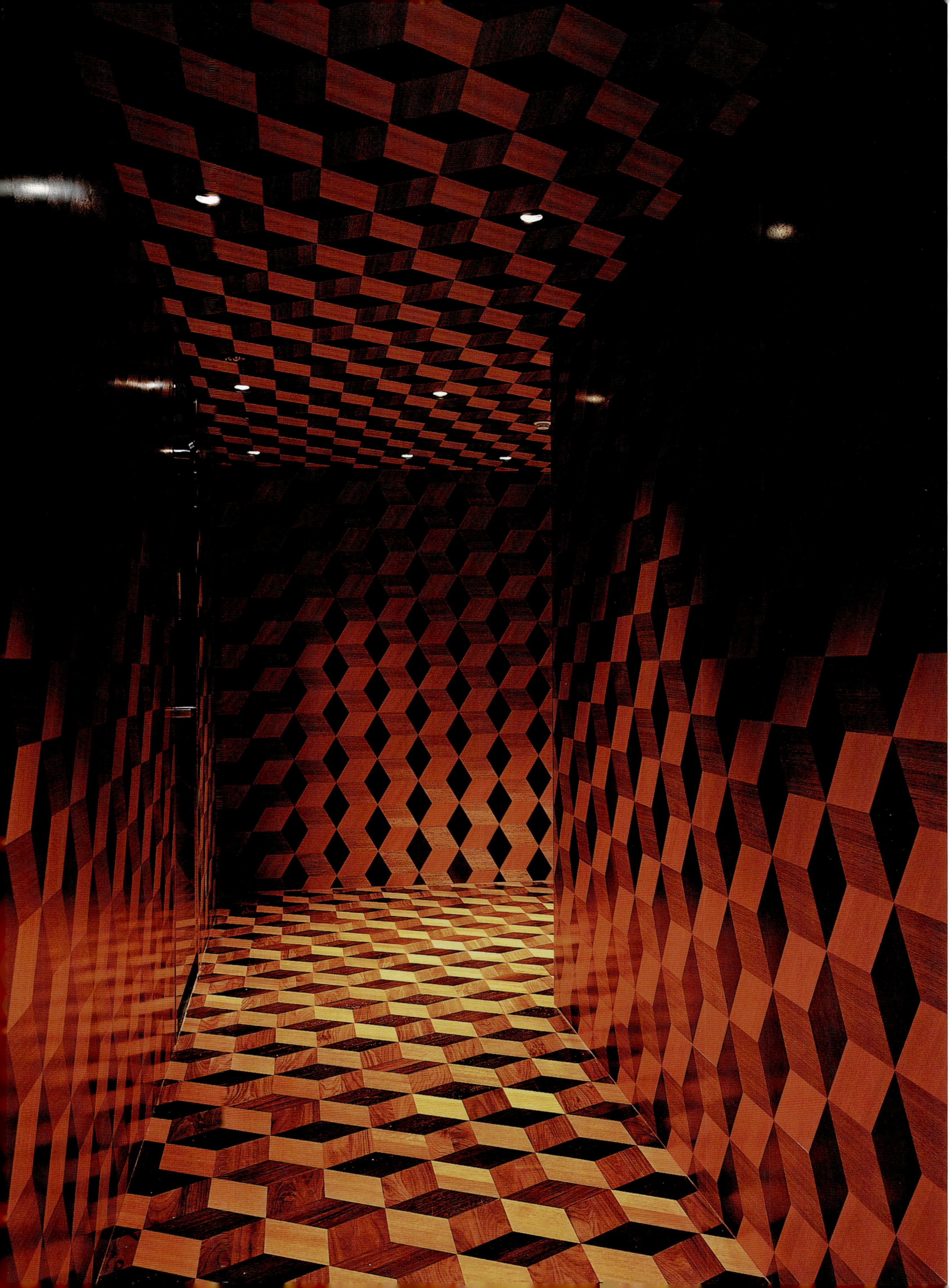

ARCHITECTURE AND INTERIORS 252

SKINS

CODES

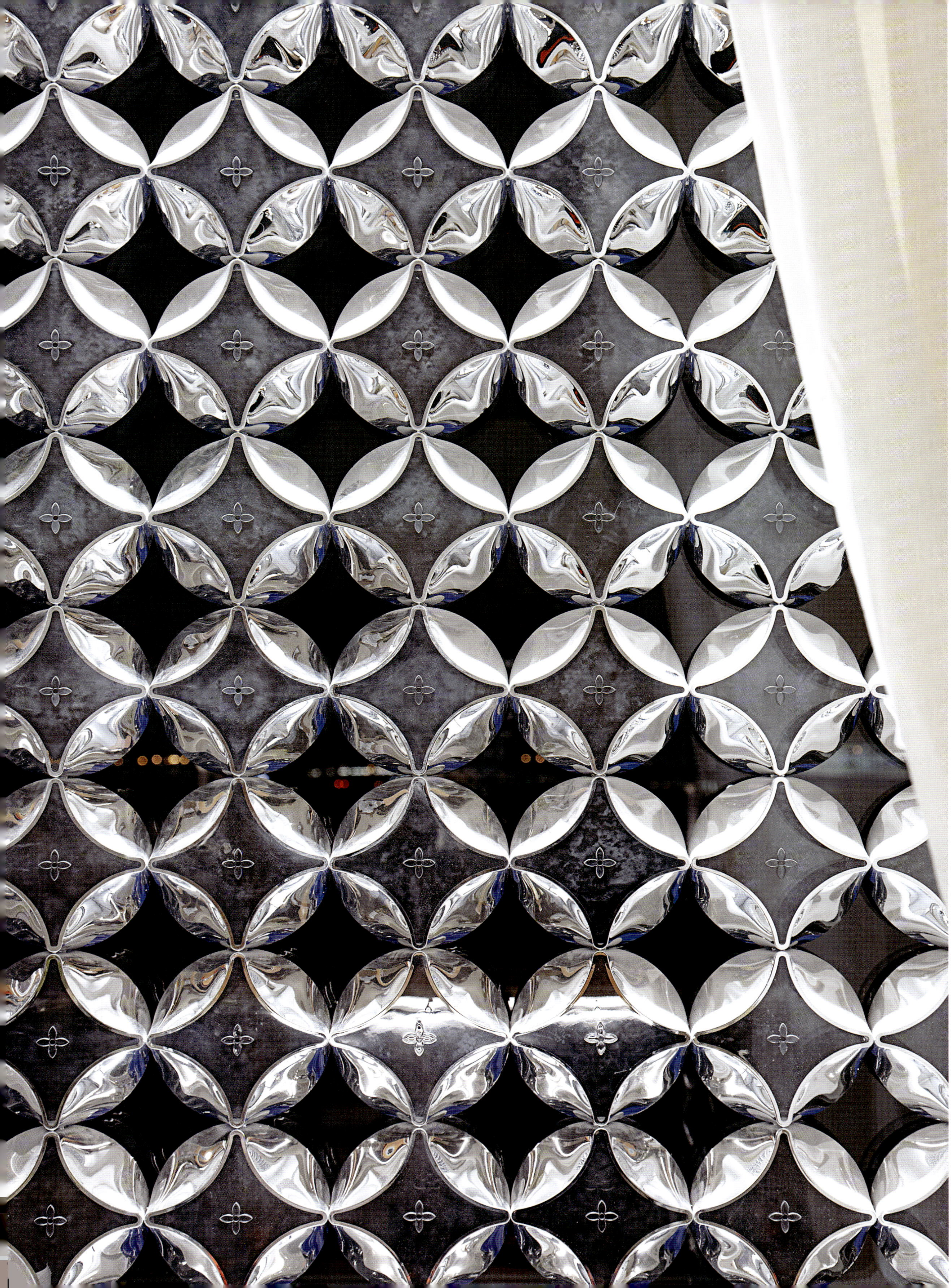

ARCHITECTURE AND INTERIORS 254

SKINS

CODES

ARCHITECTURE AND INTERIORS 255

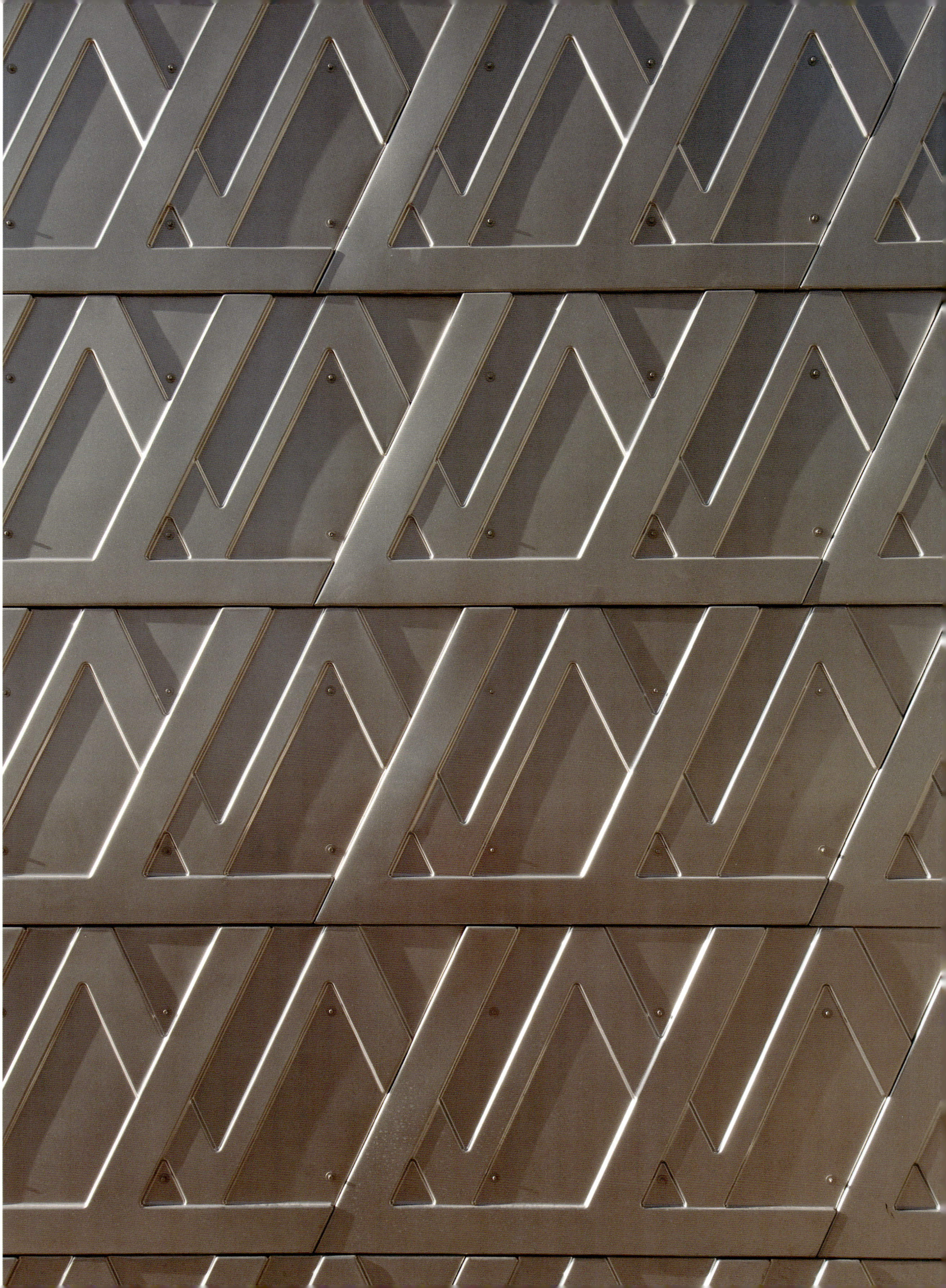

ARCHITECTURE AND INTERIORS 257

CODES SKINS

FAÇADES

Louis Vuitton's architecture is designed to produce effects through the use of circumstantial conditions. These can range from the contrast between daytime and nighttime, to the interaction of passersby. Taken together, they transform the sensory qualities of the building.

The façades, as veils, reveal something of the mystery of the buildings through their effects. The sensory qualities of their patterns and overlays are often not technologically complex, but are rather the result of a sensitive and precise juxtaposition of materials—from sheets of glass and expanded metal mesh, to enameled brick, milled metals and unfinished wood and concrete.

The temporal and transitory effects of Louis Vuitton façades, with their relatively low-tech approach, often achieve greater permanence than those façades that rely primarily on technological gestures. In many ways, this constantly evolving palette of material effects has been at the core of Vuitton's architecture since the opening of Jun Aoki's Nagoya Sakae store. And it is the combination of effects and their resulting ambiguity that have distinguished Vuitton's contemporary architectural patronage, particularly in the last decade.

p. 258 top: Louis Vuitton Kochi store, Japan, by Kumiko Inui (2003); bottom: Louis Vuitton Hamburg store, Germany (2003)
p. 259 top: Louis Vuitton Geneva store, Switzerland (2006); bottom left: Louis Vuitton Deauville store, France (2009); bottom right: Louis Vuitton Osaka Hilton Plaza Umeda, Japan, by Kumiko Inui (2004)
p. 260 Louis Vuitton Lugano store, Switzerland (2010)
p. 261 top: Louis Vuitton Singapore ION store (2009)
p. 262 Louis Vuitton Kobe Kyoryuchi store, Japan, by Barthélémy & Griño (2003)
p. 263 Louis Vuitton Seoul store, South Korea, by Jun Aoki (2000)

ARCHITECTURE AND INTERIORS

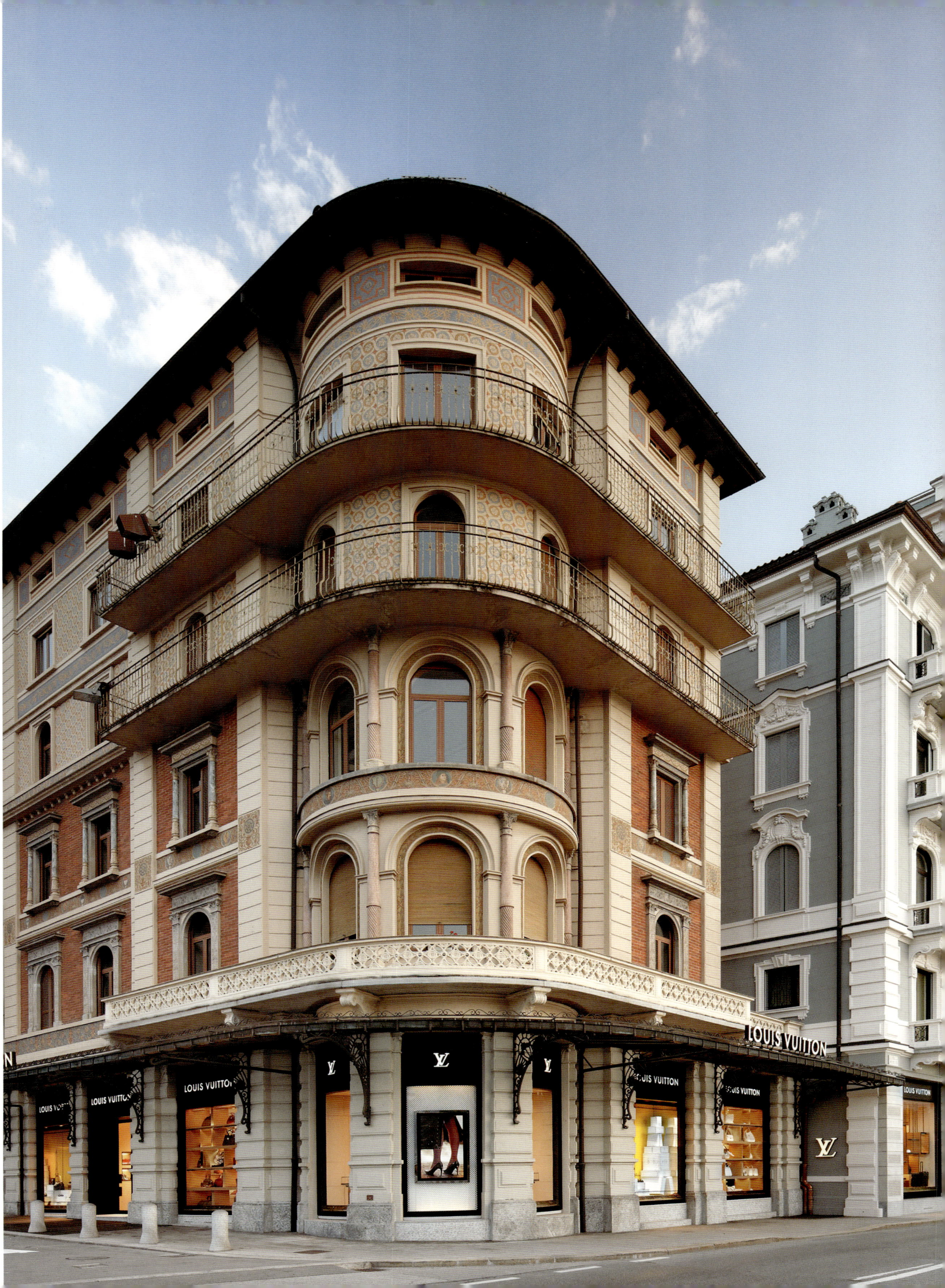
LOUIS VUITTON
LOUIS VUITTON

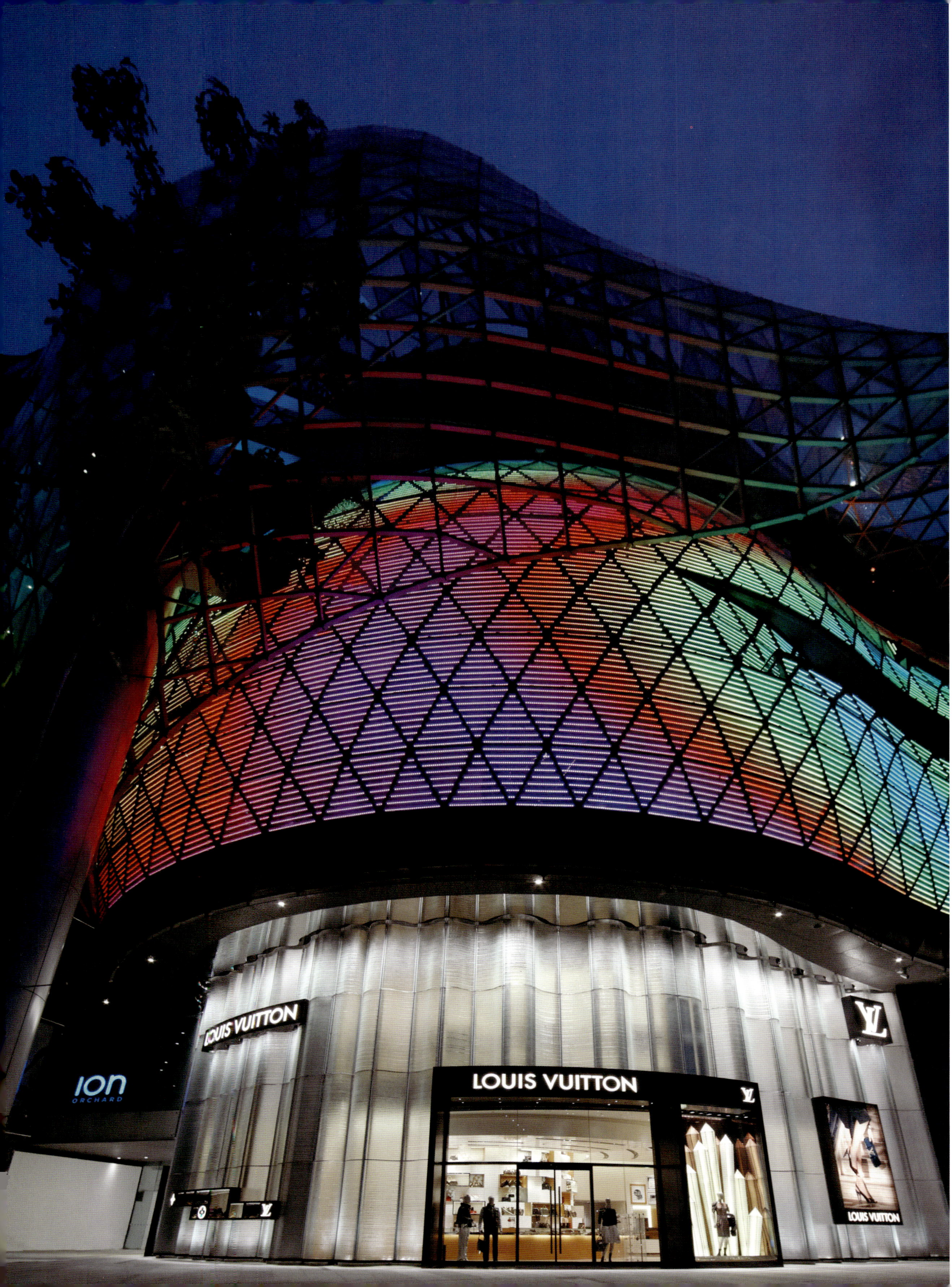
ion
ORCHARD
LOUIS VUITTON
LOUIS VUITTON
LOUIS VUITTON

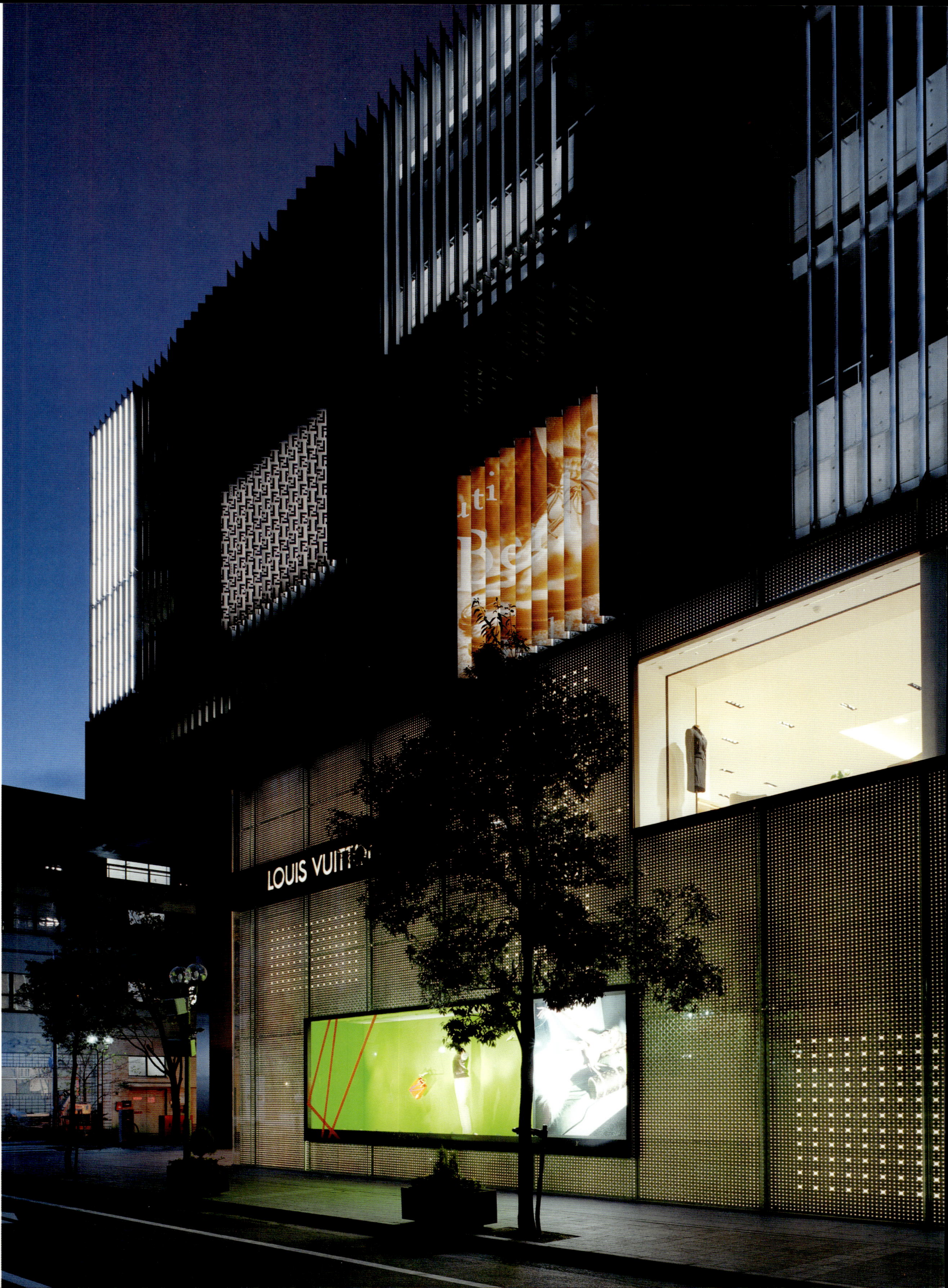
LOUIS

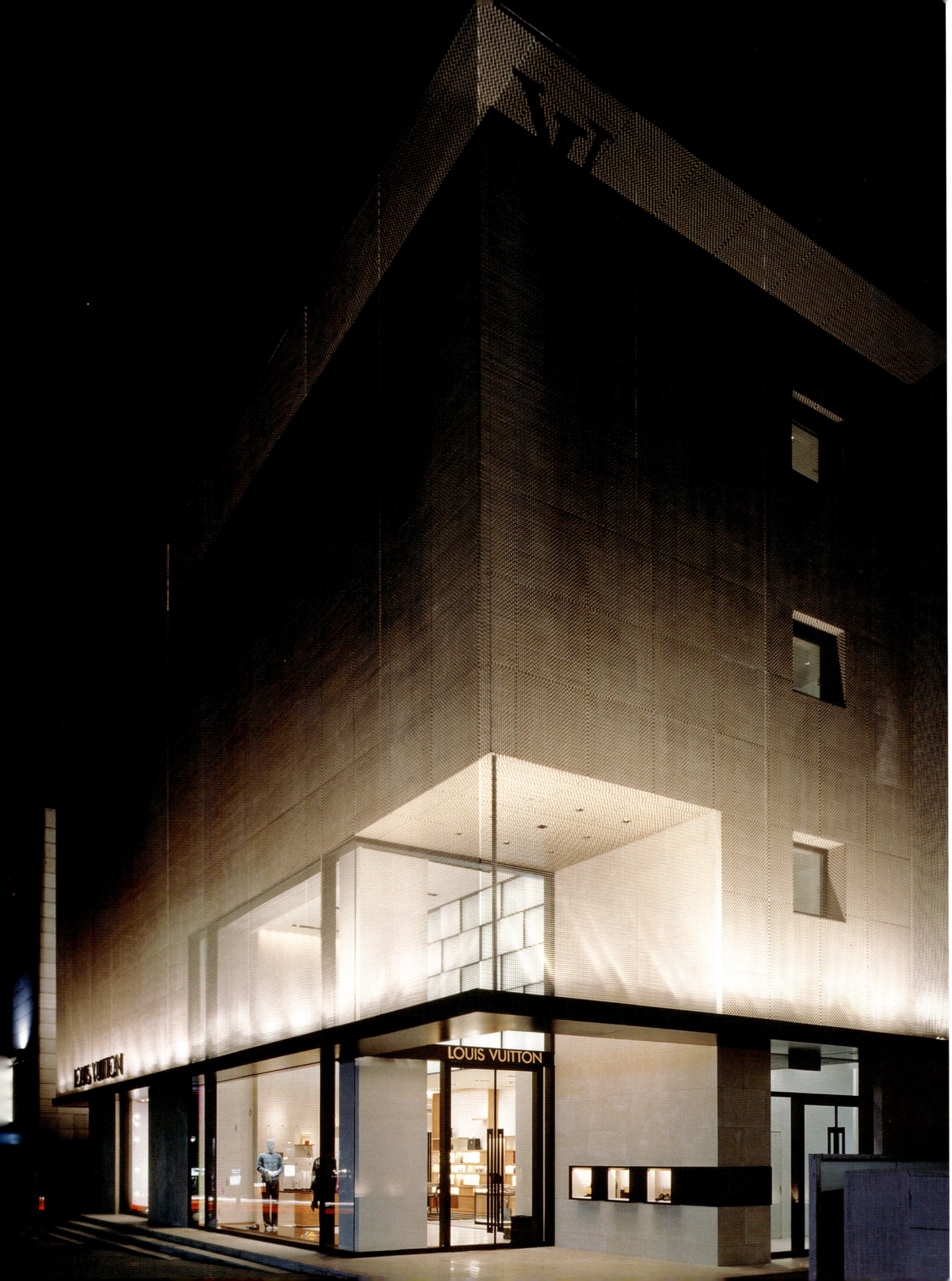
LOUIS VUITTON
LOUIS VUITTON

SIGNAGE

The Louis Vuitton logo, a key component in the identity and design of the company's products, has also been incorporated into the architecture in ways both subtle and overt. Signage is often used as in integrated element of the design rather than a separate add-on. Examples of this approach include the glass tubes that spell out Louis Vuitton on the frontage of Roppongi Hills, the projection of the LV logo on the façade of the Seoul store, and the varying degrees of transparency achieved by the melding of alabaster and aggregate on the exterior of the Namiki dori store.

More important, however, is the fact that the building design itself is becoming the sign—not through the repetition of the same materials or composition, but rather through the more complex expression of the brand, its proportions, textures and patterns. Unlike conventional retail architecture, built around literal signage and environmental graphics, the architecture of Vuitton opts to manipulate its codes through abstraction. The resulting constructions are not two-dimensional billboards, but rather spatial and material artifacts that make connections with the brand and yet simultaneously are distanced from it.

p. 264 Application of Louis Vuitton signage on the exterior of stores in Asia, North America, Europe and the Middle East
p. 266–267 detail from Fiesso D'Artico shoe atelier façade, Italy, by Jean-Marc Sandrolini (2009)

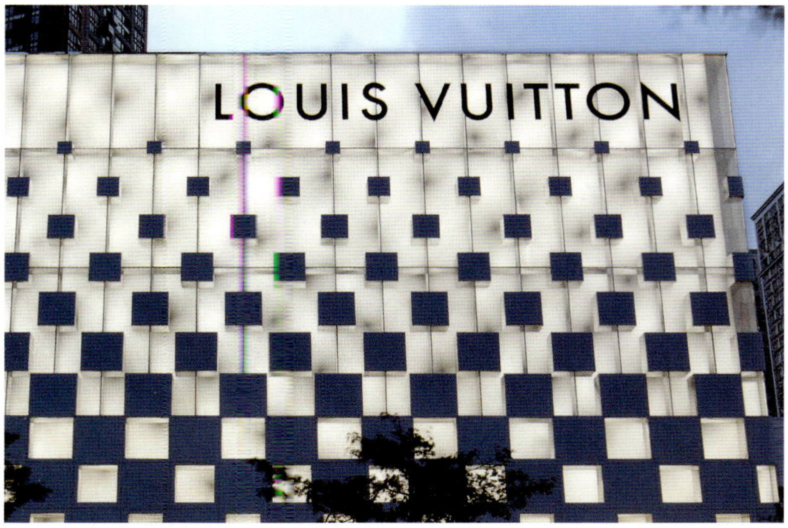
LOUIS VUITTON

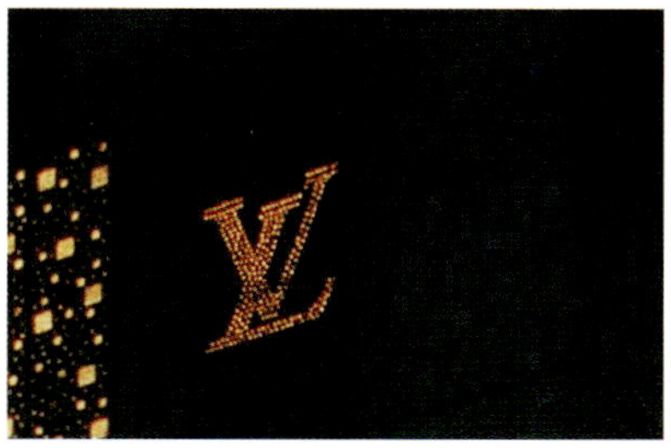

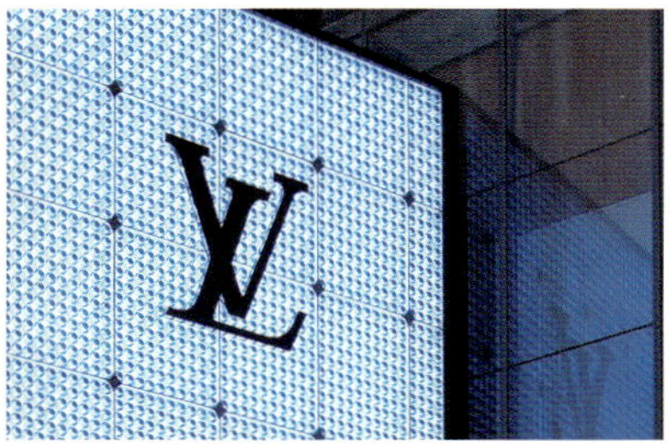

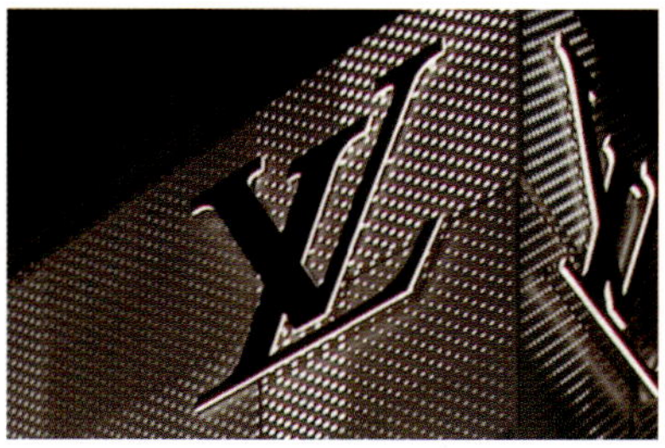

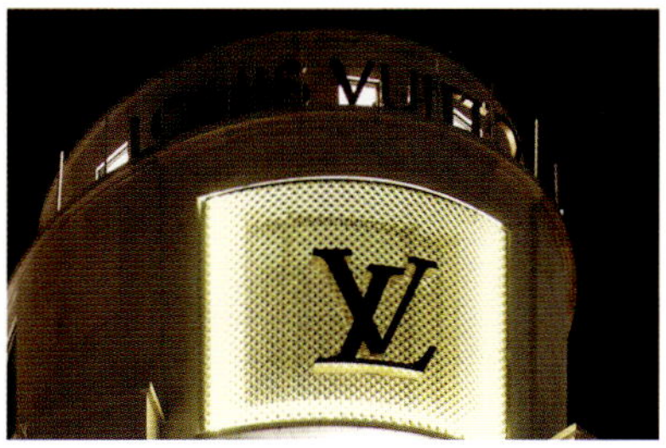

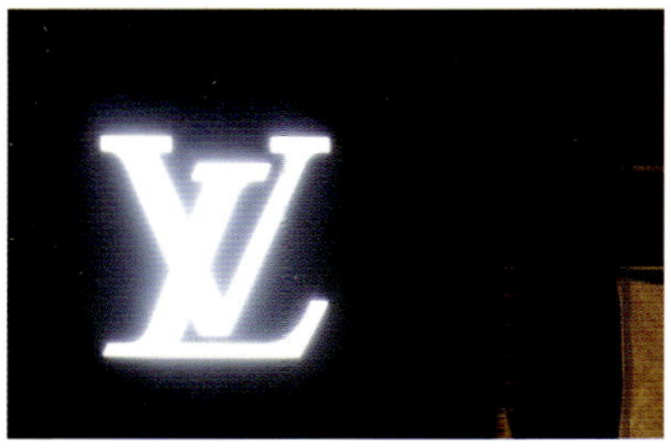

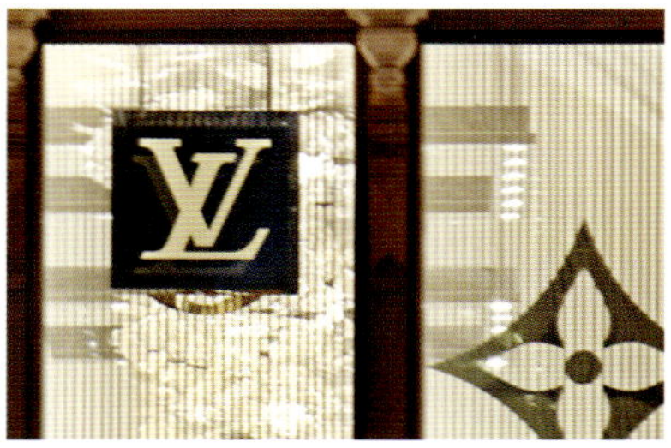

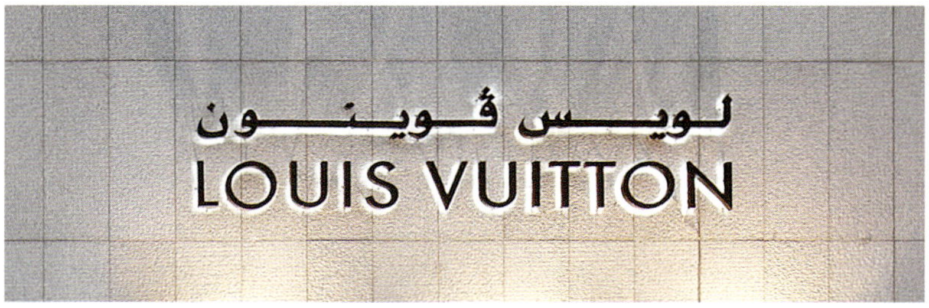
لويس فويتون
LOUIS VUITTON

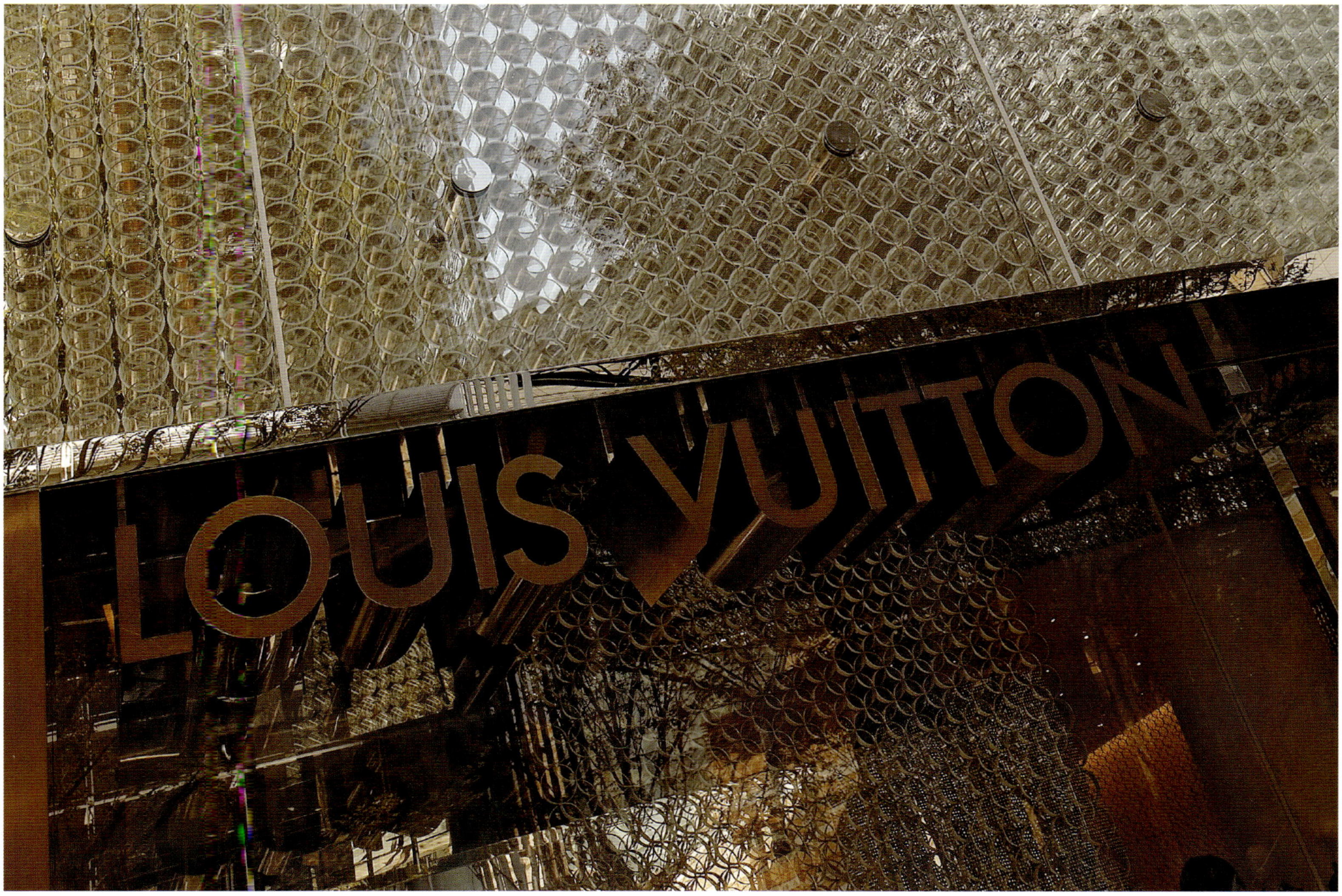
LOUIS VUITTON

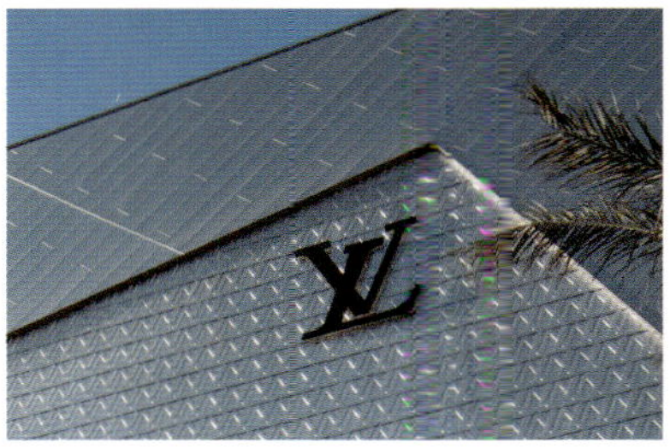

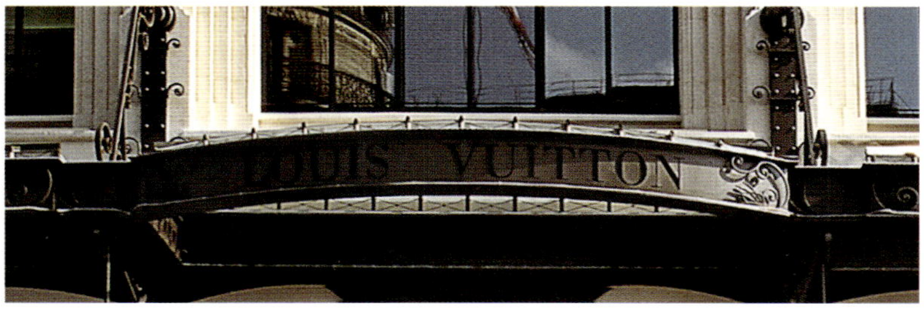

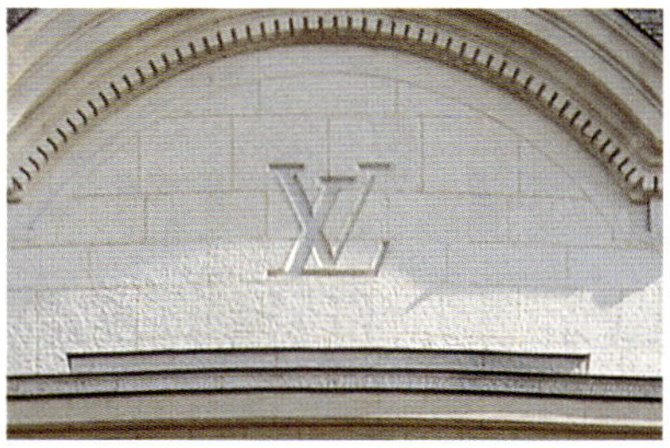

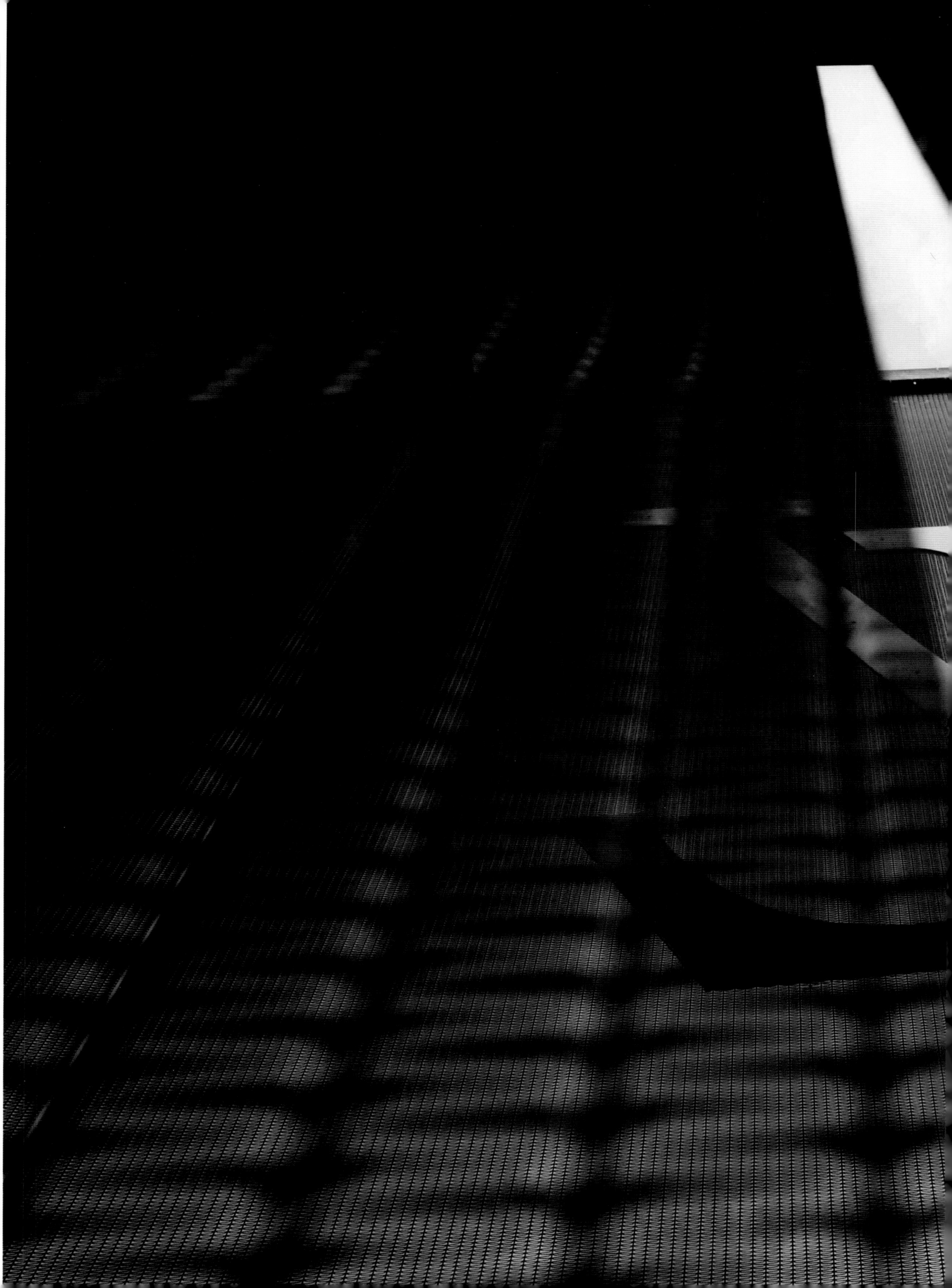

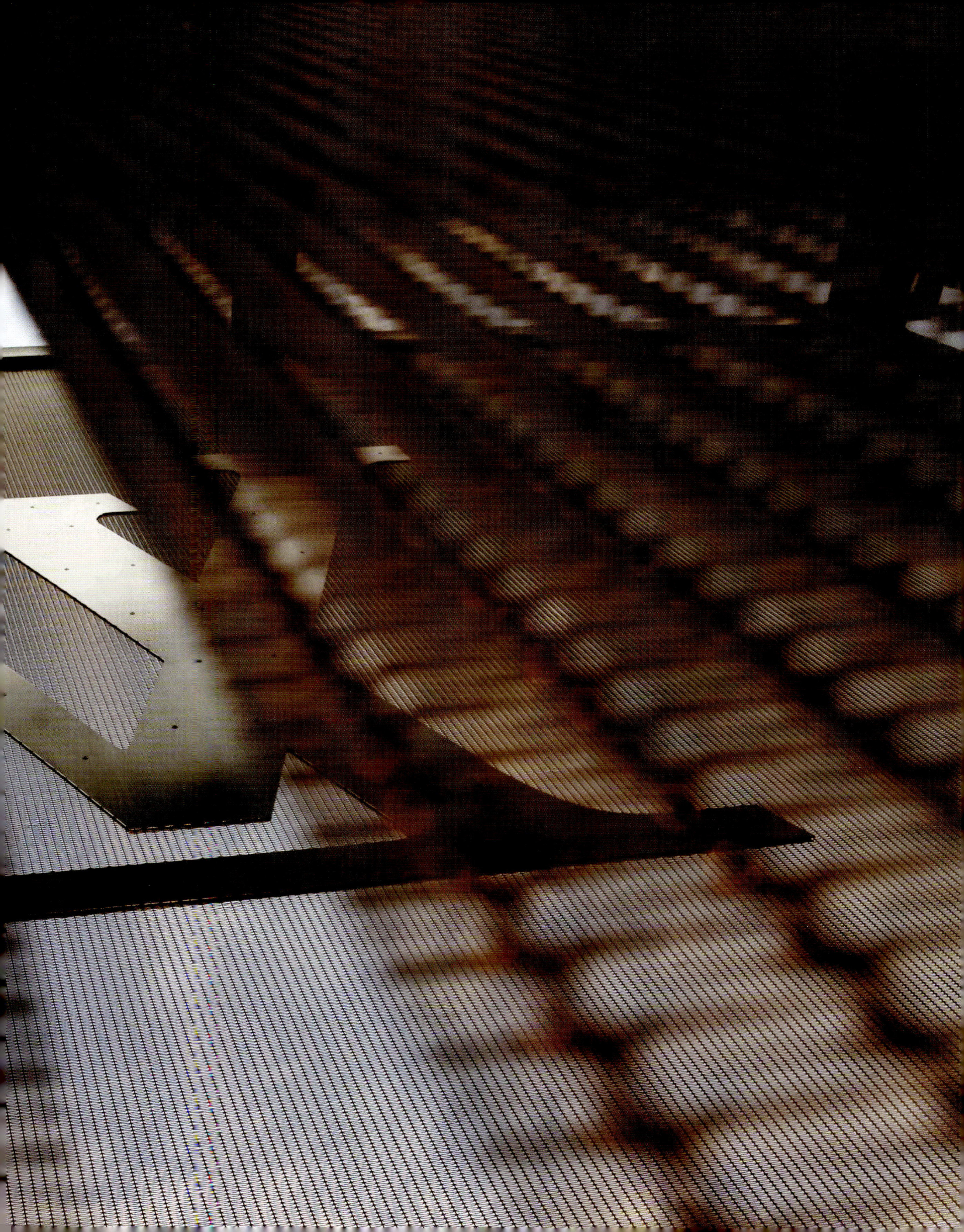

BUILDING CREDITS

JAPAN

Kobe Kyoryuchi
Project Design: Louis Vuitton Architecture Dept., Paris, Principal in charge: David McNulty, Project leader: Dak Coutts, Project architect: Marine Billet; *Project Management:* Louis Vuitton Japan, Principal in charge: Kazuhiro Takamiya, Project manager: Takuya Kanazawa; *Street address:* LV Kobe Kyoryuchi, 25 Kyomachi, Chuo-ku, Kobe-shi, Hyogo-ken 650–0034; *Total area:* 1,241 m^2; *Retail Area:* 818 m^2; *Completion date:* February 2010.

Nagoya Sakae
Façade Design: Jun Aoki and Associates, Tokyo, Principal in charge: Jun Aoki, Project Leader: Masaki Mori; *Project Design:* Louis Vuitton Architecture Dept., Paris, Principal in charge: David McNulty, Project leader: Dak Coutts, Project architect: Laetitia Perrin, Project team: Philippe Grasset; *Project Management:* Louis Vuitton Japan, Principal in charge: Kazuhiro Takamiya; *Street address:* LV Nagoya Sakae, 3–16–17 Nishiki, Naka-ku, Nagoya-shi, Aichi-ken, 460–0003; *Total area:* 889 m^2; *Retail area:* 475 m^2; *Completion date:* September 2010.

Tokyo Omotesando
Façade Design: Jun Aoki and Associates, Tokyo, Principal in charge: Jun Aoki, Project leader: Shinya Kamuro; *Project Management:* Louis Vuitton Architecture Dept., Paris, Principal in charge: David McNulty, Eric Carlson, Project architects: Marie-Eve Bidard, Laetitia Perrin; *Street address:* 5–7–5 Jingumae Shibuya-Ku, Tokyo 150–0001; *Total area:* 1,510 m^2; *Retail area:* 994 m^2; *Completion date:* November 2010.

Tokyo Omotesando 2nd & 5th Floor Expansion
Project Design: Louis Vuitton Architecture Dept., Paris, Principal in charge: David McNulty, Project leader: Dak Coutts, Project architects: Laetitia Perrin, Marine Billet, Philippe Grasset; *Project Management:* Louis Vuitton Japan, Principal in charge: Kazuhiro Takamiya; *Street address:* 5–7–5 Jingumae, Shibuya-ku, Tokyo 150–0001; *Retail area:* 276 m^2; *Total area:* 517 m^2; *Completion date:* January 2011.

Tokyo Roppongi
Project Design: Louis Vuitton Architecture Dept., Paris, Principal in charge: Eric Carlson, Project leader: Marie-Eve Bidard, Project architect: Laetitia Perrin, Studio Aurelio Clementi, Verona, Principal in charge: Aurelio Clementi, Project team: Irene Antolini, Gettina Schepis, Jun Aoki and Associates, Tokyo, Principal in charge: Jun Aoki, Project leader: Ryuji Nakamura, Project architect: Noriko Nagayama; *Street address:* Roppongi Keyaki Dori, Roppongi Hills, 6–12–3 Roppongi, Minato-Ku, Tokyo 106–0032; *Total area:* 1,147 m^2; *Retail area:* 868 m^2; *Completion date:* September 2003.

Tokyo Namiki Dori
Project Design: Jun Aoki and Associates, Tokyo, Principal in charge: Jun Aoki, Project Leader: Nagaishi Takayoshi; *Project Management:* Louis Vuitton Architecture Dept., Paris, Principal in charge: David McNulty, Project architects: Marie-Eve Bidard, Laetitia Perrin; *Street Address:* 7–6–1, Ginza, Chuo-Ku, Tokyo 104–0061; *Total area:* 1,597 m^2; *Retail area:* 838 m^2; *Opened:* September 1981; *Completion date:* September 2004.

Osaka Midosuji (Competition Proposal)
Architects: Jun Aoki and Associates, Principal in charge: Jun Aoki, Project architects: Toru Murayama, Chiaki Machimoto; *Street Address:* Osaka, Osaka Prefecture; *Site area:* 746 m^2; *Total area:* 7383 m^2; *Design Period:* 2006–2007; *Completion date:* Unbuilt.

Osaka Midosuji (Competition Proposal)
Architectural design: Shigeru Ban Architects; Principal in charge: Shigeru Ban; *MEP engineering:* ARUP; *Site area:* 746 m^2; *Street Address:* Osaka, Osaka Prefecture; *Total floor area:* 7383 m^2; *Design Period:* 2006–2007; *Completion date:* Unbuilt.

ASIA PACIFIC

Shanghai Pudong
Façade Design: Louis Vuitton Architecture Dept., Paris, Principal in charge: David McNulty, Project leader: Samuel Singer, Project architect: Fabien Hartweck; *Project Design:* Peter Marino Architect, Principal in charge: Peter Marino, Project team: Jayson Beltran, Tsuyoshi Ma; *Project Management:* Louis Vuitton Hong Kong, Principal in charge: Stuart Young, Project manager: Shirlie Kwok; *Address:* Shop L1–1, Block D, Shanghai IFC, 8 Century Avenue, Shanghai 200120; *Total area:* 1,529 m^2; *Retail area:* 987 m^2; *Completion date:* December 2009.

Hong Kong Canton Road
Façade Design: Kumiko Inui, Tokyo, Principal in charge: Kumiko Inui; *Project Design:* Louis Vuitton Architectural Dept., Paris, Principal in charge: David McNulty, Project leader: Kar-Hwa Ho, Project architect: Samuel Singer; *Project Management:* Louis Vuitton Hong Kong, Principal in charge: Stuart Young, Project manager: James Poon; *Total area:* 3,685 m^2; *Retail area:* 1,596 m^2; *Street address:* Shop G005–006, Ground floor and Level 1, Harbour City, 5 Canton Road, Tsim Sha Tsui, Kowloon, Hong Kong; *Completion date:* March 2008.

Hong Kong Landmark
Façade Design: Jun Aoki and Associates, Tokyo, Principal in charge: Jun Aoki, Project leader: Satoko Hirata; *Project Design:* Peter Marino Architect, Principal in charge: Peter Marino, Project leaders: Anne Timmerman, Maria Wilthew, Uli Wagner; *Project Management:* Louis Vuitton Architecture Dept., Paris, Principal in charge: David McNulty, Project leader: Dak Coutts, Project architect: Laetitia Perrin, Louis Vuitton Hong Kong, Principal in charge: Stuart Young, Project manager: James Poon; *Street address:* Ground Floor, Shop 7–17, Landmark Atrium, Central, Hong Kong; *Total area:* 1,558 m^2; *Retail area:* 1,068 m^2; *Completion date:* December 2005.

Macao One Central
Façade Design: Louis Vuitton Architecture Dept., Paris, Principal in charge: David McNulty, Project leader: Kar-Hwa Ho, Nathalie Fremon, Project architects: François Régis Colombani, Thibaut Bera; *Project Design:* Louis Vuitton Architecture Dept., Paris, Principal in charge: David McNulty, Project leader: Kar-Hwa Ho, Project architects: François Régis Colombani, Nathalie Fremon; *Project management:* Louis Vuitton Hong Kong, Principal in charge: Stuart Young, Project manager: Shirlie Kwok; *Street Address:* One Central, Avenida de Sagres and Avenida do Dr. Sun Yat Sen, Nape, Macao; *Total area:* 2,484 m^2; *Retail area:* 1,514 m^2; *Completion date:* December 2009.

Macao One Central (unrealized proposal)
Project Design: Zaha Hadid Architects with Patrik Schumacher, Principle in charge: Zaha Hadid, Patrik Schumacher, Project leader: Ana M. Cajiao; *Project team:* Eddie Can, Matthew Wong, Ho-ping Hsia, Maryam Pousti, Annarita Papeschi; *Street address:* Shop G27–29, 121–123, 229–231, One Central, Avenida de Sagres and Avenida do Dr. Sun Yat Sen, Nape, Macao; *Total area:* 2,400 m^2; *Completion date:* Unbuilt.

Singapore Marina Bay
Project Design: Peter Marino Architect, NY, Principal in charge: Peter Marino, Project team: Jayson Beltran, Yuuki Kitada, Masuo Nakajima, Enrique Pincay, Kihyun Son, Anne Timmerman, Uli Wagner, Simon Wutherich; *Project management:* Louis Vuitton Architectural Dept., Paris, Principal in charge: David McNulty, Project leader: Kar-Hwa Ho, Project architect: Camille Delescluse, For Louis Vuitton Hong Kong, Principal in charge: James Poon, Project manager: Andy Lau; *Street address:* #B1–38/39A & B2–36/37A, Crystal Pavillion North, 2 Bayfront Avenue, Singapore 018972; *Total area:* 3,069 m^2; *Retail area:* 2,147 m^2; *Completion date:* September 2011.

UNITED STATES OF AMERICA

Las Vegas City Center
Architects: Louis Vuitton Architecture Dept., Paris, Principal in charge: David McNulty, Project leader: Dak Coutts, Project Architect: Nadya Liebich; *Project management:* Principal in charge: John Mulliken, Project manager: Zeynep Ozandag, Pricillya Bloess; *Street address:* The Crystals, 3720 Las Vegas Boulevard South, Suite 103, Las Vegas, NV 89109; *Total area:* 3,066 m^2; *Retail area:* 1,301 m^2; *Completion date:* December 2009.

New York Fifth Avenue
Façade Design: Jun Aoki and Associates, Tokyo, Principal in charge: Jun Aoki, Project leader: Nagaishi Takayoshi; *Project Design:* Peter Marino Architect, NY, Principal in charge: Peter Marino, Project team: Maria Wilthew, Masuo Nakajima, Enrique Pincay; *Project manage-

ment: Louis Vuitton Architecture Dept., Paris, Principal in charge: David McNulty, Project architect: Bruce Ribay, Louis Vuitton Americas, Principal in charge: John Mulliken; *Street address:* One East 57th Street, New York City, NY 10022; *Total area:* 1,858 m²; *Retail area:* 1,153 m²; *Completion date:* February 2004.

EUROPE

London New Bond Street
Project Design: Peter Marino Architect, NY, Principal in charge: Peter Marino, Project team: Project team: Jason Berltran, Luis Gonzalez, Yuuki Kitada, Masuo Nakajima, Kihyun Son, Anne Timmerman, Uli Wagner, Maria Wilthew; *Project management:* Louis Vuitton Architecture Dept, Paris, Principal in charge: David McNulty, Project leader: Alain Michaux, Project architect: Izabella Kolodziejczyk; *Total area:* 2,496 m²; *Retail area:* 1,534 m²; *Street address:* 17/20 New Bond Street, London W1S 2RB; *Completion date:* May 2010.

Paris Champs-Élysées
Project Design: Peter Marino Architect, NY, Principal in charge: Peter Marino, Project leaders: Craig Greenberg, Enrique Pincay, Michael Romano; *Project Design:* Carbondale, Paris, Principal in charge: Eric Carlson; *Project management:* Louis Vuitton Architecture Dept. and Louis Vuitton Real Estate Dept., Paris, Principals in charge: David McNulty, Christain Reyne, Project leader: Frédéric Devenoge, Project architect: Izabella Kolodziejczyk; *Street address:* 101 Avenue des Champs-Élysées, 75008 Paris; *Total area:* 3,864 m²; *Retail area:* 1,906 m²; *Completion date:* June 2010.

SAINT-TROPEZ
Project Design: Louis Vuitton Architecture Dept., Paris, Principal in charge: David McNulty, Project leader: Alain Michaux, Project Architect: Abir Fawaz; *Street address:* Rue François Sibilli, 83990 Saint-Tropez; *Total area:* 373 m²; *Retail area:* 288 m²; *Completion date:* June 2010.

Maison Rome Etoile
Project design: Peter Marino Architect, NY, Principal in charge: Peter Marino, Project team: Osamu Mochizuki, Uli Wagner, Xu Zhou; *Project management:* Louis Vuitton Architecture Dept., Paris, Principal in charge: David McNulty, Project leader: Alain Michaux, Project architect: Valérie Merceron; *Street address:* Piazza San Lorenzo in Lucina 41, Rome, 00186; *Total area:* 1,960 m²; *Retail area:* 1,242 m²; *Completion date:* October 2011.

Moscow GUM
Project design: Louis Vuitton Architecture Dept., Paris, Principal in charge: David McNulty, Project leader: Alain Michaux, Project architect: Valérie Merceron; *Project management:* Louis Vuitton Europe, Principal in charge: Daniele Fumagalli, Project manager: Jane Barrett; *Street address:* Red Square 3, Moscow 109012; *Total area:* 561 m²; *Retail area:* 513 m²; *Completion date:* November 2008.

HEADQUARTERS

New York LVMH Tower
Project Design: Atelier Christian de Portzamparc, Principal in charge: Christian de Portzamparc; *Project Management:* Louis Vuitton Real Estate Dept., Principal in charge: Christian Reyne; *Function:* North American headquarters; *Street address:* 19 East 57th Street, New York, NY, 10022; *Completion date:* 1999.

Tokyo One Omotesando
Project Design: Kengo Kuma, Principal in charge: Kengo Kuma; *Project Management:* Louis Vuitton Architecture Dept., Paris, Principal in charge: David McNulty, Project manager: David Coutts, Project architect: Laetitia Perrin; *Function:* Japanese headquarters; *Street address:* One Omotesando, 3–5–29 Kita-Aoyama, Minato-Ku, Tokyo 107–0061; *Total area:* 1,510 m²; *Completion Date:* June 2003.

INDUSTRIAL SITES

Ducey, France
Project Design: Gilles Carnoy, Principal in charge: Christian Reyne, Project leader: Jean-Gabriel Coste, Project Architect: Isabelle Lemoine; *Project Management:* Real Estate Department, Principal in charge: Christian Reyne; *Function:* Leather Goods Atelier; *Street address:* Ducey 1: 188 rue de la Liberté 50301 Ducey; Ducey 2: 4, route de la Baie 50 220 Juilley; *Total area:* Ducey 1: 8,016 m²; Ducey 2: 7, 486 m²; *Completion date:* Ducey 1: September 2002; Ducey 2: May 2007.

Cergy Eole, France
Project Design: Gilles Carnoy, Principal in charge: Gilles Carnoy, Project Architect: Grégoire Gilliot; *Project Management:* Real Estate Department, Principal in charge: Christian Reyne, Project manager: Nicolas Paschal; *Function:* Logistics Warehouse; *Street address:* 4 boulevard du Moulin à Vent, 95520 Osny; *Total area:* 21,572 m²; *Completion Date:* May 2007.

Marsaz, France
Project Design: Gilles Carnoy and Grégoire Gilliot, Principal in charge: Grégoire Gilliot; *Project Management:* Real Estate Department, Principal in charge: Christian Reyne, Project manager: Céline Sidibe; *Function:* Leather Goods Atelier; *Street address:* "Les Tonnes" 26260 Marsaz; *Total area:* 8,141 m²; *Completion Date:* March 2011.

Fiesso d'Artico, Italy
Project Design: Jean-Marc Sandrolini, Principal in charge: Jean-Marc Sandrolini, Project leader: François Lefebvre; *Project Management:* Louis Vuitton, Principal in charge: Christian Reyne, Project manager: Nicolas Paschal, Rudy Novello; *Function:* Shoe Manufacturing Facility; *Street address:* Via Cavour, 35–30032 Fiesso d'Artico, Venice; *Total area:* 10,892 m²; *Completion Dates: Alma* wing (Elegant Women's): August 2008, *Speedy* wing (Sneakers): November 2008, *Nomade* wing (Mocassins): March 2009, *Taïga* wing (Classic Men's): September 2009.

ILLUSTRATION CREDITS

Unless otherwise indicated. All sketches, drawings, plans and digital renderings appear courtesy of the architects

Courtesy Jun Aoki & Associates: 30, 47, 61 left, 62, 65, 69 top

Daici Ano: 10, 14, 18, 22 top, 23, 26, 27, 28, 31, 32, 34, 36, 37, 39, 40, 41, 43, 44–45, 46, 49, 50, 51, 54, 56, 63, 64, 248–249, 250, 258 top, 259 bottom right, 262, 264 middle

Nicolas Borel: 197, 198, 199 bottom, 200, 201 top

Massimo Berruti/Agence VU': 236–237, 239, 266–267

Laurent Bremaud/LB Production: 156

© Jean-Philippe Caulliez: 217, 218 bottom, 222–223, 225, 226, 228–229

Jimmy Cohrssen: 48, 53, 58, 83, 84–85, 86, 87, 88–89, 124, 125, 134, 135, 136–137, 138, 139, 159 top, 160, 161 bottom left, 162–163, 164 top left, 169, 194, 199 top, 201 bottom, 205, 206, 207, 208 bottom, 252, 264 top and bottom

Mitsumasa Fujitsuka/HELICO Co. Ltd.,: 192, 203, 208 top, 210–211

Courtesy of Zaha Hadid: 112, 113

Vincent Knapp: 159 bottom, 161 bottom right, 164 top right and bottom, 240

© David Franzen: 126, 127 top right, 128–129, 256

Courtesy Marina Bay Sands: 115

Peter Marino Architect/Louis Vuitton Architecture Department: 179, 180, 181

Sebastian Mayer SM/AEIOU: 38

Stéphane Muratet: 13, 15, 16–17, 19, 59, 61 right, 67, 68, 69 bottom, 72, 75, 76, 77, 78–79, 80, 81, 91, 92–93, 94, 95, 96, 97, 98, 99, 100, 103, 104–105, 106, 107, 109, 110–111, 117, 120, 131, 132, 142, 145, 146, 148, 149, 150, 151, 152, 153, 154, 155, 158, 161 top, 165, 166–167, 168, 171, 172, 173, 174–175, 176–177, 183, 184, 185, 186–187, 188, 189, 214, 218, 219 top, 220, 221, 231, 232, 233, 235, 238, 239 bottom, 246, 253, 254, 255, 258 bottom, 259 top and bottom left, 260, 261, 265 middle

Nobuaki Nakagawa/Courtesy Jun Aoiki & Associates: 21, 22 bottom, 35, 251, 263

Sterling B. Plenert: 123, 127 top left and bottom

Mazen Saggar/Louis Vuitton: 227

Hiroshi Ueda: 24–25

Stuart Woods, SW Photography: 257

We would also like to extend our appreciation for all images that appear in the covers of the deluxe and trade editions of this title: Daici Ano, Stéphane Muratet, and Jimmy Cohrssen